PROCEEDINGS

OF THE

HARVARD CELTIC COLLOQUIUM

Volume 39, 2019

Edited by

Myrzinn Boucher-Durand
Elizabeth Gipson
Shannon Parker
Nicholas Thyr

Published by
The Department of Celtic Languages and Literatures
Faculty of Arts and Sciences, Harvard University

Distributed by
Harvard University Press
Cambridge and London
by the President and Fellows of Harvard University,
Department of Celtic Languages and Literatures
©2021
All Rights Reserved

ISBN: 978-0-674-25779-5

The cover design is based on the medallion of an
Early Christian belt shrine from Moylough, Co. Sligo.
Drawing by Margo Granfors

Designed and typeset by JKD Publishing
Cambridge, Massachusetts

CONTENTS

iv

PREFACE

The annual Harvard Celtic Colloquium originated in a graduate student conference convened in 1980 by students in the Harvard University Department of Celtic Languages and Literatures. Since then the conference has developed into an internationally recognized event, drawing together scholars and students from around the world to present work on all facets of Celtic Studies. The Colloquium is the oldest graduate-run conference in the field of Celtic Studies, and, true to its origins, it remains entirely run and organized by the graduate students of the Harvard Celtic department. The principal organizers of the Colloquium then become the editorial board for the publication of its proceedings.

Papers given at a Colloquium may be submitted for publication following peer review in the journal, *The Proceedings of the Harvard Celtic Colloquium (PHCC)*. The journal is distributed by Harvard University Press, which also handles subscriptions and orders for single volumes. Information on the Colloquium and *PHCC* may be found through the Harvard University of Celtic Languages and Literatures web site. The managing editor for *PHCC* may be contacted directly at phcc@fas.harvard.edu.

With the publication of this volume of *PHCC* the editors are pleased to announce a change from offset printing to digital inkjet which will allow for some limited color images. We hope this change will be of great benefit going forward, especially for articles on art history and manuscript studies. We also announce with regret that publication of the 2019 Kelleher lecture by Dr. Máire Ní Mhaonaigh has been postponed until publication of *PHCC* 40, but we look forward to its appearance in that volume. Due to the complications of the 2020 pandemic, no Colloquium was held in October 2020, so volume 40 will not appear until spring of 2023.

Acknowledgements

The editors are indebted to Professor Catherine McKenna for her advice and encouragement, and to the Celtic department staff, Ms. Mary Violette and Mr. Steven Duede, for their help with the Colloquium and administrative matters. We also wish to thank the Managing Editor of *PHCC*, and the staff of JDK Publishing for their help with the publication of this volume.

Myrzinn Boucher-Durand
Elizabeth Gipson
Shannon Parker
Nicholas Thyr

Organizers of the Harvard Celtic Colloquium 2019, and Editors of *PHCC* volume 39 (2021).

Lizards, Snakes and the Demon of Gluttony:
Oral Lore and Literature in the *Vision of Mac Con Glinne*

Barbara Hillers

Aislinge Meic Con Glinne (*The Vision of Mac Con Glinne*) has long been regarded as one of the most brilliant narratives composed in Middle Irish. Edited and translated into English by Kuno Meyer in 1892, and translated by Rudolf Thurneysen into German in 1901,[1] the saga has attracted renewed attention in recent decades, in the wake of the publication of Kenneth Jackson's edition of the text in 1990, which was followed by several translations into English.[2] More recently a conference dedicated to the text took place at University College Galway.[3]

Aislinge Meic Con Glinne (henceforth *AMCG*) straddles aspects of Early Irish literary culture that are commonly perceived as opposites; the saga combines prose and verse, deals with the monastic and the secular world, brings together upper-class and lower-class protagonists, and juxtaposes ecclesiastical learning with parody and performative orality. The setting and provenance of *AMCG* is thoroughly ecclesiastic. A significant portion of the saga is set in the bustling monastic town of Cork, and the saga's main protagonists are clerics. Its hero is a clerical student by the name of Anér Mac Con Glinne (but usually referred to only by his

---

[1] Kuno Meyer, *Aislinge meic Conglinne - The Vision of MacConglinne: A Middle-Irish Wonder Tale* (London: David Nutt, 1892); Rudolf Thurneysen, "Mac Conglinnes Vision," *Sagen aus dem alten Irland* (Berlin: Verlag von Wiegandt & Grieben, 1901), 132–149.

[2] Kenneth H. Jackson, *Aislinge Meic Con Glinne* (Dublin: Dublin Institute for Advanced Studies, 1990); Patrick K. Ford, *The Celtic Poets: Songs and Tales from Early Ireland and Wales* (Belmont, Mass.: Ford and Bailie, 1999); Lahney Preston–Matto, *Aislinge meic Conglinne. The Vision of Mac Conglinne* (Syracuse: Syracuse University Press, 2010).

[3] The proceedings of that conference are in process of being edited by Professor Máirín Ní Dhonnchadha. My contribution to that volume, "Cathal and the *lon crais*: The Oral Roots of a Literary Tale," partially overlaps with the paper presented here. The present paper brings to bear further evidence from oral tradition and from comparative literature, while the earlier contribution (which I am happy to share electronically) deals more extensively with aspects of philology and literary criticism.

1

patronymic, Mac Con Glinne) from the northern half of Ireland, who decides to improve his meagre fortune in the province of Munster. Provoked by the scant hospitality of the monks of Cork, he composes a satire which so infuriates their abbot, Manchín, that he sentences Mac Con Glinne to death. However, Mac Con Glinne manages to extricate himself, by offering to cure Cathal mac Finguine, the king of Munster, of a voracious demon in the king's stomach. He succeeds in curing Cathal, thus earning the king's patronage and his protection from Manchín's vengeful designs.

Despite its monastic setting and the ecclesiastical background of the saga's main protagonists, however, the text is not defined by the rarefied aura of the monastic *scriptorium*; quite the contrary, as it famously parodies the various genres of vernacular Irish literature, including heroic saga, voyage tales, praise poetry, genealogy and law, all the while elevating satire to a highly entertaining art. *AMCG* foregrounds oral performance and oral registers of composition; a very significant proportion of the text purports to represent Mac Con Glinne's oral compositions.[4]

In view of the saga's plebeian perspective and its engagement with oral vernacular genres it should come as no surprise that *AMCG* draws upon and incorporates an oral folk narrative. The story of how Mac Con Glinne rids king Cathal of Munster of the voracious creature in his insides is closely based on a traditional folktale found throughout Europe and further afield. In the folktale, a person unwittingly swallows a small animal–outside of Ireland it is usually a snake–and is only cured when the creature is enticed to leave the victim's body. The narrative has been assigned type 285B* in the Aarne-Thompson-Uther (ATU) index of international folktales.[5] As we shall see, it is particularly popular in Ireland, where over a hundred versions have been collected from oral tradition, most of them under the auspices of the legendary Irish Folklore Commission.

My argument here–that Cathal's cure is based on an oral narrative–is not a new suggestion. In the introduction to Kuno Meyer's 1892 edition of

---

[4] See Catherine McKenna, "Vision and Revision, Iteration and Reiteration, in *Aislinge Meic Con Glinne*," in Nagy, J.F. & L.E. Jones (eds.), *Heroic Poets and Poetic Heroes in Celtic Tradition: A Festschrift for Patrick K. Ford*. CSANA Yearbook 3–4 (Dublin, Ireland, and Portland, Oregon: Four Courts Press, 2005), 269–82.

[5] 285B* Snake Stays in the Man's Stomach, Hans-Jörg Uther, *The Types of International Folktales*, Part 1, Folklore Fellows Communications 284. Helsinki: Suomalainen Tiedeakatemia 2004).

BARBARA HILLERS

AMCG, eminent philologist and folklorist Wilhelm Wollner argued that "the central conception of the story, that of possession by a devouring demon of voracity" and "the bringing out of the monster by exciting his appetite, either through hunger or thirst" drew on oral tradition.[6] Wollner pointed to several analogues from contemporary folklore, in particular to two versions collected from Gaelic oral tradition: The first of these, from Scotland, was published in 1860 in John Francis Campbell's *Popular Tales of the West Highlands*.[7] The second version, published just two years before Meyer's edition of the *Vision*, had been collected in Ireland by Douglas Hyde.[8] Wollner argued on the basis of the Gaelic narratives that "the story of Cathal's cure is of Irish local origin."[9]

Since Wollner's time, a formidable array of documentation on this tale has been assembled. Yet, even as folkloristic evidence mounted over the course of the twentieth century, scholarly awareness of the saga's oral-traditional background seemed to recede. If we think of scholarship as a collective memory bank, then we are in danger of forgetting a very valuable lesson about the composition, function, and meaning of Early Irish literature.

My contribution to the present volume takes its departure from Wollner's insight and brings it up to date. Instead of just two folktale variants from Scotland and Ireland, we now have well over a hundred, and we can set the Gaelic variants within their wider international context. My goal is to analyse these modern-day narratives with view towards a better understanding of the medieval saga text and its relationship to oral tradition. It is not enough to simply acknowledge the existence of folklore analogues: we need to study and analyse this corpus. Thanks to the extraordinary richness of the Irish folklore record we have ample material for analysis.

Aside from demonstrating the influence of oral-traditional storytelling on one of the most self-consciously literary tales in the canon of Early Irish literature, this contribution aims to show how the use of twentieth-century

---

[6] Wollner, "Introduction," *Vision*, ed. Meyer, xiii–liii at liii.
[7] John Francis Campbell, *Popular Tales of the West Highlands* (Edinburgh: Edmonston & Douglas, 1860), 366.
[8] Douglas Hyde, *Beside the Fire: A Collection of Irish Gaelic Folk Stories* (London: D. Nutt, 1890), 47.
[9] Wollner, "Introduction," liii.

3

folklore material can enhance our understanding of a medieval text. The Irish and Scottish versions are independent witnesses to an oral narrative that was current in medieval Ireland, and a critical analysis of the modern versions can give us a fuller appreciation of the medieval text, and help us understand how the saga's Middle Irish author, as well as its subsequent redactors, engaged with the folktale, shaped it and transformed it.

The Vision of Mac Con Glinne: a text in two recensions

AMCG was composed before or around 1100, in late Middle Irish. The saga text is extant in two late-medieval manuscripts that preserve distinctly different recensions of the text. The longer and fuller recension is found in the Leabhar Breac, an early fifteenth-century vellum MS devoted primarily to vernacular ecclesiastic matter (Dublin, Royal Irish Academy MS 1230). The Leabhar Breac recension, called "B," forms the base text for both Kuno Meyer's 1892 and Kenneth Jackson's 1990 editions.[10] Jackson dates B on linguistic grounds to the last quarter of the eleventh century.[11] The shorter recension is preserved in a late sixteenth- or early seventeenth-century paper manuscript (Dublin, Trinity College MS 1337, formerly known as H.3.18). This recension, called "H," was also printed by Meyer, but has received less attention from editors and translators since.[12] H is broadly co-eval with B.

The relationship between the two recensions has significant implications for our understanding of the narrative. Although the H text is preserved in a MS compiled almost two hundred years after the Leabhar Breac, scholars are generally in agreement that H preserves an earlier and

---

[10] References to the B text in this paper are to Jackson's edition. Jackson does not provide a translation of the text. The B text was translated by Meyer, *Vision*, and, based on Jackson's edition, by Ford, *Celtic Poets*, and Preston-Matto, *Aislinge*.

[11] Jackson, *Aislinge*, xxvi.

[12] Since Jackson considered it "superfluous, in view of Meyer's more or less satisfactory text and translation" of H to include either in his own edition (*Aislinge*, xii), Meyer's edition (*Vision*, 114–129) and translation (48–55) of H are used here. Meyer's translation is not complete and less than user-friendly, at times referring the reader back to the corresponding translation of B rather than translating H. The only complete translation of H is Thurneysen's German one ("Vision," 131–147). An edition and translation of the H text would greatly facilitate the comparative study of the two recensions and is an urgent *desideratum*.

more original form of the saga than B, and that B represents an amplified reworking of the saga with much "secondary elaboration."[13]

The episodes that tell the story of how the king of Munster, Cathal mac Finguine, was cured of the *lon craís* appear to bear out this view of the relationship between the two recensions: H appears to be closer to the plotline of the traditional narrative, while B provides, in Jackson's words, "secondary elaboration," and occasionally modifies the plot to accommodate the added material.

Cathal's cure is central to the overall narrative in both recensions. It is prominently positioned, providing both the opening and the closing segments: In both recensions the saga opens with a description of Cathal's affliction, and ends with his cure. Even though extensive portions of *AMCG* are devoted to other subject matter–such as Mac Con Glinne's interactions with the monks of Cork, and his poetic journey to the land of plenty–the story of the *lon craís* provides the structural framework into which the hero's adventures have been inserted.

Recension B opens with the statement that the motivating cause for the composition of Mac Con Glinne's *aislinge*–and thus for the very existence of the saga–was the expulsion of Cathal's *lon craís*: "The reason it was composed was to expel the demon of gluttony that was in Cathal [mac Finguine]'s gullet" (*Is hé didiu fáth airicc a dénma .i. do díchur in luin c[h]raeis bhoí i mbrágait C[h]athail meic Fhinguine,* Jackson, *Aislinge,* 1; translation Ford, *Celtic Poets,* 113). Recension H concludes with the sentence, "Thus was Cathal Mac Finguine cured from his craving" (*Sic tra rohícad Cathal mac Finnguine din ginaig,* Meyer, *Vision,* 129; translation 155).

The opening of the saga offers a good illustration of the relationship between the two recensions. H begins with a short statement of Cathal's predicament:

---

[13] Jackson, *Aislinge,* xxx; Máire Herbert, "*Aislinge Meic Conglinne*: Contextual Considerations," *Journal of the Cork Historical and Archaeological Society* 110 (2005):65–72; for a different view of the relationship between B and H, see H.A. Jefferies, "The Visions of Mac Conglinne and Their Authors," *Studia Hibernica* 29 (1995–7):7–30.

THE DEMON OF GLUTTONY

Cathal mac Findguine .i. rī mōr Muman, co n-gēire chon,
col-longad chapaill. Lon crāis robōe ina medōn. Satan
domeiled leis a c[h]uitigh. (Meyer, *Vision*, 114)

Cathal Mac Findguine, a great king of Munster, with the
greed of a hound, with the appetite of a horse. A demon of
gluttony was in his inside; Satan consumed his food with
him. (Meyer, *Vision*, 148)

After this succinct statement H introduces the main protagonists, Anér mac
Con Glinne, who decides to leave his northern abode and seek his fortune
as a poet in the province of Munster.

B opens with the same opening gambit, albeit slightly amplified:

Cathal mac Finguine, rí maith ro gab Mumai; araile laech-
mál mór e-sside. Amlaid boi in laech-sin, co ngéri chon, co
longad chapaill. Sáttan, .i. lon crais boí i n-a brágait, no
meled a chuit laiss. (Jackson, *Aislinge*, 1)

Cathal mac Finguine was a good king who ruled Munster;
he was a great warrior prince. He was this kind of warrior:
greedy as a dog and hungry as a horse. Satan, namely a
demon of gluttony in his gullet, consumed Cathal's food
with him. (Preston-Matto, *Aislinge*, 2)

After that, however, B expands significantly; first, it adds a metatextual
preamble on the person, place, time and motive for the composition (§1).
Next, it pads the statement about the king's voracious appetite with further
detail: Cathal, we are told, used to eat a pig, an ox, a bullock, sixty loaves
of bread and more at one sitting (§2). Finally, B adds an entirely new
episode that explains how the demon came to inhabit the king (§3): Cathal,
B tells us, was in love with Lígach, the sister of his northern rival, Fergal
mac Máele Dúin. On one occasion, Lígach sent Cathal apples and other
delicacies which were, however, intercepted by her brother who had
malicious spells chanted over the apples before sending them on to Cathal:

So Cathal ate the apples, and they turned into magical
creatures in his guts, and those creatures in turn gathered
together and grew into a single beast which became the
demon of gluttony. And the reason that demon of gluttony

6

was created in the gullet of Cathal mac Finguine was to destroy the men of Munster in a year and a half, and it's likely it would destroy all of Ireland in another half year. (Ford, *Celtic Poets*, 114)

This episode is analysed in detail by Gwara, who offers a sustained reading of it in the light of biblical and patristic thought and imagery.[14] It is important, however, to note–as Gwara does–that the episode is found only in the B text of *AMCG* and is not present in H, which gives no account of how the *lon craís* entered the king's body. The Lígach episode should be attributed to the creative input of the B redactor and is not likely to have been a part of the traditional saga plot.

After this opening gambit, the focus in both recensions shifts away from the afflicted king and onto the good-for-nothing clerical student. Space does not allow me to follow Mac Con Glinne's adventures in the monastery of Cork, where his satirical verses send him on a headlong collision course with the abbot Manchín. Nor can we accompany him on his dream vision to the land of plenty, even though this would surely be a journey well-worth taking for a folklorist.[15] Having left our hero to his devices, we meet up again when Mac Con Glinne shows up at the house of Pichán mac Máele Finne, where Cathal is holding court. Mac Con Glinne persuades Pichán to give him a chance to cure the king. Cathal's voraciousness has brought the kingdom of Munster to the brink of ruin, and Pichán decides he has nothing to lose by allowing the wandering scholar to try his luck with the king.

In the extensive final portion of the text that deals with Cathal's cure we can observe a similar relationship between H and B as in the opening sequence: B for the most part follows the basic plotline of H, but adds additional material. It is therefore convenient to present the narrative of H first,[16] before discussing significant variations in B.

Atbert Mac Conglinne ri Pichān mac Māilfind, dā lēged dō airichthi Cathail di lesugud, robad feirde do feraib

---

[14] S. J. Gwara, "Gluttony, Lust and Penance in the B-Text of *Aislinge Meic Conglinne*," *Celtica* 20 (1988): 53–72.

[15] Wollner, "Introduction"; William Sayers, "Diet and Fantasy in Eleventh-Century Ireland: The Vision of Mac Con Glinne," *Food and Foodways* 6/1 (1994): 1–17.

[16] As printed by Meyer (1892:114–29), but incorporating his *corrigenda* (1892:206).

*Muman. Fūaslaicter di Mac Conglinne for errudus Pichāin, ocus nosfothraic ocus gabus fuathrōic occus lēinid n-gil imbiu, ocus atāidh[17] tenid do feolomain uinnsend i fiednuise Cathail cen diaidh, cen cieig, cen crithir. Nōi n-doirsi fuirri, occus dobertor nōi m-beru indfodai findcuild a bun cuill dō, occus dobertor cethri aisle senshaille occus dā muic ūrai, ocus dognī tōchtu dīb, ocus dobeir toocht senshaille etir cech dā toocht ūrsaille occus toocht ūrsaille etir cech dá toocht sensaille īerna n-esred di mil ocus do shalond. (*Meyer 1892:117*)*

Then Mac Con Glinne said to Pichán son of Máel Finn that it would be the better for the men of Munster if he were allowed to prepare the food for Cathal. On Pichán's guarantee Mac Con Glinne's fetters were loosened. He washed himself, put on an apron and a white tunic, and kindled a fire of ashwood branches in Cathal's presence, without smoke, without fumes, without sparks. There were nine openings, and nine long-pointed spits of white hazel from the base of a hazel tree were brought to him. And four joints of cured bacon were brought and two freshly slaughtered pigs, and he cut them into pieces, and he put a piece of cured bacon between two pieces of fresh pork, and a piece of fresh pork between two pieces of cured bacon, after marinating them with honey and salt. (my translation)[18]

Mac Con Glinne then extracts from Cathal a promise to listen to the recital of his dream vision of the land of plenty which the king is forced to endure without interruption, all the while hearing about the imaginary foods of the vision, and contemplating the actual food in front of him. Having finished

---

[17] Emended by Meyer from *ataidh* in the *corrigenda* (1892:206).

[18] This passage was not translated by Meyer. The use of spits in this passage is cited by Fergus Kelly in *Early Irish Farming* (Dublin: Dublin Institute for Advanced Studies, 1988, 338). I am grateful to Roisin McLaughlin for this reference, and for advice on the passage, in particular her suggestion to translate *a bun cuill* as "from the base of a hazel tree." For Thurneysen's translation of this passage, see "Vision," 135.

his recital, Mac Con Glinne brandishes the flesh-spits in front of the king and succeeds in luring out the *lon crais*:

> *Conid annsin rochromasdair a lāimh cosna dā bir bídh, ocus dosbered co bēl ind rīgh, ocus dūthraicedh a slucud etir chrand occus bīad. Corrucc fot a lāmha ūad, coroling an lon craois assa brāgait corrabā for in m-bir m-biidh, ocus corroling don bir, corrogaib imm-brāgait gilla int s[h]acairt Corcaige robōi "con coire for lār in taige, ocus roling a brāgait in gilla for in m-bior cētnae. Lāid Mac Conglinne inn m-bior issin grīsaigh, ocus lāid core ind rīgt[h]aige corrabā for in m-bir m-biid. Rucad ind rīg i n-airecal codultæ, ocus rofolmaiged in tech mōr, ocus roloiscead īarna folmugud. Ocus rolēicc in deman teora grēcha ass. Atracht in rī īarnamāirech, ocus nī bā mōamh a shāith indāss sāith mic míos. (Meyer, Vision, 128)*

Then he bent his hand with the two spits of food and put them to the lips of the king, who longed to swallow them, wood, food, and all. So he took them an arm's length from him, and the demon of gluttony jumped from his throat on to the spit, and jumped from the spit into the throat of the priest of Cork's gillie, who was by the cauldron on the floor of the house, and jumped from the throat of the gillie on to the spit again. Mac Conglinne put the spit into the embers and upset the cauldron of the royal house on to the spit. The king was taken to a sleeping-chamber, and the great house was emptied and burnt afterwards. And the demon let forth three shrieks. Next morning the king arose, and what he ate was no more but what a child of a month would eat. (Meyer, *Vision*, 154)[19]

This, according to H, is the end of the *lon crais*. Cathal has been cured of his insatiable appetite, and as a result of his intervention, Mac Con Glinne is saved from capital punishment and vindicated by a court convened to judge between himself and Manchín. Mac Con Glinne is awarded full

---

[19] For Thurneysen's translation of this passage, see "Vision," 145.

9

compensation from the monks of Cork for the treatment meted out to him, and Cathal appoints him to his personal service.

Turning to B, let us briefly describe the longer version's modifications. Up to the capture of the *lon crais*, B is broadly in agreement with H, amplifying and enhancing rather than changing the plot. B provides two significant additions which we shall return to in the context of the oral narratives: In B, Mac Con Glinne persuades the king to fast for two nights and two days, increasing Cathal's hunger pains and spinning out the narrative. B also adds the detail that Cathal is tied with ropes to the walls of the house.

The most notable difference between the two recensions lies in their depiction of the demise of the *lon crais* itself. In H, as we have seen, the creature is killed when Mac Con Glinne traps it under a cauldron and then sets fire to the hall. The compiler of B, however, succeeds in postponing the demon's exit from the tale by offering a different ending; in fact, he gives us no less than three alternative endings. The creature is trapped under the cauldron, as in H: according to "the books of Cork," B claims, the *lon crais* "was put in the cauldron, and was burned up under it" (Preston-Matto, *Aislinge*, 55). But B also alludes to a variant version according to which the demon entered the priest of Cork's gillie so that he drowned in the mill pond. After acknowledging these two variants in which the creature perishes, B relates its own version, according to which it does not. Even though the hall is set on fire, and despite being trapped under the cauldron, the creature "leaped up to the roof-tree of the royal house and the fire could do nothing to him" (Preston-Matto, *Aislinge*, 55). Mac Con Glinne then takes the opportunity to interrogate the demon who explains that he had intended to destroy Cathal and all of Ireland, but that he is powerless to do anything against Mac Con Glinne whose knowledge and poetic training, his "ability, wisdom, chastity and honor" he praises. After this fulsome eulogy of the hero, the demon "flew off into the ether . . . to join the people of hell" (Preston-Matto, *Aislinge*, 56). Once the *lon crais* is finally removed, B adds a finishing touch to Cathal's cure: The king is given a concoction of boiled milk with butter and honey.[20]

---

[20] This particular motif may be drawn from traditional folk medicine: milk, and warm milk in particular, is widely used in traditional cures in Ireland and is seen as warding off supernatural influence.

To the compiler of B, the *lon craís* is unambiguously diabolic, a creature of hell who cannot for that reason be destroyed by fire. The creature is endowed with speech and its actions are motivated by a deliberate intention to work evil. Because the devil has to yield to the superior power of God, the creature is defeated when Mac Con Glinne makes the sign of the cross and strikes at it with the Gospel book (Preston-Matto, *Aislinge,* 56). The Christian *interpretatio* of the *lon craís* in B is not of course without precedent in H; on the contrary, H explicitly refers to the *lon craís* as "Satan" in the tale's opening sequence. In view of the quintessentially monastic nature of the saga, this explicit demonization of the *lon craís* in both recensions of the text is only natural, and Meyer's translation of *lon craís* as "demon of gluttony" seems a perfect fit for Christian concepts about demonic powers on the one hand and about the vice of gluttony on the other hand. However, neither the creature's behaviour–as described in H–nor the term *lon craís* is indicative of a diabolic nature. As even a cursory glance at the etymology of *lon craís* shows, "demon of gluttony" is not a literal translation, and the Christian overtones of the English are not present in the Irish idiom.

'Demon of gluttony'? The enigmatic lon craís

Meyer's catchy rendering of *lon craís* as "demon of gluttony," which fits so perfectly into the ecclesiastic milieu of *AMCG*, was widely adopted by scholars and is used to the present day.[21] It is, however, important to bear in mind that the phrase "demon of gluttony" is not so much a translation as rather an interpretation of *lon craís*. While the second element–from *cráes* "throat / gullet"–is unproblematic (*cráes* denotes the throat or gullet, and hence, a greedy appetite), the first element, *lon*, is more elusive. As I have argued in greater detail elsewhere, *lon* can refer to a range of diverse animals, most commonly the blackbird, but also other birds and creatures

---

[21] See e.g. Gwara, "Gluttony"; Jackson, *Aislinge,* 158; Jefferies, "The Visions"; Ford, *Celtic Poets*; Herbert, "Contextual Considerations,"; McKenna, "Vision and Revision"; Preston-Matto, *Aislinge,* 2010. Wollner uses the term "demon" ("demon of voracity," "Introduction," xiii), and Thurneysen calls the creature a "devil" (*Fressteufel,* "Vision," 132).

small and large,[22] but it does not, in itself, mean "demon."[23] In both Ireland and Scotland, *lon* also carries an abstract meaning "voracity, hunger," presumably derived from its primary biological lexicon, based on the animal's behaviour. In combination with *cráes* the term might then be translated as "hunger of voraciousness" or "devouring hunger"; Ó Dónaill translates *lon craois* as meaning "insatiable, unnatural, appetite."[24]

The term *lon craís* appears to have been rare in all periods of the language. In the medieval period it appears to occur only once outside *AMCG*.[25] In modern Irish, it appears to survive only in the abstract sense of "insatiable appetite" cited by Ó Dónaill, not as referring to a living creature; the modern folk narratives do not refer to the animal protagonist by that

---

[22] In both Ireland and Scotland *lon* may denote an elk or moose deer. P. S. Dinneen, *Foclóir Gaedhilge agus Béarla* (Dublin: Irish Texts Society, 1927), lists the meaning "tape worm," which is intriguing in view of the contemporary accounts of the story featuring tapeworms; I have not found any other attestation of that meaning, however.

[23] Lexicographical references to *lon* meaning "demon" invariably refer back to *AMCG* and are clearly influenced by Meyer's rendering of *lon* craís as "demon of gluttony. Dinneen's entry for *lon craois* is explicitly derived from *AMCG* and his translation "demon of gluttony" is clearly based on Meyer. An tAthair Ó Laoghaire is similarly influenced by Meyer's translation in his bowdlerized adaptation of *AMCG,* whose title, *An Craos-Deamhan,* may be considered a back-translation into Irish of Meyer's "demon of gluttony" (Baile Átha Cliath: Muintir na Leabhar Gaedhilge, 1905). Ó Laoghaire also uses the term *lon craois* to refer to the creature, and translates the latter (in the glossary) as "demon of gluttony," indicating once again his indebtedness to Meyer's translation. See the extended discussion of the lexicography of *lon craís* in Hillers, "Cathal and the *lon craís.*"

[24] Niall Ó Dónaill, *Foclóir Gaeilge-Béarla* (Baile Átha Cliath: Oifig an tSoláthair, 1977).

[25] Within the corpus of Early Irish literature, the *lon craís* appears in one other Middle Irish narrative, in the apocryphal *Leabhar Breac Infancy Narrative*. In this text, King Herod is afflicted by an insatiable hunger, in a passage that is clearly influenced by *AMCG*. The only other pre-modern use of the idiom is in an Early Modern prose text, possibly going back to an earlier hagiographic source, which tells how Saint Columba cures Baedán of a *lon craois*; see J. C. MacErlean, ed., *The Poems of David Ó Bruadair,* vol. i (London: Irish Texts Society, 1910), 106–7. It is not clear from the text whether the *lon craois* is a physical creature living in the monk's gullet, or whether it is understood as an abstract condition of insatiable hunger.

term.[26] It is best attested in Scotland: According to Dwelly, *lon-chraois* can signify an abstract "canine appetite, inordinate desire or appetite," but it can also refer to a concrete creature, a small animal such as an insect or water creature. In several Scottish variants of the folktale, the animal protagonist is referred to as a *lon craois* (or *lon-chraois*), including the oldest version collected by Campbell, who states explicitly "The reptile . . . was called Lon Craois" (Campbell 1860:366). Based on the evidence of the modern languages, it appears that *lon crais* could refer both to the pathological condition of a voracious and insatiable hunger, and the creature which was believed to be its cause.

The use of evidence drawn from the modern languages and in particular from folklore sources offers concrete and valuable clues to our understanding the medieval term, evidence which we cannot afford to ignore. The remarkable persistence of the term *lon crais* to denote the story's animal protagonist, from the medieval saga text to Campbell's mid-nineteenth century version (published several decades *before* Meyer's translation of *AMCG*), is indicative of lexical longevity and tenacity in the context of folk belief.

In the ecclesiastical world of *AMCG* the *lon crais* took on demonic qualities which are clearly referenced within a Christian framework. Meyer's "demon of gluttony" is a reasonable rendering of *lon crais* within that framework, and, in the absence of a better alternative, will continue to be used. But it may be as well to remember that the term, as well as the creature it denoted, had a life outside the monastic world, a life that predated *AMCG* and that continued unabated in the oral stream.

The international folktale (ATU 285B*)

Wollner's suggestion that the story of Cathal's cure represented an oral traditional tale was amply born out by subsequent folklore scholarship. The narrative was classified as an animal tale in the Aarne-Thompson international folktale index, and was assigned type number 285B*. In *The Types of the Folktale*, Stith Thompson cites oral variants from Ireland, Italy, Poland, England and the US, and offers the following summary:

---

[26] It is worth noting that the terms used for the animal protagonist of the folktale, *airc* or *alp* (*airc luachra; alp luachra; airc sléibhe*) may, like *lon*, carry the meaning of voracity or greed.

13

Snake Enticed out of Man's Stomach: Patient fed salt: animal comes out for water. The patient is fed salt or heavily salted food and allowed no water for several days. He then stands with mouth open before a supply of fresh water, often a running brook. The thirsty animal emerges to get fresh water.[27]

While Thompson's summary does not specify how the snake entered the patient, versions of the story usually relate how the animal creeps into the open mouth of a person sleeping out in the open.[28] The story is bi-episodic, its movement circular: the opening move tells us how the animal gets into the body; the second move, how it is made to come back out. While the structural stability and bipartite symmetry displayed by variants of the story across languages, cultures, and even continents, legitimates its inclusion in the international folktale index, in form and contents the story shares features with traditional belief legends, and in folkloristic parlance might be more accurately defined as a folk *legend*. Versions of the story are typically short and informal and are often steeped in social realism and local detail. They are, moreover, rooted in folk belief and traditional medicine, and recent folk narrative indexes accordingly list the narrative as a legend.[29]

---

[27] Stith Thompson and Antti Aarne, *The Types of the Folktale*. Second Revision. FFC 184 (Helsinki: Suomalainen Tiedeakatemia, 1964), 84.

[28] The description of type 285B* in Hans-Jörg Uther's revised edition of the Aarne-Thompson index focuses instead on how the creature enters the man's body: "Snake Stays in the Man's Stomach: A man (woman) sleeps ... with his mouth open. A snake crawls unnoticed into his body, and he feels sick" (Uther, The Types, 167).

[29] Marjatta Jauhiainen lists the story in her index of Finnish belief legends and memorates (*The Type and Motif Index of Finnish Belief Legends and Memorates*, FFC 267 (Helsinki: Suomalainen Tiedeakatemia. 1998), 318, Q 601 and Q621), and Bengt af Klintberg lists it in his index of Swedish legends (*The Types of the Swedish Folk Legend*, FFC 300 (Helsinki: Suomalainen Tiedeakatemia, 2010), 326, R94–96). D. R. Barnes and Paul Smith survey it in "The Contemporary Legend in Literature - Towards an Annotated Checklist, part 4: The Bosom Serpent," *Contemporary Legend* 4 (2001):126–49, and Jan Brunvand includes it in his *Encyclopedia of Urban Legends*, vol. i (Santa Barbara, California: ABC-Clio, 2012).

Hans-Jörg Uther's 2004 much-enlarged revision of the Aarne-Thompson index[30] demonstrates that oral versions of the story were collected widely across Europe, the Near East (Iraq; Qatar; Israel) and North Africa (Algeria; Morocco; Egypt; Sudan), with outliers attested in other parts of Africa[31] and in India. Based on the oral attestations, the story's epicenter would appear to be Europe, where it has a very wide distribution and is attested in all major language groups. It is particularly popular in Finland, where over a hundred versions have been collected,[32] and also attested in Estonia and Poland. It is found in all major branches of Germanic (Swedish, English, German, Dutch, Frisian) and Romance (French, Italian, Catalan, Spanish, Portuguese). From Europe it was brought to the New World by European settlers.[33]

American versions have been recorded in New England from the early nineteenth century onwards, and may go back to the colonial period.[34] The story entered the literary limelight with the publication of Nathaniel Hawthorne's short story "Egotism: or, The Bosom Serpent" in 1843, apparently based on an oral version of type 285B*. Hawthorne's literary adaptation ultimately resulted in a prolific Anglo-American scholarship on the "Bosom Serpent" in oral or popular print tradition.[35] The story continued to circulate orally throughout the nineteenth century; in the twentieth century it saw renewed interest in the context of the so-called "urban legend." Few of the Anglo-American critics seem aware of the story's

---

[30] Uther, *The Types*, 167.

[31] ATU lists only one version from sub-Saharan Africa, an apparently isolated story from Namibia (Schmidt 1989). It is possible that the story came to Namibia with European colonists; on the other hand, the absence of other versions from central and southern Africa might be due to the gaps in folklore documentation.

[32] Jauhiainen, *Finnish Belief Legends,* 318, Q 601 and Q621.

[33] Primarily the Americas, but versions collected in Australia and Namibia may also be due to colonialism.

[34] See Robert D. Arner, "Of Snakes and Those Who Swallow Them," *Southern Folklore Quarterly* 35 (1971): 336–46; Richard C. Poulsen, "Bosom Serpentry among the Puritans and Mormons," *Journal of the Folklore Institute* 3 (1979), 176–89.

[35] For the most comprehensive and up-to-date list of Anglo-American scholarship on the "Bosom Serpent," see Davide Ermacora, Roberto Labanti and Andrea Marcon, "Towards a Critical Anthology of Pre-Modern Bosom Serpent Folklore," *Folklore* 127 (2016): 286–304.

presence in the international folktale index or engage with the story's international dimension, resulting in a heavily Anglocentric body of scholarhip.

Until very recently, no medieval version of the tale was known from Europe, although the story's currency in the Early Modern period is attested by a number of early printed versions, including Franco Sacchetti's Italian version written c. 1400 (Sacchetti 1795:307-13), an episode in François Rabelais" French novel *Gargantua* (1552), and Nicolas Monardes's Spanish version of 1574. Several seventeenth-century English versions have been documented by Arner.[36]

Uther's folktale index only lists a single medieval reference, the late-medieval Indian prose tale, "The King with the Snake in his Body," which combines ATU 285B* with another snake story about buried treasure.[37] It is contained in an anonymous collection, the *Pañchākhjāna Vārttika*, composed in Old Gujarati sometime between c.1200 and c. 1600, leading Uther to suggest that the story is of "Indian origin."[38] The king of Wīrpūri swallows a baby snake while taking a drink and develops terrible stomach pains. On a pilgrimage to the Ganges to seek a cure, he takes a nap, and his adviser observes the snake poke out its head through his open mouth. The adviser overhears the bosom snake converse with another snake on the ground and finds out how the king may be cured. He gives the king a concoction of crushed nutshells and salt, which kills the snake and makes the king vomit out the remains, after which he is cured.

Thanks to the collaborative effort of three Italian scholars we now understand that in fact the narrative was already known across Europe at the time the Indian version was compiled. In a paper published in 2016, Davide Ermacora, Roberto Labanti and Andrea Marcon document the story in a number of medieval languages, including Byzantine Greek, Latin, and Old Norse.[39]

---

[36] For references to ATU 285B* in Rabelais and Sacchetti, see Davide Ermacora, "Pre-Modern Bosom Serpents and Hippocrates' *Epidemiae* 5:86: A Comparative and Contextual Folklore Approach," *Journal of Ethnology and Folkloristics* 9, 2 (2015): 75–119 at 83–4 and 86. Arner, "Of Snakes."

[37] Johannes Hertel, *Indische Märchen* (Köln: Eugen Diederichs, 1983), 302–4 and 412.

[38] Uther, *The Types*, 167.

[39] Ermacora et al., "Critical Anthology."

The earliest text produced by Ermacora, Labanti and Marcon is from a Byzantine Greek collection of miracles associated with the Prophet Isaiah and dated, tentatively, to the tenth century (*Synaxarium et miracula s. Isaiae prophetae* miracle 4; Ermacora et al, "Critical Anthology," 296-7): A vineyard worker, thirsty from his labors, accidentally swallows some tadpoles when drinking polluted water. The creatures grow in his belly, making it swell terribly until he goes to the temple of Isaiah, praying for a cure. He is given oil and expels the vermin.

Around 1100, the tale was incorporated into a medieval Latin Life of St. Dominic of Silos in Spain (*Vita Dominici Exiliensis,* 3:32): A woman tired after working falls asleep in the field with her mouth open, and a snake slithers into her stomach. The snake eats all the food she consumes, and the woman wastes away. After she prays to St. Dominic, the snake leaves through her mouth; her companions kill the snake (Ermacora et al., "Critical Anthology," 293-96).

The story was also known in medieval Scandinavia. The famous Icelandic compilation known as *Morkinskinna* ('Rotten parchment'), composed c. 1220, contains a very full version in chapter 43 of the history of King Harald of Norway. A young woman is suffering from a painful, swollen belly; her father consults the king, who suggests that she must have swallowed a worm when drinking from a well. In order to cure her, the king says, she should be deprived of water, and carried outside, where she should rest next to a waterfall. The worm, driven by thirst, would come out to drink the water. The father follows the instructions, the worm comes out and is killed and the woman recovers (Ermacora et al. "Critical Anthology," 289-92).

To these three medieval texts, recorded in different language traditions on the southeastern, the southwestern, and the northern fringe of Europe respectively, we can now add *AMCG*, composed on its westernmost edge, at least a hundred years before the Gujarati tale. Taken together, these four independent attestations in medieval literature confirm that the story was well-established in Europe for a very long time. We cannot adequately address the question of origin here, but there seems no pressing reason to assume an Indian origin, given that at least three of the four medieval European texts predate the Indian version in the *Pañchākhjāna Vārttika*. In view of the super-abundant

European records, and the relatively sparse Indian attestations,[40] ATU's "Indian origin" seems somewhat of a leap of faith–a reminder, perhaps, that Benfey's *ex oriente lux* has not yet entirely lost its hold on the folkloristic imagination. Leaving aside the question of origin and migration, the important point to note is that the story was independently known from India to Ireland by the Middle Ages, illustrating the chronological depth and cross-cultural appeal of traditional narratives such as this.

ATU 285B* in Ireland and Scotland

Let us now turn to Ireland, where over a hundred versions of the folktale have been recorded. What can we learn about these modern Irish versions, and what can they teach us about *AMCG*? Most Irish versions come from the archives of the National Folklore Collection at University College Dublin (NFC). 66 versions are listed in *The Types of the Irish Folktale* under type 285B*,[41] and an additional 39 versions have come to light since. Eight versions can be added from printed sources,[42] and scrutiny of the NFC's card index revealed additional versions from the Main Manuscripts.[43] As many as 26 additional versions from the Schools' Collection have been traced, thanks to the NFC's ongoing digitization and transcription project (www.dúchas.ie), bringing the total number of versions to 105. More versions will no doubt be forthcoming once the entire collection is text-searchable.

---

[40] The story is not mentioned in Laurits Bødker's index of *Indian Animal Tales: a Preliminary Survey,* FFC 170 (Helsinki: Suomalainen Tiedeakatemia, 1991), but a version from Madras is referenced in Stith Thompson and J. Balys, *The Oral Tales of India* (Bloomington: Indiana University Press, 1958), 83, motif B784.2.1.1.

[41] Seán Ó Súilleabháin and R. T. Christiansen, *Types of the Irish Folktale,* FFC 188 (Helsinki: Suomalainen Tiedeakatemia, 1963, 57. Three of these should for various reasons be excluded: NFC 779:212 and Piers, *Westmeath*, 57, are not versions of ATU 285B*; and NFC S 925:41 is merely a copy, in manuscript, of Hyde's version in *Beside the Fire*, 46.

[42] These include six Irish versions published in the English journal *Folklore,* vol. 5 (1894), 186; vol. 10 (1899), 251; vol. 15 (1904), 460; vol. 22 (1911), 454 (two versions); and vol. 27 (1916), 422. George A. Little, *Malachi Horan Remembers* (Dublin: M. H. Gill and Son, 1943), 78–9 and note on p. 158; and Séamas Ó Catháin, *Jumping the Border* (Dublin: Phaeton, 2018), 184–5.

[43] NFC 117:209; 407:90; 541:467; 997:218 (two versions); 1168:421; S560:57; cf. 96:86; S559:21.

The tale is known in all four provinces of Ireland, with versions recorded in twenty-one counties. It appears to have been particularly popular in Munster, where forty versions were recorded. It is richly documented in both language traditions, and versions have been recorded in counties of Leinster and Ulster where English has long been the vernacular.[44] However, it is particularly well-represented in areas where Irish is still spoken, or was spoken until recently. Irish-language versions representing all Irish-speaking areas (Donegal, Mayo, Galway, Clare, Kerry, Cork and Waterford), strongly suggest that the story belonged to Gaelic storytelling tradition. This is reflected in a comparison of the two western provinces of Munster and Connacht (40 and 28 versions respectively) with the two eastern and north-eastern provinces of Leinster and Ulster (19 and 12 versions respectively).[45] It is clear that in the years after 1935, when the Irish Folklore Commission amassed the bulk of its collection, the story was very widely known. Nor should we assume that it is no longer told today: the NFC recorded its most recent version of ATU 285B* from a native of county Galway as recently as 2016.[46]

The strong Gaelic provenance of the story becomes particularly clear when we consider the Scottish material. Of the twelve Scottish versions, all but one were collected in the Gaelic-speaking Western Isles.[47] One hundred years after Campbell published the account collected in his native Islay in *Popular Tales*, the staff of the School of Scottish Studies were still able to

---

[44] Overall, more versions were recorded in the English language than in Irish. Irish-language versions predominate among the manuscripts collected by the Commission's full-time collectors, while English-language versions predominate in the Schools" Collection gathered by school children, as well as in the versions printed in English-language newspapers, popular magazines, and the journal *Folklore*.

[45] The fact that more versions were recorded in Munster and Connacht than in the two eastern provinces does of course also reflect the more intense collecting activity by the Folklore Commission on the western seaboard.

[46] Recorded on tape by Bairbre Ní Fhloinn in Moate, county Westmeath on 4.8.2016 from Michael Condren. I am grateful to Dr Ní Fhloinn for this reference.

[47] The single mainland version was collected in Scots from the great traveller storyteller Betsy Whyte (SSS SA 1973/160/1). Betsy's grandmother was a Gaelic-speaker, and Betsy has a number of items in her repertoire that are clearly derived from Gaelic folk tradition. Travellers have been credited with mediating narrative tradition between the Gaelic-speaking Highlands and the Scots-speaking Lowlands.

record oral versions of the story throughout the Isles, in Harris and Berneray, North and South Uist, Barra and Benbecula.[48] There is no indication that Campbell's published version influenced the twentieth-century versions, which vary from each other and from Campbell in details such as the name and gender of the afflicted person, the nature of the creature, and the identity of the healer.

The linguistic and geographic profile of the Scottish versions, eleven of which were told in Gaelic, confirms that the story was part of a common storytelling repertoire which Gaelic Scotland shared with Ireland, and Scottish and Irish versions of the story closely resemble each other. The story's geographic distribution and Gaelic profile in Ireland and Scotland, as well as its structural homogeneity throughout the area, all point to the story's long-established presence in Gaelic oral tradition.

Snake, lizard, newt or toad: the animal protagonist in folk belief

We have already noted the story's roots in folk belief; it adapts to local traditional beliefs about animals and their behaviour. The identity of the story's animal protagonist depends on real-life local fauna, but it also depends on what story tellers judge to be credible human-animal interaction.

As the various titles scholars have used for the story suggest,[49] the snake is the predominant animal protagonist in versions from India to the Americas and from Finland to North Africa. However, the identity of the creature is by no means homogenous. Other small animals, including frogs, lizards, eels, mice, worms and insects are also featured.

Since Ireland has no native species of snake, it is not surprising that the animal protagonist is never a snake: "In the Irish versions, it is a newt

---

[48] With the exception of the version published by Campbell in *Popular Tales,* 366, the Scottish versions are preserved in sound recordings (10 versions) and manuscript (1 version) in the School of Scottish Studies at the University of Edinburgh. One of the ten versions, collected from Donald Sinclair, has been published in English translation by Alan Bruford and D. A. MacDonald, *Scottish Traditional Tales* (Edinburgh: Polygon, 1994), 396–98 and 481: this is the only Scottish version mentioned in ATU.
[49] Snake Enticed out of Man's Stomach (AT); Snake Stays in the Man's Stomach (ATU); Bosom Serpent.

BARBARA HILLERS

or lizard, not a snake" that enters the person's stomach.[50] Ireland is not the only country where a lizard may play the role of the animal protagonist: in Finland and Sweden the lizard occurs alongside the more common snake, as it does in Germany.[51] But Ireland may be unique in consistently–overwhelmingly–favoring the lizard.[52]

Most of the English-language versions of the tale in Ireland refer to the creature as a lizard,[53] but lizards and newts are often confused in Ireland,[54] and the term "lizard" appears to denote both newt and lizard species.[55] The terms used in Irish-language versions appear to suggest that the animal in

---

[50] Seán Ó Súilleabháin and R. T. Christiansen, *Types of the Irish Folktale*, FFC 188 (Helsinki: Suomalainen Tiedeakatemia, 1963), 57.

[51] Jauhiainen, *Finnish Belief Legends*; af Klintberg, *Swedish Folk Legend*, 326, R94–6; Adolf Jacoby, "Von verschluckten Schlangen und Eidechsen," *Oberdeutsche Zeitschrift für Volkskunde* 6 (1932): 3–27.

[52] Other species (including frog and mouse) occur sporadically, but they are rare. Some recent versions of the legend I have collected feature a tapeworm, reflecting a more contemporary, urban environment, and illustrating the capacity of belief legends to adapt to present-day conditions and concerns. These contemporary tapeworm redactions occur in both urban (Belfast; Dublin) and rural contexts (county Louth) and were learned orally either at school or at home. I am grateful to Gregory Toner, Jonny Dillon and Tracy Fahey for sharing these narratives.

[53] Besides the ubiquitous term "lizard," English-language sources also offer dialect terms which seem directly related to the folk beliefs in question: In many parts of Ulster and Leinster the terms "man-keeper," "man-lepper," "man-creeper" and "man-eater" are used. The most common of these is "man-keeper," memorialized by Seamus Heaney in "Mossbawn," the poet's account of his childhood home: "This was the realm of bogeys.... we talked about mankeepers and mosscheepers, creatures uncatalogued by any naturalist, but none the less real for that" (*Preoccupations: Selected Prose 1968–78*, London: Faber & Faber, 1980, 17–27 at 18).

[54] The common lizard (zootoca vivipara) is a reptile, whereas the common newt (lissotriton vulgaris) is an amphibian, but they are of comparable size and shape. A description of the Irish newt on the website of The Herpetological Society of Ireland acknowledges that "newts are occasionally confused with the common lizard ... "; accessed 14.8.2016; https://thehsi.org/native-reptiles-and-amphibians/smooth-newt/.

[55] The term "newt" does not appear to have been used in the vernacular.

21

question was in fact a newt rather than a lizard.[56] English-language versions also seem to associate the "lizard" with a watery habitat more appropriate to the newt, as in this short version collected by a school child in county Cork:

> Long ago a man swallowed a lizard while he was drinking water. He went to the doctor to know how he could remove it, and the doctor told him to eat a lot of salt and then to go near a river. He said the salt would make the lizard so thirsty that when he would smell the flowing water he would jump out of the man and into the water. (NFC S 298:254)[57]

For all its brevity, this narrative exemplifies the story's bipartite structure: the first part explains how the animal enters the person; the second part describes what that person does to get rid of it. In the second part, the afflicted person is almost always advised and helped by a healer who typically dominates this part of the narrative. The second part reflects and reverses the action of the first: in the first part, the lizard enters the man from the water, in the second, it leaves him to return to the water. Many versions of the story are told in the context of traditional beliefs about lizards, as in this account from County Limerick:

> The only dangerous reptile we have in this country is the lizard and he is small and scarce, thank God. 'Tis hard to kill him for he is the colour of the ground . . . We always heard it said that anyone that would sleep out in the fields

---

[56] The forms *alp luachra* (Mayo), *athluachra* (Galway), *airc luachra* (Cork, Clare, Kerry, Waterford) and *eas luachra* (Kerry, Limerick) are used by the informants. The second element in all of these, *luachra* "rushes," would seem to point to the amphibian newt's watery habitat. In Donegal, the collocation *airc sléibhe* "mountain *airc*" similarly suggests boggy upland terrain. All of the terms above are variously translated as "lizard" or "newt" in printed and online dictionaries.

[57] All unpublished manuscripts are printed with kind permission from the Director of the National Folklore Collection (NFC). Manuscripts are cited by volume and page number; versions from the so-called Schools Collection are designated by S. The orthography of the originals has been retained in both Irish- and English-language texts; where necessary, editorial notes have been supplied in square brackets. Translations are my own.

was in danger of the lizard going into his mouth and creeping down his throat. Anyone that this ever happened to couldn't be fed and in no time 'twas known what was wrong with him. (NFC 1234:392-4)

Full-time collector Michael J. Murphy reported a similar dread of the lizard in the northern county of Tyrone: "The reptile is feared superstitiously, and the attitude is that it should be killed. The belief is still current that it will creep down the throat of a person sleeping outside" (NFC 1216:502). The same belief is attested by two accounts from the south-east and south-west of the country respectively: in county Waterford. Nioclás Breathnach recorded that "If a person is given to sleeping too often out under the air a lizard could get into his stomach and he'd have the appetite of two men then" (NFC 259:484). The "dangerous" nature of the animal is stressed again in an account from county Kerry: "If a person falls asleep out in a field it is very dangerous because a lizard might go into his mouth and go down into his stomach" (NFC 782:364).

The story usually opens with an account of how the animal enters the human body. In Ireland, as elsewhere, the most common way for the animal to enter the human being was to creep in through the open mouth of a person asleep in the grass. In some versions, however, the animal is swallowed as the person is taking a drink, as in the version from the Cork school child cited above ("Long ago a man swallowed a lizard while he was drinking water," NFC S 298:254). Even though the latter motif is fairly rare in Ireland, its distribution, ranging from Munster to Ulster, suggests that it may at one point have been more widely spread. The motif is also found in Scotland, where the person is said to have swallowed a frog or toad while drinking.[58] Interestingly, in Scotland the motif of the animal creeping through the sleeper's open mouth–so common in Ireland–is completely absent, indicating that the motif may have been less dominant in Ireland formerly. The competing motif of the victim's swallowing the animal accidentally while drinking may thus once have been more widespread in Gaelic tradition, particularly in Munster, where the motif occurs most often today. In Recension B of *AMCG*, the *lon crais* that afflicts Cathal is the

---

[58] The motif is found in Campbell's version (*Popular Tales*, 366), and in three versions in the archives of the School of Scottish Studies: Maclagan MS 8356/8362, SA 1968/185/B2 and SA 1968/243/B.

result of something that Cathal eats: the apples and other dainties sent to him by Lígach contain microscopic demons that combine in his stomach to form the *lon crais.*

In many versions of the folktale, the first part of the story–the account of how the animal gains access to its human host–is omitted, and the story begins *medias in res* when the afflicted person approaches the healer to seek a remedy for their mysterious complaint. This is regularly the case in Scotland, for example, where the story opens when the patient's family consults a well-known doctor. Structurally, the same can be said of *AMCG*: as the saga opens, Cathal has already been afflicted by the *lon crais.* Recension H never explains how the demon entered Cathal's body, while Recension B inserts the story of Lígach's apples in an explanatory flashback.

The effects of having ingested a live animal are usually felt instantly: the victim is said to feel pain and experience a range of symptoms, including weight loss: "she used always feel something picking her insides . . . She was in a very bad case, falling away" (NFC 1168:421). "Falling away," i.e. sudden and critical weight loss, is often invoked: "When he awoke, he felt very sick. He went home and could not eat" (NFC S 501:280), and "He grew thiner [sic] every day" (NFC S 1118:200). In many versions, the weight loss is accompanied by an unnatural, ravenous appetite: "When the man awoke he felt very sick. This sickness continued for some time although he was able to eat and drink an enormous amount. However the food and drink did him no good; the flesh was falling off his body" (NFC S 560:57). "He used to eat an awful lot and still he could not take the hunger and thirst off himself" (NFC S 572:338). The victim "could never eat enough" (NFC S 1118:2000); he had "the appetite of two men" (NFC 259:484); he "couldn't be fed" (NFC 1234:393); "*ní shásóchadh aon bídh é*" ("no amount of food would satisfy him," NFC S 612:105). The connection between ravenous hunger and weight loss is well expressed in the following account from county Laois:

> A story is told of a man who went asleep in a ditch, one day. After a long time he awoke, and he did not feel well. He was very hungry also. He rose, and went home for supper in order to appease his appetite. He eat [i.e. ate] for a very long time, but it was all no use, the more he eat, the

more he wanted; time went on, and the more he eat, the thinner he became. (NFC S 830:213)

The idea that an excessive appetite might be due to the hungry person having swallowed a small animal was clearly very much alive when the Commission's folklore collectors recorded the material. A Limerick storyteller cites as an example a neighbourhood lad, "a boy of the Hartnetts," who exhibited an unnatural appetite: "we used ask how used he ate [i.e. eat] as much and they used tell us an *eas luachra* was inside his stomach" (NFC 629:286). The same belief is still present in the twenty-first century; in county Clare a child who claims to be hungry directly after having had a proper meal is told, "you must have an *earc luachra* inside you" (Ní Gháirbhith 2013:73).[59]

The motif of ravenous hunger is not found in all or even most Irish versions of the story, but its distribution throughout the four provinces of Ireland, as well as in Scotland, suggests that it is traditional and well established. Its central importance in *AMCG* suggests that the motif was present in the oral version known to the saga author. It is worth noting that the victim's increased appetite is not believed to be due to gluttony or self-indulgence in the modern versions. The oral accounts make it quite clear that the hunger is rather caused by the rapacious animal that consumes the food intended for its human host. A Kerry storyteller refers to it as a "false appetite": "'Twas a false appetite she had ... I suppose what she used ate [i.e. eat], *he* used ate it" (NFC 1168:421; my italics). And an informant from county Clare explains: "Gach rud a d'itheadh an duine, d'alpadh an airc é uile" "Everything the person would eat, the *airc* would swallow it all" (Ní Gháirbhith 2013:73). These folk explanations echo the rationale given in *AMCG* for Cathal's unnatural appetite: "Satan, namely the *lon crais* which was in his gullet, ate whatever Cathal ate" (*Sáttan, .i. lon crais boí i n-a brágait, no meled a chuit laiss,* Jackson, *Aislinge,* 1990:1; my translation).

The Healer

The afflicted person is usually helped by a healer or a doctor, and this figure tends to become more important in the story than the afflicted person himself and to dominate the action. The seriousness of the patient's case is stressed, as he consults doctor after doctor without success: "He went to

---

[59] I am grateful to Críostóir Mac Cárthaigh for this reference.

every doctor he knew but none of them could cure him" (NFC S 830:213). In the lively account collected by Michael J. Murphy from Francis McBride in Tyrone, the family first try home-remedies before consulting doctors: "They were giving her this and that, tricking and rooting, and they took her to all the doctors of the day, and they couldn't tell what was wrong with her" (NFC 1216:502). The doctor is helpless because he fails to diagnose the cause of the suffering: " . . . he sent for the doctor, but the doctor could do nothing for him, he could not even tell him" what was wrong (NFC S 40:46). Only someone who understands the root cause of the problem can suggest a cure: "One day a man came along and told him what was wrong with him. The man asked for a cure." (NFC S 40:46). Official medicine appears to be ineffective: "The doctor gave him all sorts of medicine and it was no use" (NFC S 1118:200). The local healer, someone who has "a charm" or "the cure" succeeds where official medicine does not: "He went to all the doctors and no one of them could cure him. He went to a man who had a charm" (NFC S 501:280). An old neighbouring woman may outperform the doctors, as in Francis McBride's telling, where the newt or lizard is referred to by the local dialect form "man-keeper":

> And there was an old woman in the town and she come in and she says: "Can they not find out what's wrong with your girl?" "They cannot," she says.
> "I'll hold you," she says, "that she slep' out".
> "She did surely," she says.
> "I know what's wrong with her," she says. "She swallowed a man-keeper. I can cure that," she says. (NFC 1216:502)

In some versions the healer is said to be a high-status individual–a famous, much sought-after doctor–but in many versions the healer is just the opposite: an old woman, a local man with 'the cure', or even a complete stranger, a beggar or a tramp. In several versions it is a 'tinker,' a member of the traveller community, who cures the patient:

> *Annsin dubhairt an dochtúr dhó go dtiubhradh sé leigheas dhó agus thug ach níor éirigh leis an leigheas sin. Thárla gur casadh tinncéar leis ar an mbóthar agus d'innis sé a sgéal dhó sin freisin agus dubhairt an tinncéar leis go dtuibradh sé leigheas dhó.* (NFC S 18:248-9)

> Then the doctor told him he would give him medicine, and
> he did, but the medicine did not help. He happened to meet
> a tinker on the road, and he told him of his predicament as
> well, and the tinker said he would give him a cure.

Both motifs–of the healer having either a markedly high or low status–are found in Scotland. In most Scottish versions, the cure is attributed to a member of the aristocratic Beaton family of doctors, but we also encounter the motif of the healer as a socially marginalized figure. Betsy Whyte, a settled traveller from Montrose, tells the story as a real-life occurrence: in her version the cure is performed by her grandmother, who was a well-known traditional healer. We have seen that in both Ireland and Scotland the story taps into the tension between official medicine and traditional healing, and the oral narratives tend to valorize the non-establishment healer. In this regard, the folk legend resembles the medieval saga where the role of the healer is played not by a professional doctor or *liag* but by the social outcast Mac Con Glinne.

The Cure

In Ireland as elsewhere, the cure is commonly performed in an outdoor setting: the patient is made to eat salty food, then brought out to a stream, where the animal is induced to come out to quench its thirst, as we have seen in the version from county Cork quoted above: "the salt would make the lizard so thirsty that when he would smell the flowing water he would jump out of the man and into the water" (NFC S 298:254). This 'outdoor redaction' is predominantly found in the northern half of the country; it is the only one encountered in Leinster and Ulster, but outliers, as we have seen, can be found as far south as county Cork.

In other versions, the cure is performed indoors. In this scenario, the animal is prompted by hunger rather than thirst to leave its human host. Meat is roasted on an open fire in front of the patient to tempt the animal out: "When he got the smell of the mate [i.e. meat] he was making for it" (NFC 1168:421). What we may call the 'indoor redaction'–where an indoor setting is combined with the motif of luring the creature out with the smell of roasted meat–is dominant in Munster, where it is found in counties Waterford, Kerry, Limerick and Clare; outliers reach up north into Connacht (Galway and Mayo). The indoor redaction is not found in Leinster or Ulster, but is present in all the Scottish versions. Campbell's version of

27

1860–published thirty-two years *before* Meyer's edition–is an excellent illustration of the indoor redaction. As in other Scottish versions, the role of the healer is played by a member of the Beaton family:

> He was called to see a young lady, daughter of Mackay of Kilmahumaig, near Crinan . . . The poor young woman had an enormous appetite, which could not be satisfied, but she was reduced to a skeleton. The doctor . . . knew what her disease was, and ordered a sheep to be killed and roasted. The lady was prevented from getting any food, from which she was in great agony. She was made to sit by the sheep while it was being roasted, and the flavour of the meat tempted the toad she had swallowed to come up her throat and out of her mouth, when she was completely cured. The reptile she had swallowed was called Lon Craois.[60]

Campbell's version shares with *AMCG* a number of motifs: the victim's enormous appetite, the imposed fast, the roasting of meat, and, of course, the remarkable parallel of the animal being identified as a "Lon Craois'. Many of these motifs are also present in the twentieth-century Scottish versions. The correspondence between the Scottish and the Munster Irish versions suggests that this redaction may at one time have been known throughout Ireland, or at any rate in an area ranging from southwest Munster through Connacht and Ulster to Gaelic Scotland.

The relevance of the indoor redaction to *AMCG* is obvious: Cathal's cure takes place indoors, in Pichán's hall, and it involves Mac Con Glinne roasting pieces of meat in front of Cathal in an attempt to lure out the *lon crais*. This combination of motifs corresponds so closely to the indoor redaction that we may be confident that *AMCG* was indebted to a narrative belonging to this redaction.

This survey of the modern versions concludes with a glance at two motifs which are present only in the B redaction of *AMCG* and which may be influenced by the oral legend. The first of these is Cathal's fast. The fasting motif is found in both the indoor and the outdoor redactions; the afflicted person has to abstain either from food (in case of the indoor redaction) or drink (in case of the outdoor redaction). We have seen the motif of the imposed fast in Campbell's indoor version: –it is even more

---

[60] Campbell, *Popular Tales,* 366.

common in the outdoor redaction, where the patient is frequently said to have been denied access to water before being taken outside to a running stream.

> He [i.e. the doctor] told them to put him into a room and let him eat salt for three days. He was calling for a drink. They gave him nothing to drink. At the end of three days they took him to a river where there was a waterfall. When the mankeeper heard the water falling, it rushed out for a drink ... (NFC S 1118:200)

The imposition of a fast obviously serves to advance the climax by increasing the animal's hunger or thirst, just as it does in AMCG. The presence of the motif in Recension B may indicate the redactor's familiarity with an oral version containing the motif.

The second motif present in Recension B only is the motif of Cathal's being tied with ropes to the wall of the house:

> *At-agur téta ₇ refeda dó, ₇ do neoch ba calma don laechraid. Furmit a láma tar Cathal, ₇ ro cenglad fon samail-sin hé do shliss in rígthige. (*Jackson, *Aislinge,* 24*)*

> Ropes and cords were given to MacConglinne, and to those that were strongest of the warriors. They laid hands upon Cathal, who was tied in this manner to the side of the palace (Meyer, *Vision,* 62).

This motif is reminiscent of a curious subtype of the indoor redaction. In about half of the versions of this redaction, we encounter the motif of the afflicted person being tied and suspended from the rafters of the house:

> *Bhí fear ann fadó agus bhí sé ag obair ins a' phortach lá amháin. Do luighe sé ar an dtalamh agus do thuit a chodladh air. Bhí arc luachra ins an áit ina raibh sé ina chodladh agus chuaidh sé isteach ina bhéal agus síar ina bholag. Tháinig an fear abhaile, agus d'innis sé an sgéal go léir dá athair agus dá mháthair. Bhí sé ag cuimhneamh cad ba [chóir] dhó a dhéanamh. Do cheangail sé a chasa agus crochadh é as bárr an tíghe agus a cheann síos. Fuair siad pláta feóla agus é rósta. Cuireadh faoina bhéal é.*

Annsan fuair an arc luachra boladh na feóla agus thainig sé amach agus marbhuigheadh é. (NFC S 612:105)

Long ago there was a man, and he was working in the bog one day. He lay down on the ground and fell asleep. There was a newt in the place where he was sleeping and it went inside his mouth and down into the stomach. The man went home, and he told his father and mother everything that had happened. He [the father] thought about what he should do. He tied his feet and hung him down head first from the top of the house. They took a plate of roasted meat and put it under his mouth. Then the newt got the smell of the meat and came out and was killed.

This peculiar and distinctive motif is found in Irish and English-language versions mainly in Munster, with a small cluster of versions in county Galway. While it is not numerically common–it is found in only fifteen versions–it nevertheless appears to be firmly established throughout the distribution area of the indoor redaction. However bizarre the procedure may seem, it is described with realistic detail, and the versions all agree closely on the essential details. Even very short versions preserve the core details: "I heard of a man and they hung him over the fire and put mate [i.e. meat] frying on a pan near his head and the *eas luachra* came out" (NFC 629:286). The motif of the patient being suspended from the rafters is not likely to be of recent introduction, as the versions containing the motif do not cluster together in one locality but are distributed throughout the area of the indoor redaction (Waterford; Kerry; Clare; Limerick; Galway). Indeed, it is not an Irish invention; the same motif is found in Sweden, where the patient is "hanged by his legs with his head over a kettle."[61] In view of the stability of the motif, its wide distribution and early attestations, it is likely that it is of considerable antiquity in Ireland, and may well have been in oral circulation when the B redactor added the motif to his reworking of *AMCG*. The resemblance of this motif to the medieval text is of course not exact: there is nothing in *AMCG* to

---

[61] af Klintberg, *Swedish Folk Legend,* 326. In "Pre-Modern Bosom Serpents and Hippocrates' *Epidemiae* 5:86: A Comparative and Contextual Folklore Approach," Davide Ermacora reproduces a remarkable woodcut from a fifteenth-century German medical treatise by Hieronymus Brunschwig which depicts this procedure, *Journal of Ethnology and Folkloristics* 9, 2 (2015): 75–119 at 85.

suggest that the king is hung upside down. Nonetheless, it is possible that the detail of Cathal being tied to the wall in Recension B was prompted by an oral version containing the motif.

A version from Limerick combines the motif with the motif of the imposed fast–a combination that makes this version particularly reminiscent of *AMCG*:

> The cure in this case was to starve the man for a week and then tie him up by the legs. A panful of roast meat should then be placed under him where the lizard would be bound to get the smell of it. After a while then the lizard ravenous with hunger would throw himself out and into the pan and whoever would be in charge of the pan should throw pan and all into the fire. (NFC 1234:392)

The method of disposing of the lizard in this version is also curiously reminiscent of the saga, where the *lon craís* launches itself onto the chunk of meat held by Mac Con Glinne, who deposits both together on the hearth and upturns a cauldron over it. The fiery demise of the *lon craís* in Recension H of *AMCG* is a further indication that the saga author's oral source belonged to the indoor redaction: A significant number of indoor redactions explicitly mention the creature being killed. The presence of a wild, superstitiously feared animal inside the house may have prompted storytellers to inflict lethal action on the creature. Since an open fireplace is featured in the indoor redaction for the purpose of frying the meat to lure out the animal, a good few accounts–such as the version from Limerick cited above–make use of the fireplace as an expedient narrative device to dispatch the creature. The animal protagonist does not die in all or even most versions of the folktale, however: many versions make no mention of the creature once it leaves its human host. In the outdoor redaction especially, the creature may be presumed to just slip back into its natural habitat.

A long-lived tale

The study of medieval literary tales in conjunction with their modern folklore analogues offers benefits for the folklorist and the medievalist alike. Before we discuss in the conclusion what the folktale can tell us about the medieval saga, let us sum up the benefits for the folklorist. Our study of *AMCG* offers important evidence for the longevity of the folktale in Europe.

The existence of a literary version from the western fringe of Europe composed just before the first attestations in Spain and Iceland, and only a century or two after its first appearance in Greek Asia Minor, helps to shift the balance of probability towards Europe as the tale's epicentre.

For our understanding of the folktale's history in Ireland, the saga offers a welcome *terminus ante quem,* not only for the folktale's arrival in the country, but also for the individual motifs we have identified (insatiable hunger; involvement of a pivotal healer figure; and the motifs associated with the indoor redaction, namely fasting; roasting meat; the animal's fiery death).

Like the creature in the unfortunate victim's stomach, the folktale is long-lived and flourishes even under adverse conditions. We have seen that in some parts of Ireland, such as Clare and Galway, versions may still be collected in the twenty-first century that closely resemble those collected in the early twentieth century or the late nineteenth century. An Irish Times article about lizards from 2006 is clearly informed by traditional versions of the tale.[62] Folktales move with the times, and the tale has shown its ability to adapt to more contemporary conditions, resurfacing in an urban/suburban context as a story about tapeworm infestation. The story has a tenacious hold on our imagination: The prospect that some animal, inadvertently swallowed, would succeed in making itself comfortable inside us, partake of our food and drink, grow in size, and even produce offspring inside us, is simply too ghastly and too fascinating an idea to let go.

Conclusion: the folktale and AMCG

The author of *AMCG* did not invent the story of how Cathal was cured of the *lon crais*; he used an oral narrative which we have every reason to believe was already an old tale when the saga was composed. The oral Irish versions are not descended from the medieval saga, any more than the oral version from Madras is descended from the medieval Indian literary tale in

---

[62] "Irish folklore insists on the hazard of the "mankeeper," a creature that will creep, or leap, down one's throat (while sleeping on one's back with one's mouth open, probably snoring loudly) and give birth to young in one's stomach.... The only cure is to take a meal of salty corned beef and then lean above a pond with one's mouth ajar, whereupon the whole tribe will depart across one's tongue in desperate search of a drink" (Michael Viney, "Time for Lizards to Lie Down and Be Counted," *The Irish Times,* 5/13/2006).

the *Pañchākhjāna Vārttika.* The earliest attestation of a story, Stith Thompson reminds us, is not necessarily its source: "The fact that one may cite a literary form of a story, even a very old version, is by no means proof that we have arrived at the source of the tradition."[63] The first literary attestation of a story provides us with an important anchor in time and place, just as the first printed attestation of a word provides us with historical context: only rarely is the first attestation of a word the source of the word's subsequent attestations. The oral legend that inspired *AMCG* continued in oral circulation throughout Ireland and Scotland, with no apparent influence from the saga.[64] The modern oral versions which we have surveyed here are important because they constitute an independent witness to the oral tradition which the medieval author knew; they are our best evidence for a tradition which is of necessity undocumented.

Our analysis of the modern versions of ATU 285B* has taught us a great deal about the folktale's undocumented past, and about its relationship to *AMCG*, and it might be useful to sum up the most salient points here:

- The story's non-human protagonist, the *lon craís,* did not originate with the saga author. Its etymology suggests that the creature is firmly rooted in folk belief, and the survival in Scotland of *lon craois* to designate the animal protagonist offers testimony to the longevity of the term.
- In the oral versions, the person who performs the cure is often a lower-class character, in particular a tramp or traveller. This motif, which is found in versions throughout Ireland and Scotland, may have helped to suggest the role of Mac Con Glinne in the saga.
- The combination of motifs leading up to and culminating in the successful cure – the indoor setting, the meat roasted over an open fire, and the emergence of the *lon craís* – clearly indicates that the author's

---

[63] Stith Thompson, *The Folktale* (New York: The Dryden Press, 1946), 178.

[64] Its manuscript history would suggest that *AMCG* did not have a wide textual circulation: it is only attested in two late-medieval manuscripts, and is not found in the eighteenth- and nineteenth-century manuscripts that are known to have been in popular circulation and to have influenced oral tradition. There is no trace of any influence of *AMCG* on the modern folk versions; none of the oral versions e.g. contains any reference to the figure of Mac Con Glinne, his adventures in the land of plenty or his troubles with the monks of Cork; nor is there a single version in which the person afflicted is said to be a king.

oral antecedent belonged to what we have termed the "indoor redaction" of the story.

- The demise of the *lon crais* in *AMCG* also suggests the text's dependence on the indoor redaction: versions belonging to the indoor redaction are more likely to mention the creature being captured and killed than versions belonging to the outdoor redaction.

- We have seen that Recension B contains several additional details that may have been suggested by the folktale. The first of these is the genesis of the *lon crais,* which is unique to Recension B. In the oral versions, beside the more common form of the story according to which the animal creeps into a sleeper's open mouth, there are also versions in which the person inadvertently swallows or ingests the animal, just as Cathal ingests the embryonic demon inside the apples. The second detail is Cathal's reluctant fast in Recension B; the motif of the patient being forced to abstain from food or drink is present, as we have seen, in a significant number of folktale versions. The third and final detail that might owe something to the folktale is the motif of Cathal being tied with ropes to the timbers of the hall, which we have tentatively suggested might be inspired by versions of the folktale in which the patient is tied and hung from the rafters of the house.

- All the motifs we have identified in the saga are matched by oral versions located mainly in Munster, clustering particularly in north Munster and across the border to Galway into Connacht. This might suggest a Munster provenance for the saga's oral antecedent. One cannot, of course, assume that the modern distribution of a motif necessarily reflects its medieval distribution. However, change in distribution patterns occurs slowly and is usually traceable in the oral record. The fact that all the folktale motifs present in *AMCG* can be met with in oral versions from Munster suggests that the saga author was familiar with a Munster version of the folktale. The Munster affinities of the folktale motifs thus fit in well with the saga author's interest in, and knowledge of, the ecclesiastical and political landscape of Munster.

Having traced the outlines of the oral folktale in *AMCG*, I want to conclude with a few thoughts on the implications for our understanding of the saga. Most obviously, our analysis of the folktale demonstrates the saga's roots in oral storytelling tradition. It reminds us of the existence of an oral culture surrounding and pervading the literate monastic culture which was responsible for the production of Early Irish literature. Oral influence may be found in even such a quintessentially literate composition as *AMCG*.

Behind the saga's monastic setting, behind the voices of Latin erudition, of clerical admonition, of ecclesiastical learning, we hear other, more vernacular, voices: we hear Mac Con Glinne's satiric verses, we watch him jesting and farting in Pichán's hall, and behind it all, permeating the very plot of the narrative, we hear the voice of the oral storyteller.

Our analysis demonstrates beyond reasonable doubt the story's long continuity in Gaelic oral tradition. Continuity of tradition does not, however, imply immutability of tradition, as McKenna reminds us: "The purpose that a story serves can change with the passage of time and changing circumstances, with its migration from one cultural setting to another, and with the intentions of a storyteller, to mention just a few possible factors . . . "[65] As important as tracing the outlines of the legend in *AMCG* is to recognise the very significant transformation the story received at the hands of the literary artist. When an oral folktale enters the domain of written literature, a host of changes are likely to occur. These may include a change of the story's setting, its milieu and *dramatis personae;* its ideological or religious underpinnings, and its critical agenda, not to mention matters of literary genre and style, diction and narrative structure. The more we understand the underlying traditional narrative, the better can we appreciate that transformation.

In adapting the folktale to his own world, the author transposed it to a monastic milieu. The Christian framework of *AMCG* is evident in a myriad cultural and literary references, as Flower has pointed out: "At every turn we recognize a motive or a phrase from the theological, the historical, and the grammatical literature."[66] The author's concern with religious practices and doctrines, with Christian virtues as well as vices, with punishment and penance has been amply demonstrated.[67] The folktale's cast of characters has been adapted to the monastic milieu: most of the saga's *dramatis*

---

[65] McKenna, "Vision and Revision," 272.

[66] Flower, *Irish Tradition,* 76.

[67] Gwara, "Gluttony"; Herbert, "Contextual Considerations"; Éimear Williams, "*Aislinge Meic Conglinne*, Apples, and Byrthferth's *Enchiridion,*" *Cambrian Medieval Celtic Studies* 48 (2004), 45–73.

personae are either clerics or clerically educated, including the hero, Mac Con Glinne himself. Even the folktale's animal protagonist, the *lon crais,* is brought within a Christian framework and endowed with explicitly religious signification ("demon"; "Satan"). By elevating the hapless afflicted sufferer to royal status, the saga author sets him up as a target for his critical agenda; in the figure of Cathal, the author effectively lambasts royal greed and over-consumption: the king's voraciousness is critically portrayed as a disease, caused by a creature that is both bestial and demonic.

The most revealing indicator of the author's creative transformation of the folktale is his choice of hero. In the folktale, the main protagonist is the person who is inhabited by the creature; in *AMCG* the healer has become the main protagonist. We have seen that in the folktale, the healer is often played by a lower-class character. While the author has upgraded Cathal's role to the top of the social hierarchy, his hero remains a defiantly low-life figure. It is Mac Con Glinne the poet, the poor scholar, the satirist, the trickster, the successful quack, who is the unquestionable hero of the narrative, and there is no doubt that the creation of this vibrant, larger-than-life figure is one of the author's great achievements. Within the corpus of Early Irish literature, the choice of a lower-class character as the main protagonist and hero of the saga is unusual and significant. The author uses the energetic figure of Mac Con Glinne to express his criticism of greed and avarice in the representatives of church (Manchín) and state (Cathal).

The use of subject matter from a vernacular and lower-class milieu is in tune with the author's bottom-up perspective. The folktale is firmly rooted in folk belief–beliefs that were held by the farmers and agricultural laborers from whom the tale was recorded in the twentieth century, and that may have been held by farmers and agricultural laborers in the eleventh century. The saga author–literate and ecclesiastically educated as he is– never distances himself from this belief: there is no hint in the text that Cathal is not, in fact, inhabited by a living creature.[68]

This instance of the presence of folk belief in the saga is not an isolated example. *AMCG* opens a window onto the heterogeneous world of medieval popular belief and practice; it is an invaluable source for an understanding

---

[68] On the contrary; like the folktale, the saga offers "proof" for that belief: we watch the *lon crais* emerge from the king's mouth, thereby removing all doubt about its existence.

of medieval Gaelic folk religion.[69] Robin Flower pointed out that our hero "jests at relics, at tithes, at ascetic practices, at amulets, at the sermons and private devotions of the monks."[70] Unlike his critique of the religious establishment, however, the author's treatment of popular belief and practice strikes one as playful rather than necessarily critical; after all, the hero himself participates in and promulgates many of these practices, albeit in a parodistic fashion.

One example of the saga's use of such popular folk-religious material is in the "Apple Scene," which has been helpfully analysed by Williams.[71] In this scene Mac Con Glinne first uses his verbal skills to manipulate the king: Mac Con Glinne invokes a religious counting rhyme to trick Cathal to share his apples with him (three for the trinity; four for the four gospels; five for the five books of Moses; etc.). Despite its religious background and didactic orientation, which Williams rightly stresses, the rhyme employed by Mac Con Glinne is widely attested in oral tradition and has been assigned a place in the Aarne-Thompson-Uther international folktale index (ATU 2010 "Who knows one?"). It is best known for its place in the Jewish Passover liturgy, where it has served to entertain countless generations of children and adults. Like other aspects of the saga, the rhyme is situated at the intersection between the literate culture of official religion and the oral culture of vernacular folk religion.

The elite world of literacy in Early Ireland was not hermetically sealed from the wider currents of oral popular culture. The author of *AMCG* had access to, and shared in, the vibrant world of vernacular tradition. Like his hero, who exploits and performs popular genres, the author employs low-status folk narratives to make his point: His use of the folktale is thus part and parcel of his overall artistic strategy. The saga's humour involves the deliberate and comic juxtaposition of elite and vernacular/vulgar registers. Above all else, *AMCG* is about the playful performance of tradition; the author has more than one string to his bow, and he enjoys playing both high and low notes, to the best of his considerable abilities.

---

[69] Folk religion, in Don Yoder's classic statement, is "the totality of all those views and practices of religion that exist among the people apart from and alongside the strictly theological and liturgical forms of the official religion," "Toward a Definition of Folk Religion," *Western Folklore* 33, 1974: 1–16 at 14.

[70] Robin Flower, *The Irish Tradition* (Dublin: The Lilliput Press, 1994), 76.

[71] Williams, "Apples."

THE DEMON OF GLUTTONY

Acknowledgments

I am grateful to a great number of colleagues for helpful comments on oral and written iterations of this paper: Máirín Ní Dhonnchadha; Erich Poppe; Jacqueline Borsje; Roisin McLaughlin; Gregory Toner; Mícheál Briody; Joseph F. Nagy and Catherine McKenna.

I wish to thank the Director of the National Folklore Collection at University College Dublin for permission to publish archival materials, and to my friends and former colleagues at the NFC, Críostóir Mac Cárthaigh, Jonny Dillon, Bairbre Ní Fhloinn, Anna Bale, and Séamas Ó Catháin, who shared versions of the folktale with me or offered help in other ways. I am also grateful to the Director of the School of Scottish Studies at the University of Edinburgh for access to the School's tale archive and permission to consult and cite from its card catalogue. Margaret Mills kindly shared an Afghan version of the tale which she collected in 1975.

Frequently cited editions/translations

The following number in brackets is the footnote at first occurrence which contains the full bibliographical citation.
Ermacora et al., "Critical Anthology" [35]
Ford, *Celtic Poets* [2]
Jackson, *Aislinge* [2]
Meyer, *Vision* [1]
Preston-Matto, *Aislinge* [2]
Thurneysen, "Vision" [1]

What Did Cynddelw Know About the Old North?

Celeste L. Andrews

Characters who have their origins in the Old North (in Welsh: *yr Hen Ogledd*) can be found in many places throughout the extant body of medieval Welsh literature, including in the saga englynion cycles, in the poetry of the Black Book of Carmarthen, the Book of Taliesin, and the Book of Aneirin, and in the Triads of the Island of Britain (*Trioedd Ynys Prydein*). It is therefore curious that allusions to these characters are sparse in the work of the Poets of the Princes (*Beirdd y Tywysogion*), the court poets of the twelfth and thirteenth centuries. Allusions by these court poets to people and places from medieval Welsh tradition are some of our best and most reliable evidence of the breadth and vitality of that tradition as it stood in the late twelfth century, a crucial time in Welsh history.[1] While characters associated with the Old North are not entirely missing from the Poets of the Princes corpus, there is a notable disparity of that region's prevalence in the work of the court poets and elsewhere in medieval Welsh tradition, including in the earlier poetry but also in the triadic material that is usually thought to have been developed for the use by these court poets. This disparity raises questions about how well *cyfarwyddyd*, or Welsh storytelling material, about these characters was known to the Poets of the Princes and to what extent stories about the Old North were circulating in Wales in the twelfth and thirteenth centuries. This article aims to shed light on this issue by looking specifically at the work of a single court poet, Cynddelw Brydydd Mawr.

Cynddelw is considered to be perhaps the greatest of the Poets of the Princes. He was active between around 1155 and 1195 and sang in the courts of the most important political players of the day. He was born in Powys and his strong connection to that kingdom is evident from the content of his poetry and the long list of Powysian rulers and noblemen, both major

---

[1] The best work to date on these allusions is Rachel Bromwich, "Cyfeiriadau Traddodiadol a Chwedlonol y Gogynfeirdd," in *Beirdd a Thywysogion: Barddoniaeth Llys yng Nghymru, Iwerddon, a'r Alban*, ed. Morfydd E. Owen and Brynley F. Roberts (Cardiff: University of Wales Press, 1996), 202–218. Another important related work is D. Myrddin Lloyd, *Rhai Agweddau ar Ddysg y Gogynfeirdd: Darlith Goffa G.J. Williams* (Cardiff: University of Wales Press, 1977).

and minor, that he counted as patrons. These patrons included Madog ap Maredudd, Owain Cyfeiliog, Iorwerth Goch, and Rhirid Flaidd, among others. Outside of Powys, Cynddelw also composed poems to Owain Gwynedd and the Lord Rhys of Deheubarth, among others. In addition to these formal panegyrics and elegies, several poems in lower registers survive which are attributed to Cynddelw. The breadth of his work is remarkable.[2]

3,852 lines of Cynddelw's work have come down to us in manuscripts which survive from the Middle Ages. This is far more than any of his contemporaries; more than double the amount of surviving poetry by Llywarch ap Llywelyn (Prydydd y Moch), for instance, whose work survives in the second largest amount.[3] This large corpus is both a blessing and a curse: the wealth of information available makes it easier to ascertain the breadth of Cynddelw's knowledge of medieval Welsh tradition than any of his contemporaries, but this disparity in survival can distort our view of him and make him appear to be more unique and outstanding in his range of allusion and reference than he in fact was in his own day.[4] For this reason, I do not intend to argue that Cynddelw had access to more or different information than his contemporary poets when it came to the Old North.

Cynddelw was familiar with a number of figures associated with the Old North who are known from various texts in a handful of medieval

---

[2] Ann Parry Owen, "'A mi, feirdd, i mewn a chwi allan': Cynddelw Bryddyd Mawr a'i grefft," in *Beirdd a Thywysogion: Barddoniaeth Llys yng Nghymru, Iwerddon, a'r Alban*, 143–165, at 143–44.

[3] *Gwaith Cynddelw Brydydd Mawr I*, ed. Ann Parry Owen and Nerys Ann Jones (Cardiff: University of Wales Press, 1991), xxxiii–xxxiv.

[4] A statistical analysis comparing the number of allusions in the work of the Poets of the Princes versus the amount of extant poetry there is attributed to them would be a worthwhile future investigation, but would be complicated by questions of authorship and attribution that are still open to debate. Take, for instance, Marged Haycock's argument that Prydydd y Moch was the author of many of the anonymous poems in the voice of the "legendary" Taliesin that are extant in the Book of Taliesin (see Marged Haycock, ed. and trans. *Legendary Poems from the Book of Taliesin* (Aberystwyth: CMCS), 27–36), or the arguments discussed below regarding the authorship of the poems attributed to Owain Cyfeiliog. If Haycock's argument regarding Prydydd y Moch is accepted, we may say that he was particularly interested in the "legendary" Taliesin persona in the same way that this article argues Cynddelw was particularly interested in the Old North.

Welsh manuscripts; chiefly, the Black Book of Carmarthen, the Book of Taliesin, and the Book of Aneirin. Although these are thirteenth- and fourteenth-century manuscripts, the texts within were probably composed significantly earlier but, in most cases, attempts to secure precise dates have so far not been fruitful. We do know that Cynddelw's poetry was composed in the second half of the twelfth century. For this reason, an in-depth look at Cynddelw's allusions to the Old North material may provide a picture of what information was available to the Poets of the Princes at that time while also shedding light on this remarkable poet's relationship with material about which many questions remain. I have relied heavily in this endeavor on foundational work done by Rachel Bromwich, Ann Parry Owen, and Nerys Ann Jones, whose various works on allusions to *cyfarwyddyd* in the work of the Poets of the Princes made this investigation possible.[5]

What Cynddelw knew about material preserved in the Book of Taliesin

Five poets allude to Taliesin within the Poets of the Princes corpus for a total of six allusions.[6] One of those allusions belongs to Cynddelw, in his poem to Rhirid Flaidd and his brother:

> Ny bu warthlef kert **Kynuerching–werin**
> O benn **Talyessin**, bartrin beirtrig
> Y'm kyueteu breu, brwydyr diedig.[7]

Cynddelw refers to Taliesin as the poet of the "descendants of Cynfarch." This is a poetic way to refer to the famous king of the Old North, Urien Rheged, and his family: Cynfarch being Urien's father. It is thereby

---

[5] Rachel Bromwich, "Notes to the Personal Names" in *Trioedd Ynys Prydein: The Triads of the Island of Britain*, 4th edition (Cardiff: University of Wales Press, 2014); Bromwich, "Cyfeiriadau Traddodiadol a Chwedlonol"; Ann Parry Owen, "Mynegai i Enwau Priod ym Marddoniaeth Beirdd y Tywysogion," *Llên Cymru* 20 (1997), 25–45; Nerys Ann Jones, "*Hengerdd* in the Age of the Poets of the Princes," in *Beyond the Gododdin: Dark Age Scotland in Medieval Wales* (St. Andrews: The Committee for Dark Ages Studies, University of St. Andrews), 41–80.

[6] Owen, "Mynegai," 37. The five other allusions to Taliesin are: Elidir Sais (*Cyfres Beirdd y Tywysogion* (henceforth *CBT*) I no. 17.18n), Llywarch ap Llywelyn (*CBT* V no. 15.33n & no. 25.3n), and Einion ap Madog ap Rhahawd (*CBT* VI 25.37n).

[7] "Marwnad Rhirid Flaidd ac Arthen ei Frawd," in *Gwaith Cynddelw I*, no. 24.153–56. Bolded for emphasis.

41

established that Cynddelw refers here to the so-called 'historical' Taliesin who lived and composed in the Old North, whose patron was Urien, and not the later 'legendary' Taliesin persona, around whom another tradition had arisen removed from the Old North, which was much more widely known in the later Middle Ages.[8] Allusions to Taliesin made by other court poets are either clearly in reference to this 'legendary' Taliesin, or are ambiguous.[9] The 'legendary' Taliesin became disconnected from Urien and the Old North, and Cynddelw's allusion, therefore, is important evidence for the fact that traditions recording the 'historical' Taliesin persisted until the twelfth century, at least in the circles in which Cynddelw traveled.[10]

Similarly, from Cynddelw comes the only allusion to Argoed Llwyfain in the Poets of the Princes corpus, the site of a battle fought between Urien's forces and the Saxons according to one of the poems attributed to the 'historical' Taliesin.[11] Nerys Ann Jones understood this to mean that Cynddelw was familiar with the Taliesin poem itself, but it could simply be that he knew the story of this battle from a different source.[12] Cynddelw is also one of only two Poets of the Princes to name Urien's son, Owain mab Urien.[13] He was familiar with the tradition of Owain's ravens, a tradition that is best known from the prose tale The Dream of Rhonabwy (*Breuddwyd Rhonabwy*). Cynddelw depicts these ravens ravaging the fallen warriors of Bernicia in his poem to Owain Gwynedd.[14]

---

[8] Jones, "Hengerdd," 59–60. For the best source on the formation of this later persona see the introduction to Haycock, ed. and trans. *Legendary Poems from the Book of Taliesin.*

[9] Jones, "Hengerdd," 48. Cynddelw is the only court poet to make a connection between Taliesin and Urien.

[10] If Haycock's argument regarding Prydydd y Moch's authorship of these poems is accepted (see above note 4), the number of references to the 'legendary' Taliesin persona attributed to Prydydd y Moch would skyrocket. However, Cynddelw would continue to stand alone in his interest in the 'historical' Taliesin.

[11] "Marwnad Owain Gwynedd," in *Gwaith Cynddelw Brydydd Mawr II*, ed. Nerys Ann Jones and Ann Parry Owen (Cardiff: University of Wales Press, 1995), no. 4.107–112.

[12] Jones, "Hengerdd," 48.

[13] Owen, "Mynegai," 35.

[14] "Arwyrain Madog ap Maredudd," in *Gwaith Cynddelw II*, no. 1.27–8. These lines read: "*Marchogynt ar ueirw, ar uil urien / Marchogyon Bryneich branhes ywein!*"

Urien himself is mentioned in three poems by Poets of the Princes.[15] One of these poems was composed by Cynddelw, who mentions him twice within five lines in a poem to Owain Cyfeiliog:

> Brwydyr gygrwn gygres, bryssyws bwyd branhes
> Uch Kawres, caer amgen
> Balch ongyr, angert **Uruoen,**
> Ball ar lyw am lanneu Hafren!
> Braw rac y wryawr, g6rtwawr a gwrthwan
> A gwrtwaew yn aghen,
> Bangor toryf taerlew, llew llawen,
> Blaengar glew gletyfal **Uryen.**[16]

It is extremely interesting to note that Urien's name is spelled two different ways. The second time he names Urien, Cynddelw uses the standard Middle Welsh spelling *Uryen*, but at the first mention of him in the poem, only a few lines previous, the name is spelled *Uruoen*. This instance is the only attested example of this variant spelling of the name. An explanation for this inconsistent spelling may be found in the meter of the poem, as *Uryen* is two syllables while *Uruoen* is three.[17] It appears that this unusual *Uruoen* spelling was used to provide another syllable and fit the meter of the poem, so we can be reasonably certain that this tri-syllabic spelling or pronunciation is intrinsic to Cynddelw's poetry and not a later innovation of a scribe who copied it.

Ifor Williams thought that this tri-syllabic form of Urien's name derived from the form found in the *Historia Brittonum–Urbgen*[18]–and went so far as to suggest that it may have been the spelling the 'historical' Taliesin himself used, the implication apparently being that Cynddelw got

---

[15] Owen, "Mynegai," 37. The other two allusions to Urien in the corpus come from the anonymous author of Mawl Hywel ap Goronwy (CBT I no. 1.36n) and Meilyr Brydydd (CBT I no. 3.26n).

[16] "Canu Owain Cyfeiliog," in *Gwaith Cynddelw I*, no. 16.95–102.

[17] Owen and Jones assert that *Uruoen* is tri-syllabic in *Gwaith Cynddelw I*, note to no. 16.97 (p. 213).

[18] *Historia Brittonum* is in Latin but this can be taken as an Old Welsh form of the name. *Uruoen* and *Urien* are two reflexes of this Old Welsh form, with *Uruoen* retaining the composition vowel that *Urien* has dropped (see Kenneth Jackson, *Language and History in Early Britain* (Dublin: Four Courts Press, 1994), 647–8.)

this spelling straight from a manuscript that preserved Taliesin's spelling.[19] While I would not assume that this was the form of the name that Taliesin himself used, this unique spelling of Urien's name does raise questions about Cynddelw's source. One tantalizing possibility–though it can only be a possibility–is that he was working from a written source that preserved the old spelling.

What Cynddelw knew about material preserved in the Black Book of Carmarthen

Myrddin was known to the Poets of the Princes as one of the *Cynfeirdd* (in English: "early poets") and as a seer from the Old North, a tradition that is reflected in the allusions to him in the Poets of the Princes corpus. From poems preserved for us in the Black Book of Carmarthen, such as *Afallennau* ("the Apple Trees"), *Ymddiddan Myrddin a Thaliesin* ("the Discussion of Myrddin and Taliesin"), and *Cyfoesi Myrddin a Gwenddyd ei Chwaer* ("the Colloquy of Myrddin and Gwenddydd his Sister"), among others, there emerges what could loosely be called a 'Myrddin cycle.' According to this cycle, Myrddin was a legendary poet who fought with his lord, Gwenddolau, at the Battle of Arderydd in the Old North. Myrddin went insane during this battle and fled into the forest where he became a wild man, hence his epithet *gwyllt* or 'wild'.[20] There is no hint of Geoffrey of Monmouth's Merlinus here, the magician and prophet who was instrumental in Arthur's conception in *De gestis Britonum* and who would later become an important character in the post-Galfridian Arthurian tradition.

Myrddin is mentioned by name nine times in the Poets of the Princes corpus, far more than any other single Cynfardd.[21] Nerys Ann Jones has noted that these allusions from the twelfth and thirteenth centuries attest to

---

[19] Ifor Williams, ed. *Canu Taliesin* (Cardiff: University of Wales Press, 1960), 37–39.

[20] A good place to start for information on Myrddin is A.O.H Jarman, "The Merlin Legend and the Welsh Tradition of Prophecy," in *The Arthur of the Welsh*, ed. Bromwich et al. (Cardiff: University of Wales Press, 1991), 117–140. See also Bromwich, *Trioedd Ynys Prydein*, 458–462.

[21] Owen, "Mynegai," 35. The other eight allusions to Myrddin belong to Elidir Sais (*CBT* I no. 16.7n & no. 17.21n), Llywarch Llaety (*CBT* II 6.46n), Gwynfardd Brycheiniog (*CBT* II 25.43n), Prydydd y Moch (*CBT* V 5.62n & 24.41), Dafydd Benfras (*CBT* VI 25.4n) and Iorwerth Fychan (*CBT* VII 30.60n).

the fact that the Poets of the Princes knew "a wide range of traditions about this legendary figure."[22] Evidently, Cynddelw knew the tradition concerning Gwenddolau and Arderydd: he is one of two Poets of the Princes to name the Battle of Arderydd in his work, along with the thirteenth-century poet Llygad Gŵr.[23] Cynddelw's allusion to Arderydd does not betray knowledge any more detailed than that of Llygad Gŵr. It is interesting to note, however, that in both Cynddelw's and Llygad Gŵr's poems the location of this battle is spelled *Arderydd*, as opposed to the apparently earlier form of the place name, *Arfderydd*, which is found in the Black Book of Carmarthen.[24] This indicates that, if Cynddelw did have access to any written sources from which he took material, as speculated above regarding the spelling *Uruoen*, he did not have the same sources that made their way into the Black Book.

Turning now to Myrddin's lord, Gwenddolau, it should be noted that Cynddelw is the only one among the Poets of the Princes who alludes to him. This allusion comes in Cynddelw's apology poem to the Lord Rhys, in which he refers to Gwenddolau's "famous anger."[25] This dearth of references to Gwenddolau in the work of the other court poets is interesting because, similar to the pattern we have seen with Taliesin and Myrddin, Gwenddolau is well attested in both poetry, found in the Black Book of Carmarthen, and the Triads of the Island of the Britain. In the Triads, Gwenddolau is primarily known as the leader of the host who fought at Arderydd, but in one triad he is depicted as being in possession of two ferocious and perhaps supernatural birds and, in a related text known as the "Thirteen Treasures of the Island of Britain" (*Tri Thlws ar Ddeg Ynys Prydein*), a magical *gwyddbwyll* board.[26] Rachel Bromwich has noted that

---

[22] Jones, "Hengerdd," 45.

[23] Owen, "Mynegai," 38.

[24] Jones, "Hengerdd," 46.

[25] "Awdl Ddadolwch yr Arglwydd Rhys," in *Gwaith Cynddelw II*, no. 9.202n. The line in question reads: "*G6rtuannyar g6rtuar Gwynndoleu*."

[26] The Two Birds of Gwenddolau are found in Triad 32 (*Try Wyr a wnaeth y Teir Mat Gyflauan* / "Three Men who performed the Three Fortunate Slaughters"): "*ac yeu o eur a oed arnadunt: dwy gelein o'r Kymry a yssynt ar eu kinya6 a dwy ar eu kwynos.*" (Bromwich, *Trioedd Ynys Prydein*, 73.) Why birds belonging to this hero of the Old North would be eating corpses of the Cymry is a puzzle. For the *gwyddbwyll* board, see Bromwich, *Trioedd Ynys Prydein*, 259.

these magical possessions suggest that Gwenddolau had become a legendary figure perhaps disconnected with his "historical" counterpart.[27] If such a shift was taking place and is visible within the Triads, it is notable that it is completely absent from the extant work of the Poets of the Princes, especially since it is generally thought that these Triads were created by and for those court poets. If this were indeed the case, one would expect that a figure as well attested in the Triads as Gwenddolau would merit more than one brief reference in the extant court poetry. Such a brief reference cannot be definitively identified with either the 'legendary' or 'historical' traditions regarding this figure (if such a dichotomy existed), but I would tentatively suggest that, in invoking the anger of Gwenddolau, Cynddelw has in mind someone closer to the warlord who fought a famous battle in the Old North than the more fanciful owner of magical objects.

What Cynddelw knew about material preserved in the Triads of the Island of Britain

Before delving into a discussion of Cynddelw's references to Old North material found in the Triads of the Island of Britain, it will be helpful to briefly discuss the date and development of this corpus. Rachel Bromwich has convincingly shown that some version of a collection of triads existed by the early twelfth century, and that this collection became the core of the versions of the Triads now extant in manuscripts from the thirteenth century onward.[28] Bromwich further identified two versions of the corpus, which she termed the "Early Version" and the "White and Red Version" respectively. It is important to keep in mind that, while there is a fair amount of variation, these versions very often contain the same triads in a differing order.[29] There is no reason to suppose that a version of a triad found in the later "White and Red Version" could not have been circulating in some form during Cynddelw's lifetime in the second half of the twelfth century. As we will see, it seems likely that Cynddelw was drawing on a triadic source in a few instances.

---

[27] Bromwich, *Trioedd Ynys Prydein*, 376.

[28] Ibid., xcviii.

[29] See discussion in ibid. xi–lii.

One triad in particular is important to the discussion at hand. This is "the Three Red-Speared Bards" (*Tri Gwa(y)6rud Beird*).[30] This triad names three obscure *Cynfeirdd* whose work does not survive. These poets are Tristfardd, the bard of Urien, Dygennelw, the bard of Owain ap Urien, and Afan Ferddig, the bard of Cadwallon. All three of these figures are very sparsely attested, not only in the work of the Poets of the Princes, but in all the extant sources, so it is very remarkable that Cynddelw named all three. Afan Ferddig, who is not associated with the Old North and so will not be considered further here, is mentioned by Cynddelw in his poem to Hywel ab Owain Gwynedd, and this is the only reference to him in the work of the Poets of the Princes.[31] Additionally, in an elegy for Ednyfed, the lord of Crogen, Cynddelw says, "Tristfardd fyddaf." While it is more likely that this should be taken as "I am [or will be] a sad poet" than a reference to the personal name, it also seems possible that Cynddelw, with his demonstrated interest in the Cynfeirdd, was playing on the name of the early poet, mentioned in the "Three Red-Speared Bards" triad, whose name, if not his work, he was familiar with.[32] Aside from these obscure references, Tristfardd is only known from a fragment of a poem that survives in a late medieval copy.[33]

The reference to Owain's bard Dygynnelw is particularly significant to this discussion because Cynddelw's use of this name does not actually refer to the bard. The name Dygynnelw exists in only two places in all of medieval Welsh literature: once in this "Three Red-Speared Bards" triad, and once in an elegy Cynddelw wrote for his young son–as the name of that son![34] It is difficult to escape the thought that Cynddelw named his son after

---

[30] For the discussion of the variation in manuscript readings of this epithet, which early on read 'gwavrud' ("lordly/red-stained") but later read '*gway6rud*' ('red-speared'), see Bromwich, Trioedd Ynys Prydein, 20. Because Cynddelw never alludes to any of these figures being "red-stained" or "red-speared" the distinction is largely immaterial here.

[31] Owen, "Mynegai," 26.

[32] Jones, "Hengerdd," 44.

[33] Bromwich, *Trioedd Ynys Prydein*, 507–08. This poem is a dialogue between Tristfardd, Urien, and an unnamed woman (possibly Urien's wife).

[34] This poem is *Marwnad Dygynnelw*, which can be found at *Gwaith Cynddelw I* no. 30.

Owain's bard from the triad, and I would not be the first to suggest it.[35] Dygynnelw was clearly not a common name and the coincidence is just too great. If this is indeed the case, it is powerful evidence that Cynddelw felt some strong connection to this otherwise unknown poet from the Old North.

Another obscure figure associated with the Old North who is named in the Triads and relevant here is a certain Gleissiar Gogledd, who is said to be the father of the "Three Brave Men of the Island of Britain" (*Tri Gle6 Ynys Prydein*). Apart from this triad and Cynddelw's mention of the sons of Gleissiar in his poem to Rhirid Flaidd, this Gleissiar is entirely unknown.[36] In fact, I have included him here because of his epithet–"of the North"–but it is not clear whether he, in fact, came from the Old North, or merely North Wales. It is important to note, however, that Gleissiar is named only in the "White and Red Version" of the Triads. If Cynddelw learned of Gleissiar from a triadic source, this version of the "Three Brave Men" must have been circulating during the second half of the twelfth century.[37]

What Cynddelw knew about material preserved in the Book of Aneirin

The Book of Aneirin is the only manuscript in which the text of the *Gododdin* is preserved. No discussion of the Old North material could be complete without touching on this very early Welsh poem, which commemorates the men of Gododdin, a kingdom of the Old North. This kingdom is said to have fallen to the Saxons at the Battle of Catraeth. References to Aneirin and his work are extremely sparse in the Poets of the Princes corpus.[38] The only extant reference to Aneirin in the later Poets of

---

[35] "It is tempting to conclude that Cynddelw named his son *Dygynnelw* after the earlier *Cynfardd* attached to Owain ab Urien (concerning whom nothing is known)." (Bromwich, *Trioedd Ynys Prydein*, 336). Jones and Owen follow Bromwich in suggesting "mae'n bosibl fod Cynddelw wedi enwi ei fab ar ôl y Cynfardd hwnnw," ("it's possible that Cynddelw named his son after that Cynfardd") (*Gwaith Cynddelw I*, p. 367 (translation mine)) but, in "Hengerdd in the Age of the Poets of the Princes," Jones has dispensed with the hesitancy and takes Cynddelw's son's namesake as a simple fact (p. 44).

[36] This poem is "Marwnad Rhirid Flaidd ac Arthen ei Frawd," *Gwaith Cynddelw I*, no. 24.46n. It may be interesting to note that this is the same poem in which Cynddelw names Urien Rheged twice, discussed above.

[37] Bromwich, *Trioedd Ynys Prydein*, 361.

[38] Jones, "Hengerdd," 49.

the Princes corpus comes from Dafydd Benfras in a poem to Llywelyn ap Iorwerth.[39] Our proof that the court poets had any familiarity with the *Gododdin* at all comes almost entirely from a single poem–*Hirlas Owain*– which is attributed to the poet-prince Owain Cyfeiliog.

Owain Cyfeiliog has already been mentioned above as one of Cynddelw's many patrons. He was the nephew of Madog ap Maredudd and, after Madog's death, Owain inherited much of southern Powys from him, including the *cantref* of Cyfeiliog from which he got his epithet.[40] Two extant poems are attributed to Owain, including *Hirlas Owain*. It commemorates an expedition Owain's warband took to rescue Owain's brother, Meurig, from imprisonment in Maelor in 1156. The poem depicts the celebratory feast that took place after this expedition, with the poet addressing the cupbearer whose job it was to ensure that the drinking horn (the *hirlas*) remained full.[41] The text of the poem explicitly links the heroic deeds of Owain's warband to those of the warband of Mynyddog Mwynfawr, the lord of the Gododdin, and from verbal echoes that appear throughout the poem, it is clear that *Hirlas Owain*'s author had direct knowledge of the *Gododdin*.[42]

Additionally, the poem compares Owain's warband to that of Belyn of Llŷn which, along with the warband of Mynyddog of Catraeth, makes up two of the "Three Noble Retinues" (*Teir Gosgord Advwyn*) in the Triads.[43] Belyn is not an easy figure to pin down; his name appears in a handful of places throughout medieval Welsh literature, including in the tenth-century Welsh annal *Annales Cambriae*, and he may have been an ally of Cadwallon against Edwin of Northumbria.[44] This reference in *Hirlas Owain* is the only reference to Belyn in the Poets of the Princes corpus.[45] The forms of Belyn and Mynyddog's names used in this poem align with those found in the

---

[39] Owen, "Mynegai," 26. This reference is at CBT IV no. 25.5n.

[40] For an overview of Owain's political and military career, see Gruffydd Aled Williams, "Rhagymadrodd i Ganu Owain Cyfeiliog" in *Gwaith Llywelyn Fardd I ac Eraill o Feirdd y Ddeddegfed Ganrif* (Cardiff: University of Wales Press, 1994), 194-225 at 194–98.

[41] Williams, "Rhagymadrodd," 221.

[42] Williams, "Rhagymadrodd," 207–08.

[43] Bromwich, *Trioedd Ynys Prydein*, 70.

[44] Ibid., 287.

[45] Owen, "Mynegai," 26.

"White and Red Version" of the Triads, much like Cynddelw's reference to Gleissiar Gogledd mentioned above.[46] Again, this may suggest that the author of the poem was familiar with this particular version of the "Three Noble Retinues" triad, if not working directly from it.

This is all significant because it appears that the author of *Hirlas Owain* was probably not Owain Cyfeiliog after all, but his court poet—Cynddelw. Gruffydd Aled Williams has identified fifteen verbal correspondences between *Hirlas Owain* and various poems attributed to Cynddelw.[47] Although he concedes that it's possible that the proximity of the two men led to Cynddelw's work influencing Owain's poetry or vice versa, Williams concludes that *Hirlas Owain* is likely to share an author with that of Cynddelw's body of work–that is, that it was composed by Cynddelw himself and came to be falsely attributed to Owain Cyfeiliog later.[48] This poem is the single best example of material relating to the Old North being incorporated by one of the Poets of the Princes and, if we accept Cynddelw as its author, it becomes another example of material relating to the Old North with which he was uniquely familiar.

Conclusions

It has been shown that Cynddelw was familiar with material that has come down to us in the Book of Taliesin which links him to Urien Rheged and his son Owain, as well as material in the Black Book of Carmarthen associating Myrddin with Gwenddolau and the Battle of Arderydd. We have seen that, while figures associated with the Old North were not entirely unknown to the other Poets of the Princes, Cynddelw seems to have had a deeper knowledge of their stories, with details and specifics that are lacking across the board in the work of the other court poets. We have seen further that some lesser-known figures, such as Gleissiar Gogledd and Belyn of Llŷn, are mentioned in Cynddelw's work but not in the work of the other Poets of the Princes. It further seems likely that Cynddelw was working specifically from triads that later appear in the "White and Red Version" of

---

[46] An alternate version of this triad, in Bromwich's "Early Version," names "Mynyddawg of Eidyn" and "Melyn mab Kynuelyn" as opposed to the "White and Red" version's "Mynyddawg of Catraeth" and "Belyn of Llŷn." (Bromwich, *Trioedd Ynys Prydein*, 70.)

[47] Williams, "Rhagymadrodd," 201–04.

[48] Ibid., 205.

the Triads of the Island of Britain, judging from his references to these obscure figures. We have seen also that, if we accept Gruffydd Aled William's argument that Cynddelw was the true author of *Hirlas Owain*, he alone among his contemporaries can be shown to have known the *Gododdin*, and that he likely named his son, Dygynnelw, after the bard of Owain ap Urien.

This article began with a caution that the disparity in how much of Cynddelw's work survives relative to his contemporary poets can lead to a distortion of our view of him. The fact that Cynddelw is alone in mentioning a certain figure does not necessarily mean that that figure was unknown to his fellow court poets. Untold numbers of references have been lost. However, what we have here is not only a difference in number–the *nature* of Cynddelw's allusions to Old North figures is markedly different from those of his fellow Poets of the Princes. This is seen most starkly with the material relating to Urien and the *Gododdin*, two subjects about which Cynddelw seems to have known a great deal and for which he may have been consulting written sources. All of this probably raises more questions than it answers, and more research is needed before any firm conclusions can be reached about its implications for the transmission of traditions from the Old North in twelfth-century Wales. I am very interested to see if these patterns persist when we broaden our gaze to all of Welsh tradition and not just the Old North, or if new patterns emerge.

I would say further that perhaps we should give Cynddelw back some of his uniqueness and not assume that the work of the Poets of the Princes can be taken as a single unit when it comes to their references and allusions. They were individuals, after all, each with their own interests. The poets overall cannot be shown to know the details of stories about the Old North– but *Cynddelw* knew them. It would be arguing from silence to suggest that he somehow had more *access* to this material than his contemporaries, but I cannot help but come to the conclusion that Cynddelw was extremely *interested* in the Old North and perhaps especially with the famous poets who hailed from there and that this interest is reflected in the unique ways he interacted with this material throughout his career.

Acknowledgements

I would like to thank the organizers of HCC 39 and the editors of *PHCC* 39 for all their hard work throughout this process, especially Shannon Rose

Parker, for her insights and attention to detail. I'd also like to thank the anonymous reviewer, Catherine McKenna, and Michaela Jacques for reading this paper at various stages and offering their thoughts, advice, and corrections.

Studi var an astrou (1848): the first scientific text in the Breton language

Nelly Blanchard

The Breton Enlightenment?

The mid-nineteenth century was a time when Bretonism[1] and neo-Bardism[2] were at their height in Western Brittany[3] and for a century and a half this gave a new direction to Breton-language literature that was seeking to define, differentiate and distinguish itself from French literature.[4] During this period, in 1848, Paul Lebreton wrote and published *Studi var an astrou* [study on the stars and planets], a treatise on astronomy in Breton to educate the people of Western Brittany about the march of the universe. This was probably the first scientific text ever published in Breton. However, the 'unacknowledgement' of this text in the annals of Breton literature and writing raises the question of the author's intentions. Paul Lebreton was an

---

[1] Bretonism was based on a literary or historiographic vision of a Brittany which had become a desert at the end of the Roman invasion, and was re-celtified by Bretons from Great Britain. This embedded Brittany in an exclusively Celtic past viewed through the prism of insular Celtic countries, in opposition to the Romanist view of Armorica as an extension of Gaul, and thus a province of the Roman Empire and a fundamental part of the history of France. Bretonism therefore developed through the optic of a strong distinctiveness vis-à-vis France. About Bretonism, see Guiomar, Jean-Yves, *Le bretonisme. Les historiens bretons au XIXe siècle* (Mayenne: Société d'histoire et d'archéologie de Bretagne, 1987).

[2] The Breton neo-bardic movement is modelled on the Welsh neo-bardic and neo-druidic movement. Launching a trend for neo-bardism after a trip to Wales in 1838–1839 which had inspired Théodore Hersart de La Villemarqué (1815–1895). This inspired other Bretons to travel to Wales, notably François Jaffrennou (1879–1956), future grand druid of the Breton *Gorsedd*, who made a trip in 1899 from which he returned as a bard with the name Taldir ab Herninn. The Breton *Gorsedd* dates from 1900–1901.

[3] The Breton-speaking part of Brittany (Upper Brittany is the French-Gallo speaking region).

[4] Blanchard, Nelly and Thomas, Mannaig, "Qu'est-ce qu'une périphérie littéraire?", in *Des littératures périphériques* (Rennes: Presses Universitaires de Rennes, 2014), 20–21.

author as unknown as his texts, so who was he really? And what were his influences and motivations? This study intertwines a literature review and archival/terminological research with a study of Lebreton's astronomy approach to try to answer these questions. In addition, a comparison with other similar texts or schools of thought in Breton literature has led me to hypothesize that the Breton Enlightenment[5] did take place, but hardly left any traces.

1. Paul Lebreton: an unknown author

Absent from the anthologies

Studi var an astrou is not mentioned in any history or anthology of Breton literature: it is not cited in Hémon,[6] Rudel,[7] Abeozen,[8] Gourvil,[9] or in the anthology written by Yves Le Berre focusing on the nineteenth century.[10] However, this work was well and truly published because it is mentioned in the *Bibliographie de la France ou Journal général de l'imprimerie et de la librairie* in the chapter on diverse dialects in France,[11] and surprisingly, in a 1854 German mathematical literature review.[12] As for its author, Paul Lebreton, he is just as unknown as his work.

---

[5] The Enlightenment was an intellectual movement of the seventeenth and eighteenth centuries that promoted knowledge and its dissemination. Applying it to this small breton work seems disproportionate, but the author's intention is very much in keeping with this motivation, even with a time lag of a century.

[6] Hemon, Roparz, *La langue bretonne et ses combats* (La Baule: Éditions de Bretagne, 1947), 149 et seq.

[7] Rudel, Yves-Marie, *Panorama de la littérature bretonne des origines à nos jours* (Rennes: Imprimerie bretonne, 1950).

[8] Abeozen, [Fañch Eliès], *Istor lennegezh vrezhonek an amzer-vremañ* (Brest: Al Liamm, 1957).

[9] Gourvil, Francis, *Langue et littérature bretonnes* (Paris: Presses Universitaires de France, 1968).

[10] Le Berre, Yves, *La littérature de langue bretonne. Livres et brochures entre 1790 et 1918* (Brest: Ar skol vrezoneg- Emgleo Breiz, 1994).

[11] *Bibliographie de la France ou Journal général de l'imprimerie et de la librairie* (Paris: Pillet aîné, 1848), 334.

[12] Sohncke, Ludwig Adolph (Hger), *Bibliotheca mathematica, Verzeichnis der Bücher über die gesammte Zweige der Mathematik* (Leipzig: Wilhelm Engelmann, 1854).

Combing the civil archives

Paul Lebreton is not a recognized author in the field of the Breton language or literature linked to Brittany: he does not appear in Levot's *Biographie Breton*[13] nor in the dictionary of Breton writers edited by Lukian Raoul.[14] Could birth, death and marriage certificates provide any useful information?

As the author wrote in the Breton language, the research could be limited to Western Brittany. Additionally, on two occasions the author uses sentences and turns of phrase indicating that the work was published not long after it had been written (1848).[15] The research therefore focused on three departments in Brittany (Finistère, Côtes d'Armor, Morbihan)[16] for the period 1750 to approximately 1830. Unfortunately, as the availability of research tools varies greatly from one department to the next, crucial information may have been missed, but an initial search yielded no results for a "Paul Lebreton" and its variants[17] in this timeframe.[18]

---

[13] Levot, Prosper, *Biographie bretonne, recueil de notices sur tous les Bretons qui se sont fait un nom . . . depuis le commencement de l'ère chrétienne jusqu'à nos jours* (Vannes: Cauderan, 1852–1857).

[14] Raoul, Lukian, *Geriadur ar skrivagnerien ha yezhourien vrezhonek* (Brest: Al Liamm, 1992). However, I have recently found out online that Lukian Raoul mentions the author in a complementary note to his work, for a rather narrow readership and dating from 2015. But he points out that we do not know anything about the author: https://vdocuments.mx/raoul-lukian-anviou-a-vanke-el-levr-kentan.html, ("references missing in the first volume") accessed on 15th July 2019.

[15] Page 21: comment on the discovery of a new planet "the previous year" by Le Verrier, who had discovered Neptune in 1846-1847. And page 26: comment on the possible appearance of a comet "this year" in 1848.

[16] A "department" is a French administrative region (Finistère, Côtes-d'Armor, Morbihan, etc.) as distinguished from the traditional dialect regions associated with the local bishoprics (Léon/Leon, Cornouaille/Kerne, Tréguier/Treger, Vannes/Gwened).

[17] Paul or Pol, Lebreton or Le Breton or Breton etc.

[18] Around fifteen Paul (Le) Bretons were born or were married in Finistère during this period, but in geographic areas (Plouvorn, Landivisiau, Cléder, Crozon, Quimper, and Rédéné) that, as shall be seen later on in the article, do not correspond to the terminological markers identified in the text. There is only one Paul Breton that can be found near this zone; he was married in Saint-Martin-des-Champs in 1791 but there is

Another avenue worth exploring was the legal deposit. The book was published in Brest by Lefournier, the editor's agent, and as the work was published, the declaration can be consulted in the Finistère Departmental Archives:[19] it consists of only one line stating the title and author's name without any additional detail. Nevertheless, some interesting information can be gleaned from this document that could prove useful later on: (i) the publication date ninth of June 1848, and (ii) the planned print run of 3,000 copies, which is a high figure compared to other Breton publications of the same time period.[20]

In the absence of any direct information about the author, I must turn to the published work to shed light on the subject.

2. A treatise on astronomy to educate Bretons

Studi var an astrou: composition and content

The text is divided into thirteen parts: one foreword, ten chapters and two questions. The chapters deal with, successively, the following themes: the heavens, the four cardinal points and the telescope; sun; moon; earth; planets; stars and the milky way; comets; eclipses; high and low tides; the nautical almanac. The main questions it addresses are the possibility of going to the moon or another planet, and the existence of extra-terrestrial life (on other planets or the sun).

---

no trace of him afterwards. A targeted search on the parishes identified in the terminological research yielded no results.

[19] In the sub-series 2 T "Imprimerie, librairie, presse, dépôt légal, colportage" [Printers, bookshop, legal deposit, chapbooks] of the 2 T series "Enseignement. Affaires culturelles (1800–1940)" [Education. Cultural Affairs] are the index 2 T 11–13: Registres de déclaration et dépôts [Registers of declarations and copyrights] and 2 T 14–21: Bulletins de déclaration et dépôts [Notification of declarations and deposits].

[20] For example, the print run for *Barzaz-Breiz* by Théodore Hersart de La Villemarqué was 500 copies in 1839, 2,000 in 1845 and 2,500 in 1867. Most of the works edited by Alexandre Lédan had a print run of 1,000 copies (despite some exceptions like the 3,000 copies of *Deveriou ar c'hristen*, 1865; *An devez mad*, 1868; election-related leaflets like *Avis d'an Electourien eus ar bloas* 1848 or 4,000 copies for *Divis etre en Electourien hac an itron Republiq*, 1848; *Recit eus an darvoudou horrubl c'hoarvezet en Paris*, 1848). However, the Breton translation of the New Testament by Guillaume Lecoat was edited in 1889 and 3,000 copies were printed (as were printed for the two new editions in 1897 and 1904).

The work's key scientific features are as follows:

- Scientific popularization: the author does not claim to be an astronomer or a mathematician, but someone who popularizes science by synthesizing the ideas of experts in the field without being laden with mathematical equations that some contemporary astronomers interspersed throughout their texts.[21]

- Translation/adaptation: clearly the work does not summarize theories of astronomy published elsewhere in Breton, but those written in another language, probably French. Moreover, the choice of the word *studi* for the title of the text further reinforces the idea that the source texts were French, not Breton: for the former, translations of words such as *étude* [study], *précis* [summary], or *traité* [treatise] would have been used, and for the latter, *kentel*[22] or *lesoniou* [lesson] and the meaning of *studi* limited to intellectual work.[23] The author adapts by simplifying it and accentuating the descriptive and comparative elements with concrete ones, a popularization work in French, such as, for example, the description of the telescope:

> *An télescop so composet d'eus eun duozen hac a zo strissoc'h d'eus eur penn evit d'eus ar penn all. En peb penn eus an duozen-ze zo eur veren ac a zo teo er c'hreïz ha plateet betec mont da netra varzu ar bordou . . .*[24]

> The telescope is made of a tube, one end of which is narrower than the other. At each end of this tube is a piece of glass that is thick in the middle and flattened as much as possible around the edges . . .

---

[21] For example, Le Verrier, *Mémoire sur les variations séculaires des éléments des orbites . . .* (Paris: Bachelier, 1845); Le Verrier, *Théorie du mouvement de Mercure* (Paris: Bachelier, 1845); or Delambre, *Astronomie théorique et pratique* (Paris: Courcier, 1814) etc.

[22] *Kentel* was primarily a religion or moral lesson, and *lesoniou* academic lessons.

[23] I would like to thank Yves Le Berre for having extracted the term "*study*" in the Gothic Breton texts; rarely used in the educational sense of the term, it is essentially used in connection with intellectual endeavour, even zeal.

[24] Lebreton, *Studi var an astrou*, 6.

This aspect, along with the text's format and order, suggest that Lebreton's text was very likely modelled on an existing scientific popularization work such as Arago's *Leçons d'astronomie* (1835),[25] or Bailly's *Manuel d'astronomie* (1830).[26]

- Up-to-date information about the latest findings in the field of astronomy: the author not only makes reference to and explains heliocentrism, which had long been accepted by the scientific community,[27] but also mentions (p. 24) the astronomer Herschel,[28] who counted the number of stars making up the Milky Way, and Le Verrier's discovery in 1847 of a new planet (p.21); the latter had discovered Neptune by mathematical equations a year prior to the publication of *Studi var an astrou*.[29] Lebreton also refers to the potential advent of a new comet in 1848 (p. 28), the year he wrote his work.
- Moreover, the author introduces a connection between religion and astronomy and this is a salient feature of his text, distinguishing it somewhat from the astronomy treaties of the time.

For Lebreton, the universe, and the arrangement of the elements within it, are a result of God's creation, an order chosen and created by divine power:

> *Ma c'hadmiromp labouriou hor c'houer netra nemet d'eus*
> *ar pez a velomp en dro deomp, peguement ne admirfemp-*

---

[25] Paris, Just Rouvier et E. Le Bouvier. He is closest to this text.

[26] Paris, De Roret, third edition in 1830.

[27] The heliocentric model developed by Copernicus in 1513 and established by Johannes Kepler in 1609 had long caused controversy and religious bans in the seventeenth and eighteenth centuries. Pope Benedict XIV lifted the bans in 1741 and 1757.

[28] Herschel, William (1738–1822), British composer and astronomer of German origin. He discovered Uranus around 1780. He quantitatively analysed the Milky Way by dividing the night sky into sections for counting purposes.

[29] Le Verrier, Urbain (1811–1877), French astronomer and mathematician, discovered Neptune and was the father of modern meteorology. Neptune was the first celestial discovery made by mathematical deduction instead of observation. Le Verrier's results were published in August 1846 following two years of calculations. The German astronomers Johann Gottfried Galle and Heinrich Louis d'Arrest were the first to observe it the following month at the Berlin Observatory.

ni quet davantaj e buissançç ma c'houfemp petra eo ar steret, al loar hac oll ar pez so er firmamant!

We already admire the creations of our Creator by what we see around us, but just think how much more admirative of his power we would be if we knew what the stars, the moon, and everything in the heavens were!

The author also claims that there is a strong likelihood of extra-terrestrial life, maybe even on the sun:

Var sujet habitantet an éol, martézé alfé meur-a-hini doueti abalamour d'an domder a glé béa en astr-sé. Respont a ran penos ê êzetoc'h caout habitantet d'an éol evit lacat ar guédon da veva en fonç ar môr hac ar pesquet er voarimou. An habitantet a zo grêt d'eus ar vro en pehini e cleont beva.

About living on the sun, a lot of people may well doubt it because of the excessive heat that prevails on this star. I say to them that it is easier for people to live on the sun than for hares to live on the seabed or for fish to live in rabbit warrens. Creatures are perfectly adapted to the place where they live.

Finally, the author slips in a small sentence on page 29,[30] which has no direct bearing on an explanation of astronomy and which is indicative of the author's admiration for this perfect divine order: he encourages the reader not to fear God's justice but to admire His great work, Creation. In the context of a devout Catholic, nineteenth-century Brittany and reading between the lines, this could be taken as an anti-clerical jibe, or at least criticism of a religion based on fear–a veiled reference to Catholicism–and quite possibly a Protestant influence.

The humanistic and instructive objective: educating the people

Lebreton explains in the reader's note that he published this treatise on astronomy in Breton to educate people in the rural areas of Western

---

[30] N'ê quet an aon d'eus justiç hor C'hrouer a gle gonit dean hor c'halonou: e c'hallout, e vadeles, hac oll ar pez a velomp dirac om daoulagat a glè ober om c'haranté evit-an.

Brittany. The use of imperatives and addresses to the reader further support this approach set out in the introduction: "*Al lectur a zo necesser evit francaad ar guiêguez, diguerri ar speret, formi ar jujamant*" (p.3) [Reading is necessary to enhance knowledge, open minds and form judgement]. This approach was uncommon in nineteenth-century Breton-language literature as not only was scientific literature virtually non-existent, which in itself reveals that Breton scholars rarely shared this type of knowledge, but the published literature also fell into two categories: religious and works by neo-bardic Bretonists. Only new editions of *Buez ar sent* [The lives of saints] and some Catholic journals like *Feiz-ha-Breiz* [Faith-and-Brittany] in the Léon region or *Dihunamb!* [Wake-up!] in the Vannetais region could be found in some households, in the hands of a few people, or which were read aloud to a mostly illiterate Breton population. The neo-bardic publications never reached the Breton-speaking population of Western Brittany, as their target audience was a literary French-speaking population from Paris, or some bilingual Breton scholars wishful for an often dreamed-about Breton past based on the social order of the Pre-Revolutionary France, or for an idyllic primitive Celtic organization. This shows the extent to which Lebreton's motivations were different from those of his contemporaries.

However, a handful of Breton works can be associated with this type of pedagogical ambition, but they are marginal and leave little or no trace: some reading primers and other learning-to-read workbooks in Breton, French, and sometimes Latin that were edited between the French Revolution and the schooling laws (the Guizot Law in 1830 and the Jules Ferry Law in 1881):

- Tanguy Lejeune [Ar Yaouanc],[31] *Rudimant eus ar Finister, composet e gallec ha laqueat e brezonec, evit desqui facilament hac e nebeut amser, da barlant, da lenn ha da scriva, correctamant, evel ur grammairien / Rudiment du Finistère, composé en français, mis en Breton pour apprendre facilement et en peu de temps à parler, à lire et à écrire correctement, comme un grammairien,*[32] Brest, Malassis, 1800.

---

[31] Clerk and then schoolteacher in Plabennec, 1759–1811.

[32] "*Rudiment* of Finistère, composed in French, put in Breton to learn easily and in a short time to speak, read and write correctly, like a grammarian".

- Tanguy Lejeune [Ar Yaouanc], *An ABC pe Qenta Leur*, Brest, Gauchlet, 1801.[33]
- Y. Poullaouec,[34] *Nouvelle méthode pour apprendre à lire en peu de temps, pourvu que l'on suive la prononciation naturelle des lettres / Faeçoun neves evit desqui lenn e ber amzer gant ma vezo heuliet ar brononciation naturel eus al lizerennou,*[35] Brest, Lefournier, 1829.
- Remoinvill,[36] *[ABC]*, Brest, Lefournier, 1834.[37]
- John Jenkins, *An ABK, pe kenteliou bêrr hak eas eoit deski lenn brezonek en nebeudik amzer*[38,] Morlaix, Ledan, 1835.

Alexandre Ledan (1777-1855), the author-translator-printer and republican from Morlaix, and the author Laouënan (1781-1862), are also associated with this trend: the former was intent on diffusing leaflets and works among the Breton population,[39] and the latter was committed to

---

[33] "Alphabet book or very first book". Sold by Lefournier in Brest.

[34] School teacher in Saint-Renan then clerk for the justice of the peace. Publication based on the Jacotot approach, according to Laouënan [Yves-Marie-Gabriel], (see the PhD supplement addressed to the Société d'Emulation de Brest, fonds La Villemarqué, AD29 263J, CRBC Digital Library: LV43.053; transcription in Fañch Postic, *La langue bretonne à l'école dans les années 1830. Promotion d'un enseignement bilingue par Yves-Marie-Gabriel Laouënan*, HAL: https://hal.univ-brest.fr/hal-02137806/document).

[35] "New method for learning to read in a short time, as long as you follow the natural pronunciation of the letters." Book accessible on Gallica.

[36] Former deacon of St. Divy.

[37] Book cited by Yves-Marie-Gabriel Laouënan, cf. supra.

[38] "Alphabet or short and easy lessons to learn to read in Breton in a short time".

[39] See the publications catalogue at Ledan in Morlaix by Bailloud, Gérard, *L'imprimerie Lédan à Morlaix (1805–1880) et ses impressions en langue bretonne* (Saint-Brieuc: s.n., 1999). And the type of publications: a great many song broadsheets (*feuilles volantes*) on various subjects and usually quite cheap, informative publications on various subjects such as *Simon a Vontroulez*, adaptation of *Simon de Nantua; Beilladegou tud diwar ar méaz*, translation in 1835 of *Veillées villageoises* by de Neveu Derotrie; *Gwiziégez ar Paotr-Koz Richard*, translation in 1831 of the work of Benjamin Franklin, *La science du bonhomme Richard* (1733); translations of Aesop's and La Fontaine's Fables by Guillaume Ricou, *Fablou Esop, troët e Brezonec* (Morlaix: Guilmer, 1828), and by Pierre-Désiré De Goësbriand, *Fables choisies de La Fontaine, traduites en vers Bretons* (Morlaix: Guilmer, 1836).

sharing republican ideas of emancipating and educating the people on the history and art of their region and in their language.[40] Yet, both of these men were given a rough ride[41] or voluntarily pushed to one side by Bretonist supporters,[42] which meant that nothing or very little came of their actions and they left a rather small literary legacy behind them.

Nevertheless, going back to *Studi var an astrou*, there is a surprising and rather interesting fact to be found in *Envorennou ar barz Juluen Godest*, the memoirs of the Bard Julien Godest (1849-1932), a poor peasant from La Chapelle-Neuve (Côtes d'Armor). This self-educated author, from a predominantly oral culture, only had access to a handful of books that "good people" had given him, among which was a reading primer and this small treatise on astronomy.[43] Godest's text had borne fruit, partly because of these works published in this humanist drive to educate the people, and proves that this literary work circulated among the targeted population.

See also Hervé Peaudecerf's thesis titled, *Alexandre-Louis-Marie Lédan (1777-1855), un imprimeur breton au XIXe siècle (1805-1855)* (PhD diss., Université de Rennes 2, 2002).

[40] See Le Berre, Yves, Laouënan, Yves-Marie-Gabriel, Kastel Ker Iann Koatanskour / *Le Château de Kerjean-Coatanscour* (Brest: CRBC, 2004); and Postic, Fañch, *La langue bretonne à l'école dans les années 1830*, op. cit.

[41] Alexandre Ledan's Breton was called a "mixed jargon" by Théodore Hersart de La Villemarqué, for whom it epitomized a form of subjection of the Breton people he deplored. See La Villemarqué, "Avenir de la langue bretonne", *Revue de l'Armorique* (15/09/1842):126. On the rejection of high-society Breton by La Villemarqué, see Calvez Ronan, "Couvrir ce sein: La Villemarqué et le breton mondain", in Fañch Postic (dir.), *Bretagnes. Du cœur aux lèvres. Mélanges offerts à Donatien Laurent* (Rennes: Presses universitaires de Rennes, 2009): 141–151.

[42] The manuscript of the first Breton-language novel by YMG Laouënan had been sent by the author to La Villemarqué for submission and advice. Although La Villemarqué carefully preserved it in his archives, he never published it. It was found unexpectedly by Fañch Postic in the late 1990s.
See Le Berre, Yves, "Un rendez-vous manqué": Kastel Ker Iann, "Le Château de Kerjean (1834), premier roman breton", in Garabato, Carmen Alén (dir), *L'éveil des nationalités et les revendications linguistiques en Europe (1830–1930)* (Paris: L'Harmattan, 2005): 151–158.

[43] In due course, these works would have a place and a special resonance in this man's oral culture. See Nelly Blanchard, *Julien Godest, Envorennou ar barz Juluen Godest / Souvenirs du barde Julien Godest* (Brest: CRBC, 2020).

Lebreton was a lover of astronomy driven by a desire to develop popular education and make it widely available. Both of these objectives were explicitly set out in *Studi var an astrou* with a discreet nod to the Protestant movement that supported this democratization of knowledge, and attested by both the high print run and the fact that this poor, illiterate, Breton peasant Godest owned a copy in the 1860s and 1870s.

3. Linguistic survey

Terminological approach

The investigation can be pursued thanks to a particularity of Lebreton's text: although the treatise was written in high-brow Breton, it is very dialectologically marked. In other words, it provides the opportunity to compare the author's specific linguistic feature (essentially phonological and sometimes lexical) with the information provided by the linguistic atlases of Western Brittany.[44]

This small linguistic survey sheds light on the characteristics of a large terminological zone of Carhaix influence. [45]

- non-pronunciation of /z/ from the old voiced interdental sibilant /ð/, like *bea* (*bezañ* = to be), *bla* (*bloaz* = year), *ve* (*vez* = is), *dé* (*deiz* = day), *tigoe* (*tigouez, digouez* = arrive), *koea* (*kouezañ* = to fall), *d'ei* (*dezi* = hers), *goûd* (*gouzoud* = to know), *anaveomp* (*anavezomp* = we know); and the pronunciation of /z/ originating from the old unvoiced interdental sibilant /θ/ like *devez* (day)
- pronunciation in a full vowel for double vowels like *bla* for *bloaz* or *ê* for *eo* (is).
- *gle* (and not *dle* = must) map 164 and 166 ALBB
- *penos* [how/that] (like complement subordinate conjunction)

---

[44] *Atlas Linguistique de Basse-Bretagne* (ALBB) by Le Roux, Pierre, prepared from 1910 to 1920, and published in six volumes between 1924 and 1963; and *Nouvel Atlas Linguistique de Basse-Bretagne* (NALBB) by Le Dû, Jean, prepared from 1970 to 2000, and published in 2001 by the Centre for Breton and Celtic Research (CRBC), Brest.

[45] See Falc'hun François, *Nouvelles perspectives sur l'histoire de la langue bretonne* (Paris: Union Générale d'Editions (UGE), 1981), p. 143.

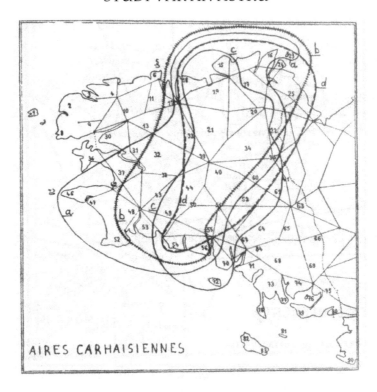

Figure 1: Map by François Falc'hun, *Novelles perspectves sur l'histoire de la langue bretonne*

We can narrow down even further where the author comes from through the linguistic traits typical of western Trégor, between Morlaix and the linguistic barrier formed by the Douron River and the strand of Saint Michel, where a relatively high number of isoglosses converge, as can be seen on the map in the figure below.[46]

---

[46] Blanchard, Nelly, "Trégor finistérien–Trégor costarmoricain. Une frontière linguistique? Quelques éléments de dialectologie à partir de rédactions de deux jeunes bretonnants en 1963", in Coativy, Gallicé, Héry, Le Page (dir.), *Sainteté, pouvoirs, cultures et aventures océanes en Bretagne(s) (V^e–XXe siècle), Mélanges en l'honneur de Jean-Christophe Cassard* (Morlaix: Skol Vreizh, 2014): 99–106.

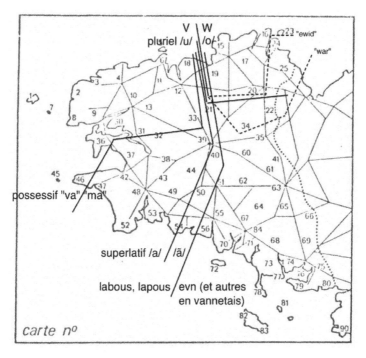

Figure 2. Frontiere tregorroise

- pronunciation as a consonant 'v' of the etymological semi-consonant 'w'[47] as in *evit* (*ewid* = for), *var* (*war* = on), *pevar* (*pewar* = four), *a velomp* (*a welomp* = we see), *ive* (*iwe* = too), *beva* (*bewañ* = to live), *bervet* (boiled)
- pronunciation of the plural as /u/ rather than as /o/[48]
- non-nasalisation of the infinitive and the superlative[49]: divertissa, essa, explica, vuia, guenta + brema
- first person singular possessive pronoun:[50] /va/ and less frequently /ma/

---

[47] See the ALBB's maps 190 and 596.

[48] See for example the ALBB's map 98 or NALBB's map 135.

[49] See the NALBB's maps 49 and 156.

[50] See the ALBB's map 172 or NALBB's map 592.

- lexical difference for 'bird':[51] /*lapus*/ and not /*i:n*/, /*evn*/
- features from the western zone of the Breton region can be added to these characteristics, the mutation of 'd-' into 'z-' (da zont, varzu, a zistrujo); the use of the term 'mintin' and not 'beure'; keeping the vowel /ɛ/ in 'êchu, êruet' (and not /a/ as in the Trégor area located in the Côtes d'Armor department).

Finally, the author uses the forms typical of the Morlaix zone of influence in the south-east area of Western Tregor,[52] which makes it possible to narrow down his origins even more. Lebreton could have come from an area comprising the parishes of Lanmeur, Garlan, Plouégat-Guérand, and possibly stretching as far as Trémel and Plufur.

- use of the vowel /ɛ/ in the first person plural of conjugated prepositions: *demp* (*deomp* = ours), *ganec'h* (*ganeoc'h* = with us)[53]
- pronunciation in full vowel of 'no/nô' (*nav* = nine)[54]
- use of the unmuted (non-mutated) sound in "z" in "querdù" (kerzu = Decembre)[55]
- muting of the central consonant in *tefal* (plan) 550 NALBB
- use of the liquid final consonant in *disquel* (*diskouez* = to show)[56]
- use of the form *hom, om* for the first person plural personal pronoun, followed by spirant mutation (*hom* fem, *hom zreit*)[57]

Sociolinguistic approach

In addition to the terminological features in his text, Lebreton uses a writing style that is characterized by a sometimes inconsistent spelling that,

---

[51] See the ALBB's map 191 or NALBB's map 214.

[52] We can also add to the list below use of the vowel /ɛ/ in "ar vêlin" (= mill), the use of the preposition "en" (for e = in), even before consonants: en touesq, en ber amzer, en pemp dervez, etc.

[53] See the ALBB's map 212.

[54] See the NALBB's map 62.

[55] See the ALBB's map 469.

[56] See the ALBB's map 170.

[57] Except on a few occasions in the fixed, so to speak, expression "hor c'houer" (our creator).

even by mid-nineteenth century standards, was marked by Latin spelling[58]. Therefore, his text deviates from the ecclesiastical standard of the time and draws instead from older spellings (which have endured in the texts from song broadsheets (*feuilles volantes*), using 'c' and 'q' for /k/, 'ç' for /s/, 'gu' for /g/ in front of 'e' and 'i', 'vo' (=/w/), but also sometimes 'so' for 'zo' and 'ê' for 'eo'.

Furthermore, the author does not seem to use Le Gonidec's linguistic or grammatical propositions either, although those propositions were becoming more and more popular particularly thanks to La Villemarqué, who was Le Gonidec's best-known disciple and the most active in publishing. At the time of the publication of *Studi var an astou*, the *Barzaz-Breiz* was on its second edition in 1845, and from 1843, the *Lizerou Breuriez ar Feiz* were published using this new spelling. Therefore, the author does not seem to be a man of the cloth as he would probably have mastered the ecclesiastic standard better, nor a neo-Bard who would probably have chosen the new purist spelling (Jean-Marie Le Scour, Gabriel Milin, Jean-Guillaume Henry). Besides, the fact that the spelling is not uniform points to an author who was not *au fait* with the mid-nineteenth century customs in this field.

In several respects, the author's Breton is reminiscent of 'high-society Breton'[59] that was, like 'clerical Breton',[60] directed at social distinction and intellectual and/or spiritual reflection, in comparison with ordinary Breton: use of the simple past tense, numerous subordinate clauses, such as the relative clauses in 'pehini' and 'pere,' more frequent use of the subject at the beginning of the sentence, direct object complements preceding the verb, loan words from French–a 'prestigious' language in the eyes of Breton speakers[61]–and specialized terms, in our case astronomical ones, which moves the text away from a more clerical Breton. The Breton of this text is equally marked by a toing and froing between local short forms and longer

---

[58] Like the use of 'c' or of 'qu' for the sound /k/, of 'gu' before an e or an i for the sound /g/, like for example 'quet' (ket), 'guenta' (genta), but also 'voar' (var or war), 'striç' (-z),

[59] For an approach of the corresponding corpus, see Calvez, Ronan, "Du breton mondain", *Annales de Bretagne et des Pays de l'Ouest* 115–3 (2008): 135–153.

[60] See Le Dû, Jean and Le Berre, Yves, *Métamorphoses. Trente ans de sociolinguistique à Brest (1984–2014)*, (Brest: CRBC, 2019), 95 and 209–222.

[61] For example: parfet, fêçon, decidet, instrui, generus etc.

standard forms,[62] a game inherited from a high-society practice looking to show the rural and urban roots of noble and bourgeois proprietors, as well as a mastery of informal and formal registers and therefore, the local and the universal. This is a cultural practice of the Breton language which reflects the bilingualism and dual culture of its speakers. Lebreton's text contains several examples of this.

4. Two contenders for a single pseudonym

There are no records of a man called Paul Lebreton in the civil archives for the specific geographical area and time period. Can we entertain the idea that this name is a pseudonym? If so, we can narrow down the potential areas the author came from, and make some educated guesses about his erudition or access to knowledge, educational and democratic motivations and possible protestant influence. Two men, at least partially, fit the bill:

- Guillaume Lejean: (1 February 1824 to 1 February 1871) from Plouégat-Guérand, the target areas based on phonological survey. Although Lejean is best known as Lamaratine's secretary in 1848, then as an explorer, geographer, and one of the founders of French modern geography,[63] he also contributed to the history of Morlaix[64] and Brittany.[65] After completing his studies at the Catholic college of Saint-Pol-de Léon (until 1841), he renounced the priesthood and became a teacher and archivist in Morlaix (1844–1847), and head of the offices of the sub-prefecture of Morlaix (1848) before specializing in geography. He had Protestant leanings, but never officially became

---

[62] For example: divezat / diveat; dervez (for numbers) / devez; lavaret / laret; gouzout / goûd; veac'h / vech.

[63] Lorain, Marie-Thérèse, *Guillaume Lejean, voyageur et géographe (1824–1871)* (Rennes: Les Perséides, 2006).

[64] *Histoire politique et municipale de la ville et de la communauté de Morlaix* (according to the manuscript of Joseph Daumesnil, mayor of Morlaix), 1846. He also wrote articles in the newspaper *Echo de Morlaix* from 1841, the first ones being written under the pseudonym of Naejel (see Gourvil, Francis, *Guillaume Le Jean. Historien, géographe, explorateur, diplomate, folkloriste*, Conference in Morlaix on 20th January 1965 (Morlaix: Imprimerie Nouvelle, 1965) 5.) Lorain, Marie-Thérèse, *Guillaume Lejean, voyageur et géographe (1824–1871)*, 37).

[65] He authored numerous notices for Levot's *Biographie bretonne* and published *La Bretagne, son histoire, ses historiens* in 1849.

Protestant, and although he had written very little in Breton, he helped
Pastor John Jenkins in his linguistic and literary studies in Breton[66].
Moreover, the civil register provides an interesting piece of
information: the surname of the author's maternal family branch was
Lebreton.[67]

- Guillaume Ricou (17 February 1778 to 12 March 1848[68]): this educated
peasant came from Trémel, a few kilometres away from Plouégat-
Guérand. He helped to enhance Breton literature with his
translations/adaptations of Aesop's Fables[69] (and with a lot of other
ground-breaking work) in which there are rather a lot of similar pelling
features as *Studi var an astrou*.[70] However, although Ricou's Breton is
extremely close to that of Lebreton's from a dialectal point of view, one
point sets them apart: Ricou's plurals ('o') are from Côte d'Armor,
whereas Lebreton's are almost exclusively '-ou'. With republican
leanings and open to evangelistic protestant ideas from Morlaix in the
first three decades of the nineteenth century, he is also known for being
Pastor John Jenkins' linguistic associate.[71] It should be noted that Ricou

---

[66] See the written correspondence between John Jenkins and Guillaume Lejean, kept
at the Morlaix municipal library, dating from 1848 to 1855. He also translated into
Breton *Historiou eus ar Bibl Santel. Testament koz* (Brest: Anner, 1853).

[67] He is the son of René Lejean (1798–1865), farmer, and of Marguerite Le Breton
(1795–1833), from Plouigneau. The couple were married on 19th November 1821 in
Plouigneau and lived in Plouégat-Guérand (Guerand Vihan). His mother died at an
early age, in 1833, so Guillaume was raised by one of his aunts on his mother's side,
Marie Françoise Le Breton (1809–1876). Guillaume had three sisters who died when
they were less than ten days old (Marie-Françoise, Marie-Françoise, Marguerite), and
two brothers (Pierre (1826 to between 1871 and 1876), François Marie (1828–1901)).

[68] Guillaume Lejean learned about Ricou's death in a letter from his friend Charles
Alexandre on 12th March 1848 (Correspondence by Guiomar, Jean-Yves, *Guillaume
Le Jean-Charles Alexandre: correspondance, 1846-1869* (Paris: Touzot, 1993) 93–
94).

[69] Ricou Guillaume, *Fablou Esop*, (Morlaix: Guilmer, 1828).

[70] For example, use of the "c" and "q", "gu" before "e" and """", "ç", "vo" (=/w/) etc.
Nevertheless, there are differences: Ricou's use of the "q" (Lebreton's "qu"), Ricou's
consistent use of the "so" for "zo", while Lebreton uses it less often.

[71] See, for example, what John Jenkins and Guillaume Lejean say in their
correspondence (in manuscript at the Morlaix library) for example, in the letter dated
22nd March 1855.

and Lejean knew each other and Lejean wrote Ricou's biographical note for Levot's Breton biography (*Biographie bretonne*) in which he makes reference to Ricou's interest in astronomy and his dream of producing a kind of popular Breton encyclopaedia,[72] in line with the Breton astronomy treatise project.

Provisonal conclusion

As the research currently stands and until further elements come to light, I would first propose that *Studi var an astrou* be considered as a work from the protestant republican mainstream of the day, originating in the area around Morlaix, notably Trémel[73] in 1830 to 1850. Second, that Lebreton is a pseudonym used to conceal the identity of an author known for his protestant leanings and therefore so as to overcome the local authority's censorship of Protestantism, in particular through their refusal to grant any requests for permission to distribute leaflets.[74] The work's high print run

---

[72] "He liked to talk, at the time, about one of his favourite dreams: an Encyclopaedia for Everyman, in the Breton language, a small book in which he would use curiosity as a ploy to direct the attention of his fellow countrymen towards common knowledge. For him, astronomy in particular, with its dreams more splendid than The Thousand and One Nights, was the powerful driver that would take this forward. But alas, this dream would never come true. Ricou, with a certain optimism, saw the start of the Revolution in February, but he would only see the beginning. He died on 12th March 1848 in Trémel, where he was buried by his friend and co-religionist M. Jenkins, evangelical pastor in Morlaix." (Levot, *Biographie bretonne*, 2: 765).

[73] Trémel's charitable organization was a Baptist establishment located between Morlaix and Lannion, which in the beginning was the community's evangelical annex founded in 1836 by the Welsh missionary John Jenkins in Morlaix and managed by Guillaume Ricou (1778–1848) who had a "Reawakening" in the 1850s, based on clerical relativism, inspired by Guillaume Le Coat (1845–1914), grandson of Guillaume Ricou, whom the Baptist Missionary Society had recognized as a minister (he was in charge of church matters, schools, the orphanage, homes for the elderly, an agricultural holding and door-to-door literature distribution).

[74] See, for example, the correspondence from John Jenkins to Guillaume Lejean, Morlaix municipal library (17 letters from 22.11.1848 to 28.09.1856), in which Jenkins, on several occasions, criticizes the libraries' and the prefecture of Finistère's refusal to grant an authorization for door-to-door selling. Another example of resistance is that of the priests: the priest of Morlaix refused to have a cemetery burial ceremony for one of the Jenkins sons (see Fichau, Jean-Gabriel, *Trémel, centre du*

suggests a significant distribution network–as was the case for the song broadsheets (*feuilles volantes*) on the market or the pamphlets and brochures distributed or sold during the door-to-door selling of Protestant material[75] carried out between 1850 and 1890 along the Brest-Rennes main road (especially in Trégor and the Monts d'Arée), then in a large area stretching from the Côtes du Nord to southern Finistère[76]–from which Godest indirectly benefited.

Additionally, the two contenders for the pseudonym, Ricou and Lejean, were selected for their ties with local Protestantism and even their participation in Protestant missions from the Morlaix-Trémel region, but also for their republican drive for educating the people. I put forward Ricou for the sociolinguistic and orthographic characteristics of his Breton, and Lejean for the terminological characteristics of his Breton and his family's maternal surname. However, Ricou died in March 1848 and was buried by Pastor Jenkins in Trémel in a non-Catholic funeral, and *Studi var an astrou* was published in June 1848. Could this publication be seen as a posthumous tribute to Ricou just three months later by Lejean, a well-connected man who would have slightly adapted it to his Finistère Breton, choosing a pseudonym for fear of publication refusals? In fact, could it be that there are two contenders for the "Lebreton" pseudonym?

---

protestantisme en Bretagne au XIXe siècle (mémoire de maîtrise, Université de Rennes, s.d., 12). It can also be observed that the Morlaix printer Alexandre Lédan stopped printing works by John Jenkins after 1835, after threats to suspend the collaboration with the bishopric.

[75] Fichau, Jean-Gabriel, Trémel, centre du protestantisme en Bretagne au XIXe siècle, 104 and seq.

[76] And strongly resembling what Pierre Flatrès has called the rebellious diagonal [*la diagonal contestataire*]–rebellious religiously and politically speaking, but culturally conservative–regions where the Catholic Church carried less weight. See Flatrès, Pierre, *La Bretagne* (Paris: Presses Universitaires de France, 1986). Thanks to a "biblical wagon" (*voiture biblique*), the door-to-door canvassers covered nearly 800 km in three months in 1887–88 (Fichau, *Trémel, centre du protestantisme en Bretagne au XIXe siècle*, 114). See also map p. 113 of Fichau, *Trémel, centre du protestantisme en Bretagne au XIXe siècle*.

Aspects of Sexual Violence in
Early Irish Literature

Matthieu Boyd

Often attributed to Oscar Wilde, but more likely from psychoanalyst Robert Michels, is the claim that "Everything is about sex, except sex: sex is about power." That seems too reductive but it does make the point that when people talk about sex they are usually talking about something else as well: power, pleasure, procreation, performativity, closeness, connection, discovery, self-discovery, self-definition, self-actualization, self-esteem, personal agency or lack thereof, and so on. A similar complexity attends the discussion of sexual violence, which is about more than uncontrolled sexual desire and usually involves issues of power, entitlement and privilege, social license to operate, and systemic features of what is often called "rape culture." A powerful recent book by Sohaila Abdulali, *What We Talk about When We Talk about Rape*,[1] evokes this range of possibilities.

This study hopes to explore the same question specifically for early Irish literature. It is inspired partly by my own experience of teaching the *Táin* and its pre-tales to students who are, perhaps as a result of recent public discourse, increasingly outspoken about and often newly sensitive to issues of consent and sexual violence. The vexed discussions among professors about putting content notes and trigger warnings on the syllabus may obscure the fact that students are often eager to confront these issues in the texts they are reading, from Ovid's *Metamorphoses*[2] to Cú Chulainn forcing

---

[1] Sohaila Abdulali, *What We Talk About When We Talk About Rape* (New York: The New Press, 2018). Among other works on this general topic, I find particular value in *Yes Means Yes! Visions of Female Sexual Power and a World Without Rape*, ed. Jaclyn Friedman and Jessica Valenti (Berkeley, CA: Seal Press, 2008).

[2] Hence the title of Madeleine Kahn's book *Why Are We Reading Ovid's Handbook on Rape? Teaching and Learning at a Women's College* (New York: Paradigm, 2005). Other discussions of this and similar pedagogical challenges include Yurie Hong, "Talking about Rape in the Classics Classroom," *Classical World* 106.4 (Summer, 2013) 669–675; Elizabeth Gloyn, "Reading Rape in Ovid's *Metamorphoses*: A Test-Case Lesson," *Classical World* 106.4 (Summer, 2013) 676–681; *From Abortion to Pederasty: Addressing Difficult Topics in the Classics Classroom*, ed. Nancy Sorkin Rabinowitz and Fiona McHardy (The Ohio State

Aífe to bear his child,[3] or Conchobor forcing himself on all the maidens in Ulster. In a comparative course that includes the Fourth Branch of the *Mabinogi*–where the rape of Goewin is treated with great seriousness, with Math insisting that he will offer compensation to the injured Goewin before he seeks it for himself–the contrast alone may be striking.

Although there is now a reasonably sized body of scholarship on women and gender in early Irish material,[4] in which sexual violence is

---

University Press, 2014), especially chapters 9 and 10 (152–186); and, for a popular audience, Katy Waldman, "Reading Ovid in the Age of #MeToo," *The New Yorker* (February 12, 2018) https://www.newyorker.com/books/page-turner/reading-ovid-in-the-age-of-metoo, and various articles in the online Classics journal *Eidolon*. In medieval studies, works of interest would include Kathryn Gravdal, *Ravishing Maidens: Writing Rape in Medieval French Literature and Law* (Philadelphia: University of Pennsylvania Press, 1991); Dianne Wolfthal, *Images of Rape: The 'Heroic' Tradition and its Alternatives* (Cambridge: Cambridge University Press, 2000); Corinne Saunders, *Rape and Ravishment in the Literature of Medieval England* (Cambridge: D.S. Brewer, 2001); Caroline Dunn, *Stolen Women in Medieval England: Rape, Abduction and Adultery, 1100–1500* (Cambridge: Cambridge University Press, 2013); *Sexual Violence and Rape in the Middle Ages: A Critical Discourse in Premodern German and European Literature*, ed. Albrecht Classen (Berlin/Boston: De Gruyter, 2011); and *Teaching Rape in the Medieval Literature Classroom: Approaches to Difficult Texts*, ed. Alison Gulley (Leeds: ARC Humanities Press, 2018).

[3] For my thoughts on this example, see Matthieu Boyd, "Teaching Early Irish Literature with Johnny Cash: How Cú Chulainn Raise (and Killed) his Son" (2013), online at https://www.academia.edu/5688333/Teaching_Early_Irish_Literature_with_Johnny_Cash_How_C%C3%BA_Chulainn_Raised_and_Killed_His_Son.

[4] Philip O'Leary, "The Honour of Women in Early Irish Literature," *Ériu* 38 (1987) 27–44; Lisa Bitel, *Land of Women: Tales of Sex and Gender from Early Ireland* (Ithaca, NY: Cornell University Press, 1996); Joanne Findon, *A Woman's Words: Emer and Female Speech in the Ulster Cycle* (Toronto: University of Toronto Press, 1997); *Constructing Gender in Medieval Ireland*, ed. Sarah Sheehan and Ann Dooley (Palgrave Macmillan, 2013). Other studies dealing with the status of early Irish women in history as opposed to literature include *'The Fragility of her Sex'? Medieval Irishwomen in their European Context*, ed. Christine Meek and Katharine Simms (Blackrock: Four Courts, 1996); Christina Harrington, *Women in a Celtic Church: Ireland, 450–1150* (Oxford: Oxford University Press 2002); Helen Oxenham, *Perceptions of Femininity in Early Irish Society* (Woodbridge: Boydell, 2015). For a

occasionally mentioned, to my knowledge there has not been a published item focusing specifically on sexual violence. This paper should be read as a preliminary effort to address the subject–one that invites correction and improvement.

My working proposal is that in the world of early Irish saga, there is what we might call rape per se, as an offense in law, and rape that also functions as a metaphor. Rape per se does not seem to be any more freighted with consequence than killing outside the kin-group: in both cases the perpetrator may need to pay compensation to the men affected by the act, and there the matter is supposed to rest. The latter situation, rape as metaphor, *does* appear to be freighted with meaning, and to be inscribed within a larger pattern that involves sovereignty, fertility, and the Otherworld. And yet, in spite of both the male-centered legalistic approach and the symbolic-metaphorical approach, both of which tend to disregard the woman's experience, there do seem to be cases where actual human emotion and trauma come through. Deirdriu's subjectivity in *Longes mac nUislenn* 'The Exile of the Sons of Uisliu' is perhaps the most clearly dramatized of female early Irish saga characters,[5] but she laments and kills herself rather than endure sexual mockery and the sexual assault that she seems to be threatened with: it may be that this contrasts with the muted condition of characters who are rape survivors rather than being of a piece with it.

Today, pop culture offers many stereotypes about strong Celtic women, but early Irish society was not a matriarchy, and early Irish literature reflects that. Characters like Medb, Deirdriu, Gráinne, and Eochaid's daughter from *Fingal Rónáin* display sexual agency that seems to fit the "strong Celtic women" stereotype, but practically all of them come to a tragic end. Meanwhile, early Irish law defines a number of sexually

---

more substantial review of the literature, see Oxenham, *Perceptions of Femininity*, 5–8.

[5] On Deirdre, see especially the recent work of Kate Louise Mathis: *The Evolution of Deirdriu in the Ulster Cycle* (PhD dissertation, University of Edinburgh, 2010); "Parallel Wives: Deirdriu and Lúaine in *Longes mac n-Uislenn & Tochmarc Lúaine ogus Aided Athairne*," in *Ulidia 3*, ed. Gregory Toner and Seamus Mac Mathúna (Berlin, 2013) 17–25; and "Mourning the Maic Uislenn: Blood, death, & grief in *Longes mac n-Uislenn & 'Oidheadh Chloinne hUisneach'*," *Scottish Gaelic Studies* 29 (2013) 1–21.

based offenses against women,[6] but the offense usually extends to the woman's kin or male legal superior, and since the payment of honor-price could easily exceed the flat "body-fine" (*éraic*), the satisfaction of that man or her kin could easily become a priority over the woman herself. As Charlene Eska, editor of the law-text *Caín Lánamna*, explains in more detail:

> In medieval Ireland, as in present times, rape was difficult to legislate. The laws divide rape into two categories, that done by physical force (*forcor*) and that done under other circumstances, such as to a woman who is passed out drunk, which is given the term *sleth*. CL [=*Cáin Lánamna*] gives the penalty due to the victim for both types of rape as the *éraic* "body-fine" (see §37). If the victim was a primary wife, girl of marriageable age, or virgin nun who had not renounced her veil, the full body-fine was paid; for a secondary wife, only half the body-fine was paid. The perpetrator also had to pay the honor-price of the woman's legal superior (e.g. husband or father), since a crime committed against the woman was considered to be a crime against him as well.[7]

> *CL* [also] discusses unions by rape, both by violence and by stealth, *lánamnas éicne* and *lánamnas sleithe*, respectively. Both of these actions were considered criminal and without the consent of either the woman or her kin. Finally, there is *lánamnas genaide* "union of mockery", which was a union of those of unsound mind. If they should be brought together for the sake of sport,

---

[6] I am not aware of any recognized sexually-based offenses against men, or of any actual rape of men in the sagas. By modern standards, Deirdriu's "two ears of shame" tactic used on Noísiu, if we interpret it as a threat to destroy his reputation with satire, is plainly coercive, while the behavior of Echaid's daughter is seen as highly problematic even within *Fingal Rónáin*. But neither would seem to be legally actionable as sexual harassment under Irish law.

[7] *Cáin Lánamna: An Old Irish Tract on Marriage and Divorce Law*, ed. and trans. Charlene M. Eska (Leiden/Boston: Brill, 2010) 13. Compare Fergus Kelly, *A Guide to Early Irish Law* (Dublin: DIAS, 1988) 134–37.

whoever brought them together was responsible for raising any resulting children.[8]

Sexual harassment of women, such as nonconsensual kissing or groping, is also against the law.[9]

The handling of *lánamnas genaide* reads as a rational and humane response to a rough environment where, presumably, that kind of activity was common enough that there had to be a law about it. In general, a man found guilty of rape that resulted in pregnancy would be expected to raise the child. Contemporary laws that assign rapists custody or visitation rights are widely considered abhorrent, on the view that the mother's emotional welfare and her bond with the child need to be protected. But early Irish law seems to assess children more as a burden than as a blessing.

A legalistic attitude toward rape–particularly the idea that an offense against a woman was primarily an offense against her kin or some man associated with her–is reflected in some of the sagas. For example, in "The Expulsion of the Déisi," Conn, son of Cormac mac Airt, gratuitously rapes Forach, daughter of Forad son of Art Corb. Her uncle Óengus Gaibuaifnech avenges the rape by killing Conn in Cormac's presence, incidentally taking out one of Cormac's eyes, but none of this concerns itself with the woman's experience: "The lack of familial permission–not the violence of the action, nor the ill-treatment of the woman–is the major element in the episode, and the cause of Conn's ultimate downfall."[10] Cormac himself, according to *Esnada Tige Buchet* 'The Musical Sounds of Buchet's House,'[11] had raped and impregnated Buchet's fosterling Ethne when Buchet apparently lacked the legal standing to give her in marriage, which would have been the responsibility of her royal father back in Leinster. Ethne fled from Cormac after one night, but the further consequences are described in terms of how Cormac accepted paternity for her son Cairbre Lifechair on the oath of the Leinstermen and how she, apparently willing to make the best of a bad situation, became Cormac's queen and demanded an enormous bride-price payable to Buchet. Ultimately, the titular joyful music at Buchet's house

---

[8] Eska, *Cáin Lánamna*, 18.

[9] Kelly, *Guide*, 137.

[10] Oxenham, *Perceptions of Femininity*, 64.

[11] "The songs of Buchet's house," ed. and trans. Whitley Stokes, *Revue Celtique* 25 (1904) 18–38, 225–27, at §12.

drowns out any lingering grief or trauma that we might detect on Ethne's part. This seems typical of how sexual violence is handled in the sagas. Where sexual violence does signify is on the level of metaphor associated with kingship. Tomás Ó Cathasaigh's analysis of the threefold death in Irish sources[12] explains this in terms of Dumézil's three functions as the punishment for a threefold violation, one effectively blasphemous (though often carried out against a sacral king), one violent, one sexual. This naturally invites the question of how the sexual violation can occur on its own and how it is punished. While some of these violations occur on a human scale–such as the homosexual relationship implicated in the death of Áed Dub as recounted in Admonán's *Vita Columbae*–others involve feminine manifestations of the pagan Otherworld, the *síd*, which is by turns nurturing and destructive.

Ó Cathasaigh's well-known article on *lommrad* in *Cath Maige Mucrama* 'The Battle of Mag Mucrama'[13] discusses human incursions on the Otherworld and Otherworld incursions on the human world that form an escalating sequence of stripping, shearing, or laying bare. Most of these are boundary disputes, where humans and Túatha Dé Danann stake claims on the others' territory and use royal or supernatural authority to reject those claims. Early in the saga, the Munster king Ailill Ólomm puts his horses to graze on a *síd*-mound, and the inhabitants respond by stripping it bare on Samain night. Ailill in turn ambushes the king of the *síd* and his daughter Áine, and rapes her while his henchman kills her father. She then sucks his ear off and says, using forms of *sáraigid* 'violates, outrages' for what he has done to her and what she will do to him, as though they are somehow equivalent moves: "You have been wicked to me [. . .] [in] violating me and slaying my father. I will cause great injury to you for it. I will leave no property in your possession when we part" (*'Olc ro bábair frim* [. . .] *mo sárugud ⁊ marbad m'athar. Not sáraigiub-sa ind .i. nocon fháicéb-sa*

---

[12] Tomás Ó Cathasaigh, "The Threefold Death in Early Irish Sources," *Studia Celtica Japonica* n.s. 6 (1994) 53–75. Reprinted in *Coire Sois, The Cauldron of Knowledge: A Companion to Early Irish Saga*, ed. Matthieu Boyd (University of Notre Dame Press, 2014) 101–120.

[13] Tomás Ó Cathasaigh, "The Theme of *lommrad* in *Cath Maige Mucrama*," *Éigse* 18 (1980–81) 211–24. Reprinted in Boyd, *Coire Sois,* 330–341. The text itself is edited and translated by Máirín O Daly in *Cath Maige Mucrama* (Irish Texts Society, 1975).

athgabáil latt in tan immo-scéram).[14] The ear-sucking could perhaps be understood as personal revenge, but the form of that revenge would be unusual, which suggests that it is best read in conjunction with Ó Cathasaigh's other examples of *lommrad* in human-Otherworld relations– that is, as symbolic. Meanwhile, the promise to strip Ailill of his property only makes sense as a threat by one who has power to carry it out. Áine thus figures primarily as a representative of the land and possibly also of Ailill's kingship, given the well-known figure of the 'sovereignty goddess' (the female personification of the sovereignty with whom the king-to-be would consummate his rule) and the connection between the land and *fír flathemon* 'the truth and justice of the ruler' that is clearly established elsewhere.[15] Whether or not we insist on reading Áine herself as a sovereignty goddess, it is clear that the destructive and possessive incursions on the Otherworld made by humans, and vice versa, can be expressed in sexual terms that are significant primarily for what they represent about how the two worlds relate to each other, and all that that implies about the conditions under which humans hold and rule the land. Ailill's rape of Áine would correspond, in terms of the larger dynamics, to the penetrative recourse of human kings to digging up *síd*-mounds when faced with an unruly Otherworld (as, for example, Eochaid Airem does in *Tochmarch Étaíne* 'The Wooing of Étaín' in an effort to retrieve Étaín from Midir[16]).

There are unambiguous instances of the 'sovereignty goddess' motif which are plainly sexual. The classic one is the story of Niall Noígiallach and the hag at the well in *Echtra mac nEchach Muigmedóin* 'The Adventures of the Sons of Echaid Mugmedón,'[17] where in lying with the hag Niall works her transformation into a beautiful blonde who explains

---

[14] O Daly, *Cath Maige Mucrama*, 38–39. The translations "violating me" and "cause great injury to you" involve the same verb.

[15] For example, in *Audacht Morainn* 'The Testament of Morann,' ed. Fergus Kelly (Dublin: DIAS, 1976), more recently translated in John T. Koch with John Carey (eds., trans.), *The Celtic Heroic Age*. fourth ed. (Aberystwyth: Celtic Studies Publications, 2003) 188–93.

[16] "Tochmarc Étaíne," ed. and trans. Osborn Bergin and R. I. Best, *Ériu* 12 (1934–8), and more recently translated in Koch and Carey, *The Celtic Heroic Age*, 146–165, at 161–162 for the digging up of the mounds.

[17] "Echtra Mac Echach Muigmedóin," ed. and trans. Whitley Stokes, *Revue Celtique* 24 (1903) 190–203.

that she is the sweetness of a sovereignty that one attains through wolfish violence. The goddess Buí, to be identified with the "Old Woman of Beare," once consort to kings, is another example.[18] In texts like *Tochmarc Étaíne*, such symbolic manifestations are as much a generative matrix as they are individual women, hence the confusing multiplicity of "Étaíns" for kings to choose from.[19] The idea of sovereignty as a woman naturally lends itself to the rendering of illegitimate kingship as an act of rape. The late text *Cath Cumair* 'The Battle of Cumair' provides an excellent illustration of this.

Cath Cumair[20] is one of a group of Irish sagas about the family of Eochaid Feidlech, king of Tara, that includes *Cath Boinde, Cath Cumair, Cath Leitreach Ruibhe, Cogad Feargusa ⁊ Conchobair*, and the shorter *Aided Meidbe*. Some of these have been analyzed by Edel Bhreathnach as tales specifically concerned with Connacht.[21] They come from late manuscripts and are largely in Early Modern Irish, but that "largely" covers the fact that they quote from or find support in early texts like the *Metrical Dindshenchus* and *Senchus na Relec* in LU, so old tradition is involved. For Karen Burgess, *Cath Cumair*:

> . . . draws upon the same now-lost traditions and in so doing, clarifies ambiguities in our surviving Middle Irish accounts [. . .] By amplifying and foregrounding certain motifs and themes, particularly those in which somatic signs serve as expressions of important and/or problematic

---

[18] See Tomás Ó Cathasaigh, "The Eponym of Cnogba," *Éigse* 23 (1989) 27–38. Reprinted in Boyd, *Coire Sois,* 155–164.

[19] Aspects of this tale, including how the episode of the multiple Étaíns also evokes the transforming hag, are discussed by Tomás Ó Cathasaigh, "*Tochmarc Étaíne* II: A Tale of Three Wooings," in *The Land Beneath the Sea: Essays in Honour of Anders Ahlqvist's Contribution to Celtic Studies in Australia*, ed. Pamela O'Neill (Sydney: University of Sydney, 2013) 129–42.

[20] "*Cath Cumair*," ed. and trans. Margaret E. *Dobbs, Revue Celtique* 43 (1926) 277–342.

[21] Edel Bhreathnach, "*Tales of Connacht: Cath Airtig, Táin bó Flidhais, Cath Leitreach Ruibhe*, and *Cath Cumair*," *Cambrian Medieval Celtic Studies* 45 (Summer, 2003) 21–42.

social relationships, the *Cath Cumair* also facilitates a deeper reading of our medieval texts.[22]

In *Cath Cumair*, specifically, the three sons of Eochaid Feidlech make war on their father. Conchobor, king of Ulster, puts them up to it, citing the disgrace to their own sons if they let themselves be expelled from Tara without a fight: apparently the hereditary entitlement to the kingship lapses if they acquiesce in their expulsion, but not otherwise. Conchobor also provides them with an army to attack their father. In this text Conchobor is presented as a source of "poisonous" advice, not at all a positive influence.

The three brothers march south. Druids come to warn them off with an appeal to filial piety, but they dismiss them. When they reach Cruachu, one of the brothers, Bres, is surveying the troops when he sees an amazingly beautiful woman approach. He speaks to her:

> *"Can as a tighidh, a ingen, ₇ créad do bheir a t-aonar tú?"*
> *"Thangusa d'agallaimh a bfuil do throchaibh ar an magh so," ar isi.*
> *"Ní troich íad amh," ar eision.*
> *"Is troich amh" ar an ingen, "óir da mádh áil leó saoghal badh faide do bheith aca no gheibhdáois cumha a righ Eirenn."*
> *"Cinnte linne amh," ar Bres, "gan comha do ghabhail uadha acht cath do thabairt dho ionnus go ma linn fein ríghe na hEirenn ₇ nach ba leision."*
> *"Is olc an chomurle sin," ar in ingen.*
> *Is annsin do chuir Bres a guala fri fód na faon-léirge ₇ do chuaidh an a gnás ₇ in a caomh-lebaidh ₇ tairnic ris taghall aice.*

"Whence come you, lady? How is it you are alone?"

"I came to talk to all the death-doomed ones on this plain," said she.

"They are not indeed doomed to death," said he.

"Indeed they are doomed," said the lady, "for, if they did

---

[22] Karen Burgess, *Disintegrating Lugaid Ríab nDerg: Medieval Irish Lore about a Legendary King* (Ph.D. dissertation, UCLA, 2004) 170–171.

desire longer life, they would take terms from the king of Ireland."

"We are indeed determined," said Bres, "not to take terms from him; but to give him battle so that we shall rule Ireland, and not he."

"That is an evil design," said the lady.

Then Bres threw her down on the sod of the sloping way and violated her.[23]

Even if the woman's assessment of the warriors' prospects is supposed to play like flirtatious banter ("negging"), Bres's reaction is sudden and shocking. The level of violence is hard to gauge: the Irish has a string of euphemisms along the lines of "engaged in intercourse with her[24] and slept with her[25] and succeeded in hooking up with her" (*do chuaidh an a gnás* ⁊ *in a caomh-lebaidh* ⁊ *tairnic ris taghall aice*). Still, there is an abrupt escalation without affirmative consent, and Dobbs's choice to cut through the verbiage with "threw her down [. . .] and violated her" seems fair enough. (Karen Burgess opts for the similarly direct "Then Bres threw her down on the ground and had intercourse with her."[26])

What is Bres thinking, on whatever level motivates this action? Unless he is a rapist in general, which we cannot know from the text, the obvious scenario is that this is punitive: the woman has cast aspersions on his cause and his ability to perform in battle, hence his manhood, so Bres intends to 'teach her a lesson.' A less likely (or complementary) option is that he is acting from a sense of doom and taking out insurance, like Éogan Mór and Art "the Lone" mac Cuinn on their way to the battle of Mag Mucrama: as

---

[23] Dobbs, "*Cath Cumair*," 302–303. Line breaks added to the Irish text. Compare the translation by Karen Burgess, *Lugaid Ríab nDerg*, 169.

[24] *Do chuaid an a gnás* alone doesn't mean rape, since in other uses it was felt necessary or appropriate to specify "not by consent but by force" (*is dachuáid ina gnáis ar sain, ní ar áis acht ar éicin, DIL* s.v. *gnás*, citing "*Ériu* xiv 157 § 11 (The Yew of the Disputing Sons (LL))").

[25] *Caomh-lebaidh* looks like *cáem* 'fair; dear' + 2 *lepaid* 'bed,' thus in effect "pleasantly [from Bres's perspective] bedded her." But compare the remarks on *cáem* and the compound *cáemmám* (for *commám*?) in Eska, *Cáin Lánamna*, 121 note a.

[26] Burgess, *Lugaid Ríab nDerg*, 169.

told in *Cath Maige Mucrama* and *Scéla Éogain ₇ Cormaic*,[27] they both impregnate women (consensually, or at least with the consent of the women's fathers) to ensure that they have sons who live after them.

There is also a third option, which becomes apparent in what follows. The woman reveals herself to be Bres's sister Clothru in disguise. This part of the story is told more briefly in Medb's death-tale, the twelfth-century *Aided Meidbe*,[28] where Clothru's approach is different: she seduces her brothers to discourage them from rebelling (in essence: "now that you have committed incest, there is no way you can possibly win, so you might as well give up"), not to cause their ruin once they did rebel. In *Cath Cumair*, her plan is the latter, presumably by getting Bres to violate the traditional ideology of *fír flathemon* in a way that removes the kingship forever from his grasp:

> *"Ort do dhon ₇ do dhuabhas,"* ar an ingen, *"is mór an col ₇ an egcóir do rinnis."*
> *"Ciodh ón, [a] ingen?"* ar Bres. *"Cia thusa?"*
> *"Clothrinn ingen Eochaidh Fheidligh misi,"* ar si, *"₇ is ar thainig dot' hath-mhilleadhsa conach biadh fiór catha agad a n-aghaidh hathar."*
> *"Do chol ₇ do chontracht ort,"* ar Bres, *"óir is agad ro bhí fios ₇ ní hagamsa."*

> "On thee be the shame and the sorrow," said the lady.
> "Great is the sin and wickedness thou hast committed."
> "How so, lady?" said Bres. "Who are you?"
> "I am Clothrinn daughter of Eochaid Feidlech," said she:
> "and I came to compass your destruction that you should not have right on your side in fighting [our] father."
> "Your sin and your curse shall recoil on you[,]" said Bres,
> "for you knew—and I did not."[29]

---

[27] Texts edited and translated by Máirín O Daly in *Cath Maige Mucrama* (Irish Texts Society, 1975).

[28] "Aided Meidbe (The Death of Medb)," ed. and trans. Vernam Hull, *Speculum* 13 (1938) 52–61.

[29] Dobbs, "*Cath Cumair*," 302–303. Compare the translation by Karen Burgess, *Lugaid Ríab nDerg*, 169.

Karen Burgess comments that "If Bres errs, it is in his hasty decision to ravish the girl and tardy inquiry as to her identity."[30] This seems true enough, but it also seems incredible that if Bres thought he had raped an ordinary woman, he would react this way to being accused of wickedness and sin. (One imagines the woman retorting "What do you mean, 'How so?'? You just raped me!") Up to this point Bres seems to have thought that his behavior was appropriate. The key to this, I would argue, is Clothru's appearance, which the text describes in elaborate detail.[31] She is fantastically alluring and wears glamorous clothes. The text says that this is because she is a famous magician (*druí*), and Burgess argues that "the idea that Clothru could deliberately alter her appearance was [. . .] an integral aspect of the figure of Clothru [. . .] in the *senchas* of medieval Ireland."[32] Bres's actions would make sense if he thought he was talking to a woman of the *síd*, and specifically the personification of sovereignty. Given his goal of seizing the kingship by force from his father, the situation seemed to call for him to take possession of the sovereignty-woman by force in the traditional way. (Although Niall in *Echtra mac nEchach* doesn't take the sovereignty-woman by force, she herself comments that she is "not obtained without battle and conflicts."[33]) When this turns out to involve a profound familial violation, it reads as an instructive metaphor about what it means to make war on his father: it is *as if* he were raping his sister. Clothru ultimately has sex with all three of her brothers, this time with more awareness and consent involved.[34] To the brothers' offense of *lèse-majesté* (a first-function violation) and open war (a second-function violation) is added this compound sexual violation that engages the third function of fertility linked to the Otherworld. Following Ó Cathasaigh, the situation calls for a threefold death. Arguably, that happens, since there are three

---

[30] Burgess, *Lugaid Ríab nDerg*, 170.

[31] Dobbs, "*Cath Cumair*," 300–303.

[32] Burgess, *Lugaid Ríab nDerg*, 170.

[33] Koch and Carey, *The Celtic Heroic Age*, 207.

[34] Burgess comments: "As *Cath Cumair* tells the story, only Bres engages in incest unawares [. . .] According to the text, despite this revelation, the three brothers lie with her anyway (*Ciodh tracht do choimh-riachtadur na ttriúr ria*)[.] Does Bres thus repeat the violation, this time fully aware of its nature? In the *Aided Meidbe*, it is clear that Clothru does not reveal her identity until she has copulated with all three of her brothers" (*Lugaid Ríab nDerg*, 209 note 108).

brothers to die: their death is threefold without having to kill the same person by multiple means. This is consistent with how the brothers are portrayed in general: they collectively accomplish a threefold conception of their son Lugaid Ríab nDerg, and their severed heads and headless bodies are placed around their father in his grave like the debris of a triune form.

This text plays on the traditional images of sovereignty in other ways as well. When the king of Tara sees the heads of his defeated sons, he says plainly "it is a pity I did not die before I survived you, and my share of sovereignty is henceforth a drink of death" (*"truagh nach bás a fuarusa* [. . .] *súl do bheinn beó do bhar n-eise ⁊ is deoch thonnaidh mo chuidse do fhlaithemhnus fesda"*)–and from then on "every movement he made a clot of blood came from his mouth" (*gach cor da ccuradh dhe is crú fola do thigeadh ar a bheol*).[35] Thus, he vomits both blood and poetry as he laments his sons. One inversion of the "drink of sovereignty" motif, which we recognize from the story of Niall and the hag, is what happens in *The Destruction of Da Derga's Hostel*: Conaire, who betrayed his charge to render justice to his foster-brothers, dies of thirst, as all but one of the rivers and lakes of Ireland withhold his drink. Here is a different twist, where the drink of sovereignty transforms into not only a drink of death, but a reverse drink, a vomit from a ruptured heart which is as unnatural as a father surviving his sons. Thus does rape function on the level of metaphor.

Cath Boinde 'The Battle of the Boyne,' a late Middle-Irish text also known as *Ferchuitred Medba* 'Medb's Husband-Allowance,' is another story about Eochaid Feidlech's family, which describes the rape of Medb by Conchobor.[36] Here the metaphor wears thin. According to this account, Eochaid had six daughters. Four of them–Mumain, Eithne, Clothru, and Medb–are described as wives of Conchobor and mothers of his children: they were given to Conchobor as part of the compensation paid by their father for killing Conchobor's father. In fact we are told that "Conchobor was Medb's first husband, and she forsook him through pride of mind and went to Tara, where the high king was" (*conad he Concobar cet fear Meadba, co ro-treic Meadb Concobar tre uabar meanman, co n-deachaid co Temraid i fail i roibi ri Eireand*).[37]

---

[35] Dobbs, "*Cath Cumair*," 332–333.
[36] "*Cath Boinde*," ed. and trans. Joseph O'Neill in *Ériu* 2 (1905) 173–85.
[37] O'Neill, "*Cath Boinde*," 176–177.

Eochaid Feidlech, in what the text calls a violation of *fir flathemon*, unseats Tindi, the king of Connacht, and replaces him with Medb in Cruachu, forcing him to live in the wilderness. However, Tindi keeps coming to visit Medb, presumably in a sexual sense as well, and together they host a regular fair at which Medb apparently tries to incite the young men of Ireland against Conchobor. Eochaid, who has been trying to hold his own fair at Tara, asks Medb to join him there. Afterward, Medb goes to bathe in the River Boyne and is surprised by Conchobor, who rapes her. This leads to war between Ulster and Tara, and Tindi challenges Conchobor to a duel. Conchobor sends a champion in his place, and the champion kills Tindi. Meanwhile, Medb is saved from the defeat of the army of Tara by Eochaid Dala, who takes her back to Cruachu, becomes her consort, and replaces the late Tindi as king of Connacht. Medb and Eochaid rule together until Ailill–a child at this point–comes to Cruachu to be fostered by Medb. When she sees Ailill grow up to be a powerful warrior and "a battle-sustaining tower against Conchobor" (*tor chongbala catha re Conconcobar*),[38] she takes him as her lover instead of Eochaid. Eochaid is unhappy and tries to have Ailill banished, but Medb makes it clear that she favors Ailill. Then Eochaid challenges Ailill to a duel and is killed, and Ailill goes on to become the king of Connacht whom we know from the *Táin*.

The secret of this text is in its conclusion: it turns out to be a kind of gloss on why Medb's seven sons, as noted in the *Táin*, are all named Maine. Medb hates Conchobor so much that she asks her druid which of her sons will succeed in killing him. Specifically, she asks: "By whom of my children shall Conchobor fall?" "You have not borne them yet, unless they be rechristened," says the druid. "Anyway, it is by Maine he shall fall" (*"Cia lais torchair Concobar don chloind?" ol si. "Nisrucais fos mina athbaisteir," ol in drai, "cid on la Maine congeoidin"*).[39] So, to have a better chance of killing Conchobor, Medb renames all her sons Maine. (Unfortunately for her, the prophecy turns out to be deceptive, and the Conchobor who is killed is not the king of Ulster, but a descendant of the king of Scotland named Conchobor mac Artuir.)

---

[38] O'Neill, "*Cath Boinde*," 182–183.
[39] O'Neill, "*Cath Boinde*," 184–185.

Medb's action here resolves an idle question that occurs to any reader of the *Táin*–why so many Maines?–but it potentially changes the way we read the whole *Táin*. Now Medb's raid on Connacht is informed not just by a rivalry between her and her husband, but by a sexual offense, and perhaps lingering sexual trauma, that sets Medb at odds with the Ulster king. While the rape of Medb, and her various sexual partnerships, could still be read as metaphors for seizing or claiming the sovereignty–an interpretation which would tie into the persistent reading of Medb as a 'sovereignty goddess'– there is also distress and agency by Medb on a human scale. Abigail Burnyeat has recently developed this idea in an unpublished presentation entitled "#MedbToo," which explores "the text's positioning of this episode both as a trigger for conflict between Conchobar and the men of Ireland, and as a key event with significant repercussions for the future relationships between Medb and her subsequent partners, in particular her marriage to Ailill." She argues that "the text places Medb's rape by Conchobar at the heart of the discord between Ulster and Connacht, providing both back-story and motivation for Medb's actions in *Táin Bó Cúailnge*, and contextualising the events of the cattle-raid within a complex narrative web."[40] Indeed, Medb's partners in *Cath Boinde* seem to be chosen explicitly for how well they will defend her against Conchobor and advance her interest in revenge against him. Such a reading might include the idea of the cattle-raid as a 'reverse rape' writ large: an aggressive penetration of Ulster's territory while Conchobor lies in a pseudo-feminine state of vulnerability, if we follow the explanation of the *ces noínden* as Macha's curse, reducing the Ulstermen to the condition of women in childbirth.[41]

Now, one might object that all of this is an after-the-fact adjustment to the *Táin* in an ancillary text that has the deliberate goal of making sense of the misogynistic presentation of Medb in the original. If so, then I would argue that still, in at least one case, a rape and its emotional consequences

---

[40] Abigail Burnyeat, abstract for "#MedbToo: *Ferchuitred Medba* as alternative *causa* for *Táin Bó Cúailnge*," *Ulidia VI/Fíanaigecht III conference (2018)*, http://www.ulidiafinn2018.scot/ulidiafinn2018abstracts.html. Unfortunately I was not able to attend this conference or to read the paper after the fact, and I hope it will be published so that these ideas become accessible in full.

[41] I do not know if Burnyeat suggested this particular idea, and further exploration of this tale and its potential relevance to reading the *Táin* should await the publication of her paper: hence my discussion of it here has been kept deliberately brief.

for the woman are integral to the basic story, even if there might be alternatives to that story where that is not so.[42] My example is *Togail Bruidne Da Derga* 'The Destruction of Da Derga's Hostel.'[43]

Early in the story, the mother of the future king Conaire is raised as an orphan in a cow shed. To keep her hidden, the herdsmen build a house with no doors or windows, only a skylight. One day a man looks in and sees her. He reports his discovery to the king of Tara, because there is a prophecy that the childless king will have a son by a woman of unknown origin. The king sends his men to break down the house and bring her back.

Meanwhile, there is an instance of the so-called '*inclusa* motif' of a woman locked away who is visited by a supernatural being who becomes the father of her child: it occurs in Greek mythology with Danaë, the mother of Perseus; in Anglo-Norman literature, with Marie de France's lay of *Yonec;*[44] and so on. Birth from this kind of anomalous union is a stock episode in the so-called 'international heroic biography,' and puts the resulting children on the fast-track to be heroes.

> *In tan didiu buí ann dadaig con-acca in n-én forsin forléss*
> *a d-dochum, & fácaib a énchendaich for lár in tigi & luid*
> *chuice & arda-gaib co n-epertsom fria: 'Do-filter chucut*
> *ón ríg do choscrad do thige & dot brith chucai ar éigin, &*
> *bia torrach úaimsea & béra mac de & ní marba eónu in*

---

[42] The alternative account in this case would be that of Lucius Gwynn (ed. and trans.), "De Shíl Chonairi Móir," *Ériu* 6 (1912) 130–143. There Conaire's mother is herself a representative of the *síd*, and there are no bird-men: she is much more aggressive in advancing Conaire's interest in the kingship.

[43] Eleanor Knott (ed.), *Togail Bruidne Da Derga* (Dublin: DIAS, 1936). I quote the translation in Koch and Carey, *The Celtic Heroic Age*, 166–167, based on the earlier translation by Whitley Stokes. For discussion, see Ralph O'Connor, *Destruction of Da Derga's Hostel: Kingship and Narrative Artistry in a Mediaeval Irish Saga* (Oxford: Oxford University Press, 2013).

[44] On *Yonec* and its Irish affinities, see Matthieu Boyd, "The Ring, the Sword, the Fancy Dress, the Posthumous Child, and the Birdman: Background to the element of heroic biography in Marie de France's *Yonec*," *Romance Quarterly* 55.3 (Summer 2008) 205–30, and John Carey, "*Yonec* and *Tochmarc Becfola*: two female *echtrai*," in *Sacred Histories: A Festschrift for Máire Herbert*, ed. John Carey, Kevin Murray, and Caitríona Ó Dochartaigh (Dublin: Four Courts, 2015) 73–85.

mac sin & bid Conaire a ainm (ar ba Mes Búachalla a h-ainmsi dano)'.[45]

Now while she was there next morning she saw a bird on the skylight coming to her, and he leaves his bird skin on the floor of the house, and went to her and captured her and said: 'They are coming to you from the king to wreck your house and to bring you to him by force. And you will be pregnant by me, and bear a son–and that son must not kill birds. And "Conaire, son of Mess Buachalla" will be his name' (for her name was *Mess Buachalla* 'the Cowherds' foster child').[46]

Then Mess Buachalla is brought to the king and has a son as predicted. The birdman's "capture" of her (expressed with the verb *ar-gaib* 'seizes, captures, takes hold of') exists somewhere on the spectrum from thrilling seduction to violent rape. The text never says how she feels about it–but I think we can guess. The clue is that while she does as the birdman says and names her son Conaire, she never tells him that he must not kill birds.

This was not for lack of opportunity. When Conaire is born, she makes a threefold request of the king to let him be raised in turn by the herdsmen who fostered her; by the two "honey-tongued" Maines; and by her (*batir h-é a trí drindrosci forsin ríg .i. altrom a meic eter theora aicce .i. na h-aiti rosn-altadar & na dá Maine Milscothacha , & ata-comnaicsi fa-deisin),*[47] and the text confirms that he was raised that way (*Alta íarum samlaid).*[48] Thus, she takes a personal role in his upbringing and would have had ample opportunity to teach him his personal *geis* and emphasize its seriousness (the nature of *geissi* in general would suggest that violating it would put his life at stake). This she never seems to do. And thus, when Conaire is a young man, he has an encounter with his father's bird-flock that moves swiftly to the brink of violence:

[45] Knott, *TBDD*, lines 91–97: quoted from the CELT edition at https://celt.ucc.ie//published/G301017/index.html.
[46] Koch and Carey, *The Celtic Heroic Age*, 168.
[47] Knott, *TBDD*, lines 104–107.
[48] Knott, *TBDD*, line 110.

*Con-acae eónu findbreca móra and, écomdige ar mét &
doath. Im-saí ina n-degaidh [. . .] & gaibid a thailm doib
asin charbad. Im-suí co m-buí oc muir ina n-deadaich.
Fos-raemet ind eóin forsin tuind. Luidseom chucu co tubart
a láim tairrsiu. Fo-fácbad na h-eóin a n-énchendcha &
imda-suat fair co n-gaíb & claidbib. Aincithi fer díb h-é &
at-n-gládastar, co n-epert fris: 'Is mise Nemglan, rí
énlaithi do athar & ar-garad dít díbrugud én ar ní fuil sund
neach napad dír dait ó a athair nó máthair'. 'Ní feadarsa',
ol seiseam, 'cosaniú sin'.*[49]*

[H]e saw great white-speckled birds, of unusual size and
colour and beauty. He pursues them [. . .] and takes his
sling for them out of the chariot. He goes after them until
he was at the sea. The birds bring themselves onto the
wave. He went to them and overcame them. The birds shed
their bird skins and turn upon him with spears and swords.
One of them protects him and addressed him, saying: 'I am
Némglan, king of your father's birds; and you have been
forbidden to cast at birds, for here there is no one that
should not be dear to you because of his father or mother.'
'Till today,' Conaire said, 'I did not know this.'[50]

The text specifically excludes the possibility of peer pressure. Conaire has
three foster-brothers–the sons of the *fían*-warrior Donn Désa–who are
active young men, and they might have gone hunting together. The foster-
brothers, with no family connection to birds, might have started hunting
some, and so got Conaire in trouble. But when Conaire goes off in his
chariot he explicitly leaves his foster-brothers playing by themselves (*Fan-
ácbat a chomaltai occa chluichiu & ima-saí a charpat & a arai co m-baí oc
Áth Clíath*[51]) before he ever sees the birds. Another possibility is that
Conaire, with youthful carelessness, forgot about his *geis*. In that case we
would have expected him to say that he forgot, but he explicitly says that
"Till today [. . .] I did not know this." If we take him at his word, he never
knew.

---

[49] Knott, *TBDD*, lines 136–148.

[50] Koch and Carey, *The Celtic Heroic Age*, 169.

[51] Knott, *TBDD*, lines 134–135.

His mother was the only one who could have told him. For Mess Buachalla to have simply overlooked this vital piece of information seems entirely unlikely. She remembered to call her son Conaire; and the *geis* was the only other information the father gave her. Since she had seen him in bird-form, she would have known that by killing a bird Conaire might accidentally kill his father. Unlike Cú Chulainn's *geis* not to eat dog,[52] hunting birds was a normal behavior in early Ireland that a young man might have been expected to engage in if he were not warned against it. The inescapable conclusion is that this was her design: she wanted her son to kill birds.

The suggestion that follows from this is that Conaire's mother was not seduced or ambiguously "taken" by the birdman, but rather raped, in a way that left her traumatized and angry.[53] She hoped her son would unknowingly kill his father's people and perhaps his father and become the instrument of her vengeance.[54] If the text seems superficially indifferent to this–and in any case her plan fails–on a deeper level it is still aware: Mess Buachalla is silenced and robbed of agency, but not wholly so.

A tentative conclusion is therefore that sexual violence, if it registers at all as an offense against women rather than against the men affiliated with them, operates as symbol rather than fact in most early Irish narratives. But it can still emerge from time to time from under the burden of silence and metaphor and, when we can perceive it as trauma with lasting effects, it has the potential to radically change our view of some of the best-known early Irish texts.

All of this bears further study.

---

[52] See my chapter "On Not Eating Dog," in *Ollam: Studies in Gaelic and Related Traditions in Honor of Tomás Ó Cathasaigh*, ed. Matthieu Boyd (Madison, NJ: Fairleigh Dickinson University Press, 2016) 35–46.

[53] Depending on when *Cath Boinde's* explanation of the seven Maines first entered the tradition, it may not be coincidental that she wants her son to be raised by two men whose identity, as expressed in their names, may be oriented towards avenging their mother's rape. I don't think that this possibility, or the larger argument about Mess Búachalla, is over-subtle: as Ó Cathasaigh demonstrated in the *lommrad* article, when one misses the subtlety of early Irish literature one also tends to miss the logic of it.

[54] Later interpretations assign a similar motive to Aífe in the *geissi* laid on Cú Chulainn's son Connla, although in the earliest version of the story it is clearly Cú Chulainn himself who chooses them: see again Boyd, "Johnny Cash."

Medieval Memory in Eighteenth-century Ireland: The Reconstruction of the Gaelic Past for an English-speaking Audience in the Writing of Charles O'Conor

Colin Brady

For both Catholics and Protestants in eighteenth-century Ireland, history played an important role in their understanding of their own identities and their position on the island as well as how they understood contemporary political issues. The Irish parliament's subordination to the British parliament and the Penal Laws, which disenfranchised Catholics legally and politically, were two of the most controversial issues of the century in Ireland.[1] In the debates surrounding these issues it is evident that contrary understandings of the history of Ireland from the time of the arrival of the Normans informed the opposing sides in the contemporary political debate.[2] Often these opinions, in turn, hinged on similarly contrary understandings of pre-Norman Ireland.[3] While for modern scholars it is important not to conflate religious identity and ethnic identity, that is not to say that eighteenth-century authors did not do so themselves. The state of civilization in pre-Norman Ireland was often treated as if it reflected on

---

[1] J.C. Beckett, "Introduction: Eighteenth-century Ireland," in *A New History of Ireland IV: Eighteenth-Century Ireland 1691–1800,* eds. T.W. Moody and W.E. Vaughan (Oxford: Oxford University Press, 1986), xxxix–lxiv at xxxix; J.G. Simms, "The establishment of Protestant Ascendancy, 1691–1714," in *A New History of Ireland IV,* 1–30, at 1, 16–20; J.L. McCracken, "Protestant Ascendancy and the rise of colonial nationalism, 1714–60," in *A New History of Ireland IV,* 105–122; R.B. McDowell, "Colonial nationalism and the winning of parliamentary independence: 1760–82," in *A New History of Ireland IV,* 196–265; J.C. Beckett, "Literature in English: 1691–1800," in *A New History of Ireland IV,* 424–470, at 456–466.
[2] William Molyneaux, *The case of Ireland's being bound by acts of parliament in England stated,* (London: F.R. Andare, 1698), 6–17; Sir Walter Harris, *Remarks on the Affairs and Trade of England and Ireland* (London: Tho. Parkhurst, 1691).
[3] Charles Lucas, *An apology for the civil rights and liberties of the commons and citizens of Dublin* (Dublin: James Esdall, 1748), 5,8.

contemporary Catholics.[4] Since the time of Gerald of Wales, the nature of pre-Norman Irish society had been used in religious and political debates and the sharp political divide that existed between different communities was reflected in extremely different collective memories.[5]

Despite having political interests that were in many ways at odds, the eighteenth century was also a time in which certain Irish Protestants and Catholics began to develop a shared national identity. Desires for greater economic and political independence from Britain and the secular outlook of the Enlightenment created shared aims for a group of Irish Protestants and Catholics.[6] Furthermore, a Romantic interest in Gaelic culture that emerged in the controversy surrounding the publication of the Ossian cycle of poetry by James Macpherson made early Irish history fashionable.[7] At the same time, the (mostly Catholic) Gaelic Irish aristocracy, which had lost its military power at the start of the previous century and was disenfranchised by the Penal Laws, had largely given up on attempts to

---

[4] A. Freeman, Barber and Citizen [Charles Lucas], *A first letter to the free citizens of Dublin* (Dublin, 1747), 2–6; A. Freeman, Barber and Citizen [Charles Lucas], *A second letter to the free citizens of Dublin* (Dublin: George Faulkner, 1747), 10.

[5] Gerald of Wales, *The History and Topography of Ireland (Topographia Hiberniae)*, ed. and trans. John O'Meara, (Portlaoise, Ireland: Dolmen, 1982).

[6] McDowell, "Colonial nationalism: 1760–82," 196–235; For further information on Protestant opposition to the Penal Laws see Ian McBride, *Isle of Slaves* (Dublin: Gill and Macmillan, 2009), 207–213; James Kelly, "Inter-Denominational Relations and Religious Toleration in Late Eighteenth-Century Ireland: The 'Paper War' of 1786–88," *Eighteenth-Century Ireland / Iris an Dá Chultúr* 3 (1988): 39–67.

[7] James Macpherson, *Fragments of ancient poetry collected in the Highlands of Scotland, and translated from the Galic or Erse language* (Edinburgh: G. Hamilton and J. Balfour, 1760); *The battle of Lora. A poem. With some fragments written in the Erse, or Irish language, by Ossian, the son of Fingal* (Edinburgh, 1762); *The works of Ossian, the son of Fingal* (London, T. Becket and D.A. Dehent, 1765); Dafydd Moore, "The Reception of the Poems of Ossian in England and Scotland," in *The Reception of the Ossian in Europe*, ed. Howard Gaskill (London: Thoemmes, 2004), 21–39; Donald E. Meek, "The Sublime Gael: The Impact of Macpherson's Ossian on Literary Creativity and Cultural Perception in Gaelic Scotland," in *The Reception of the Ossian in Europe*, 40–66; Colin Smethurst, "Chateaubriand's Ossian," in *The Reception of the Ossian in Europe*, 126–142; Clare O'Halloran, "Irish Re-Creations of the Gaelic Past: The Challenge of Macpherson's Ossian," *Past & Present* 124 (1989), 69–95.

radically alter Ireland's political status as a dominion of a Protestant English king and were instead attempting to improve their position within that kingdom. There were individuals among them who hoped to preserve Gaelic culture and further Catholic political interests through the support of sympathetic Protestants.[8]

One such individual was Charles O'Conor of Ballinagare. O'Conor lived in a cultural intersection in Irish society. He was a native Irish speaker from a formerly powerful Gaelic Irish aristocratic family in north Connacht.[9] He was a prominent participant in the Gaelic manuscript culture, but he also published a number of antiquarian writings in English including a full-length history of pre-Norman Ireland entitled *Dissertations on the Antient History of Ireland* in 1753 with a second edition in 1766.[10] As well as being an antiquarian, he was also a prolific political pamphleteer.

The O'Conors of Ballinagare were a cadet branch of the historically important O'Conors of Connacht, the most powerful family in the province and former kings of Connacht, who had produced high-kings of Ireland. At the end of the Williamite War, their estate was confiscated for their support of King James.[11] This was part of a long series of confiscations, settlements and plantations in Ireland in which land ownership changed on a large scale.

---

[8] C.D.A. Leighton, *Catholicism in a Protestant Kingdom: A Study of the Irish Ancien Régime*, (Dublin: Palgrave Macmillan, 1994), 91–92; McBride, *Isle of Slaves* 398– 405.

[9] Clare O'Halloran. "O'Conor, Charles (1710–1791), antiquary and religious propagandist." *Oxford Dictionary of National Biography*. 23 Sep. 2004; Accessed 19 Dec. 2019. https://www-oxforddnb-com.ezp-prod1.hul.harvard.edu/view/10.1093/ref:odnb/9780198614128.001.0001/odnb-9780198614128-e-20525.

[10] Charles O'Conor, *Dissertations on the Antient History of Ireland*, (Dublin: James Hoey, 1753); Charles O'Conor, *Dissertations on the History of Ireland. To which is subjoined a Dissertation the Irish Colonies Established in Britain with Some Remarks on Mr. MacPherson's Translation of "Fingal" and "Temora"* (Dublin: G. Faulkner, 1766).

[11] Charles O'Conor, Letter to Ralph Owsley, 1789, in *Letters of Charles O'Conor of Belanagare: A Catholic Voice in Eighteenth-Century Ireland,* eds. Robert E. Ward, John F. Wrynn, S.J. and Catherine Coogan Ward (Washington DC: Catholic University of America Press, 1988), 496–497.

Catholic ownership dropped from 59 percent to 14 percent of the total profitable land between 1641 and 1703.[12]

This was compounded by a diverse body of legislation that has come to be described as the Penal Laws. The 1702 Act to prevent the further Growth of Popery ensured that lands that were confiscated could not be regained by Catholics and aimed to break down Catholic land holding further. It forbade Catholics to buy land or inherit land from a Protestant. It also introduced the policy of gavelkind, which forced Catholics to divide their property among their heirs rather than allow one heir to inherit the whole property intact.[13] Land confiscation and the restrictions on land ownership effectively undermined the Catholic aristocracy's basis for power and their sources of income.

The O'Conors managed to recover a portion of their former estate through a complicated legal arrangement between themselves, a neighbouring Protestant family named the Frenches and the Trustees of Forfeited Estates. At the end of this, Charles's father Denis O'Conor held the land under a "base fee", paying an annual rent of £79 to John French.[14] This meant that the O'Conors continued to be among the elites in Catholic society but they relied on the goodwill of powerful Protestants to maintain that position. There is reason to believe that this impacted Charles's views on Jacobitism and violent resistance to Protestant hegemony in general. A 1745 diary entry reveals his disillusionment with the viability of the cause, if not its ideals. He wrote:

> *Carolus Stibhard anos a Saxoibh. Ní fidir fós ga críoch rachus ar a ghnothaidhe. Do réir gach uile chosamhlacht as críoch í ré sgriosfidhther é fén agus gach neach dár ghabh ris[.]*

> Charles Stuart now in England. What end will come of his doing is not yet known. From every appearance it will be

---

[12] J.G. Simms, *The Williamite Confiscation in Ireland: 1690–1703* (London: Faber and Faber, 1956), 196.

[13] *The statutes at large, passed in the Parliaments held in Ireland, Vol. III* (Dublin: Boulter Grierson 1765), 12–31.

[14] Charles Chenevix Trench, *Grace's Card: Irish Catholic Landlords 1690–1800* (Cork: Mercier Press, 1996), 72–73.

an end that will bring his own destruction and that of every
one that accompanied him.[15]

Regardless of his family's reduced holdings, O'Conor was still afforded an
education of a very high standard. He received both a traditional Gaelic
education and later an English academy style education. One of his early
tutors was Dominic Ó Duibhgheannáin, a member of an esteemed
hereditary learned family which included Magnus Ó Duibhgheannáin, one
of the compilers of the Book of Ballymote.[16] At seventeen, he travelled to
Dublin to attend the academy of Walter Skelton.[17] While in Dublin, he was
part of the literary circle surrounding the poet Seán Ó Neachtain and was
named among them in a poem by Seán's son, Tadhg.[18] If O'Conor was not
directly exposed to the manuscript tradition through Ó Duighgheannáin
already, he certainly was as part of the Ó Neachtain circle. The members of
the circle had access to manuscripts from the library of Trinity College
through Anthony Raymond, a Church of Ireland vicar and former lecturer
at the College who was patron to Tadhg Ó Neachtain as a scribe and
interpreter.[19]

After moving back to the family home in Roscommon, O'Conor began
writing anonymous political pamphlets. The first of these was *A counter-
Appeal, to the people of Ireland*, published in 1749.[20] It was written as a
response to William Henry's *An appeal to the people of Ireland*, which was

---

[15] Síle Ní Chinnéide, "Dhá leabhar nótaí le Searlas Ó Conchubhair", *Galvia,* 1 (1954),
32–41 at 39; Translation by Diarmaid Ó Catháin, see "Some account of Charles
O'Conor and literacy in Irish in his time" in *Charles O'Conor of Ballinagare, 1710–
91: Life and Works,* ed. Luke Gibbons and Kieran O'Conor (Four Courts Press,
Dublin 2015), 28–51 at 35.

[16] Ní Chinnéide, "Dhá leabhar nótaí," 32–41, 39; Translation by Diarmaid Ó Catháin,
see "Charles O'Conor of Belanagare: Antiquary and Irish Scholar," *The Journal of the
Royal Society of Antiquaries of Ireland* 119 (1989), 136–163 at 140.

[17] Charles O'Conor, Letter to Ralph Owsley, 1789, in *Letters of Charles O'Conor,*
496–497.

[18] For a transcription see T.F. O'Rahilly, "Irish Scholars in Dublin in the Early
Eighteenth Century," *Gadelica: A Journal of Modern-Irish Studies* 1 (1913): 156–
162.

[19] Nessa Ní Shéaghdha, "Irish Scholars and Scribes in Eighteenth-Century Dublin,"
Eighteenth-Century Ireland / Iris an dá chultúr 4 (1989): 41-54.

[20] [Charles O'Conor], *A counter-Appeal, to the people of Ireland* (Dublin, 1749).

itself a response to the Protestant Patriot ideology expressed by the editor of the *Censor*, Charles Lucas.[21] Henry opposed greater legislative independence for Ireland on the basis that, he believed, its citizens owed their liberty to its attachment to Great Britain and would lose it if that connection was weakened. A negative view of pre-Norman Irish society played an important role in his argument. He claims that:

> Whoever will please to look into the Annals of *Ireland*, and consider its Condition before it became subject to *England*, and how its barbarous Inhabitants were by degrees moulded and formed into Humanity by the *English* Laws; must confess, that before that happy Period, the whole Island seemed rather to be an Hell of Devils, than an Habitation of Men.[22]

Henry goes on to make a number of claims about the nature of pre-Norman Irish society which O'Conor contradicts in his pamphlet and later in his *Dissertations*. The first of these relates to the power of the elites over the common people. He writes

> The Tenants, if such they might be called, were of all Human Creatures the most forlorn Slaves, whose Lives were at the Mercy of their Lords; their Wives and Daughters the daily sacrifices of their Lust, and their Sons obliged to run to die in their Quarrels, whenever a sudden fit of Drunkeness or Lust disposed any one of these Tyrants to plunder another.[23]

He argues that "This condition put a stop to all Arts and Sciences, to Husbandry and every Improvement." He concludes that this is the reason for the currently underdeveloped state of Ireland's countryside.[24] In *A Counter Appeal to the People of Ireland* O'Conor draws upon a wide range of sources on early Irish history to respond to Henry's allegations. He writes:

---

[21] William Henry, *An appeal to the people of Ireland. Occasioned by the insinuations and misrepresentations of the author of a weekly paper, entitled, The censor* (Dublin: Peter Wilson, 1749).

[22] Henry, *An appeal to the people of Ireland*, 8.

[23] Ibid.

[24] Ibid.

> Liberty and *Independence* are your Birth-Rights : This
> right none but a lustful Tyrant would invade, none but an
> abject Slave would controvert : The great Charter of Nature
> gave it ; that of Antiquity kept peace with it ; and *written
> Compact* confirmed it.[25]

The "great Charter of Nature" was a familiar idea in English language discourse at the time. It referred to the natural rights enjoyed by men in the state of nature according to John Locke.[26] The "written Compact" refers to *Magna Carta Libertatum* which had long been viewed within Whiggish history as a guarantee of British liberty. The extent to which it applied to Ireland was a matter of debate, but within the patriot ideology, it was felt that it did.[27] However, the charter "of Antiquity" was not a familiar concept within the discourse of patriotism in Ireland before O'Conor's pamphlet. His explanation of this "charter of Antiquity" involves an account of the earliest settlers in Ireland. He claims that:

> *Ireland* was first inhabited by the *Damnonians* and
> *Belgians* of *Britain;* for this we have the concurrent
> Testimony of ancient Authors; similitude of customs
> renders the account highly probable, and the identity of
> Language demonstrates it.[28]

His argument for the British origin of these first settlers is seemingly based on a combination of the Gaelic historical/pseudo-historical tradition, the testimonies of Classical authors and the modern linguistic theories of Edward Lhuyd, which demonstrated the common origins of Irish and Welsh.[29] Although it seems counterintuitive to open an argument for greater

---

[25] O'Conor, *A counter-appeal to the people of Ireland*, 7.

[26] John Locke, *Two Treatises of Government,* (London Awnsham Churchill, 1690), Book II, 220–234.

[27] Lucas, *An apology for the civil rights and liberties of the commons and citizens of Dublin*, 4, 10.

[28] O'Conor, *A counter-Appeal, to the people of Ireland*, 8.

[29] O'Conor seems to be conflating the Fir Bolg and the Fir Domnann from the *Lebor Gabála* Érenn with the Belgae and the Damnoni who are listed among the people of Albion (Great Britain) in Ptolemy's *Geographia*, see *Lebor Gabála Érenn; The book of the taking of Ireland*, ed. and trans. R.A. Stewart Macalister 5 vols (Dublin: Irish Texts Society, 1932–1942), vol. IV, 63; *Lebor Gabála Érenn*, vol. IV, 6–46; R. Darcy

legislative independence for Ireland from Britain by attributing a British origin to the ancient Irish, he goes on to say:

> These *Britons* lived here *Freemen* according to the popular Plan of Government they brought along with them from their parent Country. By this migration they forfeited none of their natural Rights, any more than the latter Colonies Planted here by *Henry* II–The least suspension of these Rights never occurred, even in Speculation, in those glorious days of true Liberty. *Britain* required no subservience of her Children–; no more than *Gaul*, of *Britain*, who first Colonized that Isle.[30]

A notion of ancient pre-Roman Britons, as possessing freedom which the English had inherited was already being posited in England and it is likely that this is what O'Conor was drawing on.[31] For O'Conor the use of the word Briton in relation to the pre-Norman Irish therefore serves as proof that they were a free people and by extension that their descendants ought to be.

He then sets out contradicting Henry's image of a chaotic pre-Norman Ireland by describing a form of government that closely corresponded with an idealised version of the constitutional monarchy in place in Briton at that time.

> These British Inhabitants, together with other Colonies, who coalized with them, lived under a Monarchical form of Government, which Ollam Fodla (one of their Kings) reformed. That Legislater made this Constitution consist of three orders of Government, which took in the Regal, the Aristocratic and the Popular; attributing to each no more Power than was deemed consistent, with the Liberty and wellbeing of the other two; and the whole in their

---

and William Flynn, "Ptolemy's map of Ireland: a modern decoding," *Irish Geography* 41, no. 1 (2008), 49–69; For the common origin of Welsh and Irish see, Edward Lhuyd, *Archæologia Britannica* (Oxford, Edward Lluyd, 1707).

[30] A *counter-Appeal, to the people of Ireland*, 8.

[31] Henry St. John, Viscount of Bolingbroke, *A dissertation upon parties* (London: T. Cadell, 1732), 183.

Co-operation performing all the good that can be expected
from an equal, equitable, and well-poized Government.[32]

Luke Gibbons has argued that it would have been dangerous for O Conor
to advocate for greater independence from Britain openly in the manner
Irish Catholics had previously or to advocate for greater rights for Catholics
in Ireland.[33] By writing anonymously and adopting a Protestant Patriot
argument, he could insert this account of early Irish history that included
the Gaelic Irish into the social contract.[34] The role that early Irish history
played in this argument is visible in the examples above. This also allows
us to observe the inverse effect; how this contemporary political debate
influenced O'Conor's historical writing, which came to be of crucial
importance in the way in which the memory of early Ireland was
reconstructed in the eighteenth century.

Dissertations on the Antient History of Ireland was written as a
philosophical history.[35] It opens with an introduction that contains an
argument for the edifying value of early Irish interwoven with a summary
of Irish history throughout the period O'Conor is discussing.[36] He then sets
out describing different aspects of early Ireland in thematic chapters.
Notably, he returns to a number of themes that come up in *A Counter Appeal
to the People of Ireland* as well as topics he did not mention, but
nevertheless seem to be answering claims made by Henry in *An Appeal to
the People of Ireland.* Many of these reflected topical concerns of the period
in which he was writing such as the suitability of the land for agriculture
and religious tolerance.[37] Others were points on which there had been long
standing contention in the study of early Ireland, such as the state of learning

---

[32] *A counter-Appeal, to the people of Ireland*, 8.

[33] Luke Gibbons, "Introduction: Charles O'Conor of Ballinagare (1710–91)" in
Charles O'Conor of Ballinagare, 19–27 at 21, 22.

[34] Luke Gibbons, "'A foot in both camps': Charles O'Conor, print culture and the
counter-public sphere" in *Charles O'Conor of Ballinagare, 1710–91*, 116–132 at
122–124.

[35] John Wrynn SJ, "Charles O'Conor as a 'philosophical historian'" in *Charles
O'Conor of Ballinagare, 1710–91*, 72–80.

[36] *Dissertations on the Antient History of Ireland*, v–xxxx.

[37] *Dissertations on the Antient History of Ireland*, 65–73, 130, 157–171.

and perhaps most importantly for O'Conor, the form of government.[38] O'Conor spoke about this topic in the language of liberty and tyranny and it is referenced in almost every page of the above-mentioned introduction.[39] Only one section is explicitly described as an examination of government, but it is a topic which is mentioned frequently in other chapters.[40] Section.V is entitled "Of the *Scotish* Constitution of Government".[41] Here he writes:

> The Form of our Government was monarchical, from the Beginning; but at all Times under the Restraints of popular Councils: The chiefest in Abilities and martial Skill, was elected out of the Milesian Family (as we now call it) to govern the whole Nation.[42]

A presentist interpretation of this description is attractive. It is clear that such a description of early Ireland would function to reinforce O'Conor's own identity (that of a Gaelic Irish aristocrat), reconcile it with the present political state of Ireland and support the argument he made in *A Counter Appeal to the People of Ireland.* However, it would be a mistake to emphasise the influence of contemporary factors in O'Conor's reconstruction of early Irish government over the influence of the Gaelic historiographical tradition to which he belonged. Indeed, Geoffrey Keating had described the government of Ireland in the time of Ollamh Fodla in similarly constitutional terms:

> Feis of Tara was a great general assembly like a parliament, in which the nobles and the ollamhs of Ireland used to meet at Tara every third year at Samhain, where they were wont to lay down and to renew rules and laws, and to approve the annals and records of Ireland.[43]

---

[38] *Dissertations on the Antient History of Ireland*, 99–102.

[39] Ibid

[40] *Dissertations on the Antient History of Ireland,* xli–xlviii, 4–9, 11–13, 31, 41–42, 56–67, 100–105, 108, 115, 119–121, 126–127.

[41] *Dissertations on the Antient History of Ireland*, 73–90.

[42] *Dissertations on the Antient History of Ireland*, 73.

[43] Geoffrey Keating, *Foras feasa ar Éirinn: The history of Ireland by Geoffrey Keating D. D.* ed. and trans. David Comyn and Patrick S. Dinneen (London: Irish Texts Society 1902–1914), vol. II, 133.

O'Conor does not cite Keating as a source for his representation of early Irish government. Rather, later in the chapter he makes the following statement "Clans indeed were hereditary–that is, certain Families were vested with certain Dignities, Powers and Districts–but one Person only was to preside and govern, and that by Election: Nor were such Elections conducted irregularly, or tumultuously".[44] This statement has a footnote which says "Cuan O'Lochan's Poem [written] about the year 1020".[45] This seems to be in reference to Cúán Ua Lothcháin, an eleventh-century poet and the author of a number of the poems in the corpus referred to as the *Dinnshenchas Érenn*. Two poems in particular contain lines which seem to have influenced this statement.[46] One, the poem beginning *"Temair, Tailltiu, tír n-óenaig"* ("Temair, Tailtiu, land of assembly"), referred to as "Temair V" in E. J. Gwynn's edition, which contains the lines:

> *Ce beit ós Banbai brainig ríg amrai, ard a medair,*
> *ní fhuil rechtas ríg foraib acht a ríg techtas Temair[.]*

> Though there be over imperial Banba famous kings–high their mirth! no kingly authority is binding on them save from the king that possesses Temair.[47]

The other is the poem that begins *"A chóemu críche Cuind chain"* ("O nobles of the land of comely Conn"), referred to as "Taltiu" in the Gwynn edition, which contains the lines:

> *Ó chainiud Talten din tSéil co flaith Lóegaire maic Néil dogníthe la slúag síabra óenach cacha hóen-blíadna, La Firu Bolg, bátar and, is la Túatha Dé Danann, la maccu Míled iarsin co Pátric iar prím-chreitim[.]*

> From the lamentation for Tailtiu of the Sele to the reign of Loegaire mac Neill was held by the fairy host a fair every single year, By the Fir Bolg, who were there, and by the

---

[44] *Dissertations on the Antient History of Ireland,* 76

[45] Ibid

[46] Clodagh Downey, "The life and work of Cúán ua Lothcháin." *Ríocht na Midhe,* 109 (2008), 55–78.

[47] "Temair V" in *The Metrical Dindshencas,* ed. and trans. Edward Gwynn 5 vols. (Dublin: Hodges and Figgis, 1903–1935), vol. I, 38–45, at 44–45.

Tuatha De Danann, by the Children of Mil thereafter down
to Patrick after the first coming of the Faith.[48]

Clodagh Downey has argued that these poems were themselves part of an
eleventh-century cultural programme carried out by Máel Sechnaill mac
Domnaill to inflate the perception of the power of the king of Tara during
the period that he held the kingship.[49] It was essentially an aspirational view
of the kingship projected backwards into the pre-Christian era. But O'Conor
uses it to create an image of a king whose power is limited by a public
assembly. While the poem certainly does not depict an election, it does
depict a high-kingship that is consented to by the smaller kings who
assemble at Tara. It is important to understand that O'Conor was not
constructing his ideal image of early Ireland from nothing. To quote Jan
Assman:

> Cultural memory works by reconstructing, that is, it always
> relates its knowledge to an actual and contemporary
> situation. True, it is fixed in immovable figures of memory
> and stores of knowledge, but every contemporary context
> relates to these differently, sometimes by appropriation,
> sometimes by criticism, sometimes by preservation or by
> transformation.[50]

Returning to the contemporary context surrounding O'Conor's
reconstruction of the past, it is important not just to examine how
eighteenth-century society influenced O'Conor's writing, but also how his
writing was received and whether it can be said to have become part of the
cultural memory.[51] Unfortunately, there is not enough space for a systematic
examination of that topic here. There are a number of disparate examples
which can be pointed to and may at the least provide new avenues for further
study. In the area of political pamphleteering, Luke Gibbons has pointed
out that five years after the release of *Dissertations on the Antient History*

---

[48] Gwynn, *The Metrical Dindshencas*, vol. IV, 147–163 at 152–153.

[49] Downey, "The life and work of Cúán ua Lothcháin.", 59.

[50] Jan Assmann and John Czaplicka, "Cultural Memory and Collective Identity", *New German Critique* no. 65, (1995), pp. 125–133, p. 130

[51] Alon Confino, "Collective Memory and Cultural History: Problems of Method," *The American Historical Review*, 102, no. 5 (1997): 1386–1403 at 1390.

of Ireland, Henry Brooke released a pamphlet entitled *Essay on the antient and modern state of Ireland.*[52] Like previous Protestant Patriot pamphlets, it was basically a defence of Ireland's legislative independence but unlike many of those early pamphlets, he includes references to a supposed constitutional government that existed in pre-Norman Ireland. He wrote "Never did the Spirit of popular Freedom exert itself more powerfully or harmoniously, than in those truly parliamentary Triennial Conventions of Ireland."[53] He cites "The assiduous, exact, and candid Author of the Dissertations."[54] The influential poetry collector Charlotte Brooke (daughter of the above-mentioned Henry Brooke), also cited O'Conor, as well as Sylvester O'Halloran and Charles Vallancey, in the introduction to her *Reliques of Irish Poetry.*[55] Finally, the most obvious area to look for the reception of O'Conor's writing is in the field of antiquarianism. Clare O'Halloran has noted the influence of O'Conor on the writings of Sylvester O'Halloran, Thomas Leland and Charles Vallancey.[56] Vallancey is particularly important because of the central role he played in the founding of the Royal Irish Academy in 1785.[57] By the end of that century, three great late medieval manuscript compilations–the Book of Ballymote, the Book of Lecan and An Leabhar Breac–which had previously been held by private individuals connected to the tradition of Gaelic manuscript transmission, had been acquired by the Royal Irish Academy, a national institute of public ownership.[58]

Indeed, the foundation of the academy itself and the role it has played in preserving Irish manuscript material is a good indication of how the attitude towards the Gaelic past changed in elite spheres over the course of

---

[52] Henry Brooke, *An essay on the antient and modern state of Ireland* (Dublin: P. Lord, 1759).

[53] *An essay on the antient and modern state of Ireland*, 18.

[54] *An essay on the antient and modern state of Ireland*, 6.

[55] Charlotte Brooke, *Reliques of Irish Poetry* (Dublin: George Bonham, 1789), iii–iv.

[56] Clare O'Halloran, *Golden Ages and Barbarous Nations: Antiquarian debate and Cultural Politics in Ireland c. 1750–1800,* (Cork: Cork University Press, 2004), 38–40, 108–111; 33–35, 130,148; 37, 42–45, 51–53, 163,165.

[57] Charles O'Conor, S.J., "Origins of the Royal Irish Academy." *Studies: An Irish Quarterly Review* 38, no. 151 (1949): 325–37.

[58] Book of Ballymote RIA MS 23 P 12; Book of Lecan RIA MS 23 P 16; Leabhar Breac RIA MS 23 P 2.

the eighteenth century. English-speaking Protestant society, which had been largely hostile to Gaelic culture at the start of that century, had come to internalise parts of the history of Gaelic Ireland in their own national identity.[59] While O'Conor was only one individual involved in this process, he was a central one and understanding the image of early Ireland he wanted to convey is a useful entry point into the complex web of individuals, identities and ideologies of antiquarianism in eighteenth century Ireland.

[59] Joep Leersen, "'Why sleeps O'Conor?' Charles O'Conor and the Irish nationalization of native historical consciousness", in *Charles O'Conor of Ballinagare: Life and Works,* ed. Luke Gibbons and Kieran O'Conor (Dublin, 2015), 244–254.

COLIN BRADY

Bibliography

Primary Sources

The statutes at large, passed in the Parliaments held in Ireland, Vol. III. Dublin: Boulter Grierson 1765.

Brooke, Charlotte. *Reliques of Irish Poetry.* Dublin: George Bonham, 1789.

Brooke, Henry. *An essay on the antient and modern state of Ireland.* Dublin: P. Lord, 1759.

Gerald of Wales, *The History and Topography of Ireland (Topographia Hiberniae),* edited and translated John O'Meara. Portlaoise, Ireland: Dolmen, 1982.

Harris, Sir Walter. *Remarks on the Affairs and Trade of England and Ireland.* London: Tho. Parkhurst, 1691.

Henry, William. *An appeal to the people of Ireland. Occasioned by the insinuations and misrepresentations of the author of a weekly paper, entitled, The censor.* Dublin: Peter Wilson, 1749.

Lucas, Charles. *An apology for the civil rights and liberties of the commons and citizens of Dublin.* Dublin: James Esdall, 1748.

A first letter to the free citizens of Dublin. Dublin, 1747.

A second letter to the free citizens of Dublin. Dublin: George Faulkner, 1747.

James Macpherson, *Fragments of ancient poetry collected in the Highlands of Scotland, and translated from the Galic or Erse language.* Edinburgh: G. Hamilton and J. Balfour, 1760.

The battle of Lora. A poem. With some fragments written in the Erse, or Irish language, by Ossian, the son of Fingal. Edinburgh, 1762.

The works of Ossian, the son of Fingal. London, T. Beckket and D.A. Dehent1765.

Molyneaux, William. *The case of Ireland's being bound by acts of parliament in England stated.* London: F.R. Andare, 1698.

Charles O'Conor, *A counter-Appeal, to the people of Ireland.* Dublin, 1749.

Dissertations on the Antient History of Ireland. Dublin: James Hoey, 1753.

Dissertations on the History of Ireland. To which is subjoined a Dissertation the the Irish Colonies Established in Britain with Some Remarks on Mr. MacPherson's Translation of "Fingal" and "Temora". Dublin: G. Faulkner, 1766.

O'Conor, S.J., Charles. "Origins of the Royal Irish Academy." *Studies: An Irish Quarterly Review* 38, no. 151 (1949): 325-37.

MEDIEVAL MEMORY

Ward, Robert E., John F. Wrynn, S.J. and Catherine Coogan Ward (editors), *Letters of Charles O'Conor of Belanagare: A Catholic Voice in Eighteenth-Century Ireland.* Washington DC: Catholic University of America Press, 1988.

Secondary Sources

Assmann, Jan and John Czaplicka. "Cultural Memory and Collective Identity", *New German Critique* no. 65, (1995), pp. 125-133.

Beckett, J.C. "Introduction: Eighteenth-century Ireland," in *A New History of Ireland IV: Eighteenth-Century Ireland 1691-1800,* edited by T.W. Moody and W.E. Vaughan, xxxix-lxiv. Oxford: Oxford University Press, 1986.

"Literature in English: 1691-1800," in *A New History of Ireland IV: Eighteenth-Century Ireland 1691-1800,* edited by T.W. Moody and W.E. Vaughan, 424-470. Oxford: Oxford University Press, 1986.

Chenevix Trench, Charles. *Grace's Card: Irish Catholic Landlords 1690-1800.* Cork: Mercier Press, 1996.

Darcy, R. and William Flynn, "Ptolemy's map of Ireland: a modern decoding," *Irish Geography*, 41, no. 1 (2008), 49-69.

Downey, Clodagh. "The life and work of Cúán ua Lothcháin." *Ríocht na Midhe*, 109, (2008), 55-78.

Confino, Alon. "Collective Memory and Cultural History: Problems of Method," *The American Historical Review* 102, no. 5 (1997): 1386-1403.

Gibbons, Luke. "Introduction: Charles O'Conor of Ballinagare (1710-91)" in *Charles O'Conor of Ballinagare, 1710-91: Life and Works,* ed. Luke Gibbons and Kieran O'Conor, 19-27. Four Courts Press, Dublin 2015.

Leighton, C.D.A. Catholicism in a Protestant Kingdom: A Study of the Irish Ancien Régime. Dublin: Palgrave Macmillan, 1994.

Locke, John. *Two Treatises of Government,* (London Awnsham Churchill, 1690).

Lhuyd, Edward. *Archæologia Britannica.* Oxford, Edward Lluyd, 1707.

James Kelly, "Lucas, Charles," *Dictionary of Irish Biography.* http://dib.cambridge.org/ viewReadPage.do?articleId=a4903

Macalister R.A. Stewart (editor and translator). *Lebor Gabála Érenn; The book of the taking of Ireland,* 5 volumes. Dublin: Irish Texts Society, 1932-1942.

McBride, Ian. *Eighteenth-Century Ireland: The Isle of Slaves.* Dublin: Gill and Macmillan, 2009.

McCracken, J.L. "Protestant Ascendancy and the rise of colonial nationalism, 1714-60," in *A New History of Ireland IV: Eighteenth-Century Ireland 1691-1800,* edited by T.W. Moody and W.E. Vaughan, 105-122. Oxford: Oxford University Press, 1986.

McDowell, R.B. "Colonial nationalism and the winning of parliamentary independence: 1760-82," in *A New History of Ireland IV: Eighteenth-Century Ireland 1691-1800,* edited by T.W. Moody and W.E. Vaughan, 196-265. Oxford: Oxford University Press, 1986.

Meek, Donald E. "The Sublime Gael: The Impact of Macpherson's Ossian on Literary Creativity and Cultural Perception in Gaelic Scotland," in *The Reception of the Ossian in Europe,* edited by Howard Gaskill, 40-66. London: Thoemmes, 2004.

Moore, Dafydd. 'The Reception of the *Poems of Ossian* in England and Scotland,' in *The Reception of the Ossian in Europe,* edited by Howard Gaskill, 21-39. London: Thoemmes, 2004.

Ní Chinnéide, Síle. "Dhá leabhar nótaí le Searlas Ó Conchubhair", *Galvia,* 1 (1954), 32-41.

Ní Shéaghdha, Nessa. "Irish Scholars and Scribes in Eighteenth-Century Dublin," *Eighteenth-Century Ireland / Iris an dá chultúr* 4 (1989): 41-54.

Ó Catháin, Diarmaid "Charles O'Conor of Belanagare: Antiquary and Irish Scholar," *The Journal of the Royal Society of Antiquaries of Ireland* 119 (1989),136-163 at 140.

"Some account of Charles O'Conor and literacy in Irish in his time" in *Charles O'Conor of Ballinagare, 1710-91: Life and Works,* ed. Luke Gibbons and Kieran O'Conor (Four Courts Press, Dublin 2015), 28-51

O'Halloran, Clare. "Irish Re-Creations of the Gaelic Past: The Challenge of Macpherson's Ossian," *Past & Present* 124 (1989), 69-95.

"O'Conor, Charles (1710–1791), antiquary and religious propagandist." Oxford Dictionary of National Biography. 23 Sep. 2004; Accessed 19 Dec. 2019 .https://www-oxforddnb-com.ezp-prod1.hul.harvard.edu/view/ 10.1093/ref:odnb/9780198614128.001.0001/odnb-9780198614128-e-20525.

O'Rahilly, T.F. "Irish Scholars in Dublin in the Early Eighteenth Century," *Gadelica: A Journal of Modern-Irish Studies* 1 (1913): 156-162.

Simms, J.G., *The Williamite Confiscation in Ireland: 1690-1703.* London: Faber and Faber, 1956.

MEDIEVAL MEMORY

"The establishment of Protestant Ascendancy, 1691-1714," in *A New History of Ireland IV: Eighteenth-Century Ireland 1691-1800,* edited by T.W. Moody and W.E. Vaughan, 1-30. Oxford: Oxford University Press, 1986.

Smethurst, Colin. 'Chateaubriand's Ossian,' in *The Reception of the Ossian in Europe,* edited by Howard Gaskill. London: Thoemmes, 2004. 126-142;

St. John, Henry. *A dissertation upon parties.* London: T. Cadell, 1732.

The Life of Saint Brigid by Cogitosus

Philip Freeman

The earliest life of the fifth-century St. Brigid, Ireland's first and most famous female saint, is arguably the seventh-century *Vita Sanctae Brigidae* of Cogitosus.[1] Along with the slightly later Latin *Vita Prima* (*Vita I*) and *Bethu Brigte*, composed in Old Irish, the *Vita* of Cogitosus provides us with a hagiographical account of one of the most important figures in early Christian Ireland.

Bethu Brigte was skillfully edited with an English translation by Donncha Ó hAodha,[2] but the two Latin lives, in spite of several good beginnings over the last century by notable scholars, have never been edited. The only previous edition of value is in the *Acta Sanctorum* published in 1658 from a few mostly inferior manuscripts.[3] There have been a few studies of the manuscripts of Cogitosus, the most important being Esposito 1912/13, 1926, 1935, McCone 1982, and Sharpe 1982. There have been several important studies that focus on Brigid in Cogitosus, including Bitel 2009, Bray 2010, and Harrington 2002, as well as excellent work on the *Vita Prima*, notably Connolly 1972, 1989 and McKenna 2002. Other key secondary sources are listed in the bibliography.

The scholarly study of Brigid and the role of women in early Irish Christianity, and indeed medieval Irish historical and religious studies in general, has long been hampered by the lack of a critical Latin edition of the work of Cogitosus. There have been only a few published translations of the *Vita*, the best of these by Sean Connolly and J. M. Picard in 1987.[4] I myself have offered a translation of the *Vita* of Cogitosus as part of a recently-published anthology of writings on early Christian Ireland, but it is

---

[1] The dating of the three earliest lives of Brigid is not yet firmly settled, but I agree with the current consensus that the Vita of Cogitosus is the earliest. See Richard Sharpe, "*Vitae S Brigitae*: The oldest texts," *Peritia* 1 (1982): 81–106.

[2] Donncha Ó hAodha, *Bethu Brigte* (Dublin: Dublin Institute for Advanced Studies, 1978).

[3] *Acta Sanctorum,* February vol. 1 (1658), 135–141.

[4] Sean Connolly and J.-M. Picard, "Cogitosus's *Life of St Brigit*: Content and Value," *The Journal of the Royal Society of Antiquaries of Ireland* 117 (1987): 5–27.

by no means a critical edition.[5] The chapter divisions of my edition below follow the Connolly-Picard translation, which are based on those found within the earliest manuscripts.

There are over eighty surviving manuscripts of the *Vita* by Cogitosus dating from the ninth to seventeenth centuries, listed in the comprehensive catalog of Ludwig Bieler.[6] Over the last few years I have worked with librarians in Europe to collect high quality images of the fourteen earliest and best of these Cogitosus manuscripts. These manuscripts were chosen because of their early dates, ending in the eleventh century, and the quality of the text they preserve. Several later manuscripts were also examined, but they added little or nothing to the manuscript readings.[7] The earliest and most reliable of the fourteen surviving manuscripts of Cogitosus' work is from the Bibliothèque de la Ville at Reims in northeast France, originally housed at the nearby Benedictine abbey of Saint-Thierry.[8] This witness to Cogitosus has formed the basis of my edition with only minor changes in those cases when another manuscript seems to offer a better reading.

The complete list of the fourteen manuscripts used in this edition are:[9]

R—Reims, Bibliothèque de la Ville, MS 296 (9-10th century)

B—Berlin, Staatsbibliothek, MS 364 (10th century).

Br—Brussels, Bibliothèque Royale, MS II.2568 (10th century).

O—Orleans, Bibliothèque Publique, MS 311 (10th century).

P₁—Paris, Bibliothèque Nationale, MS Lat. 10862 (10th century).

C—Cambrai, Bibliothèque Municipale, MS 865 (10th/11th century).

L—London, British Museum, MS Cotton Nero E1 (11th century).

Bg—Bergamo, Biblioteca Civica, MS 227 (11th century)

---

[5] Philip Freeman, *The World of Saint Patrick* (Oxford: Oxford University Press, 2014), 95–128.

[6] Ludwig Bieler, "Saint Bridget" in *Manuscript Sources for the History of Irish Civilisation*, ed. Richard J. Hayes (Boston: G.K. Hall and Co.,1965), 332–334.

[7] The complete list of manuscripts is found in Bieler, "St. Bridget," 332–334.

[8] Mario Esposito, "On the Earliest Life of St. Brigid of Kildare," *Proceedings of the Royal Irish Academy. Section C, Archaeology, Linguistics, and Literature* 30, no. 11 (1912/13): 316.

[9] The dates for the manuscripts are found in the respective manuscript catalogs and in Bieler, "St. Bridget," 332–334.

M—Munich, Staatsbibliothek, MS 18854 (11th century)
N—Naples, Biblioteca Nazionale, MS VIII.B.3 (11th century)
P₂—Paris Bibliothèque Mazarine, MS 1711 (11th century)
P₃—Paris, Bibliothèque Nationale, MS Lat. 2999 (11th century)
Rn—Rouen, Bibliothèque Municipale, MS 1384 (11th century)
S—Salisbury, Salisbury Cathedral Library, MS 221 (11th/12th century)[10]

The Latin Text

VITA SANCTAE BRIGIDAE

Incipit vita Sanctae Brigidae virginis quae est Kalendiis Febrarii[11]

PROLOGUS[12]

1. Me cogitis fratres ut sanctae ac beatae memoriae Brigidae virginis virtutes et opera morum[13] doctorum memoriae litterisque tradere adgrediar. Quod opus inpositum et delicate materiae arduum parvitati et ignorantiae meae et linguae minime convenit. Sed potens est Deus de minimis magna facere, ut de exiguo olei et farinae pugillo domum inplevit pauperculae viduae.[14]

2. Itaque iussionibus vestris coactus, satis habeo meam non defuisse oboedientiam. Et ideo pauca de pluribus, a maioribus ac peritissimis tradita,

---

[10] Closely related to Cotton Nero E1, it was previously in the Bodleian Library, listed as Oxford Fell 4.

[11] *Incipit vita Sanctae Brigidae virginis quae est Kalendiis Febrarii* **R Rn**   *Incipit prologus de vita et virtutibus Sanctae Brigidae* **O P₁ P₂**   *Incipit vita Sanctae Brigidae virginis quod est Kalendis Februarii* **C L S**   *Kaldendis Februarii natale Sanctae Brigidae virginis incipit prologus* **Bg**   *Incipit vita Sanctae Brigidae virginis Kalendis Februarii* **M**   *Incipit prologus in Sanctae Brigidae* **N**. Editor's Note: With the permission of the author and for the convenience of readers, we have inserted into this Latin edition the numbering used by Sean Connolly and J. -M. Picard for their English translation. See note 4 above. Two instances of deviation from the Connolly and Picard text are marked with square brackets.

[12] **B Br** omit the Prologue entirely.

[13] *morum* omit **L Rn S**   *more* **Bg N**

[14] 1 Kings 17:8–16.

sine ulla ambiguitatis caligine, ne inoboedientiae crimen incurram, patefacere censeo.

3. Ex quibus quanta qualisque virgo virtutum bonarum florida, cunctorum oculis innotescat. Non quod memoria et mediocritas, et rusticus sermo ingenioli mei, tanti muneris officium explicare valeret. Sed fidei vestrae beatitudo, et orationum vestrarum diuturnitas meretur accipere, quod non valet ingenium ferre dictantis.

4. Haec ergo egregiis crescens virtutibus et fama bonarum rerum, ad eam de omnibus provinciis totius Hiberniae innumerabiles populi de utroque sexu confluentes, et vota sibi voventes voluntariae, suum monasterium caput paene omnium Hybernensium ecclesiarum, et culmen praecellens omnia monasteria Scotthorum, cuius parroechia per totam Hybernensem terram defusa a mari usque ad mare extensa est. In campestribus campi liffei[15] supra fundamentum fidei firmum construxit.

5. Et prudenti dispensatione de animabus suorum regulariter in omnibus procurans. Et de ecclesiis multarum provintiarum sibi adherentibus sollicitans, et secum revolvens quod sine summo sacerdote qui ecclesias consecraret et ecclesiasticos in eis gradus subrogaret esse non posse. Inlustrem virum et solitarium Conleh[16] et omnibus moribus bonis ornatum per quem Deus virtutes operatus est plurimas, convocans eum de heremo et de sua vita solitaria, et in ipsius obviam pergens, ut ecclesiam in episcopali dignitate cum ea gubernaret atque ut nihil de ordine sacerdotali in suis deesset ecclesiis accessivit.

6. Et sic postea uctum[17] caput et principale omnium episcoporum et beatissima puellarum[18] principalis felici comitatu inter se et gubernaculis omnium virtutum suam rexerunt principalem ecclesiam. Et amborum meritis suam cathedram[19] episcopalis et puellaris acsi vitis fructifera diffusa undique ramis crescentibus in totam Hybernensi insula inolevit. Quam semper archiepiscopus Hybernensium episcoporum abbatissam quam

---

[15] *lyfei* **C L Rn** *liphei* **Bg** *lifei* **M N**

[16] omit **C L Rn S** *nomine Conleeth* **Bg N**

[17] *unicum* **R B Br**

[18] *omit omnium . . . principalis* **R B Br** *omnium episcoporum et beatissimarum puellarum* **O P₁ C L Bg M N P₂ P₃ Rn**

[19] *sua cathedra* **O P₁ Bg M**

omnes abbatisse Scothorum venerantur, felici successione et ritu perpetuo dominantur.

7. Exinde ego[20] ut supra dixi a fratribus coactus, beate huius Brigidae virtutes tam eas quae ante principatum, quamque alias[21] gessit, tanto studio brevitatis, licet praepostero ordine virtutum, conpendiose explicare conabor.[22]

Explicit praefatio de sancta Brigidae virtutibus[23]

1.1. Sancta itaque Brigida, quam Deus prescivit ad suam imaginem[24] et predestinavit a Christianis nobilibusque parentibus[25] de bona ac prudentissima Ectech[26] prosapia in Scothia orta, patreque Dubtacho[27] et matre Brocca[28] genita. A sua pueritia bonarum rerum studiis inolevit. Electa enim ex Deo puella, moribus sobria aetatis ac pudicitiae plena in meliora semper crescebat.

1.2. Et quis sua opera ac virtutes quae etiam in hac aetate gessit, plene enarrare valet? Sed haec pauca et de innumerabilibus exempli causa posita demonstrabimus.

1.3. Ex inde haec cum tempus maturum advenit in opus coagli ut de turbato vaccarum lacte butyrum congregaret a matre transmissa est. Ut sicut alie femine hoc opus exercere solebant, ipsa quoque aequali modo perageret, et ut cum ceteris in tempore placito vaccarum fructum ac pondus mensuratumque butyri solitum plenissime in usum redderet.

1.4. Sed haec moribus pulcherrima et hospitalis virgo, oboedire magis volens Deo quam hominibus, pauperibus et hospitibus lac largiter et butyrum distribuit.

---

[20] *ergo* **O Bg N**

[21] insert: *quas in principatu* **O P₁ C M P₂ P₃**

[22] omit **P₁ C L M Rn S**

[23] omit *Explicit . . . virtuibus* **P₁ C L M N Rn S**. Following this are chapter titles which appear only in **R Bg P₂ P₃**

[24] Romans 8:29.

[25] omit *a Christianis nobilibusque parentibus* **P₁ C L Bg M N Rn**

[26] omit **P₁ C L Bg M N Rn S** *ectehe* **Br**

[27] *dubtocho* **B Br O P₁ C Bg M P₂ P₃ Rn** *duptocho* **Rn** *dabtoch* **Bg**

[28] *processa* **Br** *broccha O* *broicsech nomina* **P₁** *chrocha* **Bg**

1.5 Et cum secundum morem oportunum advenit tempus ut omnes redderent fructum vaccarum ad eam perventum est. Et cum cooperatrices eius monstrabant sua opera completa, quaesitum est a beata supradicta virgine, ut est ipsa similiter adsignaret suum opus.

1.6. Et ipsa matris timore pavida, cum non haberet quod monstraret, quia totum pauperibus erogavit, crastinum non procurans tempus. Tanta et inextinguibili flamma fidei accensa ac firma, ad Dominum se convertens oravit. Nec mora Dominus vocem virginis audiens ac praeces, largitate divini muneris, sicut est adiutor in oportunitatibus, adfuit. Et pro sua in se virgine confidenti, afluenter butyrum restituit.

1.7. Mirum in modum et illa hora post orationem virgo sanctissima nihil de suo opere deesse ostendens, sed super omnes cooperatrices habundas, se monstravit complesse suum officium.

1.8. Et cum plenissime inventum in oculis omnium tanti muneris miraculum innotuit et laudantes Deum qui hoc fecit tantam fidei virtutem in virginali pectore constitisse admirati sunt.

2.1. Ac non multo post cum eam sui parentes, more humano, viro desponsare volebant, illa caelitus inspirata se virginem castam exhibere Deo volens, ad episcopum sanctissimum beate memoriae Mac Caille[29] perrexit. Qui caeleste intuens desiderium et pudicitiam et tantum castitatis amorem in tali virgine, pallium album et vestem candidam super ipsius venerabile caput inposuit.

2.2. Quae coram Deo et episcopo ac altari genua humiliter flectens et suam virginalem coronam Domino omnipotenti offerens, fundamen ligneum, quo altare fulciebatur, manu tetigit.

2.3. Quod lignum in comemoratione pristinae virtutis usque ad praesens tempus viride, ac si non esset excisum et decorticatum, sed in radicibus fixum, virescit. Et usque hodie languores et morbos de omnibus expellit fidelibus.

3.1. Nec praetereundum mihi videtur commemorare de illa virtute quam haec famosissima famula Dei ac divino incessanter famulatui tradita operata est.

3.2. Nam cum illa aliquando in caldaria lardam advenientibus hospitibus coxerat cani adulanti ac flagitanti misericorditer eam tradidit.

---

[29] *machellem* **Br**   *machille* **C L Bg M N Rn S**   *maccaire* **P₂**

3.3. Et cum larda de caldaria tracta ac postea hospitibus esset divisa acsi non esset dempta plenissime reperta est.

3.4. Et valde hi qui hoc viderunt admirantes puellam incomparabilem virtute fidei et merito bonarum virtutum dignis laudibus divulgaverunt.

4.1. Et eadem messores ac operarios convocavit in messem suam. Et facta illa messorum conventione, nebulosa ac pluvialis dies illa accidit conventionis, et pluviis largiter ex nubibus effusis, per totam illam in circuitu provintiam. Ac rivulis guttarum affluentia per convalles et rimas terrarum currentibus, sua messis sola arida sine pluviarum inpedimento et turbatione perstitit.

4.2. Et cum omnes messores ipsius undique regionis pluviali die prohibiti essent sui sine ulla umbra caliginis pluvie illa die tota ab ortu usque ad occasum solis messure Dei potentia opus exercebant.

5.1. [30] Ecce inter ceteras virtutes ipsius, hoc opus dignum admiratione videtur esse et admirabile.

5.2. Advenientibus enim episcopis et cum ea hospitantibus, cum non haberet unde eos cibaret, adiuta Dei multiplici virtute, solito more habundanter ut sua poscebat necessitas. Vaccam unam eandemque tribus contra consuetudinem in una die vicibus mulsit.5.3. Et quod solet de optimis tribus vaccis exprimi, ipsa, mirabili eventu, de una sua expressit vacca.

6.1. Ecce et hanc virtutem beatitudini vestrae insinuare censeo, in qua mens pura virginalis et manus cooperatrix divina in unum apparent convenire.

6.2. Nam haec cum suas opere pastorali pasceret oves, in campestri et herboso loco, largitate nimia pluviarum perfusa, humidis vestibus domum rediit.

6.3. Et cum umbra solaris per foramina domum intrinsecus intraret, illam umbram obtusa oculorum acie, arborem fuisse transversam et fixam putans ac desuper suam complutam vestem ponens tamquam in arbore grandi et firma in ipso tenui solari umbraculo vestis pependit

6.4. Et cum ipsius domus habitatores et vicini hoc ingenti fuissent miraculo perculsi hanc incomparabilem dignis laudibus extollebant.

---

[30] Chapter 5 omitted by **Br**

7.1. Et hoc silentio opus non est pretereundum.

7.2. Cum enim haec sancta Brigida in agro iuxta gregem ovium pascendum, cura pastorali esset sollicita, aliquis nequam adolescens callide subripiens, et ipsius largitatem in pauperes conprobans et mutato semper habitu ad eam septies veniens, septem ab ea vervices in una detulit die et in secreto abscondit.

7.3. Et cum grex ad vesperum et ex more ad caulas fuerat dirigendus, duabus vel tribus vicibus diligentissime adnumeratus, sine damno sui mirum in modum totus integro reppertus est numero.

7.4. Et admirantes hi qui conscii facti fuerant, virtutem Dei manifeste factam per virginem, septem quos absconderunt vervices ad suum dimiserunt gregem. Et ille gregis numerus nec plus nec minus sed ut ante integer repertus est.

7.5. His et aliis innumerabilibus virtutibus famosissima haec famula Dei in ore omnium super omnes non inmerito sed dignis laudibus excellentissima visa est.

8.1. Mirabili quoque eventu ab hac venerabili Brigida leprosi cervisam flagitantes. Cum non haberet illa, videns aquam ad balnea paratam, et cum virtute fidei benedicens in optimam convertit cervisam et abundanter sitientibus exhausit

8.2. Ille enim qui in chana galileae aquam convertit in vinum, per huius quoque beatissime feminae fidem aquam mutavit in cervisam.

8.3. Dum autem de hac virtute dictum est, de alia admirabili commemorationem facere aptum videtur.

9.1. Potentissima enim et ineffabili fidei fortitudine, aliquam feminam, post votum integritatis, fragilitate humana in iuvenali voluntatis[31] desiderio lapsam et habentem pregnantem ac tumescentem vulvam fideliter benedixit. Et evanescens in vulva conceptus sine partu et sine dolore eam sanam ad penitentiam restituit.

9.2. Et secundum quod omnia possibilia sunt credentibus[32] sine ulla inpossibilitate innumera cotidie miracula operabatur.

---

[31] *voluptans* **Br** *voluptatis* **C L N P₂**
[32] Mark 9:23, Matthew 17:20.

10.1. Quadam enim die cum quidam ad eam salem petens veniret sicut ceteri pauperes et egeni innumerabiles venire solebant pro suis necessitatibus. Ipsa beatissima brigida in illa hora salem factum de lapide, quem benedixit, in opus poscentis sufficienter largita est.

10.2. Et sic ab ea salem portans laetus propriam domum rediit.

11.1. Et hoc potentissimum opus eiusdem divinum iungendum esse mihi videtur inter cetera quo salvatoris instar imitatrix divini nominis excelsissimam operata est virtutem.

11.2. Nam secundum exemplum Domini et haec oculos ceci aperuit nati. Sua enim nomina et opera membris Dominus largitus est suis. Quia cum de semetipso loqueretur, "Ego sum lux mundi"[33] nihilominus suis dicit apostolis, "Vos estis lux mundi" et de hisdem idem dicens intulit, "Opera quae ego facio et ipsi facient et maiora horum facient."[34]

11.3. Inde quem naturalis partus caecum protulit natum, fides eiusdem Brigide grano comparata sinapis et consimilis eidem oculos simplices et lucidos ingenti miraculo aperuit.

12.1. Haec itaque tantis virtutibus inlustris humilitate cordis et puritate mentis et morum temperantia ac spirituali gratia plena tantam auctoritatem in divino cultu et celebre nomen prae omnibus coaetaneis virginibus habere meruit.

12.2. Et quadam die cum una ex adherentibus sibi extrinsecus femina cum filia xii duodecim annos aetatis, ex naturali procreatione muta, ad eam veniret visitandam cum digna reverentia, ut omnes solebant, se inclinans et humili collo ad eius pacificum osculum procidens. Ipsa omnibus affabilis brigida ac felix conditis sale divino sermonibus eam salubriter allocuta est ac salvatoris nostri exemplo iubentis parvulos ad se venire, filie manum retinens manu sua, nesciente illa quod esset muta, et voluntatem ipsius interrogans, utrum velato capite permanere virgo, annuptus tradenda esse vellet.

12.3. Matre ipsius admonente quod sibi filia nulla daret responsa, respondens matri dixit se non dimissuram filiae manum nisi sibi prius responsum redderet. Et cum filiam secunda vice interrogaret de eadem re respondit filia sibi, dicens, "Non aliud nisi quod tu volueris agere volo."

---

[33] John 8:12

[34] John 14:12

12.4. Ac sic postea aperto ore sine lingue inpedimento et soluto ipsius vinculo sana loquebatur.

13.1. Et quibus hoc eiusdem opus nullis[35] multorum auribus antea inauditum scrupulum non moveret?

13.2. Cum enim haec animo esset intenta caelestium meditatione ut semper solebat suam de terrestribus ad caelestia elevans conversationem[36] quamdam non parvam sed grandem, lardi partem cum cane dimisit. Et cum esset inquisita, non alicubi sed in loco ubi canis solebat esse, mense transacto intacta et integra reperta est.

13.3. Non enim canis ausus est comedere depositum beate virginis, sed custos patiens lardi et idoneus, contra suum solitum morem, divina refrenatus virtute et domitus extitit.

14.1. Et[37] crescente cotidie miraculorum numero, quae vix enumerari possunt, quantum misericordie et pietatis et in pauperes elymosinarum oportune et inoportune postulantium operata est.

14.2. Nam cum aliquis indigens cibo pauperum eam rogaret, illa ad eos qui carnes coxerant, ut ab illis aliquid pauperi deferret festinavit. Et illorum unus stolidissimus famulus qui carnes coxerat insipienter partem nondum carnis coctam in albatum ipsius sinuate vestis receptaculum transiecit. Et sic illa non suffuscato mantili sed in suo candido colore manente portans pauperi tribuit.

15.1. Nec non et hoc de eius gestis felicibus admirari debet.

15.2. Confluentibus enim ad eam undique pauperibus et peregrinis ingenti fama virtutum et nimie largitatis tracti accedens inter eos ingratus quidam leprosus optimam de armento vaccam cum optimo vitulo omnium vitulorum in simul sibi donari poscebat.

15.3. Nec ipsa eius audiens preces[38] distulit, sed mox illam quam optimam didicit de omnibus vaccam et alicuius vaccae vitulum eligantem et optimum roganti infirmo voluntarie donavit. Et misericorditer suum cum illo transmittens currum per iter longum et latissimum campum, ne

---

[35] omit **B**   insert *non* **Br P₁ C M N Rn**

[36] omit *ut . . . conversationem* **P₁ C L M Rn**

[37] Chapter 14 omitted in **Br**

[38] insert *non* **C L M**

molestiam in vacca minanda infirmus longo fessus itinere sustentaret vitulum post tergum eius in currum poni precipiebat.

15.4. Et sic eum vacca lingua tangens et tamquam proprium diligens nemine eam cogente, usque ad loca destinata consecuta est.

15.5. Karissimi videtis fratres, quod et bruta contra consuetudinem famulabantur ei animalia.

16.1. Et quodam intervallo temporis alii nequissimi fures qui nec Deum nec homines verebantur de alia provintia ob latrocinium venientes et per amnem grandem facili meatu pedum egredientes, boves[39] ipsius furati sunt.

16.2. Sed eos eadem revertentes via impetus ingentis fluminis inundatione aquarum subita facta conturbavit. Non enim flumen instar muri erectum scelestissimam boum fraudem beatae brigidae per se transire[40] permisit, sed eos fures demergens et secum trahens boves de ipsorum manibus liberati loris in cornibus pendentibus ad proprium armentum ac boellium reversi sunt.

17.1. Ecce et hic virtus divina apparet.

17.2. Cum quadam die ipsa sanctissima brigida cogente aliqua utilitatis necessitate conventionem plebis visitaret in curru sedens in equis binis vehebatur. Et eum in suo vehiculo meditatione theorica caelestem agens in terris vitam suum, ut solebat, dominatorem oraret, de alto procidens loco alter bruto animo equus saliens sub curru et inrefrenatus habenis fortiter se extorquens, et de iugo semetipsum absolvens, equo altero solo sub suo remanente iugo exterritus per campestria cucurrit.

17.3. Et sic manus divina iugum pendens sine precipitio sustentans, et vidente turba ob testimonium virtutis divinae secura in suo orans vehiculo, cum uno equo sub curru posito, ad plebis conventionem discursu placabili inlesa pervenit. Et sic signis et virtutibus suam confirmans doctrinam, sermonibus salutaribus et sale divino conditis plebem hortata est.

18.1. Et hoc virtutibus ipsius videtur nobis esse deputandum.

18.2. Cum aper ferus singularis et silvestris territus et fugitivus esset ad gregem porcorum brigidae felicissimae concitus cursu praecipiti

---

[39] *bovem* **B O P₂**

[40] insert *non* **Br P₁ L Rn**

pervenit. Quem ipsa eventu inter suas cernens sues benedixit. Deinde inpavidus, ac familiaris, cum ipsius permansit grege porcorum.

[18.3.] Ecce videtis, fratres, quod et bruta animalia et bestiae sermonibus et voluntati eius resistere non poterant, sed domita et subiecta sibi famulabantur.

19. Nam cum aliquando aliquis inter ceteros offerentes ei munera, de longa veniens provincia offerret sues pingues et alios secum missos ire ad suam villam quodam longo terrarum intervallo positam rogaret, ut ab eo sues acciperent per longum itineris spatium dierum trium vel quatuor amplius prolixum cum eo suos missos transmisit comites. Ac transacto unius diei itinere in monte confinali regionum, qui proprio nuncupatur vocabulo gabor,[41] suaes suas quas in longinquis opinabantur esse regionibus, obvias contra se venire a lupis directas per viam et coactas contemplati sunt. Et sic altero die hi qui missi erant cum suibus factum mirabile narrantes domum reversi sunt.

20.1. Item de eiusdem mirabilibus gestis hoc factum videtur nobis minime praeter eundum enarrari.

20.2. Quadam enim die cum aliquis nulla subfultus scientia, vulpem per regis palatium ambulantem videret, putans illam obcaecatis sensibus suis feram esse bestiam. Et quod aulam regis familiaris et mansueta esset, variis artibus docta, agilitate corporis et subtilitate animi, regi et suis comitibus grande praestans spectaculum, ignoraret, vidente multitudine, occidit eam.

[20.3.] Et tunc ab his qui viderunt factum alligatus et diffamatus ad regem perductus est. Et rex iratus rem discens gestam, nisi sibi vulpis similis in omnibus calliditatibus quas sua vulpis operabatur, restituta esset, illum iussit occidi et uxorem et filios suos et omnia quae habuit in seruitutem redigi praecepit.

20.4. Et cum rem gestam sancta ac venerabilis brigida didicisset, tanto misericordiarum et pietatis affectu permota, currum suum sibi iungi praecipiens et ex intimo corde dolens pro ipso infelici qui iniuste iudicatus est praecibus ad Dominum profusis et per planitiem campi equitans perrexit in viam quae ad regis palatium ducebatur.

---

[41] *grabor* **Br** *cabor* **C L M Rn** *gabor liphi* **P₁**

20.5. Nec mora Dominus exaudiens ipsam suas fundentem assiduas praeces unam de suis vulpibus feris ad eam venire transmisit, quae cum velocissimo cursu per campestria veniret et beatissimae brigidae currui appropinquaret, leviter se elevans in currum intravit et sub receptaculo vestis Brigidae se constituens, sobrie cum ea in curru sedebat.

20.6. At cum ipsa ad regem veniret ut ille miser inprovidus qui illo reatu suae ignorantiae tenebatur liber et absolutus de vinculis egrederetur coepit precari. Et cum rex eius praecibus consentire noluisset obtestans se non illum dimissurum, nisi talem vulpem, tantae mansuetudinis et calliditatis qualis vulpis sua fuerat restituta sibi esset, ipsa suam protulit in medium vulpem, quae coram rege et omni multitudine totos mores et subtilitatem docibilem alterius agens vulpis in eadem forma prioris palam omnibus variis lusit artibus.

20.7. Et tunc rex haec videns placatus et eius optimates cum ingenti plausu admirantis multitudinis mirabile factum illum solui et liberum abire qui fuerat antea reus delicti iussit. Nec multo post cum sancta brigida solutione ipsius et libertate facta ad suam remearet domum, ipsa vulpis dolosa se inter turbas torquens et callide movens quae ut altera omnibus videbatur similis fugitiva ad loca deserta et silvestria ad suum antrum multis sequentibus et canibus se persequentibus inludens ac per patentes campos fugiens incolumis evasit.

20.8. Et omnes admirantes hoc quod factum fuerat privilegio sanctitatis et praerogativa virtutum multarum semper pollentem maioribus gestis sanctam venerati sunt Brigidam.

21.1. Et cum in alia die anates pectore carnali natantes in aqua et per aera interdum volitantes beata vidisset brigida eas ad se venire accerrsivit.

21.2. Quae pinnigero volatu et tanto ardore oboedientiae eius vocibus tamquam sub humana cura essent consuetae sine ulla formidine multitudines ad eam volitabant. Quas manu tangens et amplectens et per aliquantulum temporis hoc idem faciens, redire ac volare suis in aerem alis permisit.

21.3. Conlaudans creatorem omnium rerum invisibilem per creaturas visibiles cui omnia subiecta sunt animantia et cui omnia vivunt ut quidam ait officio gerendi.

21.4. Et ex his omnibus manifeste intelligi potest quod omnis natura bestiarum et pecorum et volucrum subiecta eius fuit imperio.

22.1. Et hoc eiusdem miraculum omnibus saeculis celebrandum auribus fidelium insinuandum est.

22.2. Nam cum semina saluberrima verbi Dominici ex more suae consuetudinis omnibus seminaret, vidit novem viros in forma quadam speciali vanae et diabolicae superstitionis et plausum habentes vocis ridiculae ac insaniam mentis maximam.

22.3. In quorum vis contritio erat et infelicitas, qui antiquo hosti qui in illis regnabat, votis scelestissimis et iuramentis sitientes effusionem sanguinis, antequam kalendae illius[42] mensis supervenirent venturi aliorum iugulationem et homicidia facere disposuerunt.

22.4. Quibus reverentissima et affabilis brigida melliflua verborum copia praedicavit, ut mortiferis erroribus relictis sua crimina per cordis conpunctionem et veram delerent paenitentiam.

22.5. Qui habetudine mentis suae nisi prius vana sua conplessent vota illud facere resistentes in viam suam perrexerunt. Et pro hac re fusis ad Dominum praecibus assiduis decoratae virginis volentis Domini exemplo omnes salvos fieri et ad agnitionem venire veritatis. Et egredientes illi nefarii imaginem instar viri quem debuissent iugulare contemplantes et continuo suis iugulantes lanceis et gladiis decollantes quasi post triumphum de suorum adversario et inimico cum armis sanguineis et cruentis reversi multis apparverunt.

22.6. Mirum in modum, cum neminem occiderent, illis visum est sua complesse vota. Atque cum nemo deerat de illa provincia de quo illi triumpharent, nulla dubietas pro hac re alicui persistens, largitas muneris divini per sanctam brigidam facta omnibus innotuit. Et sic illi qui antea erant homicidae per penitentiam ad Dominum conversi sunt.

23.1. Et in hoc opere per decoratam Brigidam cultu inenarrabili sacrae religionis divina manifestata est potentia.

23.2. Illam enim luguidma[43] nomine validus vir valde et virorum fortissimus, xii virorum opera per semetipsum tanta fortitudine sui corporis in una, cum vellet, laborans die et cibaria quibus xii sufficienter viri vesci possint similiter comedens. Sicut enim illorum opera facere solus sic et cibaria aequali modo unus contra plures comedere poterat. Deprecatus est

---

[42] *iulii* **O Br**   *illis* **B**

[43] *luguidmam* **B P₂**   *Quidam enim vir luguid* **Br**   *Quidam enim vir validus* **P₁**

ut pro se Dominum oraret omnipotentem ut eius ingluviem qua superflua devorabat temperaret, nec antiquam virtutem sui corporis pro hac amisisset.

23.3. Et sic ipsa causa Brigida illum benedicens et pro illo Dominum orans ipse postea victu unius viri satis contentus ac ut antea solebat, laborans sicut xii operarii operabatur, in eadem antiquam permansit virtutem.

24.1. Item inter eius opera praeclara hoc idem egregium opus et excelsum compertumque omnibus explicare debemus.

24.2. Arbor quaedam grandis et maxima ad aliquem parata usum ab omnibus qui artificia exercere solebant in silva lignorum securibus excisa est. Ad quam conventio virorum fortium propter eius molestiam et ingentem molem et loca difficillima hi quibus ramorum cum fragore suorum ruit ut deponeret ac traherent cum multis bubus et artificum machinis ad locum destinatum ut necessitas rei poscebat congregata est.

24.3. Et cum nec multitudo virorum nec vires boum et variae artificum artes movere vel trahere eam arborem ullo modo poterant, recedentibus cunctis ab ea per fortissimam fidem beatae brigidae grano sinapis similem per quam fidem ut magister caelestis organo evangelicae vocis docet montes mutantur sicut possibilia sunt omnia credentibus eam gravissimam arborem angelicae virtutis per divina ministeria nullo mortalium auxilio levantes sine ulla difficultate ad locum quem voluit sancta Brigida destinatum detulerunt.

24.4. Ac per omnes provincias tanta virtutis divinae huius excellentia devulgata est.

25.1. Et nostro occurrit animo non excludere et hanc virtutem silentio nostro, quam inter innumerabiles virtutes caeteras eadem operata est brigida venerabilis.

25.2. Quidam enim vir saecularis et gente nobilis et dolosis moribus, exardescens in alicuius feminae concupiscentiam et quomodo eius concubitu frui possit callide cogitans ac suam sentem argenteam pretiosamque in depositum sibi commendat quam dolose retraxit ille illa ignorante et eiecit in mare ut cum ipsa non posset reddere sibi esset ancilla et eius postea uteretur ut vellet amplexibus.

25.3. Machinatus est hoc perficere malum, nulla alia re ac redemptione placatu se fieri posse dicens nisi aut propria sibi sente argentea reddita aut ipsa femina in servitutem ei redacta pro causa culpabili fragilis concupiscentiae uteretur.

25.4. Et haec timens pudica femina tamquam ad civitatem refugii tutissimam, ad sanctam confugit Brigidam. Quae cum talem comperisset causam vel quid pro hac re agere debuerit cogitaret cum necdum verba complesset supervenit ad se quidam cum piscibus de flumine tractis. Et cum illorum ilia piscium excisa et aperta fuissent sentis illa argentea quam ille crudelis iaecit in mare ob causam supra dictam, in medio unius ex piscibus reperta est.

25.5. Et sic postea secura mente eam sentem secum portabat et ad conventum multitudinis pro hac culpa cum tyranno infami progrediens et monstrans sibi suam propriam sentem multis testantibus qui eam agnoscere poterant, non aliam esse sed ipsam, de qua talis sermo ferebatur, adherentem sibi feminam pudicam de manibus tyranni crudelissimi liberavit.

25.6. Et sic ille postea confitens suam culpam sanctae brigidae humiliter sua subdidit colla. Et illa ab omnibus gloriosa peracto hoc ingenti miraculo gratias agens Deo et omnia in eius gloriam faciens, domum redit propriam.

26.1. Et his miraculis gloriosum eius et clarissimum cum aliqua fideli femina hospicium in iungi debet quo prosperum iter faciens sancta brigida in Dei voluntate, in amplissimo campo breg[44] cum declinaret ad vesperum dies, ad habitaculum eius veniens cum ea pernoctavit.

26.2. Quae obviis manibus et gratulanter suscipiens et gratias omnipotenti agens Deo de felice adventu reverendissimae Brigidae tamquam Christi, cum non haberet propter suam inopiam unde ignem nutriret et cybum unde tales hospites cibaret incidens ligna telaria in quibus textura telarum operabatur in pastum ignis vitulum suae quem occidit vaccae super struem istorum ponens lignorum igni assavit cum bona voluntate.

26.3. Et caena in Dei laudibus facta et nocte adsuetis transacta vigiliis, expergescentes post illam de mane noctem, ut nullum de receptione et refectione sanctae Brigidae ullius rei sustineret damnum ipsa hospitalis, quae vitulum suae amiserat vaccae, alterum in eadem forma vitulum cum sua invenit vacca quem ut priorem ipsa dilexerat. Et telaria ligna similiter sibi pro ceteris reparata in tali forma in quantitate in qua priora fuerant contemplata est.

---

[44] omit **P₁ C L M**

26.4. Et sic sancta brigida, felici progressu et mirabili facta virtute, domui et habitatoribus valedicens pacifice in viam suam perrexit prosperam.

27.1. Et ecce in tanta miraculorum multitudine hoc eiusdem opus praeclarum admirari solet.

27.2. Tribus enim leprosis et infirmitatibus oppressis, postulantibus munus aliquodcumque ab ea accipere, vas largita est argenteum. Et ne illis esset causa discordiae et contentionis, si illi inter se dividerent cuidam in ponderibus auri et argenti conperto dixit, ut inter illos hoc vas tres ponderaret tribus aequalibus partibus.

27.3. Cum excusare se coepisset, dicens ponderare aequaliter non posse, ipsa felicissima feminarum brigida, adprehenso vase argenteo, ipsum allidit contra lapidem et confregit in tres, ut voluit, aequales et consimiles partes.

27.4. Mirum in modum cum postea ipse tres partes ipsius vasis argentei in pondere essent emensae, nulla pars alia minor vel maior, quae aliam superaret licet uno obolo de his inventa est tribus partibus. Et sic sui infirmi pauperes sine ulla iniuriae et invidiae causa inter se laeti cum suis recesserunt donis.

28.1. Secundum enim Iob[45] exemplum beatissimi numquam inopes a se recedere sinu vacuo passa est.

28.2. Nam vestimenta transmarina et peregrina episcopi Conleath[46] decorati culminis, quibus in solemnitatibus Domini et in vigiliis apostolorum sacra in altaribus et in sanctuario offerens misteria utebatur pauperibus largita est.

28.3. Et cum tempus sollemnitatis advenit secundum consuetudinem ut ipse summus populorum pontifex suis indutus esset mutatoriis vestibus, sancta Brigida, quae priora vestimenta illius aepiscopi pro Christo in forma pauperis posito donabat alia similia per omnia vestimenta prioribus, tam texturis quam coloribus, quae in illa hora a Christo quem per pauperem induebat, perlata sibi in curru duarum acceperat rotarum, tradidit pro aliis.

---

[45] *ipsius* **C L M Rn S**   *ipsius exemplum evangelii beatissimi virgo* **P₁**
[46] *concolaido* **Br**   *collodi* **P₁**   *conlei* **C M Rn S**   *cumleath* **P₂**

28.4. Voluntarie autem alia pauperibus vestimenta obtulit et haec pro eis oportune recepit. Nam cum ipsa esset vivum et felicissimum summi capitis membrum, potenter omnia quae desiderabat operabatur.

29.1. Nam et hoc eiusdem opus egregium non est praetereundum enarrari.

29.2. Quidam enim conpulsus quadam necessitate, indigens mellis sextarium eam praecatus est. Et cum ipsa Brigida mente doleret, dum non haberet paratum mel, quod illi roganti donaret, murmur apium vocum sub pavimento domus, in qua ipsa fuerat tunc, exauditum est. Et cum ille locus in quo suis apes sonabant vocibus perfossus et scrutatus fuisset, repertum est in eo quantum sufficiebat in opus poscentis.

29.3. Et sic ille ab ea recepto mellis munere quantum sibi necessitas poscebat ad sua gaudens reversus est habitacula.

30.1. Item et hoc sancta fulsit Brigida miraculo.

30.2. Quia cum regis illius patriae in qua ipsa fuit edictum per plebes et provincias, quae sub eius erant ditione et iugo, invalesceret, ut de omnibus eius regionibus et provinciis omnes populi et plebes convenirent atque aedificarent viam latam et firmam ramis arborum petris infundamen positis et munitionibus quibusdam firmissimis in gronna profunda et pene intransmeabili et in locis humentibus atque in paludibus in quibus grandis currebat fluvius, quae constructa quadrigas et aequites et currus et plaustrorum rotas et impetum populorum atque concursum undique hostium sustentare posset, convenientibus multis populis per cognationes et familias, diviserunt viam illam, quam aedificare debuerant, in partes proprias, ut unaquaeque cognatio et familia suam sibi creditam construxisset partem.

30.3. Et cum illa pars fluminis difficillima et laboriosa in sorte alicuius ex ipsis nationibus cederet eventu, ipsa natio durissimum devitans laborem, per suam fortitudinem sanctae Brigidae infirmiorem coegit nationem, ut hanc operaretur difficilem partem in structura viae et suam quam faciliorem eventu habebat partem eligens ipsa crudelis et iniusta natio aedificaret sine ulla fluminis turbatione.

30.4. Atque cum ad sanctam Brigidam suis secundum carnem cognati venissent querellosi prostratique a fortioribus sine ullo iure dispensationis[47]

---

[47] Insert *se dicerent afflici in* **R**

ipsa illis probabiliter dixisse fertur. "Abite. Voluntatis Dei est et potestas, ut ille fluvius transeat de loco in quo est et ubi vos dura opprimunt opera, in illam quam ipsi elegerunt partem."

30.5. Et cum de mane ipsius diei omnes surrexissent ad opera populi, fluvius ille quem querebantur visus est reliquisse suum antiquum locum et convallem ubi inter ambas currere solebat ripas, et transmutasse de parte ubi sanctae Brigidae natio compulsa operabatur, in illorum fortium et superborum partem, qui alios pauciores et infirmiores se iniuste et durissime operari conpellebant. Et in testimonium virtutis vestigia fluminis et vallis vacua ubi in undans et emanans antiquo currebat fluvius tempore, ipso ad alterum flumine recedente locum, ipse locus siccatus sine ullis apparet fluitantibus aquis.

31.1.[48] Non solum autem in sua vita carnali antequam sarcinam deponeret carnis virtutes operata est plurimas, sed largitas divini muneris in suo monasterio, ubi eius venerabile requiescit corpus, alias semper operari virtutes non cessat, quas nos virtutes non solum audivimus, sed oculis nostris vidimus.

31.2. Nam praepositus maximi et clarissimi monasterii sanctae Brigidae de quo in huius opusculi principio brevem fecimus mentionem, operarios et lapidum caesores quaerere lapidem et incudere molarem per loca quaecumque, ubi posset illi inueniri transmisit.

31.3. Et illi sine ulla providentia viarum difficillimam arduam ascendentes viam, ad cacumem petrosi montis perrexerunt, et elegerunt lapidem grandem in ipso montis altissimi cacumine. Et caedentes eum de omni parte in rotundum et perforatum molarem lapidem formaverunt.

31.4. Et cum praepositus de monasterio invitatus ab eis venisset cum bobus et viris ad illum montem in quo lapis formatus molaris atque cum boves secum propter arduam montis ascensionem trahere et cogere non possit, durissimum iter cum paucis illum sequentibus vix ascendere potuit.

31.5. Exinde ille cum suis comitibus et operariis dum cogitaret, quomodo illum molarem deportarent lapidem de iugo altissimi montis, cum boves in illo praerupta montis sub oneribus et iugis esse nullo modo potuerint et tunc facta desperatione, aliis ex eis descendentibus illum deserere lapidem, et eos in vanum laborasse qui illum formaverunt, ille

---

[48] **P₁ C L M Rn S** skip the next lines and begin again midway through Section 31 after *tunc facta desperatione*

praepositus prudenti dispensatione et consilio suis operariis fideliter dixit: "Nequaquam hoc ita fiat, sed hunc levate lapidem molarem viriliter et submittite in praecipitium de altissimo isto montis cacumine, in nomine et virtute reverentissimae sanctae Brigidae, quia nos nullis artificiis et viribus per ista loca petrosa et difficillima hunc grandem lapidem molarem possumus portare, nisi ipsa Brigida, cui nihil inpossibile est, secundum illud quod omnia possibilia sunt credenti, illum portaverit usque ad locum, ex quo vires boum trahere ipsum possint."

31.6. Et sic fide firma praecipitantes illum ac solum relinquentes in vallem et paulatim de monte descendens, aliquando petras devitans, aliquando traneas ac siliens et in locis currens umidis in radice montis positis, in quibus nec homines, nec boves stare potuerant pro illorum profunditate mirabili comitatu usque ad loca plana, sine ulla fragminis fractione ubi illorum erant boves cum eis progressus est. Et ex inde ex bobus usque ad molinum vectus artificiose cum altero iunctus est lapide.

31.7. Et ut plus iste molaris lapis, qui in nomine beatae directus est Brigidae, omnibus adhuc innotesceret, addidit et hoc inauditum antea et praeclarum miraculum.

31.8. Nam cum quidam paganus et gentilis ac molino vicinus suo habitaculo dolose per alium simplicem virum, ignorante molinario, qui opus moliturae exercebat, suum granum ad hunc transmisisset molinum, et quodcum inter huius molares transiectum et fusum fuisset lapides, illum supradictum lapidem molarem nullus impetus fortis fluminis et directus, et nulla aquarum vis violenta, et nulla artificum conamina movere eum ac trudere in circuitum volubilem et solitum ambitum potuerunt.

31.9. Et dum illi qui hoc viderunt de hac re cogitarent nimio perculsi stupore, tunc granum illud magi esse comperientes nullo modo dubitabant, quod ille lapis molaris, in quo sancta Brigida virtutem operata est divinam, granum gentilis hominis in farinam conprimere respuisset.

31.10. Et in illa hora tollentes foras granum ipsius pagani, et suum granum monasteriale subter molarem illum lapidem ponentes, cursus solitus et cotidianus sine ullis inpedimentis repentino reparatus est molae.

31.11. Et post intervallum temporis accidit ut iste molinus igni combureretur. Nec et hoc parvum fuit miraculum, cum ignis domum totam conbureret, et alterum lapidem, qui iunctus supradicto lapidi fuit, hunc tantum specialem sanctae Brigidae lapidem nullo modo tangere et conburere ausus est, sed sine ulla ei molestia ignis in magno molini incendio, permansit plus incolomis.

31.12. Et postea hoc viso miraculo vectus ad monasterium perductus est, et iuxta portam interioris ornati castelli quod eclesia ambitur ubi multi conveniunt populi ob venerationem beatissimae Brigidae virtutum in ipsa porta honorifice positus est. Et de fidelibus hunc Brigidae lapidem tangentibus, per quem ipsa supradictas virtutes fecit, morbos expellit et languores.

32.1. Nec et de miraculo in reparatione eclesiae facto tacendum est, in qua gloriosa amborum, hoc est, archiepiscopi Conleath[49] et huius virginis florentissimae Brigidae, corpora, a dextris et a sinistris altaris decorati in monumentis posita ornatis vario cultu auri et argenti et gemmarum praetiosi lapidis, atque coronis aureis et argenteis desuper pendentibus ac diversis imaginibus cum celaturis variis et coloribus, requiescunt.

32.2. Et in veteri nova res adnascitur actu hoc est, eclesia crescente numero fidelium de utroque sexu solo spatiosa et in altum minaci proceritate porrecta ac decorata pictis tabulis, tria intrinsecus habens oratoria ampla et divisa parietibus tabulatis sub uno culmine maioris domus. In qua unus paries decoratus et imaginibus depictus ac linteaminibus tectus per latitudinem in orientali eclesiae parte a pariete ad alterum parietem aeclesiae se tetendit. Qui in suis extremitatibus duo habet in se hostia, et per unum ostium in dextra parte positum intratur in sanctuarium ad altare, ubi summus pontifex cum sua regulari scola et his quae sacris deputati sunt misteriis, sacra ac dominica immolat sacrificia. Et per alterum ostium in sinistra parte parietis supradicti et transversi positum abbatissa cum suis puellis et viduis fidelibus tantum intrat, ut convivio corporis et sanguinis fruantur Ihesu Christi.

32.3. Atque alius partes pavimentum domus in duas aequales dividens partes a pariete orientali[50] usque ad transversum in latitudinem parietem extentus est. Et haec tenet eclesia in se multas fenestras et una in latere dextro ornatam portam, per quam sacerdotes et populus fidelis masculini generis sexus intrat in ecclesiam, et alteram portam in sinistro latere per quam virgines et feminarum fidelium congregatio intrare solet. Et sic in una

---

[49] omit **Br**   *conlei* **P₁ C M**   *conlegi* **L Rn S**   *concleah* **N**
[50] *occidentali* **Br M**   *occidentalis* **P₁ L C**

basilica maxima populus grandis in ordine et gradibus et sexu et locis diversis, interiectis inter se parietibus, diverso ordine et uno animo omnipotentem orat dominatorem.

32.4. Et cum hostium antiquum portae sinistralis per quod sancta solebat Brigida in eclesiam intrare ab artificibus suis esset cardinibus situm totam concludere portam instauratam et novam non potuit, quarta enim portae pars aperta sine conclusione et patefacta apparebat. Et si addita et iuncta ad altitudinem ostii quarta pars fuisset, tunc totam concludere portam posse altam et instauratam.

32.5. Et cum artifices alteram maius novum facere ostium deliberarent, quod totam concluderet portam, aut tabulam facere iunctam in vetus hostium ut postea sufficere posset praedictus doctor et omnium praevius artificum Hibernensium prudenti locutus est consilio: "In hac superventura nocte orare Dominum iuxta sanctam Brigidam fideliter debemus, ut ipsa nobis de mane quid in hoc opere acturi simus provideat."

32.6. Et sic orans iuxta monumentum Brigidae gloriosam noctem transegit, et de mane post ipsam surgens noctem oratione fideliter praemissa ostium antiquum trudens ac ponens in suo cardine, ianuam conclusit totam. Nec aliquid defuit de eius plenitudine nec ulla in eius magnitudine superflua pars reperta est.

32.7. Et sic illa Brigida illud extendit in altitudinem ostium ut tota porta illa sit ab eo conclusa, nec in ea ullus locus patefactus videatur, nisi cum ostium retruditur, ut eclesia intretur. Et hoc virtutis Dominicae miraculum omnium oculis videntium illam ianuam et valvam manifeste patet.

32.8. Et quis sermonem explicare potest maximum decorem huius aeclesiae et innumera illius monasterii civitatis quam dicimus miracula, si fas est dici civitas, dum nullo murorum ambitu circumdatur?

32.9. Convenientibus tamen in ea populis innumerabilibus dum civitas de quo vita in se multorum nomen accepit, maxima haec civitas et metropolitana est, in cuius suburbanis, quae sancta certo limite designavit Brigida, nullus carnalis adversarius, nec concursus timetur hostium. Sed civitas est refugii tutissima deforis suburbanis in tota Scotorum terra cum suis omnibus fugitivis in qua thesauri servantur regum et decorati culminis excellentissima esse videntur.

32.10. Et quis dinumerare potest diversas turbas et innumerabiles populos de omnibus provinciis[51] confluentes? Alii propter aepularum habundantiam alii propter suas sanitates de suis languoribus alii ad spectaculum turbarum, alii cum magnis donis et muneribus convenientes ad solemnitatem nativitates sanctae Brigidae, quae in die kalendarum februarii mensis dormiens secure sarcinam deiecit carnis, et agnum Dei in caelestibus mansionibus secuta est.[52]

Epilogue

1. Veniam peto a fratribus ac lectoribus haec legentibus immo emendantibus, qui causa obedientiae coactus, nulla praerogativa scientiae suffultus pelagus in mensum virtutum beatae Brigidae et viris peritissimis formidandum, his paucis rustico sermone dictis, virtutibus de maximis et innumerabilibus parvula intro cucurri.

2. Orate pro me Cogitoso nepote culpabili[53] Aedo[54] et ut audaciae meae indulgeatis atque orationem vestrarum di peo Domino me commendetis exoro. Et Deus vos pacem evangelicam sectantes exaudiat. Amen[55]

Explicit vita sanctae Brigidae virginis.[56]

---

[51] insert *hyberniae* **Br P₁ C L M**

[52] insert *cui est honor et gloria in saeculae saeculorum* **Br** *facit eam permanere cui est honor et gloria in saeculae saeculorum amen. Explicit vita sancta Brigidae virginis feliciter* **P₁**

[53] *cogitoso nepote culpabili* **B** *praecor ne imputetis me* **Br** *cogitos ne inputeis* **C L Rn S** *cogitoso nepote culpabilis edoni* **N**

[54] omit **B Br C L M Rn**

[55] *adiuvante Domino nostro Iesu Christo qui vivit et regnat in secula saeculorum AMEN* **Br N**

[56] omit **B Br N**

LIFE OF SAINT BRIGID

Bibliography and Further Reading

Bieler, Ludwig. "Saint Bridget." *Manuscript Sources for the History of Irish Civilisation*, edited by Richard J. Hayes, Boston: G.K. Hall and Co., (1965): 332-334

Bitel, Lisa. *Landscape with Two Saints: How Genovefa of Paris and Brigit of Kildare Built Christianity in Barbarian Europe.* Oxford: Oxford University Press, 2009.

—. "Ekphrasis at Kildare: The Imaginative Architecture of a Seventh-Century Hagiographer." *Speculum* 79 (2004): 605-27.

—. "Body of a saint, story of a goddess: origins of the Brigidine tradition." *Textual Practice* 16, no. 2 (2002): 209-28.

—. *Land of Women: Tales of Sex and Gender from Early Ireland.* Ithaca: Cornell University Press, 1996.

Bray, Dorothy. "Ireland's Other Apostle: Cogitosus' St. Brigit." *Cambrian Medieval Celtic Studies* 59 (2010): 55-70.

—. "The State of Irish Hagiography." *The Heroic Age: A Journal of Early Medieval Northwest Europe* 9 (2006).

—. "Saint Brigid and the Fire from Heaven." *Études celtiques* 39 (1992): 105-13.

—. "The Image of St. Brigit in the Early Irish Church." *Études celtiques* 24 (1987): 209-15.

Connolly, Sean. "Vita Prima Sanctae Brigitae: Background and Historical Value." *The Journal of the Royal Society of Antiquaries of Ireland* 119 (1989): 5-49.

—. "The Authorship and Manuscript Tradition of *Vita I Sanctae Brigitae.*" *Manuscripta* 16 (1972): 67-82.

Connolly, Sean., and Picard, J.-M. "Cogitosus's *Life of St. Brigit*: Content and Value." *The Journal of the Royal Society of Antiquaries of Ireland* 117 (1987): 5-27.

Esposito, Mario. "On the Early Latin Lives of St. Brigid of Kildare." *Hermathena* 24, no. 49 (1935): 120-65.

—."Cogitosus." *Hermathena* 20, no. 45 (1926): 251-57.

—. "On the Earliest Life of St. Brigid of Kildare." *Proceedings of the Royal Irish Academy.* Section C, Archaeology, Linguistics, and Literature 30, no. 11 (1912/13): 307-26.

Freeman, Philip. *The World of Saint Patrick*. Oxford: Oxford University Press, 2014.

Harrington, Christina. *Women in a Christian Church: Ireland 450-1150*. Oxford: Oxford University Press, 2002.

McCone, Kim. *Pagan Past and Christian Present in Early Irish Literature*. Kildare: An Sagart, 1990.

—. "Brigit in the Seventh Century: A Saint with Three Lives?" *Peritia* 1 (1982): 107-45.

McKenna, Catherine. "Between Two Worlds: Saint Brigit and Pre-Christian Religion in the *Vita Prima*." In *Identifying the Celtic: CSANA Yearbook 2*, edited by Joseph F. Nagy, 66-74. Dublin: Four Courts Press, 2002.

Ó hAodha, Donncha. *Bethu Brigte*. Dublin: Dublin Institute for Advanced Studies, 1978.

—. "The Early Lives of Saint Brigit." *Journal of the County Kildare Archaeological Society* 15 (1974/75): 397-405.

Oxenham, Helen. *Perceptions of Femininity in Early Irish Society*. Rochester, New York: The Boydell Press, 2016.

Sharpe, Richard. "*Vitae S Brigitae*: The Oldest Texts." *Peritia* 1 (1982): 81-106.

How was the chronology of the earliest
Welsh Latin chronicle regulated?

Henry Gough-Cooper

1. The sources

There are two groups of source texts that are witnesses to a Welsh Latin chronicle of the second half of the tenth century. The first group consists of three Welsh Latin chronicles, the Harleian, or A-text of *Annales Cambriae*, which runs from AD 445 to 977, although the last annotated annal is set at 954; the Breviate, or B-text of *Annales Cambriae*, the annals of which run from 60 BC to the late thirteenth century; and the Cottonian, or C-text of *Annales Cambriae*, the annals of which run from AD 677 to the late thirteenth century.[1] Comparison of these suggests a now-lost Latin source common to **A** and B for the annals from 445 to 954, and common to all three for the annals from c. 680 to 954.[2] Although **A** is the earliest surviving witness, the evidence of **B** and **C** shows that it does not stand at the head of the textual transmission.[3] The second group consists of the Welsh vernacular annalistic chronicles, known as *Brut y Tywysogyon* (**P** and **R**) and *Brenhinedd y Saeson* (**S**),[4] which run from AD 682 to the late thirteenth

---

[1] London, British Library, MS Harley 3859, fols. 190r–193r, written by one hand of c. 1100, henceforth **A**. London, The National Archives, MS E 164/1, pp. 2–26, written by one hand of late thirteenth century, henceforth **B**; BL, MS Cotton Domitian A I, folios 138r–155r, written by one hand of late thirteenth century, henceforth **C**. The designations A, B and C are due to the early editors: Henry Petrie and J. Sharpe, eds., *Monumenta Historica Britannica, or Materials for the History of Britain, from the Earliest Period* (London, 1848). The edition used here: Henry W. Gough-Cooper, ed., Annales Cambriae: A, B and C in Parallel, from St Patrick to AD 954 (The Welsh Chronicles Research Group, 2016), accessed November 27, 2019. http://croniclau.bangor.ac.uk/documents/AC_ABC_to_954_first_edition.pdf

[2] Kathleen Hughes, "The Welsh Latin chronicles: *Annales Cambriae* and related texts," in *Celtic Britain in the Early Middle Ages* (Woodbridge: Boydell, 1980), 67–85, at 73f.

[3] David N. Dumville *Annales Cambriae A.D. 682–954 in Parallel* (Cambridge: University of Cambridge, Department of Anglo-Saxon, Norse and Celtic, 2004), xii.

[4] Aberystwyth, National Library of Wales, MS. Peniarth 20, written c.1330, henceforth **P**; Aberystwyth, National Library of Wales, MS. 3035B (Mostyn 116),

century and beyond, and these are also held to depend on a similar lost Latin source or sources for the period 682 to 954.[5] The annals of the Welsh vernacular texts to 954 are close parallels of those in the Welsh Latin texts (**A**, **B** and **C**), with only minor variations.[6] These Welsh chronicles (**A**, **B**, **C**, **P**, **R** and **S**) form a complex of texts which are especially closely related for the period AD 445 to 954.

The **A**-text of *Annales Cambriae* appears, uniquely, as an interpolation into the recension of *Historia Brittonum* in London, British Library, Harley MS 3859, a manuscript dated to about 1100.[7] The chronicle is thought to be a text of the second half of the tenth century as its last annotated annal is for [954].[8] Without explicit chronological apparatus, its first eight annals are

---

written c. 1310x1350, henceforth **R**; London, British Library, MS. Cotton Cleopatra B.5, written c.1332, henceforth **S**. The standard editions are (P) Thomas Jones, ed., *Brut y Tywysogyon, Peniarth MS. 20* (Cardiff, University of Wales Press, 1941), (P) Thomas Jones, trans., *Brut y Tywysogyon, Peniarth MS. 20* (Cardiff, University of Wales Press, 1952), (R) Thomas Jones, ed. and trans., *Brut y Tywysogyon . . . Red Book of Hergest Version* (Cardiff, University of Wales Press, 1955, revised 1973) and (S) Thomas Jones (ed. and transl.) *Breninedd y Saesson* (Cardiff, University of Wales Press, 1971). The designations P, R and S are due to David N. Dumville, ed. and trans., *Brehinoedd y Saeson, 'The Kings of the English', A.D. 682–954: Texts P, R, S in Parallel* (Aberdeen: University of Aberdeen, Department of History, School of Divinity, History and Philosophy, 2005).

[5] J. E. Lloyd "The Welsh Chronicles," *Proceedings of the British Academy* 14, (1928), 370, 377f.; see also Thomas Jones, *Brut y Tywysogyon* 1952, xxxvi.

[6] **P**, for example, has everything that is in **A**, **B** and **C** between 684 and 953, adding only that "Rechra was harried" (*ydistriwyd rechrenn*) to its annal for 785, and that "the black Norsemen came to Gwynedd" (*doeth y normannyeid duon ywenydd*) as an annal for 892. *Rechrenn* represents the Irish genitive of *Rechra*, now Lambey Island, County Dublin. See Jones *Brut y Tywysogyon* 1952, 133, note to page 3, lines 1–3.

[7] For the date, see Dumville *Annales Cambriae A.D. 682–954 in Parallel*, vii and fn. 20. For a diplomatic transcription of the **A**-text of *Annales Cambriae*, see Egerton Phillimore "The *Annales Cambriae* and Old Welsh Genealogies from *Harleian MS 3859*," *Y Cymmrodor* 9 (1888) 141–183; for *Historia Brittonum*, see John Morris, *Nennius: British History and the Welsh Annals*, (London: Phillimore, 1980), 18–43.

[8] AD dates associated with **A** are placed in square brackets to indicate that they are editorial deductions and do not appear in the original manuscript. Similarly, see below, the editorial dates for the Annals of Inisfallen, and the corrected dates for the

empty, as are its last twenty-seven, taking the chronicle to [977]. Every tenth year is marked off, the last annal being the third after the five hundred and thirtieth,[9] suggesting the span of the 532-year Great Paschal Cycle plus one year.[10] This implied span in **A** is not found in any of the other related chronicles (**B, C, P, R** and **S**), and may not have been a feature of their source.

The 532-year Paschal cycle is a product of the 19-year (the metonic or decennovenal) lunar-solar cycle, where the moon returns to the same point in the sky on the same day of the year every nineteen years, and the 28-year solar cycle in which the ferial cycle (the 7 days of the week) and the bissextile (leap) years have a combined periodicity of 28.[11] Since the early Middle Ages, Easter has been defined as the first Sunday after the full moon (*luna XIV*) falling on or after the spring equinox; if this "14th moon" falls on a Sunday, Easter is kept on the following Sunday. The equinox and the moon are determined by calculation, not observation, but, rather than having to recalculate the date of Easter every year, cyclical tables were being produced by the third century AD.[12] One of the earliest Easter tables relevant to this paper is the 84-year *supputatio*, or *latercus*, in use at Rome in the fifth century, comprised of three twenty-eight-year solar cycles.[13] A variant 84-year table in use in Ireland and Britain until the eighth century

---

Annals of Ulster are also shown in square brackets. Dates in the manuscript of the Annals of Ulster are shown in single quotation marks, as are those in **S**.

[9] *dxxx*. The last annotated annal of the Harleian chronicle falls in the last year of the fifty-first decade (marked *dx*) [954]. The contrast between the marking of decades and the implied cycle of the paschal table is a feature that deserves more consideration–a significant apposition of the concepts of sequential and cyclical time.

[10] Molly Miller, "Final Stages in the construction of the Harleian *Annales Cambriae*: the evidence of the framework," *Journal of Celtic Studies* 4 (2004) 205–211. See also Dumville *Annales Cambriae A.D. 682–954 in Parallel*, vii. The retrograde genealogies that follow *Historia Brittonum* in the Harley manuscript, in the same hand, document the pedigree of Owain ap Hywel, king of Deheubarth, who died in 988, suggesting a compilation date 954 x 988, but probably nearer to 954.

[11] Bonnie Blackburn and Leofranc Holford-Strevens, *The Oxford Companion to the Year* (Oxford: Oxford University Press, 1999), 801–02.

[12] Blackburn and Holford-Strevens, *The Oxford Companion to the Year*, 803 and 805.

[13] Alden A. Mosshammer, *The Easter Computus and the Origins of the Christian Era* (Oxford: Oxford University Press, 2008), 204–239.

has been attributed to Sulpicius Severus (c. 363–c. 425).[14] This was thought lost until, in 1985, Dáibhí Ó Cróinín discovered an example of just such a variant 84-year table in a manuscript at Padua.[15] Cyril, bishop of Alexandria (c. 376–c. 444), compiled a 110-year table, but a 95-year table was also attributed to him.[16] It was the fact that some of the Easter dates in the Roman *latercus* were in conflict with the dates for Easter in the Alexandrian tables formulated by Cyril that led to the decision by Pope Leo the Great (c. 400–461) to reform the Paschal tables. Accordingly, Victorius of Aquitaine was commissioned to produce a paschal table on Alexandrian principles.[17] Victorius completed his work in AD 457, basing his *cursus paschalis* on the list of Roman consuls in the chronicle of Prosper, his contemporary and fellow countryman.[18] Victorius' cycle begins in the equivalent of AD 28, the year of the passion (*annus passionis*, or AP) but runs for a complete cycle of 532 years. Victorius understood that the 19-year, or decennovenal, cycle, as used in the Alexandrian tables, was fundamental to the accuracy of such a table, and that 28 such 19-year cycles constituted a perpetual calendar which returns to its starting point after 532 years. A defect of Victorius' table was that he did not take it upon himself to decide which Easter dates were correct where the Roman *latercus* differed from the Alexandrian cycle; in such cases, he supplied both dates and left it up to the pope to decide which of the alternatives was correct. A notable feature of both the 84-year tables and that of Victorius is that they had a column

---

[14] Daniel McCarthy, "The Origin of the Latercus Paschal Cycle of the Insular Celtic Churches," *Cambrian Medieval Celtic Studies*, 28 (1994), 25–49. The attribution to Sulpicius is endorsed by Warntjes, "Computus as Scientific Thought," 161; Mosshammer, *The Easter Computus*, 224; and Holford-Strevens, *The Oxford Companion to the Year*, 872.

[15] Daniel Mc Carthy and Dáibhí Ó Cróinín, "The "Lost" Irish 84-year Easter Table Rediscovered," *Peritia* 6–7 (1987–88) 227–42.

[16] Mosshammer, *The Easter Computus*, 193f.

[17] Theodore Mommsen, ed., "Victorii Aquitani cursus Paschalis annorum DXXXII" in *Monumenta Germaniae Historica Auctorum Antiquissimorum 9: Chronica minora saec. IV. V. VI. VII.*, vol. 1 (Berlin: Weidmann, 1892), 686–735.

[18] Theodore Mommsen, ed., "Prosperi Tironis Epitoma Chronicon", *Monumenta Germaniae Historica, Auctores antiquissimi: 9. Chronica minora saec. IV. V. VI. VII.* vol. 1 (Berlin: Weidmann, 1892), 341–499.

showing the *feria*, the number of the day of the week, for the first of January (for example see footnote).[19]

Victorius' *cursus paschalis* was confirmed as the official table throughout Gaul by a church council meeting at Orleans in 541.[20] In AD 525, Dionysius Exiguus (c. 470–544) calculated a new table based on Alexandrian principles.[21] His table was prefaced with the last 19 years of a 95-year table he attributed to Cyril of Alexandria. Those 19 years were numbered as "years of Diocletian" (i.e. years from the accession of the Emperor Diocletian), but his continuation was in "years of Our Lord," an innovation that was to result in later reckoning of years by Anno Domini (AD). Although the 532-year Victorian table recognised the decennovenal cycle, the Dionysian tables were often laid out in 19-year blocks, sometimes divided into an eight-year segment (the ogdoad) followed by an eleven-year segment (the hendecad). Instead of showing the *feria* for 1 January, as in Victorius' table, Dionysius gave the *concurrentes*, the number of the day of the week for 24 March. It was most probably Dionysius' method of calculating the date of Easter that was adopted by the English church after the Council of Whitby in 664, in opposition to the 84-year table of Sulpicius Severus still in use in Iona and some other Irish monasteries. The 84-year table was finally abandoned by Iona in 716, as recorded in the Annals of Ulster (henceforth AU) s.a. '715' [716]: *Pascha comotatur in Eoa ciuitate.*[22] The publication of Bede's *De temporum ratione* (725),[23] assured the final prevalence of the Dionysian *computus*, although the Victorian table was still in use well into the late eighth century. It is not certain if the reform of the British (i.e. Welsh) Easter by the cleric Elfoddw noted in **A** [768] was from

---

[19] Sunday is the first day of the week (i), but in the tables is labelled *dominica*, the following days are numbered ii, iii, iu, u, ui, and then Saturday is *sabbato*, the seventh day. Example of *feria* dating: the first of January 2020 was a Wednesday, so, in ferial terms, is the fourth day of the week, *iu f*; conversely, one can deduce that if the 1st January was a Wednesday, the year was 2014, 2020 or will be, for example, 2025.

[20] Mosshammer, *The Easter Computus*, 239f.

[21] Mosshammer, *The Easter Computus*, 59–61.

[22] Seán Mac Airt(†) and Gearóid Mac Niocaill, eds., *The Annals of Ulster* (Dublin: School of Celtic Studies, Dublin Institute for Advanced Studies, 1983).

[23] Charles W. Jones, ed., *Bedae Opera de Temporibus* (Cambridge, 1943), 175–291; for a translation and commentary see Faith Wallis, trans., *Bede: The Reckoning of Time* (Liverpool: Liverpool University Press, 1999).

the 84-year table to the Victorian table, or from one of those tables to the Dionysian table.

The dating clauses in the ninth-century *Historia Brittonum* are largely Victorian in character, by *annus passionis* and Roman consular year. Ben Guy[24] has suggested that the last of these clauses, an apparently pseudo-Victorian reckoning by fictitious consuls, may point to the approximate era of the chronicle (**A**) which follows on immediately after it in the Harley manuscript. This last dating clause in *Historia Brittonum* §66 states *Ab anno quo Saxones venerunt in Britanniam et a Guorthigirno suscepti sunt usque Decium et Valerianum anni sunt LXIX* ("From the year in which the Saxons came to Britain and were received by Vortigern, up to Decius and Valerianus are 69 years"). But in §31 it states *Regnante Gratiano secundo cum Equitio . Saxones a Guorthigirno suscepti sunt. anno CCCXLVII post passionem Christi* ("When Gratianus reigned for the second time with Equitius,[25] the Saxons were received by Vortigern 347 years after the passion of Christ," i.e. AD 375).[26] Adding the 69 years in §66 to the AD date in §31 produces 444, a year short of 445, the implied era of **A**.

The development of the annalistic chronicle in the early and central middle ages is closely associated with Easter tables, where events would be noted either in the margins of the tables or between the lines, as can be seen in this mid-tenth century Dionysian table from a manuscript written at the monastery of Einsiedeln.[27]

---

[24] Ben Guy "The Origins of the Compilation of Welsh Historical Texts in Harley 3859," *Studia Celtica* 49 (2015) 21–56, at 41.

[25] Mommsen, "Victorii Aquitani cursus Paschalis annorum DXXXII," 686–735. The Victorian table shows Gratianus and Equitius as consuls in (AP) CCCXLVII and CCCXLVIII, but this was the third time that Gratianus had been consul; so we should probably take the statement in *Historia Brittonum* §31 as meaning "the second time that Gratianus had been consul with Equitius," i.e. AP CCCXLVII, or AD 375.

[26] Morris, *Nennius: British History and Welsh Annals*.

[27] Reginald L. Poole, *Chronicles and Annals: A Brief Outline of Their Origin and Growth* (Oxford: Clarendon Press, 1926). Dáibhí Ó Cróinín, "Early Irish Annals from Easter Tables: A Case Restated," Peritia vol. 2 (1983), 74–86.

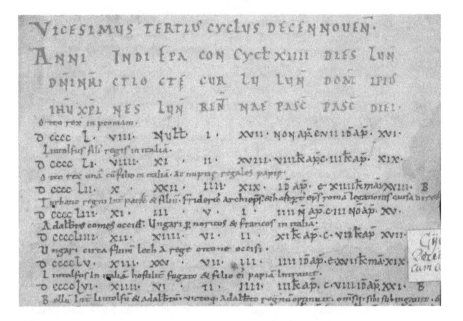

Fig. 1: Codex Einsiedelnensis 29, p.97, detail. Annals interpolated in an Easter table. The columns show 1) the AD date (showing the years AD 950–956); 2) the indiction; 3) the lunar epact; 4) the *concurrentes*; 5) the 19-year lunar cycle; 6) the Julian calendar date of the Easter full moon; 7) the Julian calendar date of Easter Sunday; 7) the lunar age at that date. The annals have been written in above the lines of the paschal table.

A is unusual as a free-standing chronicle in still displaying multiple paschal reflexes.[28] The chronicle's explicit interest in Easter runs from its first annal, Pope Leo's reform of Easter in 455 (**A** [453]), through the first Easter celebrated in Northumbria after the Council of Whitby of 664 (**A** [665]), up to the later eighth century and Elfoddw's reform of the Welsh Easter in [768].[29]

---

[28] David N. Dumville, "*Annales Cambriae* and Easter", *The Medieval Chronicle* 3 (2004), 40–50. But see the discussion of The Annals of Inisfallen"s use of data from paschal tables, both Victorian and Dionysian, below.

[29] Elfoddw is on his first appearance [768] just described in **A** as "that man of God", but on his death in [809] "bishop of the Venedotian region", i.e. Gwynedd.

HENRY GOUGH-COOPER

It is clear from external dating and the implied Great Paschal Cycle frame of the chronicle that the first year of **A** is AD 445, the first year of the hendecad (the last eleven years) of the nineteen-year lunar-solar cycle starting in AD 437. Molly Miller[30] pointed out that [445] is exactly seventeen 19-year cycles before the annal noting Elfoddw's reform of the British Easter in [768].

1 (Og.)	(437)				(532)		570	589		627		665	684
2		457											
3										629			
4				516			573			630			
5							574		612	631	650	669	
6					537				613	632			689
7								595					
8			501			558							
9 (Hen.)	(445)			521					616				
10									617				
11							580				656		
12						562					657	676	
13		468			544			601			658		
14													
15							584						
16					547						661		
17	453								624		662		
18	454							606		644		682	
19								607	626	645		683	

Fig. 2i: the distribution of the annotated annals in A mapped onto the twenty-eight 19-year cycles of a Great Paschal Cycle running from 437–683

Annals in plain black font, annals with no external parallels except in [B], [C],[P], [R] or [S]; annals in red, underlined, a hypothetical chronicle of 798–854 consisting of purely Welsh events (also in [B], [C],[P], [R], or [S]); annals in green boldface, annals with parallels in the Irish chronicles, but not necessarily Irish events; shaded area [617]– [777], the greatest extent of Kathleen Hughes' proposed North British chronicle.

---

[30] Molly Miller, "The Disputed Historical Horizon of the Pictish King-lists", *Scottish Historical Review* 58 (1979), 1–34 at 23.

1 (Og.)		**722**		760		*798*	*817*							**950**
2	**704**								856	875	**894**	**913**		**951**
3										876	895			
4										877		**915**		
5						*840*				878				**954**
6					784	*822*						**917**		
7		**728**					*842*			880				
8									862		**900**	**919**	**938**	
9(Hen.)				768		*825*	*844*			882			**939**	
10			**750**			*807*			864		**902**	**921**	**940**	
11						*808*			865		**903**			
12	**714**					*809*			866	**885**	**904**		**942**	
13						*810*	*848*						**943**	
14		**735**	**754**			*811*	*849*			**887**	**906**		**944**	
15	**717**	**736**				*812*	*831*	*850*	869		**907**			
16	**718**			775		*813*			870		**908**		**946**	
17			**757**	776	795	*814*			871		**909**	**928**	**947**	
18				777	796		*853*							
19	**721**			778		*816*	*854*		873	892				

Fig. 2ii: the distribution of the annotated annals in A mapped onto the twenty-eight 19-year cycles of a Great Paschal Cycle running from 704–954

Annals in plain black font, annals with no external parallels except in [B], [C],[P], [R] or [S]; annals in red, underlined, a hypothetical chronicle of 798–854 consisting of purely Welsh events (also in [B], [C],[P], [R], or [S]); annals in green boldface, annals with parallels in the Irish chronicles, but not necessarily Irish events; shaded area [617]– [777], the greatest extent of Kathleen Hughes' proposed North British chronicle.

Kathleen Hughes considered that annals began to be kept at St. David's in the late eighth century, and that, soon after, these were extended backwards to include items from an Irish source, and from a North British chronicle with some North Welsh entries,[31] and that the annals were arranged at some time between then and 954 in the form of a 532-year cycle.[32] Molly Miller,

---

[31] Kathleen Hughes, "The Welsh Latin chronicles: *Annales Cambriae* and related texts," *Celtic Britain in the Early Middle Ages* (1980), 67–85, at 70f.

[32] Hughes, "The Welsh Latin chronicles," 85.

in a paper published posthumously,[33] argued for two periods of work on the
A-text, the later period being that of the final redactor or compiler working
between 954 and 977 (the last year of the 532-year "frame"), and the earlier
being that of their predecessor who still had an interest in the 84-year cycle.
The two dates Miller identified as evidence for the start of 84-year cycles
were 759 and 843, where **A** shows signs of a dislocation.[34] It is doubtful that
anywhere in Britain was still using 84-year tables as late as 759, and, in any
case, Elfoddw's reform of the British Easter in 768 would have been based
on a Dionysian 19-year table probably with its first year as AD 760.[35]
However, Miller was surely correct in identifying an earlier compiler for
the late-eighth to mid-ninth century annals, and in pointing to Abergele and
Gwynedd as being the probable locale of the creation of the ninth-century
annals,[36] rather than St. David's as Hughes had thought. David Dumville
showed that the Irish material, while providing the foundation of **A** down
to 613, as Hughes recognised, extends right through to the fifth decade of
the tenth century, and an Irish source is in use down to at least 887.[37]
Dumville also endorsed Miller's conjecture on evidence for the 84-year
cycle in **A**, and the possible Abergele locale for "a North Welsh source"
used by the final compiler. Dumville concluded that sometime between 954
and 977 the Harleian chronicle, **A**, was created "essentially as we have it"[38]
by combining material from a North Welsh source chronicle with extracts
from an Irish chronicle, a chronicle kept at St. David's from about 800
onwards, and perhaps a North British chronicle (if that was not already part

---

[33] Molly Miller, "Final Stages in the Construction of the Harleian *Annales Cambriae*:
the evidence of the framework," *Journal of Celtic Studies* 4 (2004), 205–211.

[34] I will argue that these "dislocations" are the result of simple scribal error (see n. 71).

[35] Miller's speculation that there might have been a Welsh tradition of starting the 19-
year cycle with a hendecad is unconvincing (Miller, "Final stages," 207f); there is no
evidence for such an unorthodox procedure.

[36] Miller, "Final stages," 211.

[37] David Dumville, "When was the 'Clonmacnoise Chronicle' Created? The Evidence
of the Welsh Annals," in Katherine Grabowski and David Dumville, *Chronicles and
Annals of Medieval Ireland and Wales: the Clonmacnoise-Group Texts* (Woodbridge:
Boydell, 1984), 209–226, at 211f. The situation in the tenth century becomes less
certain, as the evidence suggests more information passing from Wales to Ireland than
from Ireland to Wales.

[38] Dumville, "*Annales Cambriae* and Easter," 47f.

of the North Welsh source or the Irish text). Dumville thought it unlikely that **A** itself was extracted from a 532-year cycle, but that the annals from about 800 may have been recorded in decennovenal tables.[39] In a recent paper, Ben Guy has summed-up much of the research to date,[40] concluding that the 532-year frame is a feature inherited from the ninth century Abergele chronicle, rather than a product, as Miller and Dumville saw it, of the "final redaction" of the later tenth century.[41]

2. A chronicle of 854?

A chronicle of 854 may lie at the core of the **A**-text and its sisters, **B** and **C**. This is in red, underlined, in Fig. 2ii. These three 19-year cycles commencing at [798] are distinctive in several ways. Most importantly, the chronology here, relative and absolute (by external dating), is fairly consistent over all the versions of the chronicle, both the Welsh Latin annals (**A**, **B** and **C**) and the vernacular chronicles (**P**, **R** and **S**).[42] Furthermore, in contrast to the annals that precede them and those following, these three cycles note purely Welsh events, only one of which has a parallel in the Irish chronicles ([816]: the death of Cynan ap Rhodri). In the preceding annals, the three nineteen-year cycles for 703 to 759 contain only two or three Welsh events.[43] Furthermore, the annals from [807] to [814] represent the longest continuous sequence in the chronicle. Finally, after [854] there

---

[39] Dumville, "*Annales Cambriae* and Easter," 48.

[40] Ben Guy, "The Origins of the Compilation of Welsh Historical Texts in Harley 3859," *Studia Celtica* 49 (2015), 21–56.

[41] However, mid-ninth-century computists in north Wales would have been quite able to construct a retrospective sequence of 19-year cycles going back from 768 to 445 (or, indeed, from 854 to 437), but they would not necessarily have seen an immediate need for extending this all the way through to 977 to form a complete Great Cycle of twenty-eight 19-year cycles.

[42] The chronology of **P** and **S** falters slightly after '815' where they go a year ahead for '817' (=[816]), '818' (=[817]), '819' (=[818]) and '823' (=[822]) but resynchronises at '825' = [825].

[43] The possible third is the "consecration of the church of St Michael" [718], which might refer to the church at Abergele. See Guy, "The Origins," 29; for St Michael dedications in Gwynedd, see Molly Miller, *The Saints of Gwynedd* (Woodbridge: Boydell, 1979), 127, note 20.

appears to be a chronological disjunction before the subsequent annals (see below).[44]

This chronicle of 854 might have extended back before 798. Elfoddw, whose death is noted in [809], reformed the British Easter in [768], and it would be logical for him to have introduced nineteen-year tables commencing in 760.[45] Seven out of the nine annals from [760] to [796] record Welsh events. Of the annals starting in the *primus decennouenalis* year [722], the death of a king of Alclut, Beli, son of Elphin, is also recorded by the Annals of Ulster[46] under this year, and the events of [735] to [760] all appear under their 'correct' years, whereas the annals for [775] to [795] all appear to be a year in advance of the true AD year.

There are three copies of paschal tables for 798 to 854 in the papal archives, issued at Rome presumably shortly before 798.[47]

---

[44] **B** and the Welsh vernacular texts also record some accurate astronomical data, a solar eclipse of 807 and two lunar eclipses of 810 and 831, which do not appear in **A** or **C** but are very likely to have been in their common source.

[45] It is highly unlikely that Elfoddw possessed a full Dionysian table for 532 to 1063; the practice from the seventh century onwards was to extend the tables by 95 years, following on Dionysius's precedent (Dionysius's original table ran from 532 to 626), or for shorter multiples of 19 years (see Immo Warntjes, "The Irish in Early Medieval Europe," 165f). The earliest known Welsh 532-year table (for the twenty-eight 19-year cycles from AD 1064) is preserved in a manuscript of the late eleventh century, Dublin, Trinity College, MS. A. 4. 20: see Hugh Jackson Lawlor, ed., *The Psalter and Martyrology of Ricemarch*, 2 vols. (London: Henry Bradshaw Society, 1914). The only other early Welsh reference to the nineteen-year cycle is in the Old Welsh computus fragment in Cambridge University Library MS. Add. 4543 (AD 930 or earlier); for the date, see Helmut Gneuss and Michael Lapidge, *Anglo-Saxon Manuscripts* (Toronto: University of Toronto Press, 2014), p. 44.

[46] Mac Airt and Mac Niocaill, *The Annals of Ulster*, s.a. '721' [722].

[47] Immo Warntjes, *The Munich Computus: Text and Translation* (Stuttgart: Franz Steiner Verlag, 2010), 339.

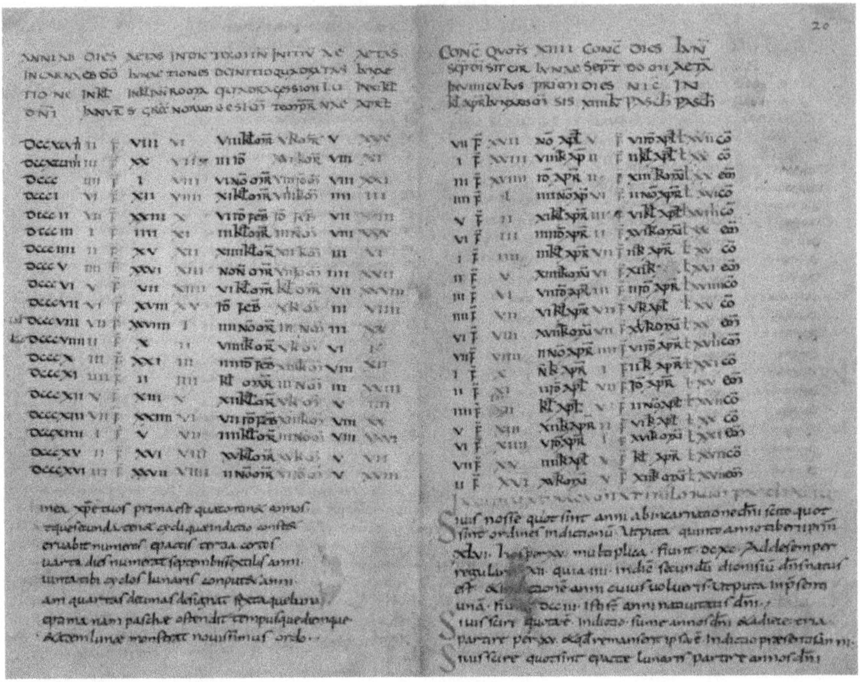

Fig. 3: Vatican, Biblioteca Apostolica, Pal. Lat. 1447 ff. 19v-22r: 19v and 20r shown. First 19-year cycle, 798–816. This is one of three tables for the years 798–854 in the Vatican archives: the other two are in Vatican, Biblioteca Apostolica, Reg. Lat. 1260 ff. 112r –114r, and Vatican, Biblioteca Apostolica, Pal. Lat. 1448ff. 13v–16r, probably issued in, or shortly before, 798. Transitional between Victorian and Dionysian tables, they include data from both traditions. The columns are 1) The AD date; 2) the weekday (*feria*) of 1st January; 3) the epact (age of the moon) of 1st January; 4) the indiction; 5) the Julian calendar date of the *terminus quadragesimae*; 6) the Julian calendar date of the *initium quadragesimae* (the beginning of Lent); 7) the lunar age at that date; 8) the epact of 22 March; 9) the *concurrentes*; 10) the lunar cycle; 11) the Julian calendar date of the Easter full moon; 12) the weekday of that date; 13) the Julian calendar date of Easter Sunday; 14) the lunar age at that date.

These are hybrid Victorian-Dionysian tables, showing attributes of both the table of Victorius of Aquitaine, adopted as canonical in Gaul and Francia at the synod of Orléans in 541, and the tables based on the principles of Dionysius Exiguus that were gaining favour in the seventh and eighth centuries. These hybrid tables appear, therefore, to signal a transition between the two traditions, the Victorian tables that were rapidly becoming obsolete, and the Dionysian-style tables that were the new standard.

There may also be evidence from Ireland for the issuing of these tables. The Annals of Inisfallen (henceforth AI)[48] have only sporadic indications of chronological data before 798. For example, under the year AI [435][49] the ferial (day of the week) for the 1st of January is noted: *Kl. .iii. f. Orosius & Cirillus in doctrinam floruerunt* (Kalends, the third *feria*. Orosius and Cyril flourished in teaching)*;* and under AI [437] the lunar epact and the start of the above-mentioned Cyril of Alexandria's 95-year table: *Kl. .ix. l. initium circuli magni* (Kalends, the sixth of the moon. Beginning of a Great Cycle).[50] The chronicle then states occasional ferial and lunar data–e.g. AI [440] *K. .ii. f., xii. (l.)*–up to AI [454] after which a bare "Kl." is given for each year up to AI [798], although first years of decennovenal cycles, *Kl. initium circuli*, are noted at AI [608] and AI [779], which are possibly the remnants of what was once a more continuous chronological apparatus. But at AI [798] accurate ferial and lunar data start to be supplied, and bissextile ("leap") years marked off. The bissextile data are partially corrupt, but there are accurate ferial and lunar epact data for the years 798, 817 and 855.[51] AI [798] *Kl. Initium cicli. secunda feria .ix. luna* (the data is for Victorian AP CCXXXVIIII; but although the start of a 19-year cycle is noted (*initium cicli*), the older Victorian tables were not generally divided into 19-year cycles).

---

[48] Seán Mac Airt, ed., *The Annals of Inisfallen (MS. Rawlinson B. 503)* (Dublin: Dublin Institute for Advanced Studies, 1944).

[49] The editorial AD dates in square brackets are those supplied in Mac Airt, *The Annals of Inisfallen*.

[50] Dionysius Exiguus' 95-year table was a continuation of Cyril's earlier table. See Alden A. Mosshammer, *The Easter Computus and the Origins of the Christian Era* (Oxford: Oxford University Press, 2008), 65–67. The invention of Victorius' table is noted at [457], *Kl. uictorius scripsit ciclum pascha.*

[51] The presence of Irish scholars passing through Gwynedd and visiting the court of Merfyn Frych in the first half of the ninth century is attested by the Bamberg cryptogram; see James F. Kenney, *The Sources for the Early History of Ireland: Ecclesiastical*, rev. ed. (Dublin: Four Courts Press 1968), 556. Merfyn's son and successor, Rhodri, had a relationship with the Irish scholar Sedulius Scottus of Liége (fl. 848 x 860); Kenney, *The sources*, 554f.

AI [799] *b. Kl. .iii. f .xx. luna.* (Victorian AP CCXL; ferial and moon, marked erroneously as bissextile)
AI [800] *Kl. .iiii. f .i. luna.* (Victorian AP CCXLI; the true bissextile.)
There follow fifteen bare kalends, and then:

AI [816] *b. Kl.* (CCLVII; marked correctly as bissextile);
AI [817] *Kl. .u. f., .ix. luna* (Victorian AP CCLVIII; *primus decemnouenalis,* but not marked as such);
(bissextile years noted correctly at 820, 824, 836, 840, 844, 848 and 852)
AI [846] *Kl. .uii. f., .x. l.* [Victorian AP CCLXXXVIII = AD 847, but correctly *.xi. l.*]
AI [855] *Kl. .iii. f., ix. luna* (Victorian AP CCXCVI; *primus decemnouenalis,* but not marked as such).[52]

The chronological data for 798 onwards in the Annals of Inisfallen are intensive compared to the data for the preceding centuries, suggesting a fresh impetus in recording such data. Both the nature of the [798]–[854] section of the Harleian chronicle, **A**, and the detailed chronological data provided in the Annals of Inisfallen from AI [798] onwards may reflect the papal initiative in issuing revised tables for 798–854, even though the Welsh Latin annals have not preserved any explicit chronological data for this period.

After the annal in **A** for [854], international notices recommence with the death of Kenneth MacAlpine (Cineadh m. Alpin, *rex pictorum*), with which is synchronised the death of Jonathan, *princeps* of Abergele (in North Wales). This is placed under the year of the paschal cycle corresponding to 856. But Kenneth McAlpine is generally held to have died in 858 (AU, s.a. '857').[53] This annal perhaps indicates a retrospective notice where the precise date of both events was not known to the later compiler. The notice of Jonathan's death is unusual, the only item in the chronicle about Abergele or its primates, and has led David Dumville to suggest,[54] and Ben Guy to

---

[52] AI subsequently gives data for the *primus decennovenal* years 874, 893 and 931 and 988. The lacuna in the annals between 969 and 972 is reminiscent of the "skewed" Great Paschal Cycle in **A**, 445+532, in that it strongly suggests an ancestor of AI consisted of a chronicle that ran from 437 to 969 (i.e. 437+532 = 969).

[53] The date 858 is probably correct. See Alex Woolf, *From Pictland to Alba: 789–1070* (Edinburgh: Edinburgh University Press, 2007), 103.

[54] Dumville, *Annales Cambriae*, ix, n. 46.

speculate at more length,[55] that the hypothetical chronicle of 854 could be an Abergele record, and this may well be the case. The focus from [798] to [854] is primarily on events in North Wales.[56] But the evidence for this chronicle stretching further back to the early eighth century is weak.[57]

3. The compilation from the mid-fifth century to the late eighth century

On the hypothesis that a chronicle of 854 was the starting point of the chronicle, the annals for the earlier centuries appear to be a scholar's compilation, but whether it is of the ninth or tenth century remains in question. Kathleen Hughes observed that the structure of the chronicle for the fifth to the eighth centuries was given by annals that had parallels in the so-called "Chronicle of Ireland," hypothesised to have been compiled in Iona until about AD 740 and then have been continued in Ireland to AD 911.[58] Annals in **A** that have parallels in the Irish chronicles are shown in bold in fig. ii. These start with a pairing that also occurs in the Annals of Ulster and the Annals of Inisfallen: Pope Leo I's change of the date of Easter, **A** [453], and the birth of St Brigid in the following year, **A** [454]:

A has:

A [453] *Pasca commvtatur super diem dominicum cum papa leone . Episcopo rome .*

---

[55] Guy, *The Origins*, 29f. Guy considered the "Abergele" chronicle ran to [856], as that is where it records the death of Jonathan. If Jonathan did have something to do with the authorship of the chronicle of 854, he was remembered afterwards as such rather than being the last entry in it.

[56] [854] records the death of, Cygen, king of Powys, in Rome. Cyngen was the last of his line; after his death, his brother-in-law, Rhodri Mawr of Gwynedd, seems to have assumed the kingship of Powys. See Peter Bartrum, *A Welsh Classical Dictionary*, (The National Library of Wales, 1993), s.n. Cygen ap Cadell ap Brochwel.

[57] It may be noted that after Dionysius' initial table for 532–626 ran out, at least one 95-year continuation was written for 627–721, and Coelfrith writing to Nectan, a king of the Picts, in 710 suggests a further table could be made for 722–816. This last 95-year table would have been current in 768, at the time of Elfoddw's reform. See Immo Warntjes, "Computus as Scientific Thought," 166.

[58] Kathleen Hughes, "The A-text of *Annales Cambriae*," in *Celtic Britain in the Early Middle Ages* (Woodbridge: Boydell, 1980), 89f. See also Dumville, "The Evidence of the Welsh Annals," 209–226. Dumville argued for the continuing use of Irish annals down to [887] or perhaps [942] (211).

A [454] *Brigida sancta nascitur.*

The Annals of Ulster (AU) has these same events under the years 451 and 452:
AU '451' *Pasca Domini uiii Kl Mai celebratum est* .[59]
AU '452' *Hic alii dicunt natiuitatem Sanctae Brigidae* .

Inisfallen (AI) under its annals corresponding to [454] and [455]:
AI [454] *Kl. .xxui. l. Pascha in .uiii. Kl. Mai.*[60]
AI [455] *Hic alii dicunt natiuitatem Sanctae Brigidae* .[61]

Irish annalistic chronicles typically note simply the *kalendis ianuariis* (often just a "K" or "Kl." demarking the years) and the ferial numbers of the Victorian table without any other chronological data (for example, the AD or AP year, or the lunar epact).[62] The simplest explanation for the two-year displacement between AU and **A** is a misreading of an Irish source chronicle's *ii feria* and *iii feria* (the *feria* for AD 451 and 452) for *u feria* and *ui feria* (the feria for AD 453 and 454) in a Victorian table, thus:

---

[59] *uiii kl. Mai* is the alternative Easter date, *graeci*, for anno CCCCXXVIII, i.e. AD 455, in the Victorian table.

[60] *xxui. lune* is the lunar epact for 453 in the Dionysian table; see Faith Wallis, trans., *Bede: The Reckoning of Time*, 402. Alternatively, *xxui* could be a scribal error for *xuiii*, the Victorian lunar epact for 455.

[61] Daniel Mc Carthy considers 451 an authentic annal for the reform of Easter; this is equivalent to Nick Evans' CPI year 454; see Nicholas Evans *The Present and the Past in the Medieval Irish Chronicles* (Woodbridge: Boydell, 2010), 235f. The actual AD years the date of the Roman Easter had to be changed were 444 and 455. *Chronicon Scotorum* (https://celt.ucc.ie//published/G100016/index.html; henceforth CS) places the birth of St Brigid at CS [439], which is also Mc Carthy's preferred date. See Daniel Mc Carthy, *Chronological Synchronisation of the Irish Annals*, 2005, accessed November 27, 2019:
https://www.scss.tcd.ie/misc/kronos/chronology/synchronisms/Edition_4/K_trad/Sync h_tables/s0425-0487.htm

[62] Daniel P. Mc Carthy, *The Irish Annals: Their genesis, evolution and history.* (Dublin: Four Courts Press, 2008), 8.

Kalends of January ferial data in the Irish source chronicle:	*Anni passionis* (AP) (AD equivalent) years in the Victorian table:
kal. Ian. d. ii feria (1ˢᵗ January, a Monday)	*Anno CCCCXXIIII* (AD 451)
kal. Ian. d. iii feria (1ˢᵗ January, a Tuesday)	Anno CCCCXXV (AD 452)

misread by the Welsh compiler as:

kal. Ian. d. u feria (1ˢᵗ January, a Thursday)	*Anno CCCCXXVI* (AD 453)
kal. Ian. d. ui feria (1ˢᵗ January, a Friday)	*Anno CCCCXXVII* (AD 454)

The Welsh compiler, misreading *u* for *ii* and *ui* for *iii* in the source, would then have referred back to a Victorian table to see under which AP years the annals should be placed.[63] The modern edition of the Annals of Inisfallen

---

[63] There is some slight evidence in **A** for the use of an Irish-style "kalends of January" source; under [630] we read *Guidgar uenit et non redit . kalendis . ianuariis . Gueith meicen et ibi interfectus est et guin cum duobus filiis suis. Catguollaun autem uictor fuit.* It is doubtful that *kalendis ianuariis* here refers to the date of the battle of *Meicen* (Hatfield), which Bede says was fought on the twelfth of October, and may have been taken over by automatic copying from an Irish-style chronicle. For Bede's date, see Bertram Colgrave and R. A. B. Mynors, eds., *Bede's Ecclesiastical History of the English People* (Oxford: Clarendon Press, 1969), 202–3 (henceforth, HE). Another explanation for **A** placing the change of Easter in [453] could be that this is the year when Pope Leo wrote to the Emperor Marcian in June 453 about the date for Easter of 455 (Jacques Paul Migne, ed., *Patriologia Latina*, Vol. 54, *Sancti Leonis Magni, Romani Pontificis, Opera Omnia, Epistolae* [Paris, 1846], Letter CXXI). However, this does not explain the discrepancy between the Irish and the Welsh dates, if the Welsh compiler was indeed depending on an Irish chronicle for his fifth and sixth century structure. AU seems to be noting the change of date for 455 but has placed it in the year of the pope's letter of June 451 in which he raised the matter of the disputed date of the Easter of 455 with Bishop Paschasinus (Migne, *op. cit.*, Letter LXXXVIII). Pope Leo's letters are dated by day of the month and consul (i.e. for 451, *8 kal. Julii, Adelfio*; for 453, *7 kal. Julii, Opilione*). The sources the compiler was working with may not have provided either AP or AD dates, or indeed consular years, the earliest Irish annals perhaps giving only the ferial number for the 1ˢᵗ of January

places the Easter reform under [454] where it has *Kl. .xxui. l(unae). Pascha in .uiii. Kl. Mai.* (Kalends, 26th of the moon, Easter on the 24th of April). Twenty-six is the the the age of the moon on 22 March, the *concurrentes*, for AD 453 in the Dionysian tables.[64] AI's chronology appears to have gone a year in advance after the Council of Chalcedon AI[451] by the insertion of an annal about the death of the emperor Marcian under AI[453], who in fact died in 457. Before the erroneous insertion of the obituary for Marcian, the source of the Annals of Inisfallen may have placed the Easter reform under 453, and this would match **A**'s note of the reform at [453].

The death of St Patrick is noted in **A** at [457], which is in perfect agreement with the Annals of Ulster and the *Chronicon Scotorum*. But the Welsh chronicle, unlike the Irish chronicles, does not qualify this as the old (*senex*) Patrick and has no later obituary for the saint. The Irish sources, as they now stand, all place the saint's principal obituary in the last decades of the fifth century.

A [457] *Sanctus Patricius ad dominum migratur.* (St Patrick goes to the Lord.)

AU '457'. *Quies senis Patricii, ut alii libri dicunt.* (The repose of the old Patrick, as other books say.)

AU '461'. *Hic alii quietem Patrici dicunt.* (Here others say the repose of Patrick.)

AU '491' [492].[65] *Dicunt Scoiti hic Patricium archiepiscopum defunctum fore.* (The Irish state here that Patrick the Archbishop died.)

AU '492' [493]. *Patricius archiapostulus [(vel) archiepiscopus et apostolus Scotorum] quieuit 16 kl. Aprilis, .c.xx. anno etatis sue, .lx. autem quo uenit*

---

year (and that was easily prone to scribal error). While the Victorian tables (and the earlier 84-year paschal tables) give the ferial number for the 1st of January, the Dionysian tables give the *concurrentes*, the ferials for 24 March. At a time of transition between the tables (750–850), this might lead to confusion. For example, the "concurrent" for 455 in the Dionysian tables is stated as 5 (*u*), and the *kal. ianuarii* ferial for 453 (AP CCCCXXVI) is also 5 (*u*).

[64] 26 (*xxui*) could be a possible misreading of 18 (*xuiii*), the lunar epact for AD 455. But would AI plausibly have Dionysian data here? The alternative ("Theophilian") Easter date and moon in the Victorian table is *VIII kal. Mai, lun. XXII. XXII* could just possibly have become *XXVI* by scribal error.

[65] After its annal for 487, AU has omitted a year so that its stated AD years have to be increased by one: so, '488' = [489], etc.

ad Hiberniam anno ad babtistandos Scotos. (Patrick, arch-apostle, [or archbishop and apostle] of the Irish, rested on the 16th of the Kalends of April in the 120th year of his age, in the 60th year after he had come to Ireland to baptize the Irish.)

AI [496] *Quies Patricii h-i .xui. Kl. April, anno .cccc.xxxii. a Pasione Domini.* (Kl. Repose of Patrick on the 16th of the Kalends of April in the 432nd year from the Passion of the Lord; *Annus passionis* CCCCXXXII = AD 459/460).[66]

A synchronises the birth of St Columcille with the death of St Brigid [521]; in the Irish annals these are separated by three to four years. The amalgamation of the two events might be due to misreading a source that noted the birth of Columcille on the same day that Buite m. Brónaig died.[67]

A [521] *Sanctus columcille nascitur. Quies sanctae brigidae.*
AU '518' [519] *Natiuitas Coluim Cille eodem die quo Bute mc. Bronaigh dormiuit.*
AU '522' [523] (Hand 2) *Buithi mc. Bronaigh obiit. Colum Cille natus est.*
AI [521] *Natiuitas Coluimb Chille (&) dormitatio Buti m. Bronaig.*
AU '523' [524] *Quies sancte Brigite anno .lxx. etatis sue.*
AU '525' [526] *Dormitatio sancte Brigite anno lxx. etatis sue.*
AU '527' [528] *Uel hic dormitacio Brigide secundum Librum Mochod.*
AI [524] *Quies sanctae Brigitae.*

The implied dates of the subsequent parallels in **A** are fairly close to those in the Irish chronicles ([468] St Benignus, [501] St Ebur, [558] Gabran m. Domangairt, [562] Columba's voyage to Britain, [570] the death of Gildas), but only four out of the twenty annals agree exactly with external dating.

Of the British items in **A**, two are synchronised with plagues ([537] Camlann; [547] death of Maelgwn Gwynedd). Maelgwn Gwynedd stands at the head of a genealogical chain that leads to Hywel Dda (died [950]). Camlann [537] is placed a decade before Maelgwn [547], and Badon [516] about two decades before Camlann, both of which placings look artificial.

---

[66] This annal in AI at [496] apparently noting the death of Patrick "in the 432nd year from the passion of Our Lord," i.e. AD 460, appears to contradict its position in the annals" chronological sequence.

[67] Buite m. Brónaig, founder of Monasterboice, County Louth, Ireland. Pádraig Ó Riain, *A Dictionary of Irish Saints* (Dublin: Four Courts Press, 2011), s.n. Buithe.

A [516] *Bellum badonis.* (This has no Irish parallel. Badon is noted in *Historia Brittonum* in the battle-list of Arthur but not Camlann.[68])
A [537] *Gueith camlann . . . Et mortalitas in brittannia et in hibernia fuit*; possibly synchronized with AI [537] *Perditio panis*; AU '535' [536].
A [547] *Mortalitas magna in qua pausat mailcun rex genedotae*; Possibly the plague noted in AU '548' [549]; AI [551].

There are also two North British, perhaps Ionan, items:

A [558] *Gabran filius dungart moritur*;[69]
noted in AU '557' [558]; '559' [560].
A [562] *Columcille in brittannia exit*;
noted in AU '562' [563]; AI [563]; Bede 565 (HE iii. 4).

At [601] there appears to be a "catch-all" for late entries to the "Heroic Age" of the fifth and sixth centuries. This notes a synod at Chester, and the deaths of Pope Gregory (12 March 604) and St. David of Menevia (whose death the *Chronicon Scotorum* places at [589]).[70] The four later-medieval bishoprics are referenced by **A** noting Deiniol of the Bangors (Bangor) [584], David (St. David's) [601], and Kentigern (St. Asaph) and Dyfrig (Llandaff) [612]. The seniority of Deiniol is suggestive, while David is made senior to Kentigern and Dyfrig. But the appearance of David as a subsidiary item in [601] and the pairing of the latter two, Kentigern and Dyfrig, is perhaps a sign of late eleventh or early twelfth century interpolation.

The chronology of these early annals might depend on marginal notes in 84-year Easter tables.[71] The Padua *latercus*, the 84-year insular *computus*

---

[68] Morris, *Nennius: British History and the Welsh Annals*, §56.

[69] Gabran and his son Aedan feature in Welsh legend. See Rachel Bromwich, ed. and trans., *Trioedd Ynys Prydein: The Triads of the Island of Britain*, 4th ed. (Cardiff: University of Wales Press, 2006), 272f.

[70] Mac Niocaill, *Chronicon Scotorum*; William M. Hennessy, ed. and trans., *Chronicum Scotorum. A Chronicle of Irish Affairs, from the earliest times to A.D. 1135, with a supplement containing the events from 1141 to 1150*, Roll Series 46 (London, 1866).

[71] Molly Miller"s conjecture that there might be evidence in **A** for the use of 84-year tables commencing in AD 759 and 843 (Miller "Final stages," 208f.; and Dumville "Annales Cambriae and Easter," 43f.) was vitiated by the nature of the insular 84-year

154

rediscovered by Dáibhí Ó Cróinín, has been shown to have its first year in 438.[72] The second iteration of this cycle would be 606 to 689, and it is possible that the annals [606] to [689] do outline such a cycle.

The Padua *latercus*:	438 – 521
Hypothetical First iteration:	522 – 605
Hypothetical Second iteration:	**606 – 689**
Hypothetical Third iteration:	690 – 773

As has been noted above, Iona converted to the Dionysian *computus* in the second decade of the eighth century (AU '715' [716]: *Pascha comotatur in Eoa ciuitate*). The 84-year cycle was almost certainly obsolete in Wales by 768, but possibly earlier. Elfoddw's reform of 768 may have been from the ambiguous Victorian table to the Dionysian-style one. However, as we have seen, Victorian-style dating clauses still prevail in the ninth-century *Historia Brittonum*.

There is a decided divergence between the Welsh annals and both the Irish annals and Bede's dates (*Historia Ecclesiastica*) for the events of the 640s, where the displacement in the Welsh annals is difficult to account for.

---

table discovered in 1985 at Padua (see Mc Carthy and Ó Cróinín, "The "Lost" Irish 84-year Easter Table Rediscovered"; Miller's "Final Stages" paper was published posthumously, and the Padua *latercus* was not identified until after her death). The first year of the Padua table is equivalent to AD 438, so that further iterations would not have begun in 759 or 843. The "corrections" Miller noted in in the MS (three annals inserted *post-scriptum* at [756], [757] and [758]; and two annals inserted at [841] and [842]) are more likely to be amendments to very similar scribal eye-skips from like to like. The scribal eye-skip is made very clear by Dumville's tabulated analyses of the two instances (Dumville, "*Annales Cambriae* and Easter," 44): the first scribal error is where the copyist, in turning over a leaf, has omitted a blank annal and an annotated annal, and has jumped to another blank and annotated pair in his exemplar (in fact, the pattern here is two blank annals and an annotated annal followed by a similar blank-blank-annotated triplet again, so that the copyist has had to insert an extra blank annal at the top of the column on the new leaf); the second is where the careless copyist has skipped, again, from a blank and annotated pair of annals to the next blank and annotated pair, and has then had to go back and insert the omitted pair in their proper place by writing them into the margin of the column.
[72] Mc Carthy, "The Origin of the Latercus Paschal Cycle of the Insular Celtic Churches." Mc Carthy and Ó Cróinín, "The "Lost" Irish 84-year Easter Table Rediscovered."

A	AU	Bede (HE)[73]
[627] Belin moritur.		
[629] Obsessio Catguollaun.		
[630] Gueith meicen (Edwin killed).		
[631] Bellum cantscaul (Cadwallon falls).	'630' [631] (Edwin killed).	
[632] Strages sabinae (Iudris slaughtered).	'631' [632] (Cadwallon killed).	
	'632' [633] (Iudris killed).	633, October 12th, Edwin killed.
		634, first year of Oswald.
	'638' [639] (Oswald killed).	
		642, August 5th, Oswald killed.
		643, first year of Oswiu.
[644] Bellum cocboy (Oswald killed)		
[645] Percussio demeticae regionis (St. David's burnt).		

Fig. 4: The 19-year cycle 627 to 645 in AC, AU and Bede

In the segment in **A** from [606] to [689] there are only two annals out of the twenty that agree with external dating, the rest are mostly one year in advance or in arrears, while three ([644], [645] and [650]) are two years in

---

[73] Colgrave and Mynors, eds., *Bede's Ecclesiastical History*. For the arguments for accepting the veracity of Bede's chronology, see Susan Wood "Bede's Northumbrian Dates Again," *English Historical Review* 98 (1983), 280–296.

advance of the true AD date.[74] After 689 there is a lengthy lacuna.[75] The eighth century sees chronological accuracy improving, with eleven annals of the twenty-one in agreement with external dating, of which the cogent sequence from [735] to [760] has already been noted.

In general, the pattern in this first three and a half centuries of annals in **A** is to pair events in one annal, or pair events to an immediately preceding or succeeding annal, which suggests pairing the uncertain with the certain (or the more certain), so that we see this sort of pattern emerging where items also found in the Irish annals (bold lettering) are often preceded or succeeded by British items in the adjacent year.

[**453**]/[**454**]	Pope Leo reformed Easter / St Brigid born.
[573]/[**574**]	Battle of Arfderydd / Brendan of Birr died.
[606]/[**607**]	Bishop Cynog buried / Aedan 'map' Gabran died.
[612]/[**613**]	Kentigern and Bishop Dyfrig died / *Caer Legion*, Sylyf ap Cynan fell; Iago, son of Beli, slept.
[616]/[617][76]	Ceredig died / Edwin started to reign.
[**626**]/[627]	Edwin baptized / Belin died.
[629]/[**630**]/[**631**]/[**632**]	Cadwallon besieged. *Meicen*, Edwin and sons killed / *Cantscaul*, Cadwallon fell. The strife on Severn; Idris slaughtered.
[**644**]/[645]	*Cocboy*, Oswald and Eawa fell / The hammering of Dyfed, St. David's monastery burnt.

---

[74] The Annals of Inisfallen also appear to misdate Oswald's death to [644].

[75] Ecgfrith (died 685) is unaccountably omitted from the sequence of Northumbrian rulers which commences in **A** with Edwin's accession [617], his baptism [626] and death [630]; his successors, Oswald's and Oswiu's deaths [644] and [669]; and continues with Aldfrith [704] and Osred [717]. Ecgfrith and the catastrophe at *Lin Garan* (Dunnichen/Nechtansmere, 20 May 685) are noted twice in the *Historia Brittonum*, §57 and §65.

[76] Edwin's first regnal year on Bede's system; see Susan Wood, "Bede's Northumbrian dates again", 286.

[656]/[**657**]/[658]	*Gaius Campus* / Penda killed / Oswiu came and took plunder.
[**661**]/[662]	Cummine *fota* / Brocmail died.
[682]/[**683**]/[**684**]	Great plague in Britain, Cadwalladr ap Cadwallon died /
	Plague in Ireland / A great earthquake in Man.
[**717**]/[718]	Osred died / Consecration of the church of St Michael.
[**721**]/[722]	Hot summer / Beli ab Elphin died; the Britons won three battles.
[**735**]/[736]	Bede died / Ougen, king of the Picts, died.
[775]/[**776**]/[777]/[778]	Ffernfail ab Ithael died / Cinaed, king of the Picts, died /
	Abbot Cuthbert died / The South Britons laid waste by Offa.
[**795**]/[**796**]	The first coming of the gentiles to (the south of) Ireland/
	Offa (Mercia) and Maredudd (Dyfed) died; battle of Rhuddlan.

Isolated annals are more unusual. Of these fourteen singletons, only two have no Irish parallel, and are legendary British events (italicized).

[**457**]	Patrick goes to the Lord.
[**468**]	The death of Bishop Benignus
[**501**]	Bishop Ebur rests in Christ.
[*516*]	Battle of Badon.
[**521**]	St. Columba born; the death of St. Brigid.
[**537**]	Battle of Camlann; a mortality in Britan and Ireland.
[**544**]	The sleep of Ciaran.
[**547**]	A great mortality; Maelgwn, king of Gwynedd, ceased.
[**558**]	Gabran, son of Dungart, died.
[**562**]	Columba came (*exiit*) to Britain.
[**570**]	Gildas died.

158

[*580*]	Gwrgi and Peredur died.
[**584**]	War against Man; the burial of Daniel of the Bangors.
[**589**]	The conversion of Constantine to the Lord.

Kathleen Hughes posited a "north British chronicle" running from [617] to [777] (see Fig. 2i and 2ii).[77] But, as we have seen, this crosses a boundary between two periods of the chronicle with distinct characteristics, indicated by the lacuna from 690 to 703 and the omission of Ecgfrith (died 685) from the series of Northumbrian rulers. Furthermore, the seventh century ([617] – [689]) appears to give the view from North and East Wales of the wars of the Welsh and their Mercians allies against Northumbria, with only eight out of twenty-four annals being "northern" in character, whereas in the eighth century to [777] twelve out of the seventeen annals are decisively "northern," including annals noting the deaths of three kings of Strathclyde ([722], [750], [760]), two kings of the Picts ([736], [776]), and a battle between the Picts and the Britons ([750]).[78] So, rather than an homogeneous "north British chronicle" running from [617] to [777], there appears to be a North Welsh chronicle running from [617] to [689], and a North British chronicle running from [704] to [777].

4. The last century, 855 to 954

The Harleian chronicle from [855] to [954] pursues the themes introduced by the hypothetical chronicle of 854. There is only one reference to St. David's (Menevia, Mynyw) before 800, after that the St. David's interest becomes somewhat stronger:

---

[77] Hughes, *The A-text*, 94f, and more explicitly in *The Welsh Latin Chronicles*, 72f. See also now Thomas Charles-Edwards, *Wales and the Britons: 350–1064* (Oxford 2013), 346–359.

[78] Nicholas Evans, "The Irish Chronicles and the British to Anglo-Saxon Transition in Seventh-century Northumbria," *The Medieval Chronicle* 7 (2011), 15–38, found little evidence for direct connection with the seventh-century Irish parallels: the latter describe the same events but with very different wordings and accounts, with Welsh names for the locations of battles.

[645] The monastery of David (*cenobium dauid*) is burnt.

[810] The burning of Mynyw.

[840] Bishop Nobis reigns in Mynyw.

[873] Nobis dies.[79]

[906] Mynyw (St. David's) stormed or broken into (*fracta est*).

[907] Gorchewyl dies (possibly a bishop of Mynyw; **B** calls him *episcopus*).

[908] Asser dies (probably never bishop of Mynyw).

[944] Lunberth, bishop in Mynyw, dies.

[946] Eneurys, bishop of Mynyw, dies.

And the descent of Hywel Dda and his family from Merfyn ap Gwriad is noted in some detail:

[844] †**Merfyn Frych** ap Gwriad.	**Great-grandfather**.
[877] †**Rhodri Mawr** ap <u>Merfyn Frych.</u>	**Grandfather**.
[877] †Gwriad ap Rhodri Mawr.	Uncle.
[892] †**Hyfaidd** ap Bleddri	Father-in-law's father.
[894] **Anarawd** ap Rhodri ravages Ceredigion.	Uncle.
[903] †Merfyn ap Rhodri Mawr.	Uncle.
[903] †**Llywarch** ap Hyfaidd	Father-in-law.
[904] †**Rhodri** ab Hyfaidd	Father-in-law's brother.
[909] †**Cadell** ap Rhodri Mawr.	**Father**.
[915] †**Anarawd** ap Rhodri Mawr.	Uncle.
[919] †**Clydog** ap Cadell.	**Brother**.
[928] **Hywel Dda** goes to Rome.	**Himself**.
[939] †Meurig (ap Clydog ap Cadell?).	Nephew?
[939] †Hyfaidd ap Clydog ap Cadell.	Nephew.
[943] †Elise ab Anarawd.	Cousin.
[943] †**Idwal Foel** ab Anarawd.	Cousin.
[946] †Cyngen ab Elise ab Anarawd.	Cousin[once removed].
[950] †**Hywel Dda** ap Cadell ap Rhodri Mawr.	**Himself.**
[954] †Rhodri ap Hywel Dda.	**Son.**

---

[79] Asser tells us his kinsman, Bishop Nobis, was expelled from his see by a king *Hemeid*, who is almost certainly Hyfaidd ap Bleddri who died in [892]. See William Henry Stevenson, *Asser's Life of King Alfred* (Oxford: Clarendon Press, 1904), §79, p. 65. The otherwise obscure Catgueithen, who was expelled [862] and died in [882], is possibly another ecclesiastic.

HENRY GOUGH-COOPER

Parallels to events (and, indeed, notices of Irish rulers) also found in the Irish annals appear again; there are eight of these parallels in the three 19-year cycles after 854, compared with only one, and that concerning a Welsh prince,[80] in the three previous cycles. However, the evidence now suggests more information being passed from Wales to Ireland ([816], [877], [909], [915], [917], [950]) than from Ireland to Wales ([878], [887], [942]).

The annal for [856], as noted above, appears to be two years short of the true AD date for the death of Kenneth McAlpine (858), and there is a possible lacuna of two to three years in all the Welsh chronicles between [854] and [858]. Curiously, the Anglo-Saxon chronicles also have a lacuna between 855 and 860.[81] Comparing the various sources here perhaps allows us to reconstruct the true chronology of the annals after allowing for the leap from 854 to 858.

AC A, B, C, P and **S**, 854–867 schema.
Evidence for a lacuna at the end of the chronicle of 854:

True AD	A	B	C	P	S
854	[854] †Cinnen rex.	†Cengen.	†Eygen	(850+4)	'854'
(855?)	(empty annal)	(three missing	(three missing		
(856?)	(two missing annals?)	annals?)	annals?)		
(857?)					
858	[856] †Cemoyoth rex; †Ionathan princeps.	Ceinod; Ionathan.	(empty)	(850+6)	'856'
(859?)	(empty annal)	(empty)	(empty)		
(860?)	(empty annal)	(empty)	(empty)		
(861?)	(empty annal)	(empty)	(empty)		
	(empty annal)		(empty)		
	(empty annal)		(empty)		
862	(missing annal?)	†Mailsachlen	†Matusalem	'860'	'860'
(863?)	[862] Catgueithen	Catweithen	(empty)	(860+2)	'862'
(864?)	(empty annal)	(missing?)	(empty)	(860+3)	'863'
(865?)	[864] Duta	Dutta	(empty)		
			(empty)		
(866?)	[865] †Cian	†Chian	†Kenan	(860+5)	'865'
867	[866] York	York	York	(860+6)	'866'

---

[80] **A** [816] Cinan rex moritur; AU '815' [816] Conan m. Ruadhrach rex Britonum.
[81] Michael Swanton, ed. and trans., *The Anglo-Saxon Chronicles* (London: Phoenix Press, 2000), henceforth ASC.

From [862] to [919] the annals appear to be one year in <u>arrears</u> of the true AD date;[82]
From [938] to [954] the annals appear to be one year in <u>advance</u> of the true AD date.

In **A**, the annals from the later ninth century to the second decade of the tenth show a general tendency to be a year in arrears of the external dates. For example, the death of Rhodri ap Merfyn is noted at **A** [877], AU '877' [878]; the death of Alfred, king of Wessex at **A** [900], 899 (HBC[83]; but ASC 901); of Asser at **A** [908], 908/909 (BEASE[84]); Æthelflaed at **A** [917], 918 (HBC). Only the siege of Alclud (Dumbarton) **A** [870] accords with AU '869' [870], and the death of Cadell ap Rhodri **A** [909] with CS [909].

After 930, this trend is reversed, with the annals being placed one year in advance of the true AD dates. So, Brunanburh is noted at **A** [938] for 937 (ASC); the death of Æthelstan at **A** [940] for 939 (27 October: HBC); the death of Eadmund at **A** [947] for 946 (26 May: HBC); Hywel Dda at **A** [950], AU '949' [950].

This underlines the conjecture, first mooted by Molly Miller,[85] that the 532-year Great Paschal Cycle frame of the Harleian text is an artificial and secondary feature of the annals, with which the compiler of **A** has struggled to synchronise the annals of his source or sources. The last notated annal of **A**, [954], falls rather too neatly on the last year of its 51st decade, marked "dx." None of the extant versions of the chronicle of 954, the hypothetical source of **A**, are wholly accurate copies of their source, but this source can possibly be reconstructed by comparing **A**, **B** and **C**. The only section of the chronicle which was almost certainly derived directly from an actual paschal table is the "Abergele" chronicle of 854.

The lapse in the annals from 922 to 936, during which there is only one annal at [928] suggests that there could be at least two different periods of

---

[82] The annals at [921] and [928] appear to be "true" by comparative annal count but lack external confirmation.

[83] E. B. Fryde et al., *Handbook of British Chronology* (Cambridge: Cambridge University Press, 2003).

[84] Michael Lapidge et al., *The Blackwell Encyclopaedia of Anglo-Saxon England* (Oxford: Blackwell, 2001).

[85] Molly Miller, "Final Stages."

compilation here, or perhaps a compilation from two different sources.[86] Most perplexing is the persistent chronological error in the annals closest to the presumed date of the compilation of the chronicle (954–5). This suggests that the chronology of the paschal cycle was no longer understood, or that the chronicle, or the various sources for it, had become separated from its paschal table or tables, and there was then a botched attempt at a reunion. Misreading of annalistic notes written between the lines of a paschal table cannot be ruled out, where the annals written between the lines could be read either (correctly) as referring to the year below (i.e. the annals are written above the line), or (erroneously) to the year above (see Fig. 1).

The only indication of the paschal cycle in the other Welsh Latin chronicles for the fifth to tenth centuries is in **C**, where its annal c8 notes the first year of a decennovenal cycle (AD 684), but this was almost certainly inserted as part of the wholesale restructuring of an ancestor of **C** in the early thirteenth century.[87] There are certainly at this stage no signs of the paschal cycle in **B** or in the Welsh vernacular chronicles. **B** has a single annal noting the first year of a decennovenal cycle, b1201 *1179* (= AD 1178).[88] **P** and **S** have the first years of decennovenal cycles indicated in some of their annals for the eleventh and early twelfth centuries (**S** '1024' = 1026; **P** and **S** '1062' = 1064; **P** and **S** '1081' = 1083; **S** '1100' = 1102). This appears to indicate that the source of **P** and **S** for the later eleventh and early tenth century was structured by 19-year cycles, but without an AD apparatus, and that the attempt to add an AD apparatus at some later date (possibly as late as the end of the thirteenth century) was largely unsuccessful. The continuous chronological apparatus of **S**, (*Brenhinoedd y Saeson*), goes severely awry after 890, dropping two or three years behind the true AD date, probably because it was attempting to follow the same source as **B**, or **B** itself, which is deficient in annals (too few years) after [885].[89]

---

[86] A final run of annals extracted from a 19-year cycle running from 931 to 950 would be a distinct possibility.

[87] For an analysis of the decennovenal apparatus of **C**, see Henry Gough-Cooper, "Decennovenal Reason and Unreason in the C-text of Annales Cambriae," *The Medieval Chronicle* 11 (2018), 195–212.

[88] The stated chronology of **B** is a year in advance here. **C** also notes this *primus decemnouenalis* of 1178, (c498).

[89] Compared with the 510 annals in **A** from [445] to [954], **B** has only 504.

Conclusion

This analysis seems to show that a North Welsh chronicle of 854 was probably the basis from which the extant tenth-century Welsh chronicle was compiled, and that the annals for 798–854 were copied directly from annalistic notes in an actual paschal table, probably consisting of three 19-year cycles, 798–816, 817–835, 836–854, kept somewhere in northern Wales. This would seem to be the earliest Welsh annalistic chronicle, and its chronology was regulated by the Easter table or tables in which it appeared as glosses to the paschal data. This was extended backwards after 854 to incorporate reasonably chronologically accurate annals for the eighth century dependent on a north British source, possibly a Northumbrian set of annals, or annalistic notes, which found their way to north Wales, possibly via Mercia, and into which were interpolated a few Welsh events, the north British notices extending from [704] to [777] followed by some Mercian events of the late eighth century. The Welsh historical horizon in the ninth century would seem to have extended back not much beyond the mid-eighth century, perhaps only as far as the death of Rhodri Molwynog [754]. Before 700 lies the final period of the British 'heroic age,' the wars with the Northumbria kingdom of the seventh century.[90] Although the chronology for these wars probably depends on an Irish annalistic chronicle, the content appears to be from a Welsh narrative source or sources. Before 615, and back to the mid-fifth century, the annals are heavily dependent on an Irish annalistic source with which some legendary Welsh material has been synchronised. The fact that Irish parallels start to appear again after the mid-ninth century might indicate that in its entirety this fifth to eighth century preface to the chronicle of 798–854 was a tenth century compilation. A major component of the chronicle for the last century (854–954) is the tracing in some detail of the descendants of Merfyn ap Gwriad (died [844]) down to Hywel Dda ap Cadell and his son Rhodri ap Hywel

---

[90] There is a marginal note in the manuscript of **C** against its annal for 689 *anno domini dclxxxix Britanorum regni finis* ("In the year of the Lord 689, the end of the kingdom of the Britons"). The Welsh vernacular annals, **P**, **R** and **S** commence at this juncture as continuations of Geoffrey of Monmouth's *De gestis Britonum*, in which the last British king, *Cadualadrus*, dies in Rome in 689; Michael D. Reeve (ed.) and Neil Wright (transl.), *The History of the Kings of Britain* (Woodbridge: Boydell, 2009), *Liber XI*, §206. **A** does not contain the Galfridian reflexes evident in **C**.

(died [954]), and this, coupled with the increased St. David's interest, suggests the whole was indeed a tenth-century compilation written to reflect the hegemony of Hywel's kingdom of Deheubarth over most of Wales, in which St. David's was now the preeminent episcopal see.[91]

The chronological evidence is for a Chronicle of 854 (the "Abergele" chronicle) and for a Chronicle of 954 (a St. David's chronicle, ancestral to **A, B, C, P, R,** and **S**). The Chronicle of 854 consisted of three 19-year cycles 798–854. The Chronicle of 954 was a scholarly compilation made up from the expanded Chronicle of 854 (extended backwards from 768 by 19-year increments to include Pope Leo's Easter reform of 455 and populated with items from an Irish chronicle, Welsh legend and heroic history of the seventh century, and an eighth century North British chronicle supplemented with a few Welsh and Mercian notices), and two continuations of it, the first from c. 858 to c. 920, the second from c. 935 to c. 950. The whole was then 'enshrined' in a frame of 532+1 years, symbolic of Christian unity and orthodoxy. In assigning annals to this 532-year cycle, the final redactor made several chronological errors, including failing to correctly synchronise his two annalistic sources for the last century (855–954) with the years of the cycle.

---

[91] **A** does not make explicit the connection between Merfyn Frych ap Gwriad (d. 844) and the earlier dynasty of Gwynedd. Merfyn's claim to the throne of Gwynedd was probably through marriage to Esyllt, the daughter of the previous ruler, Cynan Dindaethwy ap Rhodri Molwynog (d. 816; Bartrum, *A Welsh Classical Dictionary*, s.n. Merfyn Frych ap Gwriad). The contest in Môn between Merfyn's father-in-law, Cynan ap Rhodri, and Hywel Farf-fehinog ap Caradog is recorded in **A** [813], [814], [816]. Ancestors of Cynan ap Rhodri are noted, with some gaps in the generations, back to Maelgwn Gwynedd whose death **A** places in [547]. The whole of **A** provides a broad genealogical conspectus of the two dynasties of Gwynedd; but the second, the dynasty founded by Merfyn Frych, while covering a shorter period, is much more detailed and continuous than the first. So, it may be that this was the later ninth-and tenth-century view of notable rulers of Gwynedd prior to Rhodri ap Merfyn, whose claim to Gwynedd was through his mother's line, rather than a dynastic record as such.

Visualising the Elite in Early Irish Society

Mary Leenane

Early Irish literature advances a variety of characters with some appearing quite fleetingly and others fulfilling more pivotal roles. Cultivated in an evolving socio-political and ecclesiastical cultural matrix, such characterisations are not static but multifaceted. However, these are often moulded around an understanding of the crux of a character, such as Cú Chulainn's depiction as the warrior-hero of the so-called Ulster Cycle. A highly complex figure, evidence reveals a biographical emphasis in portrayals of him, perhaps reflecting a desire to create a more 'realistic' figure. Cú Chulainn's attachment to a specific landscape, namely Emain Macha and the region to the south of this, conceivably, also cultivates a more coherent and plausible personage.[1] Surviving evidence points to an appreciable effort to visualise not only Cú Chulainn but also other high-status figures, such as Conchobar, Medb, Cormac mac Airt, and Conaire Mór.[2] A somewhat peripheral and largely understudied area, this material merits consideration as a facet of early medieval character and narrative

---

[1] A biographical impetus as an aspect of character creation for at least some Ulster Cycle figures is advanced in Mary Leenane, "Character creation in the Ulster Cycle," in *Proceedings of the Second European Symposium in Celtic Studies, Bangor University*, ed. Raimund Karl and Katharina Möller (Hagen/Westfalen: Curach Bhán, 2018), 103–17. Mary Leenane reviews Cú Chulainn's case in detail in a forthcoming publication arising from the paper, "Tracing Cú Chulainn's characterisation in the Ulster Cycle," presented at the Fifth International Conference on the Ulster Cycle, 18–20 March 2016, Maynooth University. Mary Leenane argues for an underlying theme of landscape as a component of characterisation in a forthcoming article stemming from the paper, "Positioning characters in the Ulster Cycle," presented at the joint meeting of the Ulster and Finn Cycle Conferences, 13–17 June 2018, Sabhal Mór Ostaig, Isle of Skye.

[2] Of a corpus of twelve well-known tales from the Ulster Cycle, Ranko Matasović, identifies seventy descriptive passages with thirty-nine of these referring to men and six to women, confirming interest in this kind of material, "Descriptions in the Ulster Cycle," in *Ulidia 2: Proceedings of the Second International Conference on the Ulster Cycle of Tales, National University of Ireland, Maynooth, 24–27 June 2005*, ed. Ruairí Ó hUiginn and Brian Ó Catháin (Maynooth: An Sagart, 2009), 95–105 at 96–7.

166

creation. Entries of this kind broadly concur, underlining physical beauty and fine, colourful clothing as a mechanism to express the notion of authority; an important societal concern. Representations of Cú Chulainn serve as a good platform from which to establish the main thrust of these kinds of written visualisations. Some consideration will also be given to descriptions of other significant personages and to evidence from legal texts. It is proposed in this paper that these depictions can be better understood when considered alongside contemporaneous illustrations of male forms, attested in the religious iconographies of the insular illuminated gospel books and the Irish high crosses. Additionally, this interdisciplinary approach offers insight into male perceptions of male beauty, broader society and the narrative creation process.

Firstly, we will look at references to Cú Chulainn's appearance in early Irish prose material from the Ulster Cycle in order to get a sense of the way in which he is visualised by medieval writers who were predominantly, if not exclusively, male. Varying in date, these range from brief references to one or two features, to more substantial descriptions, confirming different approaches in the treatment of this kind of material. For example, *Brislech Mór Maige Muirthemne* includes this information, but other early tales, like *Verba Scáthaige*, *Forfess Fer Fálgae* and the oldest account of *Tochmarc Emire*, do not.[3] However, Emer and Úathach are smitten with the hero in the latter text, intimating his pleasing aspect; possibly an established part of his persona often with no need for a concomitant description.[4] The original beginning of the tale, which is now lost, may have supplied this detail. While some variations are apparent, extant data points to at least some

---

[3] Proposed as a reworked eighth-century tale, Bettina Kimpton's edition and translation of the text is used here, *The Death of Cú Chulainn: A Critical Edition of the Earliest Version of Brislech Mór Maige Muirthemni with Introduction, Translation, Notes, Bibliography and Vocabulary* (Maynooth: School of Celtic Studies, 2009). Perhaps a little earlier, Patrick L. Henry's edition of Verba Scáthaige is consulted here, "Verba Scáthaige," *Celtica* 21 (1990): 191–207. Reference is to Kuno Meyer's edition of Forfess Fer Falgae, again dating to the eighth century, "Forfess Fer Fálgae," *Zeitschrift für celtische Philologie* 8 (1912): 564–5. Likewise, an eighth-century date can be proposed for the earliest account of Tochmarc Emire and again Kuno Meyer's work is consulted here, "The oldest version of Tochmarc Emire," *Revue Celtique* 11 (1890): 433–57.

[4] Meyer, "The Oldest Version of *Tochmarc Emire*," 442–7.

underlying themes in the visualisation of Cú Chulainn and other important figures. Arguably, idealised appearances are proffered through descriptions of high-status figures, particularly males, in documentary sources.

Táin Bó Cúailnge (hereafter: the *Táin*) offers the most complete portraiture of Cú Chulainn in the prime of his life, immediately after his ferocious *ríastrad* or 'distortion' towards the latter part of the tale:

> *Faircsi trí folt fair: dond fri toind cind, cróderg ar medón, mind órbude ardatugethar. Caín cocarsi ind fuilt sin co curend teóra imsrotha im c[h]lais a chúlaid, comba samalta 7 órṡnáth cach finna fathmainnech forscaílte forórda dígrais dúalfota derscaigt[h]ech dathálaind dara formna síar sell sechtair. Cét cairches corcorglan do dergór órlasrach imma brágit. Cét snáthéicne don charmocol cummascda hi timthacht fria chend. Cethri tibri cechtar a dá grúad .i. tibre buide 7 tibre úane 7 tibre gorm 7 tibre corcra. Secht ngemma do ruthin ruisc cechtar a dá rígrosc. Secht meóir cechtar a dá choss, secht méoir cechtar a dá lám co ngabáil ingni sebaic, co forgabáil ingne griúin ar cach n-aí fo leith díib-sin.*

He seemed to have three kinds of hair: dark next to his skin, blood-red in the middle and hair like a crown of gold covering them outside. Fair was the arrangement of that hair with three coils in the hollow in the nape of his neck, and like gold thread was each fine hair, loose-flowing, bright golden, excellent, long-tressed, splendid and of beautiful colour, which fell back over his shoulders. A hundred bright crimson ringlets of flaming red-gold encircled his neck. Around his head a hundred strings interspersed with carbuncle-gems. Four shades (?) in each of his cheeks, a yellow shade and a green, a blue shade and a purple. Seven brilliant gem-like pupils in each of his noble eyes. Seven toes on each of his feet; seven fingers on

168

each of his hands with the grasp of a hawk's claws and the
grip of a hedgehog's claws in each separate toe and finger.[5]

Aside from the recording of his additional digits, this account focuses
very much on Cú Chulainn's head and face, with specific mention of his
multi-pupiled eyes, multi-hued cheeks, and hair. *Serglige Con Chulainn,
Fled Bricrenn* and the considerably reworked Middle Irish version of
Tochmarc Emire offer slightly less detailed profiles. The latter two texts
display significant parallels and these also note his fine apparel. These three
tales outline his colourful aspect, multiple pupils, blackened eyebrows, and
his unusual hair, though the latter is omitted in *Tochmarc Emire*. His blood
red lips are confirmed in *Síaburcharpat Con Culainn* with his teeth likened
to a shower of pearls in *Tochmarc Emire* and *Fled Bricrenn*, traits also
assigned to other characters in early Irish literature.[6]

The detailed description from the *Táin*, provided above, displays a
disproportionate interest in his hair, noting its hue, condition, length, and

---

[5] I will largely focus on the first recension of the text here though conscious of the
potential of gaining further insights through a comparative analysis of material from
the second recension. The edition used is that of Cecile O'Rahilly, ed. and trans., *Táin
Bó Cúailnge, Recension I* (Dublin: Dublin Institute for Advanced Studies, 1976), ll.
2342–53, 189. This lengthy description largely parallels the account of the hero in
Recension II of the *Táin*, Cecile O'Rahilly, ed. and trans., *Táin Bó Cúalnge from the
Book of Leinster* (Dublin: Dublin Institute for Advanced Studies, 1967) at ll. 2344–56.
The latter offers the only detailed profile of the child hero to include his physical
features, with the first recension highlighting only his clothing of a hooded tunic, blue
mantle secured with a silver brooch, ibid., ll. 1198–207, O'Rahilly, *Táin Bó Cúailnge,
Recension I*, ll. 818–9. Arguably, the coalescing of boy and adult profiles in
Recension II reflects a later fine tuning of this aspect of his persona.

[6] These details occur as follows in *Serglige Con Culainn,* Myles Dillon, *Serglige
Con Culainn* (Dublin: Dublin Institute for Advanced Studies, 1953), 21–2; *Fled
Bricrenn*, George Henderson, *Fled Bricrend*, Irish Texts Society 2 (London and
Dublin: Irish Texts Society, 1899), 62–3; the later account of *Tochmarc Emire*,
Anton G. van Hamel, *Compert Con Culainn and other stories*, Mediaeval and
Modern Irish Series 3 (Dublin: Dublin Institute for Advanced Studies, 1933), 16–
68 at 25; *Síaburcharpat Con Culainn*, Richard I. Best and Osborn Bergin, *Lebor
na hUidre:* Book of the Dun Cow (Dublin: Hodges, Figgis, 1929), 278–87 at 279
and the latter also mentions his dark eyebrows, a feature also attested in *Mesca
Ulad*, J. Carmichael Watson, *Mesca Ulad*, Mediaeval and Modern Irish Series 13
(Dublin: Dublin Institute for Advanced Studies, 1941), 24.

style. Its tri-colouration is somewhat of a standout feature with the sparkling, golden, outer layer attracting the most attention. Whether Cú Chulainn's hair is described as wavy or curly, or groomed into what could be three shoulder-length coils, it is sometimes likened to a golden crown by onlookers, such as Fer Diad in the *Táin* and Erc mac Cairpre in his early death tale, *Brislech Mór Maige Muirthemne*.[7] A highly visible if not defining trait, this crown is not unique to Cú Chulainn but one shared with noble men, such as Conchobar in the tale, *Aided Chonchobuir*, and Níall Noígiallach in Cúán Úa Lothcháin's poetic account of Níall's life.[8]

The attribution of at least some of the observations on Cú Chulainn's splendid appearance to women intimates his appeal to the opposite sex. The women of Munster and Connacht clamber up onto the shoulders of the menfolk to catch a glimpse of the hero after he displays himself to the women of Ulster in the previously mentioned extract from the *Táin*. Úathach is rendered speechless upon seeing his *delb* 'shape' in the earliest account of *Tochmarc Emire*. In the later reworked version of the text, the women equally adore him on account of *ar chaími a gnúise, ar sercaigi a dreiche* 'the beauty of his face and for the irresistibility (lit. loveableness) of his appearance.'[9] The text adds that he is bestowed with the gift of beauty

---

[7] O'Rahilly, *Táin Bó Cúailnge, Recension I*, ll. 2959–65; Kimpton, *Brislech Mór Maige Muirthemni*, 19. Fand also acknowledges the unusual threefold coloring of his hair in *Serglige Con Culainn*, Dillon, *Serglige Con Culainn*, 21. Alternatively, he appears to have bright, red, curly hair in *Fled Bricrenn*, Henderson, *Fled Bricrend*, 62.
[8] Kuno Meyer, *The Death-Tales of the Ulster Heroes*, Todd Lecture Series 14 (Dublin: Royal Irish Academy, 1906), 8; Maud Joynt, "Echtra mac Echdach Mugmedóin," *Ériu* 4 (1910): 91–111 at 94–5. Lug mac Ethnenn and Conchobar are also described as having long, curly, golden hair in the *Táin*, O'Rahilly, *Táin Bó Cúailnge, Recension I*, l. 2093, ll. 3593–4. Elatha, king of the Fomori, is also adorned with shoulder-length, golden hair, Elizabeth Gray, ed. and transl. *Cath Maige Tuired: The Second Battle of Moytura*, Irish Texts Society 52 (London: Irish Texts Society, 1982), 26.
[9] O'Rahilly, *Táin Bó Cúailnge, Recension I*, ll. 2335–70; Meyer, "*Tochmarc Emire*," 446; van Hamel, *Compert Con Culainn*, 21. Translation from Damian McManus, "Good-looking and irresistible: the hero from early Irish saga to classical poetry," *Ériu* 59 (2009): 57–109 at 69–70. Leborcham acknowledges his fair countenance in his early death tale, Kimpton, *Brislech Mór Maige Muirthemni*, 14–5 and Feidelm is equally impressed with his appealing visage in the *Táin*, O'Rahilly, *Táin Bó Cúailnge, Recension I*, ll. 71–2.

and this is noted as one of his three failings along with being too young and too daring. Indeed, evidence intimates a little more emphasis on the beauteous aspect of his persona in this later version of the *Tochmarc Emire* tale.[10]

Lóeg mac Riangabra's counsel to Cú Chulainn to seek grooming from Emer in preparation for his contest with Fer Diad in the *Táin* underlines a preference for a carefully manicured male appearance. It is anticipated that Fer Diad will present similarly, freshly bathed and beautified. Here, his groomed aspect is deemed important to the predominantly male audience who come to witness the fight. Fer Diad also expresses an interest in Cú Chulainn's appearance prior to the fight, asking his charioteer to describe him. Fer Diad duly criticises him for extolling Cú Chulainn's beautiful presentation too highly.[11] Extant prose texts are not short on references to the delightful appearances of elite men, and it seems that this attribute was important, if not prioritised as an essential trait by the medieval writers, who were largely writing to a male audience. Arguably, this quality is equally important, if not more so, to men. As mentioned above, Cú Chulainn's pleasing aspect is announced in several different tales, inculcating this as an important part of his persona. Conchobar's and Noísiu's appealing aspect is also detailed in the *Táin* and *Longes mac nUislenn*, respectively, and the collective beauty of the Ulster warriors is confirmed at the start of *Tochmarc Emire*.[12]

While the intention in this paper is not to interpret each individual feature, these descriptions of Cú Chulainn underline his striking–even exceedingly seductive–appearance endorsing his heroic status while delineating another facet in his characterisation. Arguably, only this hero's body can accommodate such 'extra' features as many pupils, dimples, and tresses of hair infused with an array of colours. His scintillating beauty sets him apart from other figures and is designed to amaze the medieval imagination. Interestingly, the attributes assigned to Cú Chulainn display parallels with the portrayal of female beauty in early Irish literature. For

---

[10] van Hamel, *Compert Con Culainn*, 21–2.

[11] O'Rahilly, *Táin Bó Cúailnge, Recension I*, ll. 2806 –14, ll. 2943–76.

[12] Ibid., ll. 3591–623; Vernam Hull, *Longes mac n-Uislenn: The Exile of the Sons of Uisliu*, The Modern Language Association of America 16 (New York: The Modern Language Association of America, 1949), 45, 50; van Hamel, *Compert Con Culainn*, 21.

example, the *femme fatale* of the narrative, *Longes mac nUislenn*, Deirdriu, is furnished with long, curling, blonde hair, reddish cheeks, pearly-white teeth, and blood-red lips. Feidelm also has long styled (braided) hair, blackened eyebrows, red lips, pearly-white teeth–even multiple pupils–in the *Táin*.[13]

The hair and facial features of kings are somewhat similarly represented. Conaire Mór's perfect form, notably his eyes, hair, and whiteness are extolled in the saga, *Togail Bruidne Da Derga*.[14] The whiteness of Cormac mac Airt's body and teeth, the redness of his lips, the colour of his cheeks, eyes, and eyebrows all affirm his suitability for royal office in the tale, *Echtra Cormaic*. Damian McManus rightly argues for an emphasis on a facial aspect rather than an Olympian frame, on beauty rather than brawn, on "dazzling colours but in particular on dazzling brightness: not of the king's regal bejewelled attire, but of his body itself."[15] The paltry concern with the physique of male heroic figures, especially Cú Chulainn's, would no doubt surprise a modern audience. The advancing of colourful, ornate, and pretty features appears to align more naturally with female characters. However, this effeminate sense of beauty is not only shared by elite men but is intrinsic to the idealised perceptions of them. These writings likely reflect the concerns and perceptions of the male dominated religious houses in which they are created, and it is important to appreciate this. At the very least, an aesthetic kind of beauty is prioritised for elite men in the literature, and this might intimate the male writers' admiration and, perhaps, desire for such idealized male forms. Although it is not possible to delve further into the potential evidence for homoerotic leanings as a factor in these written depictions, this will be explored in a subsequent study. This will also include a consideration of the possible influence of classical

---

[13] Hull, Longes mac n-Uislenn, 43–44; O'Rahilly, *Táin Bó Cúailnge, Recension I*, ll. 29–39.

[14] Eleanor Knott, *Togail Bruidne Da Derga*, Mediaeval and Modern Irish Series 8 (Dublin: Dublin Institute for Advanced Studies, 1936), 32.

[15] Whitley Stokes, "The Irish ordeals, Cormac's adventure in the Land of Promise, and the decision as to Cormac's sword," *Irische Texte* 3 (1891): 183–229 at 186. See McManus, "Good-looking and irresistible," 57–74 for a further discussion of the representation of beauty in early Irish literature. The dazzling whiteness of Cú Chulainn's breast is underlined in the Táin, O'Rahilly, *Táin Bó Cúailnge, Recension I*, l. 2354–6.

sources on the development of ideas and imageries around male beauty on the continent and in early Irish society. Crucially, it would be interesting to ascertain the kinds of similarities and differences in the visualisation of heroes, such as Cú Chulainn and Achilles. Ranko Matasović remarks that "in none of the four authors that constituted the school curriculum of the Middle Ages (Terence, Virgil, Sallust and Cicero) do we find any descriptions even remotely resembling typical descriptions in the Ulster Cycle. If they use descriptions at all, Roman authors are more interested in the moral characteristics they are writing about."[16] Suetonius is viewed as somewhat of an exception in the provision of this kind of detail for Augustus in *De Vita Caesarum* with a concern for the impact of a man's physical features on his moral character. Nevertheless, mention of Achilles' snow-white countenance and shiny-golden locks in the *Achilleid* seems familiar–even alluding to prevailing ideas concerning heroic appearances. A late Roman mosaic from La Olmeda in Spain broadly concurs with this perception of Achilles, thus offering insight into the currency of heroism at the time.[17]

Returning to the early Irish material, it seems that fine clothing further enriches resplendent physical appearances and so an account of Cú Chulainn's clothing follows the lengthy description in the *Táin*, cited above, of his body. Most notably, this centres around his five-folded, bordered, purple mantle which is secured with a brooch of mixed metal:

---

[16] Matasović, "Descriptions in the Ulster Cycle," 102–5. The influence of classical works on the Ulster Cycle literature, and indeed characters, is worth noting. See Brent Miles, *Heroic Saga and Classical Epic in Medieval Ireland* (Woodbridge: Boydell & Brewer, 2011); Ralph O'Connor, *Classical Literature and Learning in Medieval Irish Narrative* (Woodbridge: D.S. Brewer, 2014); Michael Clarke, "Achilles, Bryhtnoth, Cú Chulainn: continuity and analogy from Homer to the medieval north," in *Epic interactions: perspectives on Homer, Virgil and the epic tradition presented to Jasper Griffin by former pupils*, ed. Michael Clarke et al. (Oxford: Oxford University Press, 2006), 243–71; Máire Ní Mhaonaigh, "The Hectors of Ireland and the Western World," in *Sacred Histories: A festschrift for Máire Herbert*, ed. Kevin Murray and Catríona Ó Dochartaigh (Dublin: Four Courts Press, 2015), 258–68.

[17] "Statius Achilleid 1," Classical Texts Library, accessed November 30, 2019, https://www.theoi.com/Text/StatiusAchilleid1A.html; "Mosaic of the Oecus Achilles in Skyros," Villa Romana La Olmeda, accessed November 30, 2019, https://www.villaromanalaolmeda.com/en/villa/image/download/high-resolution/mosaic-oecus-achilles-skyros.

Gabaid-seom dano a dílat n-óenaig n-imbi in láa sin. Baí dá étgud immi .i. fúan caín cóir corcorglan corthorach cóicdíabuil. Delg find findargit arna ecor d'ór intlassi úasa bánbruinni gel imar bad lóc[h]rand lánsolusta nád chumgaitis súili doíni déicsin ar gleóraidecht 7 glainidecht. Clíabinar sróil sirceda ré chnes congebethar dó co barrúachtar a dondfúathróci donddergi míleta do ṡról ríg.

So on that day he [Cú Chulainn] donned his festive apparel, namely, a fair mantle, well-fitting, bright purple, fringed, five-folded. A white brooch of silver inset with inlaid gold over his white breast as it were a bright lantern that men's eyes could not look at by reason of its brilliance and splendour. Next to his skin he wore a tunic of silky satin reaching to the top of his dark apron, dark-red, soldierly, of royal satin.[18]

This kind of apparel largely represents the fundamental tenets for the narrative expression of elite status across early Irish literature. Comparable depictions survive for Fergus, Medb, and Conchobar, and these are underlined at various points in Recension I of the *Táin* with all wearing purple mantles predominantly secured with a brooch.[19] Cormac mac Airt is also dressed in an expansive purple mantle adorned with a gem-encrusted brooch in *Echtra Cormaic*, and Elatha's garment is embellished with gold and similarly fastened in the tale, *Cath Maige Tuired*. The king of the Uí Maine, Eochu Rond, dons a purple fourfold cloak, hemmed with gold, in the story, *Fled Bricrenn ocus Loinges mac nDuíl Dermait*, and a gold border is also found on Noísiu's purple mantle in *Longes mac nUislenn*.[20] *Brat* most commonly describes a mantle in the literature but other terms

---

[18] O'Rahilly, *Táin Bó Cúailnge, Recension I*, ll. 2352–60, 190.

[19] Ibid., ll. 1302–4, ll. 3206–8, ll. 3594–6.

[20] Stokes, "The Irish ordeals," 186; Gray, *Cath Maige Tuired*, 26. The colour of Elatha's mantle is unspecified. Karina Hollo, *Fled Bricrenn ocus Loinges mac nDuíl Dermait and its Place in the Irish Literary and Oral Narrative Traditions: a Critical Edition with Introduction, Notes, Translation, Bibliography and Vocabulary*, Maynooth Medieval Irish Texts 2 (Maynooth: Department of Old and Middle Irish, National University of Ireland Maynooth, 2005), 54; Hull, *Longes mac n-Uislenn*, 50.

including *fúan* also occur, and *delg* frequently denotes a brooch with *éo* and others also attested. A detailed study of the terms used, their context and etymologies would prove useful but is beyond the remit of this paper.[21]

Purple is clearly aligned with the noble classes and evidence further points to a hierarchical perception of colour. The colours of the mantles of Cormac's three companies at the start of the *Táin* are status-defining; the highest-ranking company don purple mantles while dark-grey and varicoloured ones are reserved for the second and third companies, respectively.[22] The archaeological picture around clothing is unclear owing to a dearth of artefacts. However, if we look to the continent, we can better understand the written visualisations of noble ranks in purple mantles. The special positioning of purple is redolent of its association with imperial authority in the Roman world. Tyrian purple was extracted from the *Murex* seashell, found in the Eastern Mediterranean, and this pigment was an immensely prized commodity, the supply of which was tightly controlled. It was unlikely that Tyrian purple, or materials stained with it, would have reached the western seaboard in any sizable quantity. Nevertheless, this would not have prevented the adoption of the concept of reinforcing elite hierarchies using strong exotic colours. The Old Irish for purple dye, *corcur*, is an early borrowing from Latin *purpura*, indicated by the substitution of a 'c' for a 'p', confirming the Irish monastic community's familiarity with this colour, and more specifically its prestige.[23] This term is used quite freely to capture the colour of the mantles of many important figures, including Medb, Cú Chulainn, Conchobar, Cormac and Eochu Rond etc.

---

[21] Some observations on the terms used to denote brooches are offered by Niamh Whitfield, "More thoughts on the wearing of brooches in early medieval Ireland," in *Irish art historical studies in honour of Peter Harbison*, ed. Colum Hourihane (Dublin: Four Courts Press, 2004), 70–108 at 93–5. A more detailed consideration on the wearing of brooches is also provided.

[22] O'Rahilly, *Táin Bó Cúailnge, Recension I*, ll. 9–16. A similar approach manifests in the accounts of the various factions coming together to support Ulster later in the *Táin*, ibid., ll. 3589–861. We might also look to *Bruiden Da Choca*, where the hues of the mantles, ranging from blue, speckled to purple, allow Cormac Connloinges to segregate three hundred warriors into three groups, Gregory Toner, *Bruiden da Choca*, Irish Texts Society 61 (London, Irish Texts Society, 2007), 106–7.

[23] Damian McManus, "A Chronology of Latin Loan-Words in Early Irish," *Ériu* 34 (1983): 21–71 at 42, 48.

Other materials, such as lichens, dog-whelk, berries, and mixtures of pigments might have been used to stain cloths purple, though with varying degrees of success.[24] The production of dark, vibrant colours may have sufficed, effectively fulfilling the regal connotations of Tyrian purple and, indeed, the dark-red hue dominating the mantles of religious elites in the Book of Kells might be viewed in this light (7v, 32v [Fig. 3], 292r), and we will return to this.[25] Conceivably, the meaning of *corcur/corcair* may not be simply limited to a single colour, but rather a more generic term to imply a wider range of colours, perhaps of a vibrant blue, red or purple hue, yet crucially, intimating superior status.

Legal evidence broadly endorses findings from the narrative literature. The eighth-century legal text dealing with fosterage, *Cáin Íarraith* "The law of the Fosterage Fee," attempts to regulate appropriate clothing. Gem-encrusted, gold brooches are recommended for the sons of provincial kings and silver ones for the sons of lower ranking ones. Clothing of purple (*corcra*) and blue (*gorm*) is prescribed for kings' sons, red (*derg*), grey (*glas*) or brown (*donn*) for the sons of lords, and black (*dub*) and white (*find*) is reserved for the sons of commoners.[26] This is not to say that this system was rigorously applied, but rather this text reinforces perceptions of the ideal, while intimating a concern for appearance. Broadly contemporary archaeological records display similar concepts. Evidence confirms the use of brooches as status symbols, with the late seventh or early eighth-century pseudo-penannular Tara brooch being one of the finer and more recognisable exemplars, though few survive. Interestingly, like Cú Chulainn's brooch recounted in the *Táin*, this Tara brooch is also of

---

[24] See Niamh Whitfield, "Dress and Accessories in the Early Irish Tale 'The Wooing of Becfhola,'" in *Medieval clothing and textiles 2*, ed. Robin Netherton and Gale R. Owen-Crocker (Woodbridge: Boydell Press, 2006), 1–34 at 12.

[25] See images at "Digital Collections: TCD MS 58," Trinity College Dublin, accessed November 30, 2019, https://digitalcollections.tcd.ie/home/index.php?DRIS_ID=MS58_003v.

[26] Daniel A. Binchy, *Corpus Iuris Hibernici* (*CIH*) (Dublin: Dublin Institute for Advanced Studies, 1978), v, 1759.165.21–4; *CIH* v 1759.12–15. See also Fergus Kelly, *Early Irish Farming* (Dublin: Dublin Institute for Advanced Studies, 1997), 263. *Audacht Morainn* reiterates the centrality of clothing to good appearance noting the just ruler's responsibilities towards the production of pleasing garments, Fergus Kelly, *Audacht Morainn*, (Dublin: Dublin Institute for Advanced Studies, 1976), 8.

silver/silver gilt with gold insert panels and additional gemstones. These brooches are preceded by a larger number of zoomorphic penannular archetypes, such as the Ballinderry brooch; a specialised secular production found at a royal crannog site at Ballinderry, Co. Offaly.[27] The survival of other visually appealing–even status-defining metal objects–such as the Moylough belt shrine, the Lagore buckle, and various religious items, including the Derrynaflan Silver Paten, and the Derrynaflan Chalice, confirms a wider societal interest in the aesthetic.[28] Many of these objects boast mixed metals, gemstones, coloured enamels, and millefiori patterns. Interestingly, the intricate design and colouring on Matthew's gown on 21v in the Book of Durrow is reminiscent of these millefiori patterns, and the red and yellow enamel 'squares' or 'tiles' of the similarly dated Moylough belt shrine, reflecting a cross-fertilisation of ideas designed to impress and awe audiences.[29]

---

[27] O'Rahilly, *Táin Bó Cúailnge, Recension I*, ll. 2354–6. Fulfilling a similar function beyond Ireland, the Late Roman period witnesses a transitioning from round unelaborate functional brooches to the wearing of more opulent exemplars by those of varying rank according to Whitfield, "More thoughts on the wearing of brooches in early medieval Ireland," 70–2. For a consideration of the development of brooch styles in early Irish tradition, see Niamh Whitfield, "The "Tara" Brooch: An Irish Emblem of Status in Its European Context," in *From Ireland Coming: Irish art from the Early Christian to the late Gothic Period and Its European context*, ed. Colum Hourihane (Princeton: Princeton University Press, 2001), 211–47. The Ballinderry crannog and associated brooch are discussed by Hugh O'Neill Hencken, "Ballinderry crannog no. 2," *Proceedings of the Royal Irish Academy* 47C (1942): 1–76 at 34–8, figs.12–14.

[28] For a detailed appreciation of the Moylough Belt-Shrine, see Michael J. O'Kelly, "The Belt-Shrine from Moylough, Sligo," *Papers in Honour of Liam Price, Journal of the Royal Society of Antiquaries of Ireland* 95, (1965): 149–88. A detailed account of the various finds at the royal site at Lagore is provided by Hugh O'Neill Hencken, "Lagore crannog: an Irish royal residence of the 7th to 10th centuries A.D," *Proceedings of the Royal Irish Academy* 53C, (1950): 1–247. For a consideration of the Derrynaflan Hoard, see Michael Ryan, "The Derrynaflan Hoard and Early Irish Art," *Speculum* 72, (1997): 995–1017.

[29] Images available at "The Library of Trinity College Dublin," Trinity College Dublin, accessed November 30, 2019, https://www.tcd.ie/library/exhibitions/durrow/ and "A History of Ireland in 100 Objects, a selection," An Post, The Irish Times, National Museum of Ireland, Royal Irish Academy, accessed November 30, 2019, http://100objects.ie/moylough-belt-shrine/. The Iron Age bog bodies

Further insight into the written visualisations of Cú Chulainn and other high-ranking figures from early Irish prose material can be gleaned from the illuminated insular gospel books. It has been observed earlier in this paper that documentary accounts often highlight a pretty facial aspect, including golden hair, and vibrant, if not purple, mantles secured with a brooch. Arguably, a similar intent is expressed in the eighth-century Book of Dimma with prominence also given to the face, hair, and clothing of Matthew, Mark, and Luke. Their golden hair, though styled differently, intimates grooming with the delineation of at least some facial features a little more clearly, most notably the eyes and eyebrows (see Fig. 1).[30]

Their hands and feet seem disproportionately small and delicate with little shoes or booties. Their clothing, construed in three sections; an inverted heart-shaped top, a roughly horseshoe central section and a pair of wing shapes at the bottom, is designed to imply a generous garment of distinctly coloured sections, with finished hems worn over a tunic. The eighth-century Book of Mulling contains more colourfully-illustrated evangelists wearing layered clothing of distinct robe 'folds' replete with edging, with more refined hands; details which are suggestive of enhanced artistic skills. Presumably, this book was produced in a better-resourced and networked monastic house. Again, the representation of their hair is interesting, and though infused with different dyes, Matthew and Mark sport shoulder-length, groomed hair while John's is shorter but golden (see Fig. 2).[31]

---

demonstrate an earlier concern for the aesthetic with the Clonycavan man's upwardly, styled hair achieved using imported "hair-gel" while the hands of the Old Croghan man are smooth with manicured nails. For further discussion, see Eamonn P. Kelly, "An Archaeological Interpretation of Irish Iron Age Bog Bodies," in *The archaeology of violence: interdisciplinary approaches*. The Institute for European and Mediterranean Archaeology Distinguished Monograph Series 2, ed. Sarah Ralph (Albany: State University of New York Press, 2012), 232–40.

[30] See folio 30 "Digital Collections: TCD MS 59," Trinity College Dublin, accessed November 30, 2019, https://digitalcollections.tcd.ie/home/#folder_id=1659&pidto page=MS59_054& entry_point=30.

[31] See folio 12v "Digital Collections: TCD MS 60," Trinity College Dublin, accessed November 30, 2019, https://digitalcollections.tcd.ie/home/#folder_id= 1648& pidtopage= MS60_032&entry_point=32. A chalk white pigment is used extensively in this manuscript, including on the hands, feet and face of the evangelists, Susie

Figure 1. Book of Dimma, MS 59, p. 30

Bioletti and Allyson Smith, "The pigments of early Irish manuscripts," in *An Insular Odyssey: Manuscript culture in early Christian Ireland and beyond*, ed. Rachel Moss, Felicity O'Mahony and Jane Maxwell (Dublin: Four Courts Press, 2017), 114–27 at 123–6.

Figure 2: Book of Mulling, MS 60 fo. 12v

Of a similar date, the Book of Kells signifies a further advancement in illustrative skills and resources, proposing more 'realistic' portraitures but in a similar vein. We find a more sophisticated and cosmopolitan Christ, of slim build, manicured, long hair, of a yellow/golden colour, pronounced eyebrows, beautiful clothing with elongated, elegant hands and feet (see Fig. 3).[32]

Figure 3: Book of Kells, MS 58 fo. 32v

---

[32] See folio 32v "Digital Collections," Trinity College Dublin, accessed November 30, 2019, https://digitalcollections.tcd.ie/home/#folder_id=14&pidto page= MS58_291v&entry_point=64.

Here, Christ dons a dark beard. Overall, these imageries are not incongruous with the written visualisations discussed, with a pretty, colourful facial aspect again prioritised coupled with vibrant clothing of an outer covering garment or mantle worn over a tunic.

These religious portraitures arguably echo, to some degree, the illustrations of the *Codex Amiatinus* (*c*. AD 700), the earliest Latin Vulgate version of the Bible, and perhaps the most accurate surviving copy of St. Jerome's late fourth-century text. This codex was produced as part of a three-copy commission at the monastery at Monkwearmouth-Jarrow, Northumbria, and with little Hiberno-Saxon influence, it was seemingly modelled on late Antique copies–possibly even St. Jerome's own.[33] This deeply influential manuscript looks to antiquity and not to contemporary society to conjure up images of distinguished church leaders. These church books reflect a global vision of the church with God and the evangelists at the top, and these imageries are contrived within the context of a wider European learned landscape. These manuscripts are exclusively ecclesiastical artefacts conceived by, and for, an elite religious grouping of ordained priests and abbots. This literate part of society not only read the texts but also understood their greater symbolisms. Harping back to antiquity, the figures in the *Codex Amiatinus* are clothed in a toga-like garment which wraps around the body, leaving the right hand free, and fastening over the left arm, with a reddish-hue dominating. A similar fastening method is apparent in the imageries in the Book of Kells and the Book of Mulling.

With some palpable resemblances in the written depictions and the portraitures of the illuminated insular gospel books, some distinct differences also emerge; most significantly, the absence of brooches in the portraitures. Nonetheless, if we look to related iconographies carved into the Irish high crosses, religious elites are again dressed in tunics and mantles, but here there is the noticeable inclusion of brooches in at least some instances. The insignia of elite secular office, this alternative feature

---

[33] See Cecila Chazelle, for an appreciation of this manuscript, "Ceolfrid's gift to St. Peter: the first quire of the *Codex Amiatinus* and the evidence of its Roman destination," *Early Medieval Europe* 12 (2003): 129–58. The Mediterranean style of the Ezra portrait, arguably, anticipates its Mediterranean/Roman destination while also demonstrating allegiance to Rome and orthodox doctrine, ibid.,147–8.

is worthy of further consideration. Brooches are attested on the mantles of the religious figures on the West Cross at Kells and, most notably, on the sculpture of Christ on Muiredach's Cross at Monasterboice–high crosses that typically postdate the gospel books by over one hundred years (see Fig. 4).[34]

Figure 4: J. Romilly Allen's sketch of Arrest of Christ scene, Muiredach's cross

In contrast to the closed focus of the gospel manuscripts, these crosses are intrinsically connected with the wider secular community. Kings serve as patrons for a number of the crosses with Flann Sinna, of the Clann Cholmáin, for example, sponsoring the early tenth-century Cross of the

---

[34] John Romilly Allen's sketches of both scenes are reproduced with discussion by Whitfield, "More thoughts on the wearing of brooches in early medieval Ireland," 71–4. The Arrest of Christ scene on Muiredach's Cross is accessible at "Muiredach's High Cross, Monasterboice, Co. Louth," *Irish Archaeology* accessed November 30, 2019, http://irisharchaeology.ie/2017/05/muiredachs-high-cross-monasterboice-co-louth/ and the Baptism of Christ scene on the West Cross at Kells can be viewed at "Holy Well," Ireland's Holy Wells accessed November 30, 2019, http:// Irelands holywells.blogspot.com/2013/06/saint-columbas-well-kells-county-meath.html.

Scriptures at Clonmacnoise.[35] The tenth century is noted as a time of flux around the notion of royal authority and, arguably, this influences the representation of high-status figures on the high crosses and in the literature.[36] Although the high cross imageries typically advance biblical scenes, a very distinctive and evolving native style is palpable.[37] Thus, brooches became emblematic for both elite religious and secular offices, and so, Christ on Muiredach's Cross could be mistaken for a secular prince. Despite some variation in the representation of religious elites in the manuscripts and high crosses, broadly speaking, these are depicted as well-dressed and finely groomed, implying the Church's acceptance of their portrayal as wealthy ecclesiastics.

Overall, evidence intimates substantial agreement in the representation of secular and religious elites: an idealised male form defined by the beautiful appearance of groomed, long, golden hair, delineated eyes and eyebrows, which dons an expansive, bordered, colourful mantle worn over a tunic. At least some of the narrative material might hint towards more specific similarities. Cú Chulainn's outer golden, wavy or coiled, shoulder-length, styled–if not crown-like–hair aligns well with royal personages, including Conchobar. Arguably, it is also reminiscent of Christ's illustrated tresses in the Book of Kells (see Fig. 3).[38] This attribute is also highlighted in Cú Chulainn's early death tale, *Brislech Mór Maige Muirthemne*, a text which, conceivably, offers a more Christ-like hero–even a 'death' journey–

---

[35] See Tomás Ó Carragáin, "Skeuomorphs and spolia: the presence of the past in Irish pre-Romanesque architecture," in Making and Meaning in Insular Art: Proceedings of the fifth International Conference on Insular Art held at Trinity College Dublin, 25–28 August 2005, ed. Rachel Moss (Dublin: Four Courts Press, 2007), 95–109 at 105.

[36] For further discussion, see Máire Herbert, "*Rí Érenn, Rí Alban*, kingship and identity in the ninth and tenth centuries," in *Kings, clerics and chronicles in Scotland*, ed. Simon Taylor (Dublin: Four Courts Press, 2000), 62–72.

[37] These somewhat contrasting representations will be explored in a forthcoming article, by Mary Leenane, emanating from the paper, "Functional or symbolic? A consideration of cloak and brooch wearing in early Irish literature," presented at the 41st California Celtic Conference, 14–17 March 2019, University of California, Berkeley.

[38] See earlier discussion of Cú Chulainn's hair and fn. 7. See folio 32v at "Digital Collections: TCD MS 58," Trinity College Dublin, accessed November 30, 2019, https://digitalcollections.tcd.ie/home/#folder_id=14&pidtopage=MS58_291v&entry_point=64.

that is somewhat comparable to the Passion of Christ. Perhaps, it would not be unreasonable for Cú Chulainn's physical appearance, or an aspect of it, to be aligned with Christ's. A similar case might be argued for *Aided Chonchobuir* in which news of Christ's crucifixion triggers the death of the king, Conchobar, whose golden hair is also underscored somewhat prominently.[39] Significantly, archaeological evidence supports a concern with appearance, most notably grooming, with the survival of many fine combs, many of which are decorated, at royal sites, such as Ballinderry and Lagore,[40] These depictions of seemingly contrasting secular and religious figures, are largely rooted within the same social, political and ecclesiastical milieu and, heavily indebted to idealised perceptions of a pretty–even angelic beauty–it is not surprising to find parallels in expressions of this kind.

Arguably, evidence from the literature reveals a more substantial concern with the portrayal of appearance and its significance. Indeed, we see indications of this in Cú Chulainn's case. The prose text, *Síaburcharpat Con Culainn*, presents an unfamiliar Cú Chulainn, emerging from hell with shorn or clipped black hair rather than his usual long-styled hair with an outer 'golden crown'. This alternative depiction is best understood in light of the tale's concern with promoting the Christian faith as Cú Chulainn, an exponent of the heroic pagan lifestyle, is denigrated and confined to the past.[41] The once irresistible hero with the long, glistening, golden locks is metamorphosed into a much darkened, clipped and reprimanded–even humiliated–less appealing personage. This unsavoury transformation also distances him from the more typical imagery associated with elite ecclesiastics. The manipulation of Cú Chulainn's appearance here confirms its importance to his persona while reiterating the medieval writers' interest in physical features. Elsewhere, evidence points to a further manipulation of his usual physique in the context of his *ríastrad* or 'distortion.' When consumed by this *ríastrad*, most notably in the *Táin*, traits of beauty and

---

[39] Meyer, *The Death-Tales of the Ulster Heroes*, 8.
[40] See Hencken, "Ballinderry crannog," 129, 140, 148, 156–7, 163–4 and Hencken, "Lagore crannog," 184–90. For a detailed discussion of combs, see Mairead Dunleavy, "A classification of early Irish combs," *Proceedings of the Royal Irish Academy* 88C, (1988): 341–422, The Iron Age Bog bodies vouch for an earlier concern with–even styling–of hair. See footnote 30.
[41] Best and Bergin, "*Síaburcharpat Con Culainn*," 279.

prettiness are abandoned to present an alternative unrefined and more barbaric side of Cú Chulainn. Typically, these underline changes to his hair, eyes, and mouth rendering him into a frightening one-eyed, bristly, short-haired spectre. His distortion upon arriving to Emain Macha as a young boy is described as follows:

> *Ríastartha immi-seom i sudiu. Indar lat ba tinnarcan asnort cach foltne ina chend lasa comérge conérracht. Indar lat bá hoíbell tened boí for cach óenfinniu de. Iadais indara súil dó conárbo lethiu indás cró snáithaiti, Asoilgg alaile combo móir beólu midchúaich. Doérig dia glainíni co rici a hóu. Asoilg a beólu coa inairddriuch combo écna a inchróes.*

> Thereupon he became distorted. His hair stood on end so that it seemed as if each separate hair on his head had been hammered into it. You would have thought that there was a spark of fire on each single hair. He closed one eye so that it was no wider than the eye of a needle; he opened the other until it was as large as the mouth of mead-goblet. He laid bare from his jaw to his ear and opened his mouth rib-wide (?) so that his internal organs were visible.[42]

His physical transformation is more pronounced when, as a young adult, he experiences a ferocious distortion later in the *Táin* and this is recorded in detail. The following morning, Cú Chulainn acknowledges his dishonourable and undignified appearance and moves quickly to erase this image, displaying himself in all his finery to the womenfolk and learned men.[43] As a hero very much embedded in Ulster society, this more unpredictable and threatening side to Cú Chulainn is circumscribed so as not to interfere with his role as chief guardian.

If we probe the literature a little more, evidence suggests a more pointed treatment of key items of dress, most notably mantles and brooches. Items like these may be insinuated at career-defining moments for Cú Chulainn and others more clearly. Upon receiving his spear, shield, and chariot, prematurely at the age of seven, Cú Chulainn embarks on an

---

[42] O'Rahilly, *Táin Bó Cúailnge, Recension I*, ll. 428–34, 137.
[43] Ibid., ll. 2245–79, ll. 2335–70.

exceedingly successful expedition, returning victorious, but in a fit of rage, to Emain Macha in his final *macgním* or 'boyhood deed'.[44] Cooled off when immersed in three vats of water, Cú Chulainn is subsequently clothed in the official costume of a hooded tunic and blue mantle, secured with a silver brooch by the Queen Mugain, before sitting at Conchobar's knee. In effect, this dressing represents his ceremonial induction into the position of chief Ulster warrior at Emain Macha. Cú Chulainn, when he appears as the older hero of the *Táin*, is generally 'upgraded' to a purple mantle, and a brooch of silver and gold which is, arguably, in acknowledgement of further great exploits. Poignantly, the first fold of Cú Chulainn's mantle fails in his death tale, *Brislech Mór Maige Muirthemne*, causing him to drop his brooch, and while appearing to don his mantle thereafter, his brooch is not mentioned. Lamenting the hero later in the text, his wife, Emer, notably, comments that he arrayed himself unfittingly so that his shield fell, his horse avoided him, and his brooch wounded him.[45] By inference, he is no longer able to bear the appropriate insignia of his elite position.

Similar themes also emerge for some royal figures, and examples are attested in narrative material outside of the Ulster Cycle. Firstly, to Cormac mac Airt, whose father, on the eve of battle, leaves his sword, golden thumb ring, and assembly garment with Cormac's mother in *Scéla Éogain ocus Cormaic*.[46] This *timthach* 'covering, garment or cloak', qualified with the noun *óenach* can be understood as an 'assembly garment,' and it is reasonable to interpret this as a type of covering mantle–even part of the official clothing of a king. Legal evidence reiterates the concept of official royal dress, outlining a substantial fine equalling the king's honour-price to atone for his shame at having to appear without it.[47] Significantly, *Scéla Éogain ocus Cormaic* places the baby Cormac in a specially crafted yew vessel with a purple garment, reaffirming his royal associations. Cormac's

---

[44] Ibid., ll. 608–821.
[45] Kimpton, *Brislech Mór Maige Muirthemni*, 31.
[46] Tomás Ó Cathasaigh, *The heroic biography of Cormac Mac Airt*, (Dublin: Dublin Institute for Advanced Studies, 1977), 119–23.
[47] *CIH*, 469.19–23. See also Fergus Kelly, *A guide to early Irish law*, (Dublin: Four Courts Press, 1988), 166–7. Legal material details a fine of a purple cloak worth seven ounces of silver along with a hooded tunic for the satirising of King Cernodon of Ulster, placing emphasis again on the idea of appropriate clothing, Myles Dillon, "Stories from the law tracts," *Ériu* 11 (1932): 42–65 at 45.

destiny to follow in his father's footsteps is delineated more clearly not only by the passing down of specific items to him, including clothing, as stated above, but by the conferring of these onto him at the appropriate time, as he embarks on his journey to the royal seat of Tara, and also as he comes of age so that these 'fit' him. Arguably, by donning this regalia, Cormac is already slotting into the role of king as the incumbent, Lugaid mac Con, effectively announces his own demise by giving the wrong judgment concerning compensation arising from the eating of the Queen's woad by a farmer's sheep. Bearing the attire of royal office, Cormac quickly issues the just judgment, crucially, upon arriving at Tara, confirming his new positioning as king.

A similar case can be argued for Conaire Mór's coming to the kingship in *De šíl Conaire Mór* and the early Middle Irish text, *Togail Bruidne Da Derga*.[48] Though there is considerable variation in detail, official royal clothing features at the point of ascension in both narratives. The former text sees Conaire greeted with a set of items assigned to the kingship of Tara, namely a chariot with horses of the same colour, a mantle fitting only the rightful king, two flagstones, and the Stone of Fál. The successful king must negotiate these and, following his mother's instructions, Conaire enters the chariot, putting on the king's mantle, and it is confirmed that this fits him, denoting his ascension to the kingship. Clothing is also central to Conaire's ascension in *Togail Bruidne Da Derga* in which an earlier revelation that the next king of Tara will appear naked with a stone and sling, duly prompts Conaire to appear in this guise. Prior to this, the text confirms that he possesses the same raiment, armour and colour of horses, as his foster brothers, the descendants of Donn Désa. As the naked Conaire proceeds to Tara, three kings await him on his journey and dress him in *étach ríg* 'royal clothing.'[49] His stripping sets him apart from his foster brothers and his previous societal positioning, in preparation for his garbing in kingly garments in line with his new role as king. Like Cormac, Conaire is dressed in royal clothing *en route* to Tara before assuming the kingship. Although differing accounts are offered for Cormac and Conaire, similar intent is expressed with the emphasis on a mantle-type garment as a constituent of royal dress–even of inauguration–for both men. Somewhat

---

[48] See Lucius Gwynn, "*De 'Síl Chonairi Móir*," *Ériu* 6 (1912): 130–43.

[49] Knott, *Togail Bruidne Da Derga*, 4–5, Ibid., 5.

comparable themes are revealed for some female figures associated with sovereignty, such as Mór Muman who is aligned with the kingship of Munster. Fíngen mac Áeda instructs his wife to cede her purple mantle and brooch to Mór, marking Mór Muman's repositioning as Queen in the tale, *Mór Muman ocus Aided Chuanach meic Cailchíne*. Níall Noígiallach's union with the 'ugly hag' prompts her transformation into a beautiful sovereignty figure, replete with purple mantle secured with a bright silver brooch, marking the beginning of his reign at Tara and perhaps also her rejuvenation in the text, *Echtra mac nEchach Muigmedóin*.[50]

To conclude, evidence reveals an emphasis on colourful and defined facial features, along with groomed, golden, long hair, as being pivotal to the representation of high-ranking males, most notably Cú Chulainn, in early Irish literature. Cú Chulainn's beautiful features are noted in several different texts confirming their centrality to his characterisation as the warrior-hero *par excellence* of the Ulster Cycle. His pretty countenance is further embellished through his dressing in an expansive, bordered, purple mantle which is adorned with a brooch of mixed metal. This visualisation of Cú Chulainn is underpinned by an idealised perception of the male form that is conceived in male dominated religious houses. The most appealing features and clothing are reserved for the most esteemed, and these serve as a mechanism to confirm high-status. This paper proposes that religious iconographies in the illuminated insular gospel books and on the Irish high crosses can help us to better understand the textual descriptions of Cú Chulainn and at least some other high-ranking personages. The portraitures of the gospel books present a groomed and refined male form, garbed in a vibrant, colourful, outer garment, that is reminiscent of the written visualisations of secular males. These written and illustrative visualisations favour an aesthetic sense of beauty that also infiltrates metal artefacts of a comparable date. Interestingly, medieval writers undermine Cú Chulainn's beauteous–even clerically aligned–profile to offer divergent portrayals of him in *Síaburcharpat Con Culainn*, and when he is consumed by his *ríastrad* elsewhere. His pretty aspect is discarded, and thus he is distanced from any religious associations for these alternative representations of the

---

[50] Thomas P. O'Nolan "Mór of Munster and the tragic fate of Cuanu son of Cailchin," *Proceedings of the Royal Irish Academy* 30C (1912–13): 261–82 at 262–3; Whitley Stokes, "*Echtra mac nEchach Muigmedóin*," *Revue Celtique* 24 (1903): 190–207 at 198–200.

hero. While brooches are fundamental to the narrative expression of elite status in the literature, this is not the case in the gospel books, but they do adorn the clothing of at least some ecclesiastics on the Irish high crosses. These stone artefacts were largely created in the tenth century, a time of flux around the notion of secular authority. The crosses are very much intertwined with secular affairs with royal figures sponsoring at least some of these, and it seems that dynastic status symbols recognised by the general population, most notably brooches, infiltrate these depictions of important church leaders. While luxurious apparel, often including brooches, affirms elite status in a simplified way, the literature is more revealing–even delineating royal insignia–particularly in the case of Cormac mac Airt and Conaire Mór and some female sovereignty figures. Evidence advances the notion of a mantle-type garment, along with a brooch in some instances, as a constituent of royal dress–even inauguration. At the very least, this interdisciplinary study has revealed interesting connections and linkages between various visualisations of the elite in early Irish society. Crucially, this has provided a fresh insight into this aspect of the narrative material and demonstrates the value in adopting an interdisciplinary approach.

Chaos or Comrades? Transatlantic Political and Cultural Aspirations for Ireland in Nineteenth-century Irish American Print Media

Fiona Lyons

In 1872 Michael Logan, a Galway born native who moved to the United States [hereafter the US] in the 1870s, wrote a letter to the New York *Irish World*. [1] He called for the establishment of an Irish class to teach the Irish language in order to "maintain Irish ideas and Irish nationality in their integrity."[2] Logan, a trained teacher, stood true to his word and created an Irish language class in Brooklyn in 1873[3] and the establishment of the Philo-Celtic Societies across the US stemmed from this. The first was established in Boston in 1873, Brooklyn followed suit soon after, and by the end of the 1890s there were approximately fifty Philo-Celtic Societies and language classes across the US.[4] By sending a letter to the *Irish World* Logan highlights an evolving relationship between print media and reader in Irish American society. Sociolinguistic engagement such as this provides an insight into the Irish speaking community in the US in the nineteenth century, conveying aims and ambitions for the Irish language on a transatlantic basis. As Wittke has stated, Irish American journalism was an important service "to blend the cultural memories of the past with the immigrant's hopes for the future."[5] It also acted as a means to allow the immigrant to adjust to American life while remaining knowledgeable about,

---

[1] See Fionnuala Uí Fhlannagáin, *Mícheál Ó Lócháin agus an Gaodhal* (Dublin: An Clochomhar Tta, 1990), 11, 14.

[2] "A Practical Suggestion," *Irish World*, May 25, 1872.

[3] See also Kenneth E, Nilsen, "The Irish Language in New York 1850–1900", in *The New York Irish*, ed. Ronald H. Bayor, Timothy J. Meagher (Baltimore and London: The Johns Hopkins University Press, 1996), 252–74 at 268.

[4] The New York branch of the Ossianic Society had been formed before this in 1859 and many figures who were members of this branch such as John O'Mahony, Michael Doheny, Michael Cavanagh, David O'Keeffe and Thomas D. Norris were also members of later Philo-Celtic Societies. They also played an active role in the pre-revival of the Irish language in the US.

[5] Carl Wittke, *The Irish in America* (Baton Rouge: Louisiana State University Press, 1956), 202.

and involved with, Irish affairs.[6] With the growth of Irish language classes and societies in the US, print media was becoming an important resource for the Irish language speaker and enthusiast. The Philo-Celtic Societies used the journalistic forum via their corresponding secretaries to send reports to the print media for updating fellow society members, or general admirers, of their work and progression. They often encouraged new members to join classes, attend entertainments, and noted their disapproval to current members regarding lack of attendance. Print media also became a forum to voice opinion and to create debate and discussion on Irish language matters. With the establishment of Gaelic departments and columns in Irish American print media, Irish language lessons and grammar exercises for readers began to appear. The first Irish language column began in the New York *Irish American* newspaper in 1857 printing stories, poems and manuscript material until 1861 when "Self Instructions in Irish" began. Irish language material has been found in a wide range of print media forums across the US in the nineteenth century such as the *Celtic Monthly* (New York), *Donohoe's Magazine* (Boston), the *Citizen* (Chicago), the *Irish American* (New York), *An Gaodhal* (Brooklyn), the *Irish Echo* (Boston), and the *Monitor* (San Francisco).[7] Letters to editors of these

---

[6] Timothy McMahon, *Grand Opportunity: The Gaelic Revival and Irish Society, 1893–1910* (New York: Syracuse University Press, 2008), 182.

[7] Kenneth E. Nilsen, "The Irish Language in nineteenth century New York city," in *The Multilingual Apple: Languages in New York City,* ed. Ofelia García and Joshua A. Fishman (New York & Berlin: Mouton de Gruyter, 1997), 53–71; Nilsen, "The Irish Language in New York, 1850 – 1900,"; Matthew Knight, "Gaels on the Pacific: The Irish Language Department in the San Francisco Monitor, 1888–91," *Éire-Ireland* 54, no. 3 (2019): 172–199 at 175–6; Regina Uí Chollatáin, ""Thall is Abhus" 1860–1930: The Revival Process and the Journalistic Web between Ireland and North America," in *Language Identity and Migration: Voices from Transnational Speakers and Communities,* ed. Chloe Diskin, Jennifer Martyn and Vera Regan (Oxford: Peter Lang, 2016), 353–379; Regina Uí Chollatáin, "Athbheochan Trasatlantach na Gaeilge: Scríbhneoirí, Intleachtóirí agus an Fhéiniúlacht Éireannach," in *Litríocht na Gaeilge ar fud an Domhain. Cruthú, Caomhnú agus Athbheochan. Imleabhar 1,* ed. Ríona Nic Congáil, Máirín Nic Eoin, Meidhbhín Ní Úrdail, Pádraig Ó Liatháin and Regina Uí Chollatáin. (Dublin: LeabhairCOMHAR, 2015), 277–309; Dorothy Ní Uigín, "An Iriseoireacht Ghaeilge i Meiriceá agus in Éirinn ag Tús na hAthbheochana: An Cúlra Meiriceánach," in *Léachtaí Cholm Cille XXVIII,* ed. Ruairí Ó hUiginn (Maynooth: An Sagart, 1998), 25–47 at 28.

newspapers, journals and magazines show readers using the columns as a learning aid. An example of this is a letter from Nóra Breathnach, an eleven-year-old girl from Clare, Ireland. She sent a letter to Michael Logan, the editor of *An Gaodhal*, in 1888 thanking him for the journal's Irish lessons as through this she learnt to read and write the language; "Cuirim chugat an leitir beag seo le buidheachas a thabhairt dhuit fá 'n tíodhlacadh mór a bronnais orm, eadhon, gur fhóghluim mé le teanga mo dhúthchais a sgríobadh agus a léigheamh thré do pháipeur, An Gaodhal."[8]

Irish American print media, cultural societies and language classes also had a symbiotic relationship with one another. Some societies would use the newspapers or journals and their Gaelic departments in their language classes or use the columns whilst waiting on textbooks to arrive; "while waiting for the books, members have signilled (sic) their intention of relying on the *Irish American*, as the first lessons are to appear therein, as taught at Philo-Celtic schools."[9] The relationship between press and society was also noted in a society report in the *Brooklyn Daily Eagle* in 1879 mentioning that the Brooklyn Philo-Celtic Society "gratefully acknowledge[s] the powerful assistance of the press in the furtherance of [their] exertions."[10] Thomas O'Neill Russell, founding member of Conradh na Gaeilge/the Gaelic League in Dublin in 1893 and "official representative" of Aontacht na Gaeilge/the Gaelic Union in Dublin in the US in 1882 also noted in the Boston *Irish Echo* in June 1886 that the Irish American press "has now almost as much influence in Ireland as the native Irish press has."[11] Whilst this study looks at the journalistic forum in the pre-revival of the Irish language,[12] the usage of print media by language societies as a means

---

[8] "An Effective Mode of Promoting the Cultivation of the Irish Language," *An Gaodhal,* February 1888; "I send you this small letter to thank you for the great favour which you have bestowed on me, to wit, I learned to write and read the language of my country through your paper, the Gael," translation accompanied the printed latter in *An Gaodhal.*

[9] "The Irish Language, Philo-Celtic Society, New York," *Irish American*, June 15, 1878.

[10] "Celtic Literature: The Eagle Complemented for Shedding Some Light on It," *Brooklyn Daily Edge*, March 27, 1879.

[11] "The Irish Parliament and the Irish Language," *Irish Echo*, June 1886.

[12] Regina Uí Chollatáin, "The Irish-Language Press: Tender Plant at the Best of Times?" in *The Edinburgh History of the British and Irish Press,* Volume 2,

to communicate their ideas and objectives was also used in the revival movement in Ireland. The Gaelic Union began *Irisleabhar na Gaedhilge* in 1882 and the Gaelic League established *An Claidheamh Soluis* in 1899, for example. In the US the *Irish Echo* was established by the Boston Philo-Celtic Society and *An Gaodhal* by the Brooklyn Philo-Celtic Society. This paper in particular will focus on the analysis of nineteenth century Irish American print media sources c.1857-1897 and will explore how the journalistic forum was used to express political and cultural aspirations for Ireland concerning the Irish language.

Cultural Aspirations

As aforementioned, the New York *Irish American* began printing an Irish language column entitled "Our Gaelic Department" in 1857 which featured Irish language lessons and "Self Instruction in Irish" began on February 2, 1861.[13] These "Self Instruction in Irish" exercises had been previously published in the *Nation* newspaper in Dublin, however, the *Irish American* had been printing various material in the Irish language in the paper for a year prior to this which they refer to on April 17, 1858:

> The Dublin *Nation* of March 20, has the annexed remarks upon the revival of ancient Irish literature, which will in future be a regular feature in that journal, as it has been for the past year in the *Irish American*. It is a source of no little gratification to us to find that our example has already begun to produce good effects, and that we may now calculate with certainty on a combined, vigorous effort, on

---

Expansion and Evolution, 1800–1900, ed. Martin Conboy and David Finkelstein (Edinburgh: Edinburgh University Press, 2020), 357–376 at 357, describes the term "revival" in the context of the Irish language as one "used to denote the late nineteenth-century rise of literary talent and work allied to a strong political nationalism and a revived interest in Ireland's Gaelic language and literary heritage."

[13] The editor of this column was Michael Doheny, and John O'Mahony until 1858. Both took part in the Young Irelander movement in Ireland, were exiled to New York in the late 1840s/early 1850s and were native Irish speakers. "Boru," William Russell, was another editor of the column in the 1860/70s. My thanks to Matthew Knight for this information. See also Nilsen, "The Irish Language in New York, 1850 – 1900," 260–1; "Irish Music: A "Gaedhlic Idyll" in New York," *Irish American*, December 6, 1884.

both sides of the Atlantic, to rescue from oblivion the
venerable tongue of our beloved Fatherland . . .[14]

The importance of rescuing the vernacular from extinction often arose from
questions of identity, nationality and patriotism. As Uí Chollatáin has
commented "language was the tool for communication but in the context of
the Revival [and the pre-Revival in the US] it was also an emblem of
community and identity."[15] This is observed in articles in the Irish American
press regarding the importance of education as it was hoped that recognising
the value associated with learning the Irish language would encourage its
increased usage in both scholarly work and printed matter. The language's
antiquity was also often compared to the scholarship of Greece and Rome
to spark such patriotism and interest with the general public. Patrick Pearse
referred to this in his lecture "The Intellectual Future of the Gael" given in
October 1897 for the Inaugural Address of the New Ireland Literary
Society:

> What the Greek was to the ancient world the Gael will be
> to the modern; and in no point will the parallel prove more
> true than in the fervent and noble love of learning which
> distinguishes both races. The Gael, like the Greek, loves
> learning, and like the Greek, he loves it solely for its own
> sake . . . When love of learning is so deeply implanted in
> the heart of the Gael that not even persecution, penury, and
> degradation can eradicate it, surely it ought to blaze
> forthwith ten-fold brilliancy when the night is past and the
> morn is come.[16]

Another means to portray the featuring of the Irish language in global
scholarship was when contributors and editors would mention European
colleges around the world where the Irish language was studied:

> [I]s fios duinn go múintear í a mórán de na h-ard-scolaibh
> is cludhamhla agus is aoisde céim san Európ. Múintear í

---

[14] "The Celtic Tongue," *Irish American*, April 17, 1858.

[15] Uí Chollatáin, "'Thall is Abhus'," 357.

[16] P.H. Pearse, *Three Lectures on Gaelic Topics by P. H. Pearse* (Dublin: M.H. Gill &
Son, 1898), 56.

'san bh-Frainc agus 'san n-Gearmain, Múintear í san Róimh..."[17]

Similarly, the presence of many Irish books and manuscripts in said colleges was noted to further emphasise the intellectualism of the Irish language; it was not a language of barbarianism and poverty. O'Neill Russell wrote in a letter to the editor of the Boston *Pilot* in 1878, that the great German scholar Zeuss "never saw any of the Irish manuscripts in Ireland or England; he did not want them: he had plenty of Irish manuscripts nearer to him in Germany, France, Switzerland, Italy, and Spain."[18] This was similarly expressed by a Mr. Edwin L. Abbett at the annual public meeting of the Gaelic Society in New York in 1887 who remarked that:

> Irish priests were welcomed at the most enlightened courts of Europe, while going back and forth on their pilgrimages to Rome. With such a historic record, it would seem as if their language should be deemed worthy of preservation and study by their race to day (sic). Should we not reverently point to, and link ourselves with the past; and, if we have a country, and a language, why not cultivate and reverence the latter as we do the former from which we derive it? The field is open. Why not harvest, and why not glean?[19]

de Brún notes that the past "cannot be restored miraculously or seamlessly reintegrated into the present. It can, however, re-emerge through a creative renewal in which the past ceases to be a static burden and becomes instead part of a dynamic dialogue with the present."[20] In this context the previous assumption that the Irish language represented ineptness could be presently modified to one of intelligence and learning. This was attempted by appreciating the study of Irish, as aforementioned,

---

[17] "Our Gaelic Department," *Irish American,* July 16, 1887; "We know that Irish is taught in many of the most famous and oldest schools in Europe. It is taught in France and in Germany. It is taught in Rome . . ." translation the author's own.

[18] "The Irish Language," *Pilot,* August 31, 1878.

[19] "Teanga agus Ceoil," *Irish American,* June 4, 1887.

[20] Fionntán de Brún, "Escaping the "Shower of Folly": The Irish Language, Revivalism, and the History of Ideas," *Maynooth Philosophical Papers* 9, (2018): 43–58 at 55–6.

and also highlighting the relationship between Irish and Catholicism. Brian Ó Conchubhair conveys that in the Irish revival many believed that Irish was a true Catholic language as in the minds of the Irish speakers Catholicism linked them to a pure and glorious past.[21] Catholicism was also utilised as a means to inspire the Irish to speak their vernacular as it was a language which should be held as "a sacred and honoured possession by all."[22] Pearse also referred to this connection in his 1897 address remarking that:

> The hunted priests and schoolmasters of the seventeenth and eighteenth centuries carried about with them from cave to cave, and from glen to glen, not only copies of the Gospels, but copies of the Greek and Latin classics, and volumes of old Gaelic poetry, history, and romance . . .[23]

Pearse places emphasis here on the utilisation of Gaelic poetry by Priests in a parallel fashion as the Gospel was used for learning. Articles in Irish American journalism would also refer to saints or the Irish priests who travelled across Europe as missionaries as examples of instances where the Irish tongue was widely appreciated and supported. This, therefore, led to questioning why the Irish people would ever turn their back on their vernacular if it was once spoken by the most learned of scholars. The value placed on studying the Irish language arising from its connection with Catholicism is seen in a letter to the editor of the New York *Irish World* from Thomas J. Shahan, Professor of Early Church History in the Catholic University of America, in 1894 when he wrote that the Irish language:

> . . . was the tongue of Patrick, Bridget and Columbia and has been sanctified by long use in the mouths of the most

---

[21] Brian Ó Conchubhair, *Fin de Siècle na Gaeilge: Darwin, an Athbheochan agus Smaointeoireacht na hEorpa* (Connemara: An Clóchomhar, 2009), 33–4; " . . . creideadh go forleathan go raibh dlúthnasc idir teanga agus leanúnachas staire, ach tuigeadh chomh maith go raibh bá faoi leith idir teangacha áirithe agus creidimh áirithe . . . Dé réir na tuisceana seo, is teanga Chaitliceach í an Ghaeilge toisc gur mhúnlaigh Caitligigh na hÉireann, idir naoimh agus phobal, í."

[22] See J. M. Synge, *Aran Islands and Connemara* (Dublin: Mercier Press, 2008), 31–2, as quoted in Ó Conchubhair, *Fin de Siècle*, 34.

[23] P.H. Pearse, *Three Lectures on Gaelic Topics by P. H. Pearse* (Dublin: M.H. Gill & Son, 1898), 56.

eminent saints and the most learned doctors. It is saturated in its structure and in its monuments with the purest and most spiritual Catholicism and for those reasons alone deserves a place in an institution destined to be the mouthpiece of the Catholic Church in America.[24]

Martin P. Ward also associated the Irish language with Catholicism in his letter to the editor of the San Francisco *Monitor* in 1888 in which he mentioned that he was glad to see the beginning of the revival of his "grand old mother tongue in which St. Patrick preached" and that when he enters the "gates of glory [he] does not think St. Peter will reprimand [him]; and when [he] meet[s] St. Patrick and Bridget, [he] will say '*go dea mar tha shiv.*'"[25] The understanding of the Irish language in Heaven was also referred to by Edward J. Rowe, corresponding secretary of the Irish American Philo-Celtic Union, in a society report to the New York *Irish American* in 1879. He wrote that at a meeting of the West 25th Street School Father McAleer,[26] Reverend Pastor of St. Columba's Church in New York, spoke of how well Irish is understood in Heaven and how St. Patrick mastered the Irish language and "converted, through that language, the whole people of Ireland."[27]

Whilst referring to the Irish language as a Catholic language was often a means to spark patriotism and interest for the revival and cultivation of the language, it was also an interference at times. Michael Logan, editor of the Brooklyn *An Gaodhal,* responded in an editorial to a letter from Patrick A. Dougher regarding the founders of a night-school movement in Ireland to teach the language some years ago. Logan remarked that the "falling off in the percentage of the Irish Catholic immigrant" was due to the shame and embarrassment the Irish immigrants felt regarding their vernacular when they came to the US. This led them to speaking English rather than Irish in

---

[24] "University to have an Irish Chair," *Irish World*, November 24, 1894.

[25] "From a True Son of the Gael," *Monitor*, March 28, 1888; *go dea mar tha shiv* is phonetically spelt for the Irish *go dté mar atá sibh*, and translates to English as *how are ye.*

[26] McAleer was also president of St. Columba's Irish School in New York from 1878–80 and died in 1881.

[27] "The Irish American Philo-Celtic Union," *Irish American*, June 21, 1879.

order to assimilate easier into American society. The exact thing Irish revivalists and enthusiasts wished to eradicate:

> The Irishman came here [the US]; he never saw the Irish alphabet, nor believed there was such, and therefore could not instruct his children. Self interest (sic) and anti-Catholic surroundings whispered into the ear of the Irish-American youngster that his father[s] were utterly ignorant and no better than the Indian, and the youngster, seeing the apparent proof in his own parent, swallowed the bait, and hence the large number of the Mac's and O's in this country who are the inveterate enemies of Irishism and Catholicism, there being in this city alone over thirty Anglican ministers bearing purely Celtic names. Had Gaelic literature been published and circulated, the youngster could see for himself and his parent's ignorance would not affect him.[28]

Logan places blame on the lack of Gaelic literature being published and similarly displays an "us versus them" mentality between the Irish in the US and the Irish in Ireland.[29] Whilst this type of comparison could result in questions surrounding the best efforts and practices for the revival and cultivation of the language on a transatlantic basis, it also showed how the Irish in the US could motivate and encourage those in Ireland to cultivate and revive their vernacular. In a letter published in the *Irish American* in 1884 Professor Frederick L. O. Roehrig, Professor of Sanskrit at Cornell University, wrote to the President of the New York Society for the Preservation of the Irish Language highlighting the importance of the efforts for the Irish language in the US for Ireland:

> It is not so much for the Irish in *this* country [the US] that their language should, from an absolute necessity, be carefully kept up as a living tongue, to preserve their nationality;–but the great object should be to show to the

---

[28] "Editorial," *An Gaodhal*, November 1890, 43–4.

[29] See also Kerby A. Miller, *Emigrants and Exiles: Ireland and the Irish Exodus to North America* (New York: Oxford University Press, 1985), 106, for an "us versus them" mentality in the context of the Catholic *Gaeil* and the Protestant *Sasanaigh*.

people of the mother country,–of Ireland,–what is the next important thing to do that they may not cease to be a nation distinct from their conquerors and oppressors. For, in Ireland, the people will look up to their countrymen in America to see what they will do when wholly unrestrained and free. And this should be to teach them to love, to cultivate, to preserve and perpetuate their venerable mother-tongue,–so superior to the greatest number of the languages spoken all around them on European soil, for its antiquity, its originality, its unmixed purity, its remarkably pleasing euphony and easy, harmonious flow, its poetical adaptation, musical nature and picturesque expressiveness; its vigorous vitality, freshness, energy and inherent power; its logical, systematic, regular and methodically constituted grammar; its philosophic structure and wonderful literary susceptibility.[30]

The support the US could give to the revival movement in Ireland would have been beneficial in numerous ways. The first was ideological. As seen previously in the context of education and Catholicism the Irish in the US were supporting and encouraging the study of the Irish language instead of belittling its value and scholarly contribution as many believed they should do. This in particular was acknowledged by Douglas Hyde in the lecture he gave to the New York Gaelic Society published in the Chicago *Citizen* in 1891 on his return from his year of lecturing at the University of New Brunswick in Canada. The "communicated" article in the *Citizen* writes that Hyde claimed:

> [N]othing has done more to help the cause of the language in Ireland than the interest that is being taken in it in America. He said that there are very many speaking it and studying it in Ireland at present, who, had they not been excited by hearing of how many in America were taking an interest in it, would never, probably, have given it a thought.[31]

---

[30] "The Irish Language," *Irish American*, May 17, 1884.
[31] "Mr. Douglas Hyde," *Citizen*, June 27, 1891.

In terms of methodology, the establishment of a Celtic Chair in the Catholic University in Washington in 1895 would have been a huge boost of morale for the Irish as it signified a step towards Irish, or Celtic, as an exam subject in Universities. Rev. Father Richard Henebry (Risteard De Hindeberg) was chosen to occupy the chair and in the early 1890s when this appointment was being discussed in Irish American journalism there was general widespread support from societies and readers:

> Both in this country [Ireland] and amongst our kith and kin across the ocean the Celtic spirit and the Celtic ideals are, thank goodness, as fresh and fruitful as ever.[32]

> The Gael congratulates the Hibernians on the appointment of Father Henebery (sic) to the Professorship of their Keltic Chair in the Catholic University. Father Henebery (sic) is the right man in the right place . . . Professor Henebery (sic) is a county Waterford man and is a natural Irish speaker.[33]

> With this example of a chair in Gaelic established in an American Catholic university, and of the Celtic professorships in all the principal universities of Germany and other continental countries, it is not to be doubted that similar chairs will be established in all the Catholic colleges of Ireland, so is to perfect the system of Gaelic education begun in the primary schools of the country.[34]

In the article aforementioned from the *Citizen* when Hyde gave his lecture in New York in 1891, he also presented a practical method on how the US could help Ireland in the promotion of the Irish language. Hyde suggested that if six Irish speakers from the US were sent over to Ireland, and particularly to the Irish speaking regions in Ireland, throughout the winter months they could visit houses speaking Irish. This would display the importance and value placed on the language by others outside of Ireland as well as demonstrating to children in these houses that it was a

---

[32] "The Irish Language," *Irish American*, December 17, 1894.
[33] *An Gaodhal*, September 1895, 44.
[34] "The Gaelic Language," *Irish World*, November 22, 1895.

positive thing to be able to speak their national tongue. This would be invaluable to the Irish in Ireland as they saw the US as a "fatherland from which they are to take their teaching."[35] Fr. James Keegan who was born in Leitrim, Ireland, in 1859 and left for the US in the 1880s also attempted to aid the Irish language movement in Ireland on a transatlantic basis. Michael C. O'Shea, editor of the Boston *Irish Echo* (May 1889-May 1890) described him in an editorial as "a Celtic scholar so well known as our able correspondent" and Hyde cited him as "among the foremost of those who were working unceasingly in the cause of their country's [Ireland] language and literature."[36] In August 1890 Keegan wrote a letter to John Glynn, editor of the *Tuam News* in Galway. In his encouragement for the language movement in Ireland he wrote that they should work "quietly in union" and that they "have no time to lose" in case the language ceased to be spoken in Ireland, "if that evil day should ever come."[37] He also offered suggestions on how the movement in Ireland could progress and prosper:

1. We must get the language and culture into schools and colleges;
2. We must open the entire Irish national press daily, weekly and monthly to contributions in Irish;
3. We must publish Irish books, ancient middle and modern. Also we must compile and publish cheap and good text books;
4. We must circulate Irish literature;
5. We must gather funds for the carrying out of the projects here laid down.[38]

---

[35] "Mr. Douglas Hyde," *Citizen*, June 27, 1891.

[36] "Editorial," *Irish Echo*, November 1889; "Mr. Douglas Hyde," *Citizen*, June 27, 1891.

[37] National Library of Ireland, MS 3254, Letters to John (Mc) Glynn, of the Tuam News, with some to J. Mc Philpin of the same, and some associated correspondence mainly relating to the Irish language, incl. letters, essays, etc., in Irish by Rev. Eugene O'Growney; other correspondents include Canon Ulick Bourke and Rev. Euseby D. Cleaver. c. 1863–1894.

[38] National Library of Ireland, MS 3254, Letters to John (Mc) Glynn, of the Tuam News, with some to J. Mc Philpin of the same, and some associated correspondence

FIONA LYONS

The majority of his suggestions in 1890 were in fact fulfilled by the Gaelic League in later years. Irish became necessary for matriculation in the University of Ireland from 1913 onwards,[39] many English language newspapers contained Irish language columns,[40] literature was printed in the Irish language as well as textbooks for use in classes, and Hyde undertook a tour of the US in 1905/06 to raise funds for the Gaelic League back in Ireland with the help of John Quinn.[41] As well as having similar cultural aspirations for the future of the Irish language the Irish linguistic community in the US provided those in Ireland with hope, encouragement and a framework from which they could draw ideas and methodology for their own revival movement.

Political Aspirations

The importance of the national language to the nation was also a common theme in writings at this time to spark patriotism amongst readers to convince them to appreciate and speak their vernacular. Without the cultivation and revival of the Irish language many believed that Ireland would never have a successful future nor would she ever be free from English rule. Jean-Christophe Penet in reference to the German philosopher Johann Gottlieb Fichte mentions that:

---

mainly relating to the Irish language, incl. letters, essays, etc., in Irish by Rev. Eugene O'Growney; other correspondents include Canon Ulick Bourke and Rev. Euseby D. Cleaver. c. 1863–1894.

[39] See Regina Uí Chollátáin, "Language Shift and Language Revival in Ireland," in *Sociolinguistics in Ireland*, ed. Raymond Hickey (Hampshire & New York: Palgrave Macmillan, 2016), 190.

[40] See Nollaig Mac Congáil, "Saothrú na Gaeilge ar Nuachtáin Náisiúnta Bhéarla na hAoise seo caite: Sop nó Solamar?" in *Féilscríbhinn Anraí Mhic Giolla Chomhaill*, ed. Réamonn Ó Muireadhaigh (Dublin: Coiscéim, 2011), 112–191; Aoife Uí Fhaoláin, "Language revival and conflicting identities in The Irish Independent, 1905–1922," *Irish Studies Review* 22, no. 10, (2014): 63–79; Aoife Whelan and Regina Uí Chollatáin, "The Irish Language in the Regional Revival Press," *The Irish Regional Press, 1892–2012*, ed. Ian Kenneally and James T. O'Donnell (Dublin: Four Courts Press, 2018), 91–104.

[41] See Úna Ní Bhroiméil, *Building Irish Identity in America, 1870–1915: The Gaelic Revival* (Dublin: Four Courts Press, 2003) and Neil Comer et al., *Douglas Hyde My American Journey* (Dublin: UCD Press, 2020).

In his writings, Fichte stated that the culture of the German nation, and more importantly its language, made it holy because they enabled it to preserve its original purity. Fichte thereby turned German into what he called an Ursprache, an original language, which he considered to be the most distinctive sign of nationality, since it made the very soul of the German nation–its Volksgeist–stand out. We can therefore clearly see how, in Fichte's organic conception of the nation, the national language, its voice, became physically tied to the nation's very soul. And that was precisely why Fichte warned that to deprive a nation of its original language was to deprive it of the very means to express its soul and its own vision of the world, which consequently stopped it from becoming independent.[42]

This is also seen in the writings of Thomas Davis, founder of the Dublin newspaper the *Nation* who wrote in 1843 that "to lose your native tongue and learn that of an alien, is the worst badge of conquest–it is a chain on the soul. To have lost entirely the national language is death."[43] Politics, identity and language were often connected with one another in the Irish American journalistic forum of the nineteenth century.[44] In the September issue of the Boston *Irish Echo* for 1886 an article appeared entitled "No Irish Language, no Irish Nation." The title itself is self-explanatory and the first line stated that, "no nation that lost its language ever became a nation again." Likewise, in the *Brooklyn Daily Eagle* in 1878 Michael Logan wrote a letter to the editor as corresponding secretary of the Brooklyn Philo-Celtic Society stating that the object of the society was the "cultivation and preservation of the Irish language" but that in order to claim a distinct nationality Irish people "ought to be able to show some proof of their ancient autonomy." He also made use of Tacitus' expression "the language of the conqueror in the mouth of the conquered is ever the language of the slave" delineating that "no nation is wholly subdued till it yields its

---

[42] Jean-Christophe Penet, "Thomas Davis, 'The Nation' and the Irish language," *Studies: An Irish Quarterly Review* 96, no. 384 (Winter 2007): 433–43 at 435.

[43] Thomas Davis, "Our National Language," *Nation,* April 1, 1843.

[44] See Ní Bhroiméil, *Building Irish Identity in America*; Fionnuala Uí Fhlannagáin, *Finíní Mheiriceá agus an Ghaeilge* (Dublin: Coiscéim, 2008).

language; for 'the language of the conqueror in the mouth of the conquered, is the language of the slave'."[45] He emphasised here that the idea of speaking the English language in favour of speaking the vernacular would allow the country to remain in a world of suffering and injustice instead of prospering with their own national language. Whilst Logan mentions in the same report that the word 'Philo' means lover and has no political affiliation, his strong association of language loss with conquest suggests otherwise. Logan repeats his sentiment in a report from the Brooklyn Philo-Celtic Society sent to the New York *Irish American* in 1878 when he remarked that the knowledge of the Irish language was an essential factor for nationality and patriotism:

> I cannot, for the life of me, see how men have the cheek to proclaim themselves advocates of Irish nationality and ignore the national tongue. If they are content with the English language and English manners what is this commotion about Irish nationality? If you leave out the language where is the distinctive national characteristic? . . . Keep the trunk of the tree in a sound condition and there is no fear but it will shoot forth strong and vigorous branches.[46]

Often when the cultivation and revival of the Irish language was mentioned in Irish American print media the lack of support by political figures in Ireland would also be acknowledged. A key example of such is seen in a letter to the editor of the Boston *Irish Echo* from Thomas O'Neill Russell in 1886 in which he stated that "the native Irish parliament, would be bound to take some steps towards giving the Irish language national recognition."[47] He also referred to the obligation of this new native Irish parliament,[48] according to the beliefs of the Chicago *Citizen*, to establish

---

[45] "The Irish Language: A Society for its Preservation," *Brooklyn Daily Eagle*, April 21, 1878. It is probable that Logan is referring here to the idealisation of the slave implying a struggle and loss of voice and power against a higher power; ie. the Irish against British rule.

[46] "Brooklyn Philo-Celtic Society," *Irish American*, September 7, 1878.

[47] "The Irish Parliament and the Irish Language," *Irish Echo*, June 1886.

[48] O'Neill Russell's reference to the "new Irish government" stems from his belief that the passing of the Home Rule bill would create "the new Irish, or as it should be

Gaelic chairs in colleges throughout Ireland as well as stressing that a knowledge of Irish should be necessary for those who wish to enter professions such as lawyers, doctors and teachers in Ireland.[49]

In the aforementioned article in the *Citizen* regarding the lecture Douglas Hyde gave in New York in 1891 it was similarly communicated that Hyde was "justly severe on the Irish parliamentarians for not having done something for the language, and for not taking even a little interest in it. Hardly one of them has open his mouth about anything connected with the language or his country for nearly half a score years."[50] Hyde had previously written a letter to the editor of the *Irish Echo* in December 1887 conveying that when he speaks of the case of the Irish language it is the same as what he would say for the cause of Ireland as both causes go hand in hand;

> agus nuair a derim do chúis na Gaedheilghe is ionnann é
> agus dá n-deurfain do chúis na h-Éirionn mar is dóigh liom
> go bh-feicean tu go soilléir, mar fheicimid-ne, go
> d-téidheann an dá chúis lámh air láimh.[51]

The sentiment Hyde portrays in both articles echoes that of O'Neill Russell in 1886 as they conveyed similar criticisms and ambitions for the future of the language with political connections. Hyde's sentiments, published in Irish American journalism, is interesting given the non-political stance he vocally took in his presidency of the Gaelic League up to 1915. He wrote in his 1918 memoir that he felt "satisfied in [his] own mind that the rigid non-political attitude was the one thing that saved the League during the first dozen years, for everyone had a good word to say of it and nobody spoke against it" and that he:

---

more correctly called, the native Irish parliament . . ." The bill he refers to was the Government of Ireland Bill 1886 which was voted against in the House of Commons on June 8, 1886.

[49] "The Irish Parliament and the Irish Language," *Irish Echo*, June 1886.

[50] "Mr. Douglas Hyde," *Citizen*, June 27, 1891.

[51] "LITIR O'N G-CRAOBÍN AOIBÍNN," *Irish Echo*, December 1887; "and when I speak for the cause of Irish it's the same as what I would say about the case of Ireland and I suppose that you see clearly, as we see, that the two causes go hand in hand." My sincere thanks to Dylan Bryans for his suggestions on this translation.

... had reiterated to the public over and over again that the
League <u>was</u> only a language movement, and that so long as
I was in it I would never consent to its being made anything
made else . . . I myself was pledged before the country,
pledged to the very teeth, to keep the League out of politics,
and I had absolutely <u>no choice whatever</u> left but to retire
from it when I thought it was becoming political.[52]

Aside from this example of Hyde's personal reaction to the politicisation of
the Gaelic League in Dublin it also offers a noteworthy contrast to the
lecture he gave in New York in 1891 in which he laid much blame on the
lack of action and acknowledgment those associated with Irish politics at
the time gave to the Irish language and its cultivation. The lack of
recognition given to the language by those in political power is also
expressed in O'Neill Russell's lecture to the New York Philo-Celtic Society
in 1878. The article published in the *Irish American* mentions that in his
lecture he stated that "Emancipation failed; Fenianism failed; and if the
present [language] movement is not persevered in, all hope for Ireland is
lost."[53] In terms of the failure of Emancipation O'Neill Russell clarified that
Daniel O'Connell contributed more than any other man could to destroying
Irish nationality as although he could speak the Irish language "to
perfection" he made only one Irish speech in his career. He continued and
remarked that throughout O'Connell's forty-year public career "more than
a million of the Irish people ceased to speak Irish, while thousands of
Irishmen learnt to read English, solely for the purpose of being able to read
O'Connell's speeches."[54] This highlights the importance of reading Irish
matter for the survival of the language, echoing Keegan's previous plea for
the creation of literature in Irish and Logan's criticism of the lack of printed
Gaelic literature. The benefit of featuring the Irish language in print for its
cultivation and revival, and to political autonomy, is reiterated by O'Neill
Russell at a Fourth of July oration held at Bay Bridge, Chicago, in 1880. He

---

[52] University College Dublin Department of Irish Folklore, MS SOD/4/X/1961,
Douglas Hyde Memoir, 1918; emphasis in the original.
[53] "The N. Y. Philo-Celtic Society: Public Meeting in Support of the Irish Language
Revival," *Irish American*, September 21, 1878.
[54] "The N. Y. Philo-Celtic Society: Public Meeting in Support of the Irish Language
Revival," *Irish American*, September 21, 1878.

spoke in Irish and mentioned that Irish freedom wouldn't be long gotten once the first newspaper was printed in Irish and once the language had reclaimed its deserved respect freedom would soon be assured:

> An uair a g-clóbhuailtear an cead paipéar nuaidheacht go léir a n-Gaedhilig deirfidh mé nach m-beidh saoirse fad uainn; agus an uair a m-beidh meas cheart againn air teangain ar d-tíre, beidh Fáine lar mhóir na saoirse ag dealrughadh go fíor."[55]

Examples such as these from Irish American print fora convey how easily political ideology was associated with the cultivation and revival of the language and in turn the necessity of the language's survival for the future success of the nation. It also reveals the importance of the role of journals and newspapers in the creation of a new Irish psyche and hybrid identity. As Uí Chollatáin states "links to the native language formed part of the identity chain which was developed through the use of the language itself."[56] Journals and newspapers facilitated a space for debate, discussion, criticism and encouragement regarding linguistic and cultural matters. They also became "significant vehicles" where the Irish language and culture, with occasional political links, could "flourish and develop."[57]

Conclusion

The press allowed both communicator and reader to interact with one another. Ideas could become "a basis for practical action"[58] and the public sphere could engage with political and linguistic writings offering their own interpretations and perspectives. Through the journalistic forum the public sphere began to realise their identity, nationality, importance and worth in

---

[55] "A Polyglot Pic-nic," *Irish American*, July 17, 1880; "When the first newspaper is printed completely in Irish I will say that freedom isn't far from us ; and when we have the proper respect for the language of our country, the dawning day of freedom shall truly be upon us." My sincere thanks to Dylan Bryans for his suggestions on this translation.

[56] Uí Chollatáin, "'Thall is Abhus'," 354. See also Ní Bhroiméil, *Building Irish Identity in America.*

[57] Uí Chollatáin, "The Irish-Language Press: Tender Plant at the Best of Times?," 357.

[58] Declan Kiberd and P.J. Matthews, *Handbook of the Irish Revival* (Dublin: Abbey Theatre Press, 2015), 25.

the world on both a national and international level in the formation of a cultural, national and political consciousness. This incorporates Benedict Anderson's theory of an imagined community as the Irish American linguistic community began to recognise themselves as a group on a transnational basis rather than a fragmented society alone in their cultural and political aspirations for Ireland.[59] Questions of identity and the relationship between language and nationalism often arose in the Irish American journalistic forum which aided in the creation of a Irish language reading public giving the normal everyday citizen or immigrant the opportunity to practice writing Irish as well as offering their own opinion on societal matters.[60] It gave them a public profile to write, discuss, debate and communicate cultural and political objectives for Ireland which the Irish language community in Ireland and the US collectively envisioned on a transnational and transatlantic basis.

Acknowledgements

My thanks to the Irish Research Council for funding this research under the Government of Ireland Postgraduate Programme. I am also very grateful for the comments and suggestions from the reviewer.

---

[59] See Benedict Anderson, *Imagined Communities: Reflections on the Origin and Spread of Nationalism* (London & New York: Verso, 2016).
[60] See also McMahon, *Grand Opportunity: The Gaelic Revival and Irish Society, 1893–1910.*

CHAOS OR COMRADES?

Bibliography

"A Polyglot Pic-nic," *Irish American*, July 17, 1880

"A Practical Suggestion," *Irish World*, May 25, 1872.

"An Effective Mode of Promoting the Cultivation of the Irish Language," *An Gaodhal*, February 1888.

"Brooklyn Philo-Celtic Society," *Irish American*, September 7, 1878.

"Celtic Literature: The Eagle Complemented for Shedding Some Light on It," *Brooklyn Daily Edge*, March 27, 1879.

"Editorial," *An Gaodhal*, November 1890, 43–4.

"Editorial," *Irish Echo*, November 1889.

"From a True Son of the Gael," *Monitor*, March 28, 1888.

"Irish Music: A "Gaedhlic Idyll" in New York," *Irish American*, December 6, 1884.

"LITIR O'N G-CRAOBÍN AOIBÍNN," *Irish Echo*, December 1887.

"Mr. Douglas Hyde," *Citizen*, June 27, 1891.

"Our Gaelic Department," *Irish American,* July 16, 1887.

"Teanga agus Ceoil," *Irish American*, June 4, 1887.

"The Celtic Tongue," *Irish American*, April 17, 1858.

"The Gaelic Language," *Irish World*, November 22, 1895.

"The Irish American Philo-Celtic Union," *Irish American*, June 21, 1879.

"The Irish Language, Philo-Celtic Society, New York," *Irish American*, June 15, 1878.

"The Irish Language," *Irish American*, December 17, 1894.

"The Irish Language," *Irish American*, May 17, 1884.

"The Irish Language," *Pilot*, August 31, 1878.

"The Irish Language: A Society for its Preservation", *Brooklyn Daily Eagle*, April 21, 1878.

"The Irish Parliament and the Irish Language," *Irish Echo*, June 1886.

"The N. Y. Philo-Celtic Society: Public Meeting in Support of the Irish Language Revival," *Irish American*, September 21, 1878.

"University to have an Irish Chair," *Irish World*, November 24, 1894.

An Gaodhal, September 1895, 44.

Anderson, Benedict. *Imagined Communities: Reflections on the Origin and Spread of Nationalism*. London & New York: Verso, 2016.

Comer, Neil, Liam Mac Mathúna, Máire Nic an Bhaird, Brian Ó Conchubhair and Cuan Ó Seireadáin. *Douglas Hyde My American Journey*. Dublin: UCD Press, 2020.

Davis, Thomas. "Our National Language," *Nation,* April 1, 1843.

de Brún, Fionntán. "Escaping the "Shower of Folly": The Irish Language, Revivalism, and the History of Ideas." *Maynooth Philosophical Papers* 9, (2018): 43-58.

FIONA LYONS

Kiberd, Declan and P.J. Matthews. *Handbook of the Irish Revival*. Dublin: Abbey Theatre Press, 2015.

Knight, Matthew. "Gaels on the Pacific: The Irish Language Department in the San Francisco Monitor, 1888–91." *Éire-Ireland* 54, no. 3 (2019): 172–199.

Mac Congáil, Nollaig. "Saothrú na Gaeilge ar Nuachtáin Náisiúnta Bhéarla na hAoise seo caite: Sop nó Solamar?" In *Féilscríbhinn Anraí Mhic Giolla Chomhaill*, edited by Réamonn Ó Muireadhaigh, 112–191. Dublin: Coiscéim, 2011.

McMahon, Timothy. *Grand Opportunity: The Gaelic Revival and Irish Society, 1893–1910*. New York: Syracuse University Press, 2008.

Miller, Kerby A. *Emigrants and Exiles: Ireland and the Irish Exodus to North America*. New York: Oxford University Press, 1985.

National Library of Ireland, MS 3254, Letters to John (Mc) Glynn, of the Tuam News, with some to J. Mc Philpin of the same, and some associated correspondence mainly relating to the Irish language, incl. letters, essays, etc., in Irish by Rev. Eugene O'Growney; other correspondents include Canon Ulick Bourke and Rev. Euseby D. Cleaver. c. 1863–1894.

Ní Bhroiméil, Úna. *Building Irish Identity in America, 1870–1915: The Gaelic Revival*. Dublin: Four Courts Press, 2003.

Ní Uigín, Dorothy. "An Iriseoireacht Ghaeilge i Meiriceá agus in Éirinn ag Tús na hAthbheochana: An Cúlra Meiriceánach." In *Léachtaí Cholm Cille XXVIII*, edited by Ruairí Ó hUiginn, 25–47. Maynooth: An Sagart, 1998.

Nilsen, Kenneth E. "The Irish Language in New York 1850–1900." In *The New York Irish*, edited by Ronald H. Bayor, Timothy J. Meagher, 252–74. Baltimore and London: The Johns Hopkins University Press, 1996.

Nilsen, Kenneth E. "The Irish Language in nineteenth century New York city." In *The Multilingual Apple: Languages in New York City*, edited by Ofelia García and Joshua A. Fishman, 53–71. New York & Berlin: Mouton de Gruyter, 1997.

Ó Conchubhair, Brian. *Fin de Siècle na Gaeilge: Darwin, an Athbheochan agus Smaointeoireacht na hEorpa*. Connemara: An Clóchomhar, 2009.

Pearse, P.H. *Three Lectures on Gaelic Topics by P. H. Pearse*. Dublin: M.H. Gill & Son, 1898.

Penet, Jean-Christophe. "Thomas Davis, 'The Nation' and the Irish language." *Studies: An Irish Quarterly Review* 96, no. 384 (Winter 2007): 433–43.

Synge, JM. *Aran Islands and Connemara*. Dublin: Mercier Press, 2008.

Uí Chollatáin, Regina. ""Thall is Abhus" 1860–1930: The Revival Process and the Journalistic Web between Ireland and North America." In *Language Identity and Migration: Voices from Transnational Speakers and Communities*, edited by Chloe Diskin, Jennifer Martyn and Vera Regan, 353–379. Oxford: Peter Lang, 2016.

CHAOS OR COMRADES?

Uí Chollatáin, Regina. "Athbheochan Trasatlantach na Gaeilge: Scríbhneoirí, Intleachtóirí agus an Fhéiniúlacht Éireannach." In *Litríocht na Gaeilge ar fud an Domhain. Cruthú, Caomhnú agus Athbheochan. Imleabhar 1*, edited by Ríona Nic Congáil, Máirín Nic Eoin, Meidhbhín Ní Úrdail, Pádraig Ó Liatháin and Regina Uí Chollatáin, 277–309. Dublin: LeabhairCOMHAR, 2015.

Uí Chollatáin, Regina. "The Irish-Language Press: Tender Plant at the Best of Times?" In *The Edinburgh History of the British and Irish Press, Volume 2, Expansion and Evolution, 1800–1900*, edited by Martin Conboy and David Finkelstein, 357–376. Edinburgh: Edinburgh University Press, 2020.

Uí Chollatáin, Regina. "Language Shift and Language Revival in Ireland." In *Sociolinguistics in Ireland*, edited by Raymond Hickey, 176–197. Hampshire & New York: Palgrave Macmillan, 2016.

Uí Fhaoláin, Aoife. "Language revival and conflicting identities in The Irish Independent, 1905–1922." *Irish Studies Review* 22, no. 10, (2014): 63–79.

Uí Fhlannagáin, Fionnuala. *Fíníní Mheiriceá agus an Ghaeilge*. Dublin: Coiscéim, 2008.

Uí Fhlannagáin, Fionnuala. *Mícheál Ó Lócháin agus an Gaodhal*. Dublin: An Clochomhar Tta, 1990.

University College Dublin Department of Irish Folklore, MS SOD/4/X/1961, Douglas Hyde Memoir, 1918.

Whelan, Aoife and Regina Uí Chollatáin. "The Irish Language in the Regional Revival Press." In *The Irish Regional Press, 1892–2012*, edited by Ian Kenneally and James T. O'Donnell, 91–104. Dublin: Four Courts Press, 2018.

Wittke, Carl. *The Irish in America*. Baton Rouge: Louisiana State University Press, 1956.

Late modernism and Irish-language poetry: the INNTI project, and the Black Mountain poets of North Carolina

Liam Mac Amhlaigh

"An Sceimhlitheoir"

Tá na coiscéime   anna tar éis filleadh arís.
B'fhada a gcosa gan lúth gan
fuaim.

Seo trasna mo bhrollaigh iad
is ní féidir liom
corraí;

stadann tamall is amharcann siar
thar a ngualainn is deargann
toitín.

Táimid i gcúlsráid dhorcha gan lampa
is cloisim an té ar leis
iad

is nuair a dhírím air féachaint cé atá ann
níl éinne
ann

ach a choiscéimeanna
ar comhchéim le mo
chroí.[1]

This essay begins with the short, intense poem "An Sceimhlitheoir" (the title possibly best translated as "The Terrorist"). Written by Michael Davitt (1950–2005), lynchpin of the Irish-language INNTI poets, in the year after the publication of his second collection *Bligeard Sráide* (1983),[2] it was first published as an addendum in the *Selected Poems/Rogha Dánta*

---

[1] Michael Davitt, *An Tost a Scagadh* (Dublin: Coiscéim, 1993), 12.

[2] Michael Davitt, *Bligeard Sráide* (Dublin: Coiscéim, 1983).

collection in 1987,[3] and then fully anthologized in his third collection, *An Tost a Scagadh* in 1993. Belonging to an imagist tradition of late-modernist poetry, and similar in style to poems written by his slightly later contemporary, Áine Ní Ghlinn (1955–), the poem demonstrates a composer, as distinct from simply a poet or a writer, at work. The composition is drawn from short sharp components, weaved together from distress, rooted in contemporary reality, and focused on an immediate and potentially ongoing dilemma, but with the backdrop of an attempted cathartic emancipation; all that fused with lyrical expression, and contemporary rhythm. While it possesses a regular "irregular" structure, this psychological statement conjures up a very specific set of images and places us in an immediate and present danger.

The word *sceimhlitheoir* has a more regularly-quoted meaning within the public language in Ireland in the last 70–80 years, but the personal concept of *sceimhle* "terror" is at the heart of a word recaptured here as one not necessarily restricted to organised crime. With his careful choice of words, Davitt gets us to think in terms both personal, national and global.

"An Sceimhlitheoir" is one of a number of poems penned by poets associated with INNTI where a modernist style of writing can be seen. One could ask how much of this "modernism" in their poetry was a conscious decision on their part to either confirm or re-imagine tradition for both the writer and reader alike; or do these threads simply provide Davitt, in this case, with an exhortation through a formula of words in a language that he lived, loved and lamented to varying degrees? In the opaque nature of a perception of a threat behind his shoulder, can the reader detect, as with other poems from this time, a cry for help from the point of view of the poet and for his audience?

The regeneration, renewal and reinvigoration of Irish-language poetry that occurred during the early to late 1970s had as much to do with the times themselves, as with the poets writing within them. Recognised movements such as The Beats, The Confessionalists, through to The Martian Poets all scaffolded a mixture of hardy perennials and new voices in Ireland. The Irish-language INNTI publication/project grew out of University College

---

[3] Michael Davitt, *Selected Poems 1968–1984 Rogha Dánta* (Dublin: Raven Arts Press, 1987).

Cork in the late 1960s, with Davitt, as its de facto leader, the Ginsberg of the piece, playing a very important role in this new order.

While there may have been a space for such a 'school' of writing in the wider sphere of Irish-language poetry at that time, the group's ability to examine wider socio-cultural environs and utilise them to convince the reader of a broader form of poetic expression in the language is very telling. To better understand their impact, it is pertinent to look at a school of poetry on the other side of the Atlantic in that light: the poets from Black Mountain, North Carolina, and Robert Creeley (1926–2005) especially, who in his time was a pupil, poet and editor of *The Black Mountain Review*. The spontaneity of verse and strong links to imagist, modernist poetry allow the social development of a group of poets such as those of Black Mountain College to be a good yard-stick for the growth of a similar group, and poetic style, in the INNTI project in the Irish language.

This short essay draws a cursory comparison between the imagist, late-modernist poetry of the two groups at a reach of approximately twenty years from each other. In terms of INNTI, and without in any way wishing to reduce the stature of Nuala Ní Dhomhnaill (1952–), Liam Ó Muirthile (1950–2018) and Gabriel Rosenstock (1949–), this essay prioritises Michael Davitt's efforts in his critical role as leader and director of both sections of the INNTI project and it forms part of a larger body of work to analyse the corpus of poetry of the leader of the INNTI poets, its underpinnings and its influence on those around him.

Modernism, and its place in Irish-language poetry

In general terms, many international literatures have seen modernist writings inspired by urbanization and industrialisation and by the locating of an authentic response to a world that is ever-changing; in doing so, the reader can often see a sense of fragmentation and disillusionment in the work. One need only look at T.S. Eliot's (1888–1965) long poem *"The Waste Land,"*[4] to see a search for redemption and renewal in a sterile and spiritually empty landscape.

As Lauren Arrington has pointed out, many scholars have shown a critical reticence to consider even English-language Irish writers as modernists on account of modernism being associated with

---

[4] T. S. Eliot, *The Waste Land* (New York: Horace Liveright, 1922).

internationalism; that, in turn, has been interpreted as precluding a reading of such writers in a national context. For example, Yeats's canonical position as Ireland's national poet was a considerable stumbling block in assessing his developing style in his middle and late poetry from a modernist lens. The opposite, however, is the case for Beckett if you consider how detached from Ireland as a nation he had once become.[5]

If modernism, in the arts, was a radical break with the past and a concurrent search for new forms of expression, particularly in the years following World War I, Irish-language literature, and its poetical canon especially, is a very different case-study entirely. While there has been a reasonably consistent stream of academic commentary as regards recognisable modernist, and to a lesser-extent post-modernist, tendencies in Irish-language prose of the twentieth century, there is far less analysis of such features in Irish-language poetry of the same time period.

Louis de Paor has argued that such a modernist era began in Irish-language poetry in the late 1930s and continued until the arrival of the INNTI poets in the late 1960s, from which point he identifies a shift from the "modernist" to what he simply describes as the "contemporary". He refers to this thirty-year period as a "late adaptation of European modernism; an Irish variant of ideas that dominated the art, literature and philosophy of Continental Europe in the first half of the twentieth century."[6] Post-World War II poetry therefore in the Irish-language did not quite share the same lull as there may have been in Ireland within poetry in the English language. In such an assessment, it can certainly be argued that the work of Máirtín Ó Direáin (1910–1988), Seán Ó Ríordáin (1916–1977) and Máire Mhac an tSaoi (1922–) bestows on Irish-language poetry a quietly-felt revolution in terms of thematic thought, structure, and sense of language and place.

As we know, many simple mechanisms or conventions feature in modernist poetry including disrupted syntax, irregular sentence structure, and a stream of consciousness presentation where the poet presents the thoughts that come to their mind without regard to sequence or logic.

---

[5] Lauren Arrington, 'Irish Modernism,' in *British and Irish Literature* (DOI: 10.1093/obo/9780199846719-0069, 2012), 1.

[6] Louis de Paor (ed.), *Leabhar na hAthghabhála/Poems of Reposession* (Cork/Inverin: Bloodaxe Press/Cló Iar-Chonnacht, 2016), 18.

Modernist poets can often also convey a sense of alienation from the world; distanced from its experiences and its marvels, and a latent visual imagery. The poetic corpus of the triumvirate to which de Paor refers would benefit from further critical analysis of their function as modernist poets (in the same way as with Barry McCrea's recent experimental analysis of Ó Ríordáin's work within a minority language backdrop in his monograph *Languages of the Night* (2015)).[7] That is not to argue their status as poets of a European-influenced modernist era in Irish-language poetry; indeed Ó Ríordáin's *Eireaball Spideoige* (1952)[8] is a seminal collection from that modernist perspective, bringing a psychologically complex and often bleak form of poetry to bear.

However, in this article I would suggest that although Ó Direáin (*et al*) facilitated the opening-up of the writing of poetry in Modern Irish after the war, some of the modernist conventions mentioned above are potentially more intrinsically connected with the later group of INNTI poets, who had more in common with some of the American modernists starting with Eliot, and Pound (1885–1972), and continuing on to cummings (1894–1962), Stevens (1879–1955) and Williams (1883–1963) *et al*.

In this instance, it is important to note the significance that ought to be placed on the techniques of the visual arts. Re-centering poetic expression on abstract designs was the key to enabling a departure from a reliance on mimetic principles. Anglo-American poetry drew more on the aesthetic principles of non-representational arts therefore providing a model for a new poetic language which, in part, assisted the INNTI group of poets in breaking the Irish-language mould. Likewise, post-modernism's traditional association with an awareness of societal and cultural transitions after World War II, and the rise of mass-mediated consumerist popular culture in the 1960s–1970s, may also assist us in better-categorising the INNTI poets. In keeping with the Anglo-American influence, this essay argues that the modernist style most closely associated with Michael Davitt's work, and INNTI as a whole, is that which originates with imagism, best enunciated

---

[7] Barry McCrea, *Languages of the Night: Minor Languages and the Literary Imagination in Twentieth-Century Ireland and Europe* (Yale: Yale University Press, 2015).

[8] Seán Ó Ríordáin, *Eireaball Spideoige* (Dublin: Sáirseal & Dill, 1952).

by Pound at the start of the twentieth century (see below). It is also a style shared by the Black Mountain Poets.

INNTI and its origins

The INNTI movement of poetry reimagined the poetical landscape of the Irish-language in a short, sharp burst, evident with the first broadsheet published in 1970, and lasting a short few years (which we might refer to as 'INNTI na hOllscoile/University INNTI'), before Davitt reconvened the troops later in that decade to continue this project outside of a university setting, which we might classify as 'INNTI an phobail/Community INNTI'.

On the publishing of Liam Ó Muirthile's collected works in 2013 by Cois Life, *An Fuíoll Feá,*[9] Mícheál Ó hAodha reflected that the INNTI group "went at high and long-established walls with sledgehammers."[10] In stating that everything was grist to their mill, Ó hAodha states that poets such as Davitt and Ó Muirthile absorbed a range of influences as diverse as the aforementioned Beats, the new register of rock music–Cohen, Dylan, the Beatles–and even *sean-nós*, long before the latter became fashionable or even acknowledged as a form of "world music". He feels that they were eager to break with conventions and established norms, both literary and philosophic; that they took a delight in undercutting the establishment and providing a platform for hitherto marginalised or neglected sensibilities and viewpoints; that they wanted to use the "forgotten" language (the Irish-language) in a contemporary setting; to kick back against the *status quo.*

However, it is safe to say that the 'INNTI na hOllscoile' poets maintained a variety of mentors or sources of inspiration. Nuala Ní Dhomhnaill looked to John Berryman (1914–1972) and Adrienne Rich (1929–2012), Ó Muirthile preferred Jacques Prévert (1900–1977) and French poetry in general, Leonard Cohen (1934–2016), and later Robert Lowell (1917–1977). Gabriel Rosenstock read literary publications such as the *London Magazine, Akzente* from Germany, along with the works of Indian poets such as A. K. Ramanujan (1929–1993).

Davitt, on the other hand, functioned practically *sui generis*–he neither craved or needed any inspiration at all. As Louis de Paor states: "[Davitt]

---

[9] Liam Ó Muirthile, *An Fuíoll Feá* (Dublin: Cois Life, 2013).

[10] Mícheál Ó Aodha, 'The Old Boot Resouled,' in *Dublin Review of Books* (accessed 1st November 2019), https://www.drb.ie/essays/the-old-boot-resouled (2013).

acknowledges Ó Ríordáin, Ó Direáin, imitates ee cummings, translates George Mackay Brown (1921–1996), quotes Heinrich Heine (1797–1856), and insists that the songs of Bob Dylan (1941–) set the standard for poetry, but his debt to each of these is minimal."[11] Davitt was not, by reputation, a voracious reader. In current terms, he had read what was required to be read on educational curricula but did not engage in reading as a past-time. What he did read, or indeed what might have been shown or recommended to him, he devoured at a rapid pace. In eschewing the inclination to read widely, as the years progressed, he was more inclined to 'associate' himself with, rather than be influenced by, any number of well-known poets in America, France, England and beyond, mainly in a fraternal way, if he was already of the view that they maintained a well-known creative reputation. Davitt was very interested, and indeed inspired by (Allen) Ginsberg (1923–1997), but not by the poetry of Ginsberg. Therefore the reader finds the majority of INNTI poets mentored, at least in part, by modernists, while the leader of the INNTI movement consumed modernism merely through osmosis. It is also important to point out Davitt's editorial role with *INNTI*, the publication, preceded the first published collections by himself, Ó Muirthile, and Ní Dhomhnaill by over ten years; therefore, the written production of INNTI that was marshalled by Davitt represented these writers' greatest influence on the reader for that number of years.

Robert Creeley and The Black Mountain Poets

This brings us to the other consortium of poets discussed by this article, located in America: The Black Mountain Poets, from the short-lived experimental college in North Carolina of the same name. These poets favoured open forms, sudden and unexpected imagery and diction, and remarkable freedom in prosody. The Black Mountain College was established in 1933 as an experiment in situating the creative arts in a private educational institute. The College was founded by John A. Rice (1888–1968), an eminent and yet controversial scholar that had left Rollins College in Florida, and who wished to establish a new educational space based on John Dewey's (1859–1952) progressive educational approach. The College was established at the same time as artists were being persecuted across Europe, parallel to the commencement of Adolf Hitler's

---

[11] de Paor, *Leabhar na hAthghabhála*, 261.

regime, and the closure of the Bauhaus school in Germany, and it is interesting that a stream of both staff and students came to the College from Europe in these years, based, in part, on those reasons. The College existed for twenty-three years, and in that time, a recognisable group of poets grew—either teacher or students or in some cases both–who were especially progressive, particularly in the later years. Charles Olson (1910–1970), Robert Creeley, Robert Duncan (1919–1988), Denise Levertov (1923–1997) and Ed Dorn (1929–1999) are often the most noted disciples, and similar to the INNTI generation, there was a great variety between the poets in terms of style, personal interest, and approach, while they shared Olson's common philosophy of "projective verse".

Olson and Creeley are particularly noteworthy for this essay; Olson taught in the College for eight years between 1948 to 1956, and he was the final director of the College, even if his efforts did not save the College from closure. It was Olson, particularly, that developed this creative input in his well-known essay 'Projective Verse' in 1950,[12] praising the open form very highly, the instantaneous composition, and the importance of the deliverer of such poetry "os ard" (or "out loud"), something which ties with INNTI's Liam Ó Muirthile when he said: "it is the sounds of Irish poetry that move us in mysterious ways. The language itself has a strange hold on us, beyond reasonableness."[13]

Creeley was a student in the College originally, and then later taught alongside Olson. He drew on the example of William Carlos Williams and Pound, and their type of verse that also espouses the same imagism that in my view the Black Mountain poets share with INNTI. These verses from Creeley's poem "For Love" being a good example:

> Love, what do I think
> to say. I cannot say it.
> What have you become to ask,
> what have I made you into,

---

[12] Charles Olson, "Projective Verse" [1950], in *Collected Prose*, eds., Donald Allen & Benjamin Friedlander (Berkeley: University of California Press, [1950], 1997), 239–249.

[13] Liam Ó Muirthile, "Offshore on land: Poetry in Irish Now," in *A New View of the Irish Language,* eds. Caoilfhionn Nic Pháidín & Seán Ó Cearnaigh (Dublin: Cois Life, 2008), 140–151, 149.

companion, good company,
crossed legs with skirt, or
soft body under
the bones of the bed.

Nothing says anything
but that which it wishes
would come true, fears
what else might happen in

some other place, some
other time not this one.
A voice in my place, an
echo of that only in yours.[14]

    Creeley's sharp vignette created from the interpersonal dynamic shows a very human side to the images created; they are conveyed in a fluctuating way which highlights the many choices that life produces; choices that at times rest very heavily on many softer fragile words in print. The fragility of the humanity presented is ever more evident in the purposeful contemporary image created by the sparing use of text, as also evidenced in Davitt's "An Sceimhlitheoir" at the outset of this discussion.

    Creeley's singular importance is established in his time as the editor of the publication *The Black Mountain Review*, which commenced from an invitation from Olson. Just like *INNTI* (the publication), the *Review* emphasised the complete aesthetic: visual art in addition to the potential bareness of the printed word. Creeley and Olson's combined roles of creative force, and poetic lightning rod within the Black Mountain group both merge into one person in INNTI: into Michael Davitt. As Olson confirms Creeley's mantra of: "form is never more than an extension of content,"[15] Davitt, and the three other poets in University INNTI facilitated this very idea in remoulding the pre-existing form in a way in which it did not follow any pre-prepared pattern from any one source. Creeley also functions as a bridge as far as the Beat poets are concerned, always mentioned as critical mentors to the INNTI generation, in facilitating the

---

[14] Robert Creeley, "For Love," in *Poetry,* 98.2, 76–78 (1961).
[15] Olson, *Collected Prose*, 240.

Beats as an advisor, and it is to them that he dedicates the seventh and final edition of the *Review*.

Imagism

As we have seen in Davitt's *"An Sceimhlitheoir,"* and Creeley's "For Love," the concept of the visual vignette is important to both groups in this discussion: where an image (or images) can be generated from a vary sparing use of language in the text of the poem, an approach applied by many imagist poets. Imagist poetry designated free verse a legitimate poetic form and went on to play an influential role in a number of poetry circles and movements such as the Objectivist poets who came to prominence in the 1930s under the auspices of the aforementioned Pound and Williams. The March 1913 issue of *Poetry* contained two essays entitled *A Few Don'ts by an Imagiste*[16] and *Imagisme*[17] and in the first essay, Pound laid out some ground rules for what an imagist poem should contain:

1. (the) Direct treatment of the "thing," whether subjective or objective.
2. To use absolutely no word that does not contribute to the presentation.
3. As regarding rhythm: to compose in sequence of the musical phrase, not in sequence of the metronome.[18]

As a consequence, imagists preferred to use the language of common speech, embracing free verse and ignoring concerns regarding poetic metre. There was a focus, however, on the rhythm of phrases: known as "new rhythms." Their choice of subject tended to reflect real life, writing about a world that the poet inhabited, describing real people and real places, whether or not they directly named them.

At the time that Pound explained the preferences of imagism above, more traditional poets produced images through very detailed description, connecting them to a philosophical concept or theme; the imagist poet,

---

[16] Ezra Pound, "A Few Don'ts by an Imagiste," in *Poetry: A Magazine of Verse,* ed., Harriet Monroe (Chicago: Harriet Monroe, 1913), 1.6: 200–206.

[17] F.S. Flint, "Imagisme," in *Poetry: A Magazine of Verse,* ed., Harriet Monroe (Chicago: Harriet Monroe, 1913), 1.6: 198–200. This article was, in fact, drafted by Pound, and then re-written by Flint.

[18] Pound, *A Few Don'ts by an Imagiste,* 201.

however, makes no reference to the themes that were the focus of the image at all; they attempted to allow the created image to stand *sua sponte*.

After this initial developing of the concept of imagism in modernism, Pound's description was taken one step further by Olson in 1950 (see above), as he stated: "One perception must immediately and directly lead to a further perception."[19] These features are consciously visible in Black Mountain poetry as the imagist framework developed from Pound to Olson, and from Olson to Creeley, as Navero states: "More so than any other Black Mountain or Beat writer, Creeley has proposed a poesis of continual nascense amidst the varied and indefinite occasions of an immediate reality, while retaining the formal attention and integrity of the original impulse toward imagist concision and epiphany."[20] Again, as we see in examples such as the poem "Severed Head":

> In my head I am
> walking but I am not
> in my head, where
>
> is there to walk,
> not thought of, is
> the road itself more
>
> than seen. I think
> it might be, feel
> as my feet do, and
>
> continue, and
> at last reach, slowly,
> one end of my intention.[21]

Creeley manages to make the single frame/the photograph count for the image in the same way as the syllable is primary in his deliverable composition. It is a compact rhythm, that heightens emotion, and yet

---

[19] Olson, *Collected Prose*, 240.

[20] William Navero, "Robert Creeley: Close. In the Mind. Some Times. Some What:" in *boundary* 2 (Durham: Duke University Press, 1978), 2.6/7 (6.3 – 7.1), 347–352, 349.

[21] Robert Creeley, "Severed Head," in *Words* (New York: Charles Scribner, 1967), 36.

paradoxically, normalises it in a similar way to Frank O'Hara's theory of personism,[22] where he suggests what is personal to the poet is projected into forms of art. As Navero states in reference to Creeley's significant collections,[23] "This hard-edged, compact and muscular interior rhythm pervades the emotional terrain of *For Love* and *Words*."

Creeley's work shows the Black Mountain poets to be a good case study with the INNTI generation, especially in these imagist roots. As stated, it cannot be said that Davitt was influenced by one particular imagist writer (in the same manner as Creeley) but that the modernist approach that imbued other literatures with imagism did likewise in the Irish-language through INNTI, and specifically through Davitt. Davitt was a master of how to state such sequential ideas visually through words; he understood the vignette, the snapshot, that picture-perfect visual, with an albeit slightly more self-conscious approach in later collections of work.[24] He could also produce a very tight, compact, syllabic rhythm as he demonstrated particularly in this first three published collections.

As regards the vignette, as Mitchell states: "there were two possible uses: one was to use the vignette symbolically to provide information and the other was to use it to direct the audience's attention."[25] Both functions can be seen in Davitt's work, supporting two general backdrops: the personal vignettes, a little like a television drama serial in poems when specific occasions in his own life were involved, and impersonal vignettes, similar to documentary films, when Davitt stretches his vision into the greater public sphere. Davitt's poem "Ó mo bheirt Phailistíneach" catches this two-sided coin very well. Similar to a cold journalistic camera focusing on the barbaric work of the death squads,[26] Davitt puts us at an impersonal threshold; we stay at the edge having opened the door, a little like a curtain

---

[22] Frank O'Hara, "Personism: A Manifesto," in *Yugen* (New York: Totem Press, 1961), 7.27–29, 29.

[23] Navero, boundary, 351.

[24] Liam Mac Amhlaigh, "Amharcfhínéid na teilifíse i bhfilíocht Mhichael Davitt," in *Ó chleamairí go ceamaraí: an drámaíocht agus an teilifís.* eds., Éadaoin Ní Mhuircheartaigh, Pádraig Ó Liatháin and Síle Denvir (in press, Dublin: Cló Léann na Gaeilge, 2021).

[25] Mitch Mitchell, *Visual Effects for Film and Television* (Oxford: Focal Press, 2004), 53.

[26] Tadhg Ó Dúshláine, *Anois Tacht an Eala* (Dingle: An Sagart, 2011), 69.

at the start of a drama, and the spotlight shines in, as in the first verse he states:

> Bhrúigh mé an doras
> oiread a ligfeadh solas cheann an staighre
> orthu isteach:

The cameraman, the poet, is not making a judgment; simply placing the bare image in front of us; there is no hint of the horror to come as he focuses simply on the mess of the room, and he continues:

> na héadaí leapa caite díobh acu
> iad ina luí sceabhach
> mar a thiteadar
>
> a gúna oíche caite aníos thar a mása
> fuil ar a brístín lása, as scailp
> i gcúl a cinn
>
> a hinchinn sicín ag aiseag ar an bpiliúr,
> putóg ag úscadh as a bholgsan
> mar fheamainn ar charraig,
>
> ae ar bhraillín,
> leathlámh fhuilthéachta in airde.
> Ó mo bheirt Phailistíneach ag lobhadh sa teas
> lárnach.[27]

If the camera initially seems apathetic by its distance at the threshold, the text of the poem is anything but apathetic as the horror becomes more apparent when the camera focuses on the visceral distress of the girl's body in verses three and four. Davitt directs the vignette back to the personal in the last line comparing and referring to his own two children "ag lobhadh sa teas lárnach" ("decaying in the central heating"). A very strong emotional statement is made by the end, both privately and publicly, in the sparing use of language combined with the latently strong vignette and the tight, rhythmic structure. In this way, Davitt capably follows Pound and Olson's imagist styles in both the direct treatment, and the sequence of perception.

---

[27] Michael Davitt, *Bligeard Sráide* (Dublin: Coiscéim, 1983), 29.

Similar to Creeley, Davitt's poetry is filled with many other examples of modernism at work through imagism, such as the aforementioned "An Sceimhlitheoir:" the chilling, "Athchúirt ar Chúl an Tí" (from his first collection *Gleann ar Ghleann* (1981),[28] which is also a play on the title of Seán Ó Ríordáin's poem "Cúl an Tí"), the corporeal liquid that pours from love in the sexually-driven "Lúnasa" from *Bligeard Sráide* (1983) and the public exhortation in "Iarsholas" from *Scuais* (1998)[29] referencing the Irish presidential term of Mary Robinson. He reflects this imagism through a mix of divergent voices; calling upon multiple perspectives to provide striking visual imagery, in the same way in which Caitríona Ní Chléirchín in her 2011 paper from *Léachtaí Cholm Cille*, describes, as she refers to it, the paintwork of the INNTI poets, viewing Davitt as the most committed.[30]

Davitt's work contributed to University INNTI being imbued with an imagist approach that is, nevertheless, of its own time: parts of the period from 1945 to 1965 in the United States reflected in late 1960s Ireland. INNTI therefore functions as a counterpoint to Black Mountain, providing a parallel, intertwining development of late-modernist poetry based on imagist principles that have been consumed by osmosis. This article, however, does not attempt to analyse the tradition of European modernism that is also infused in the INNTI generation by their reading of previous twentieth century Irish-language poets. This noteworthy combination of influences from two distinct modernist traditions has been experimentally described as "bimodernism" and will benefit from further exploration.[31]

---

[28] Michael Davitt, *Gleann ar Ghleann* (Dublin: Sáirseal & Ó Marcaigh, 1981).

[29] Michael Davitt, *Scuais* (Inverin: Cló Iar-Chonnachta, 1998).

[30] Caitríona Ní Chléirchín, "INNTI: Ealaín, Focalphéintéireacht agus Meanma na Réabhlóide," in *Léachtaí Cholm Cille XLI: filí INNTI go hiontach,* eds., Tadhg Ó Dúshláine & Caitríona Ní Chléirchín (Maigh Nuad: An Sagart, 2011), 83–112, 109.

[31] Liam Mac Amhlaigh, "Tá na coiscéimeanna tar éis filleadh arís: leanúnachas agus nua-aoiseachas san fhilíocht iarChadhnach," in *Léachtaí Uí Chadhain 1980–2020,* eds., Liam Mac Amhlaigh & Caoimhín Mac Giolla Léith (in press, Dublin: Cló Léann na Gaeilge, 2020).

LIAM MAC AMHLAIGH

Conclusion

In a talk in 2018 concerning Máirtín Ó Cadhain's posthumously-published text *Barbed Wire*,[32] Alan Titley referred to its potential for comparison with Joyce's *Finnegan's Wake*, and he entertained us with the possibility that both Joyce and Ó Cadhain could equally liberate and imprison us at the same time in such texts. Albeit that the modernist debate that surrounds the INNTI group of poets is very much one of social, linguistic, and ideological emancipation, at differing points during his published corpus, Michael Davitt also hints that writing poetry both imprisoned and liberated himself and the other INNTI poets.

This writer would argue that some of these features are bound up in tradition, and the expectation of same, and while an understanding of tradition shifts continuously, Irish-language literature always engaged with tradition, and invented, reinvented, subverted, and repositioned itself on many occasions in light of the contemporary order. While scholarship grapples with what type of 'modernism' relates to the INNTI group of Irish-language poets, this work demonstrates a yet-to-be named category of poetical invention, and restatement, where tradition is re-imagined, and imagination is re-purposed: signposts on a modernist journey. The future naming of this category hints at a modernising voice, drawing on a collage of both late-modernist and post-modernist influences by osmosis.

The greater context of committed experimentalism concentrated in a single geographical location with a self-conscious sense of community, as described by Alan Golding,[33] as being crucial for understanding the ethos of Black Mountain poetry, is also equally as critical to UCC, and the community based around 'University INNTI'. Finally, in the words of

---

[32] Alan Titley, "Barbed Wire and Finnegan's Wake," Reimaging Traditions: IASIL Conference (unpublished conference contribution, Nijmegen: IASIL, July 2018).
[33] Alan Golding, 'The Black Mountain School,' in *The Cambridge Companion to American Poets,* ed., Mark Richardson (Cambridge: Cambridge University Press, 2015), 340–354, 342.

Ó Ríordáin's sparring partner Máire Mhac an tSaoi as she describes the launch of *INNTI* 11[34] in 1988:[35]

> The writing of verse in modern Irish is by any reckoning a mysterious phenomenon: a living literature in a fast-dying minority language, a literature with almost no spoken linguistic hinterland to draw on, which has not even the cultural and cultic status of Hebrew or Latin: by all the rules it should not happen, and yet it has. Poetry in Irish today is recognisably vital and valid, elegant and economical in expression, contemporarily relevant, and yet all the criteria by which it can be judged are established from beyond the grave.

INNTI helped to instil that specific "validity and vitality" in Irish-language poetry at the beginning of the 1970s and onwards, in conscious commentaries on life, the public and the private, the inner, and the outer; providing a visceral image-based canvas for the artform of the poetic word to re-configured. Further work to compare and contrast their underpinnings to those of the Black Mountain Poets will benefit our understanding of late modernist poetry, on both sides of the Atlantic.

---

[34] *INNTI 11*, ed. Michael Davitt (Dublin: Preas Innti Teoranta, 1988).

[35] "The Clerisy and the Folk: a review of present-day verse in the Irish language on the occasion of the publication of *Innti* 11," in *Poetry Ireland Review* 24, 33–35, 33 (1988).

The Conceptualization of Nationhood in Early-Seventeenth Century Irish: A Frame-Semantic Approach

Peter McQuillan

This essay will re-examine two words in seventeenth-century Irish that I have previously discussed elsewhere; **cine** 'descendants, a people' and **pobal** 'people, a people,' in terms of their contribution to the development of the concept of Irish nationhood.[1] I want to return to them using a more cognitive-linguistic based approach, that of frame semantics. To begin to justify my methodology, I am going to juxtapose two quotes. The first is from a scholar of nations and nationalism (Steven Grosby) in response to the question that he poses, "what is a nation?"[2]

> The nation is a community of kinship, specifically a bounded, territorially extensive, temporally deep community of nativity[.]

The nation as a form of kinship, therefore, is conceived of as a family vastly extended over space (territory) and time (history, myth, legend),[3] representing a "social relation of collective self-consciousness" reinforced by a shared culture.[4] "Nation-as-family" is a pervasive metaphor to be discussed below; Grosby suggests that territoriality, or "territorial descent", the shared identification with a common territory and its culture, is what distinguishes nationality from ethnicity in that it facilitates the assimilation of more than one ethnic group to this "family."[5]

---

[1] Peter McQuillan, "Nation as word and concept in seventeenth-century Irish", *Eolas. Journal of the American Society for Irish Medieval Studies* 8 (2015): 71–88; "Nation as *pobal* in seventeenth-century Irish", in *Early Modern Ireland: New Sources, Methods and Perspectives*, ed. Sarah Covington, Vincent Carey and Valerie McGowan-Doyle (Abingdon: Routledge, 2019), 113–29.

[2] Steven Grosby, *Nationalism: A Very Short Introduction*, (Oxford: Oxford University Press, 2005), 14.

[3] Grosby, *Nationalism*, 7.

[4] Ibid. 10.

[5] Ibid. 14, 43–4; more generally on ethnicity and nationhood, see Anthony D. Smith, *The Ethnic Origins of Nations*, (Oxford: Blackwell, 1986), on territoriality 134–8 especially. See also Adrian Hastings, *The Construction of Nationhood. Ethnicity,*

THE CONCEPTUALIZATION OF NATIONHOOD

"Nation" is a complex idea; yet, as "nation-as-family" indicates, it is predicated upon immediate everyday experiences of kinship and socialization, as well as the cultural practices in which we routinely participate. Our everyday experiences are crucial to our making sense of our world and meaning is constructed through the interface of body, mind, and that world. The words of language are the symbolic representations of this interface. This means that, ideally, we want an approach to language and to meaning that is holistic, that integrates all these elements into as seamless an epistemological continuum as possible. The approach best fitted to such a program in my view, is cognitive semantics. Evans lays out what he calls the "guiding principles of cognitive semantics" as follows:[6]

- **Cognition is embodied:** The conceptual structure of our minds reflects our bodily experience of the world
- **Semantic structure reflects and interacts with this conceptual structure:** The words we use refer to concepts in our minds
- **Meaning representation is encyclopedic:** Meaning originates in a structured inventory of general knowledge which represents our experience of the world
- **Meaning construction is conceptualization:** Specific words help us pick out what aspects of that knowledge we need in order to construe particular situations

These principles are the background to **frame semantics**, the approach to meaning that forms the basis of this essay. This will be further discussed in the next section below.[7]

Religion and Nationality, (Cambridge: Cambridge University Press, 1997), especially 167–84.

[6] Vyvyan Evans, *A Glossary of Cognitive Linguistics*, (Edinburgh: Edinburgh University Press, 2017, 99). See also by the same author his overview essay "Cognitive linguistics", (online: *WIREs Cogn Sci* 2012, 3:129–141. doi: 10.1002/wcs.1163).

[7] Foundational texts in cognitive linguistics include Ronald W. Langacker, "An introduction to cognitive grammar", *Cognitive Science* 10 (1986): 1–40; *Foundations of Cognitive Grammar* vol. 1 *Theoretical Prerequisites* (Palo Alto: Stanford University Press, 1987); George Lakoff, *Women, Fire and Dangerous Things. What Categories Reveal about the Mind* (Chicago: University of Chicago Press, 1987); & Mark Johnson, *Metaphors We Live By* (Chicago: University of Chicago Press, 1980).

This brings me to my second quotation, from the historical semanticist Dietrich Busse.[8] Busse describes his research program as "a historical-semantic epistemology," the aim of which is to explicate how what he calls "social knowledge" affects a diachronically oriented lexical semantics. This entails the broadening of semantic scope, of the "epistemic conditions," that give rise to meaning. This is essentially the cognitive linguistic program with a more specifically diachronic focus. As Busse asserts:[9]

> This kind of 'rich' semantics or 'depth semantics' cannot limit itself to elucidating the 'obvious,' as it were, epistemic elements of lexical and textual meanings. It must also explain the underlying, hidden knowledge that is normally overlooked because it is considered self-evident.

This is the kind of historical "depth semantics" that I hope to apply below. The idea of depth brings us back to Grosby's quote with which we opened. Let us begin by looking at frame semantics.

Frame semantics and FrameNet

"Meaning representation is encyclopedic": encyclopedic knowledge, however, consists of potentially vast, inchoate bodies of information about the world. The role of linguistic forms is to help us identify and access the smaller more manageable coherent areas of knowledge that we need in order to interpret particular situations. Frame semantics is the idea first advanced by Fillmore that we understand what words mean because when we use them they evoke particular scenarios, "frames", in our minds

---

More recently, see Lakoff, *Ten Lectures on Cognitive Linguistics* (Leiden and Boston: Brill, 2018). For state-of-the-art overviews of current research trends, see *The Oxford Handbook of Cognitive Linguistics*, ed. Dirk Geeraerts and H. Cuyckens (Oxford: Oxford University Press, 2010) and *The Cambridge Handbook of Cognitive Linguistics*, ed. Barbara Dancygier (Cambridge: Cambridge University Press, 2017). For cognitive approaches to lexical semantics, see Dirk Geeraerts, *Theories of Lexical Semantics* (Oxford University Press, 2010), 183–272; John R. Taylor, "Lexical Semantics", in *The Cambridge Handbook*, 246–61.

[8] Dietrich Busse, "Conceptual history or the history of discourse? On the theoretical basis and questions of methodology of a historical-semantic epistemology", in *Global Conceptual History. A Reader*, ed. Margit Pernau and Dominic Sachsenmaier (London: Bloomsbury, 2016), 107–32.

[9] Busse, "Conceptual history", 117.

through which we contextualize them.[10] Semantic structure reflects conceptual structure: frames are schematizations of our experiences, which our words reflect and allow us to access. The relationship between semantic (lexical) and conceptual structure is thus reflexive: a word evokes a frame, the combination of word and concept in turn evokes other words that give a different perspective on the same frame. A well-known example is 'buying and selling', which involves two participants, 'buyer' and 'seller', as well as two entities: what is being bought and sold ('merchandise') and how it is being paid for ('money'). Each of these words represents a concept that plays its own unique semantic role within the frame while helping to establish the set of relationships that obtain between it and other elements that constitute the frame.[11] Lakoff calls this scenario the "commercial event" frame.[12] Different individual words like 'buyer' and 'seller' highlight different aspects of that scenario, while simultaneously evoking each other and thus suggesting the entire coherent area of knowledge. Now the 'meaning' of a word is the particular access that it provides to the conceptual structure that underlies it (meaning construction is conceptualization).

Frames thus constitute a structured inventory of encyclopedic knowledge;[13] in addition they organize this inventory in respect of the lexicon. Lakoff makes the further point that the structure of frames is recursive. He points out that the commercial event frame makes use of other ideas, like "desire" and "possession," so that typically we buy things because we want or need to have them. In other words, a frame does not

---

[10] Charles J. Fillmore, "An alternative to checklist theories of meaning", *Proceedings of the First Annual Meeting of the Berkeley Linguistics Society* (1975), 123–31; "Frame semantics", in *Linguistics in the Morning Calm* (Linguistics Society of Korea, ed. 1982), 110–37; William Croft and D. Alan Cruse, "Frames, domains, spaces: the organization of conceptual structure", in *Cognitive Linguistics* (Cambridge: Cambridge University Press, 2004), 7–39.

[11] For a comparison between frames and the earlier more structurally oriented semantic 'fields', see Brigitte Nerlich and David D. Clarke, "Semantic fields and frames: historical explorations of the interaction between language, action and cognition", *Journal of Pragmatics* 32 (2000): 125–50.

[12] For a particularly succinct characterization, see George Lakoff, *Ten Lectures on Cognitive Linguistics* (Leiden and Boston: Brill, 2018), 37–8.

[13] See Langacker, *Foundations*, 57.

exist in isolation but draws on other broader or deeper frames as well.[14] We can adduce another instance here in relation to the commercial frame which consists of the fact that commercial exchange is only one type of exchange and can be subsumed under a more general frame of "reciprocality."[15] There are two aspects to frames, therefore. The first is frame-internal: the relationship between the concepts within the frame and the words that evoke them. The second is frame-external: the relationship between individual frames, or bundles of concepts. This is how the structure of our encyclopedic knowledge is built up: just as words evoke frames, so frames evoke other frames, which gives us our "inventory" whence we draw meaning.

How do we decide what frames to select or what to call frames? The answer is empirical and is based on the analysis of human language.[16] Since semantic structure reflects conceptual structure, it is reasonable to expect that words evoking the same frame will occur in close discursive and textual proximity to one another. Housed in Berkeley at the International Computer Science Institute since 1997, the Berkeley FrameNet computational lexicographical project has created an on-line lexical resource, using computer-assisted annotation of a large corpus of example sentences from contemporary English.[17] Its aim is to apply the theoretical and methodological understandings of frame semantics to this corpus of about 122 million words.[18]

In FrameNet, frames are made up of two basic constituents. First, we have the **frame elements (FE)**, the relevant conceptual entities that

---

[14] Or as Lakoff puts it: "more and more primitive ideas", *Ten Lectures*, 38; see also Geeraerts *Theories of Lexical Semantics*, 224–9.

[15] In FrameNet, RECIPROCALITY is a 'parent' frame of the COMMERCIAL TRANSACTION frame.

[16] Croft and Cruse, "Frames, domains, spaces", 14.

[17] See http://framenet.icsi.berkeley.edu; also Charles J. Fillmore, Christopher R. Johnson and Miriam R.L. Petruck, "Background to FrameNet", *International Journal of Lexicography* 16, 3 (2003): 235–50. The lexical database, as of 2016, contained more than 13,000 lexical units (the combination of a word and its meanings), about 7,000 of which are fully annotated, in more than 1,000 hierarchically related semantic frames.

[18] FrameNet uses both the electronic British National Corpus (100 million words) and the American National Corpus (22 million words) databases.

participate in the frame. Second, we have the **lexical units** (LU), the items that give linguistic expression to these entities and the relationships between them.[19] As they are conceptual rather than lexical, frame elements are considered to be relatively language-independent. Conventionally, these are depicted in uppercase (BUYER, SELLER etc.) to distinguish them from the lexical units, combinations of words and their senses, whose symbolic realizations are language-specific (e.g. English *buyer*, *seller*, but German *Käufer*, *Verkäufer*).[20] Annotated sentences then exemplify how the frame elements relate semantically and syntactically to the various frame-evoking lexical units.

I propose now to assess what frame semantics and FrameNet can offer in terms of the diachronic semantics of **cine** and **pobal** in relation to the conceptualization of nationhood in seventeenth-century Irish. As is conventional, frame names will be uppercase.

A note on authors and sources

In the two sections that follow, most of my examples are taken from the work of the Jesuit-trained secular priest Seathrún Céitinn (*angl.* Geoffrey Keating).[21] Having been educated in France, like so many of his Irish Catholic contemporaries, Céitinn returned to Ireland around 1610. In 1634, he completed his seminal narrative history of Ireland from pre-historic times to the arrival of the Anglo-Normans in the twelfth century, *Foras Feasa ar Éirinn* (The Foundation of Knowledge on Ireland).[22] As

---

[19] See for example Geeraerts *Theories of Lexical Semantics*, 224–9.

[20] Several projects are underway to build FrameNets parallel to the English-language project for languages around the world, including Spanish, German, Chinese, and Japanese. See also Collin F. Baker, "FrameNet, current collaborations and future goals", *Language Resources & Evaluation* 46 (2012): 269–82, especially 279–82.

[21] For Céitinn, see Bernadette Cunningham, *The World of Geoffrey Keating. History, Myth and Religion in Seventeenth-Century Ireland* (Dublin: Four Courts Press, 2002); "Keating, Geoffrey (Céitinn, Seathrún)", *Dictionary of Irish Biography* (online Cambridge University Press/Royal Irish Academy; accessed 06/26/2020) for a concise summary.

[22] For text and translation, see *The History of Ireland by Geoffrey Keating D.D.*, 3 vols., ed. David Comyn and Patrick S. Dinneen (London: Irish Texts Society, 1902–08). For context, see Breandán Ó Buachalla, "*Annála Ríoghachta Éireann* agus *Foras Feasa ar Éirinn*: an comhthéacs comhaimseartha", *Studia Hibernica* 22–23 (1982–3):

Bradshaw has emphasized, this is the first Irish national history; what makes it so is the grafting of the author's own historic community, the Old English, descendants of the Anglo-Normans, onto the pseudo-historical schema of the Gaelic Irish *origo gentis*, as represented by the medieval *Lebor Gabála Érenn* (*Leabhar Gabhála Éireann* (The Book of the Taking of Ireland), as legitimate members of the Kingdom of Ireland.[23] That kingdom is now constituted by the merger of the two ethnicities on the island prior to the New English re-conquest of the sixteenth and seventeenth centuries: Gaelic Irish and Old English, the latter the descendants of the Anglo-Normans.

Towards a frame analysis of cineadh (cine)

Let us first review the relevant lexicographic information for the medieval and early modern Irish periods based on the electronic Dictionary of the Irish Language:[24]

(1) Verbal noun **cineadh** (verb **cinidh** 'is born') '(act/state of) being born'; when followed by the prepositions **de** 'from' or **ó** 'of', the verb means 'descends/is descended from'

(2) Noun **cineadh** (based on the verbal noun), also with the form **cine** reflecting evolving pronunciation: (a) 'offspring, descendants, children' (always plural); (b) 'tribe, race'

This gives us three lexical units (a combination of word form and word sense): 'being born'; 'offspring'; 'a people' (incorporating tribe and race as an extension of offspring). Each of these semantic units evokes its own

---

59–105; Brendan Bradshaw "Geoffrey Keating: Apologist for Irish Ireland", in *Representing Ireland: Literature and the Origins of Conflict 1534–1600*, ed. Brendan Bradshaw, Andrew Hadfield and Willie Maley (Cambridge: Cambridge University Press, 1993), 166–90.

[23] For the text, see *Lebor Gabála Érenn: The Book of the Taking of Ireland* ed. R.A. Macalister (Dublin: Irish Texts Society, 1938); see also John Carey, *A New Introduction to Lebor Gabála Érenn* (London: Irish Texts Society, 1993); Most comprehensively, see R Mark Scowcroft, "Leabhar Gabhála Éireann Part I: the growth of the text", *Ériu* 38 (1987): 81–142; "Leabhar Gabhála Éireann Part II: the growth of the tradition", *Ériu* 39 (1988): 1–66.

[24] *eDIL: Electronic Dictionary of the Irish Language*, ed. Gregory Toner, Máire Ní Mhaonaigh, Sharon Arbuthnot, Marie-Luise Theuerkauf and Dagmar Wotko (www.dil.ie, 2019), s.v. *cinid* and *ciniud* (accessed online 12/26/2019).

frame, and in two of three cases here, the apposite frame is available in FrameNet: BEING BORN and KINSHIP. Here I present in a very summarized form both of these frames in FrameNet, recalling that frame elements (FEs) are the conceptual units that comprise the frame: [25]

- BEING BORN: FE **child**; LU *be born, come into the word*
- KINSHIP: FE **alter** + **ego** = **relatives**[26]; LU *mother father son ancestor descendant* (etc.)

Let us now consider the following example, also from the eDIL entry for *ciniud*. This is from a medieval gloss on a law text:[27]

> **Ciniud** *iar tuistiu .i. geinemain do o maithir iar na tuisti o athair*
>
> being born after being procreated i.e. his being born from a mother having been conceived from a father

From this we could construct the following frame, adapting it to a more early-modern spelling; the conceptual elements are uppercase:

Frame elements: MOTHER FATHER CHILD
Lexical units: *máthair* 'mother' (noun (n)) *athair* 'father' (n) *tuistiu* 'procreation' (verbal noun (vn)); *cineadh* (*ciniud*) 'being born' (vn) *geineamhain* (*geinemain*) 'being born' (vn)

In FrameNet, this scenario would actually evoke at least three frames. BEING BORN is most directly evoked by the verbal nouns **cineadh** and *geineamhain* (to give the 'classical' early modern Irish spellings); the addition of the lexical units *máthair* 'mother' and *athair* 'father' directly evoke the further frame BIRTH SCENARIO (on which BEING BORN is one perspective, GIVING BIRTH another). Mother and father further suggest a SEXUAL REPRODUCTION SCENARIO frame, confirmed by the verbal noun *tuistiu* 'engendering, procreating'.

---

[25] In the interests of economy, I ignore here the valency relations (the possible combinations between entities within frames based on their semantics and syntax) that obtain.

[26] FrameNet employs here the terminology current in anthropology, so for example *my* (ego) *brother* (alter).

[27] The translation is my own.

It is also interesting in this connection that the glossator feels the need to explain **cineadh** in the sense 'being born' with its more common synonym, *geineamhain*. In fact, the dictionary entry for **cineadh** above is the only example I have found of its original verbal noun sense of 'being born'. **Cineadh** much more commonly directly evokes the second original frame above, KINSHIP, as do the words *máthair* and *athair*, also occurring commonly with other KINSHIP-evoking items like *mac* 'son', *sinsear* 'ancestor', *clann* 'children' *síol* 'seed' and *sliocht* 'descendants'. In other words, 'being born' shifts to 'what has been born', but always in the collective sense ('children' never 'child').

The KINSHIP frame is comprised of people of course, and we recall that our third sense of **cineadh** above was 'tribe' or 'race'. FrameNet has a frame PEOPLE but as its definition makes plain, it is not fit for purpose here: "This frame contains general words for Individuals, i.e. humans. The Person is conceived of as independent of other specific individuals with whom they have relationships and independent of their participation in any particular activity." The nation on the other hand (or the "race" or "tribe" for that matter) is "a social relation of collective self-consciousness."[28] We need something that captures the idea of "collective self-consciousness." Consider the following passage from *Foras Feasa ar Éirinn,* in which Céitinn begins discussion of the ethnic origins of the Irish nation. (In the interests of space and clarity of exposition, I will give English translations with the relevant Irish vocabulary highlighted in the course of the essay. Target words and expressions for the particular passage are in bold; supporting words and expressions are in italics):[29]

> Of the origins (**bunadhas**) of the children of Míl (*Clann Míleadh*) . . . /of their genealogy (*geinealach*) . . . In order, truly, that we should be able to trace the origin of the Scotic[30] nation (**cineadh Scoit**) to its root (**préamh**), i.e. to Japheth, (we find) the two most distinguished sons (*mic*) Japheth had, that is to say, Gomer and Magog. Moses, in

---

[28] Grosby, *Nationalism*, 10.

[29] Comyn, *History*, vol. I, 224–6; 225–7 (editor's translation).

[30] I adhere to this rendering of Céitinn's editors, as there seems to be no viable alternative in English. There is an adjective *Scoitic* in medieval Irish derived from Latin *Scotticus*, which is used occasionally of the Irish language (eDIL *s.v. Scoitic*).

the tenth chapter of Genesis, where he records the propagation (*craobhsgaoileadh*) of the posterity (*sliocht*) of Japheth, sets down that Gomer had three sons (*mic*) . . . however, he does not mention specially the children (*clann*) of Magog according to their names. Nevertheless, as it is on the antiquaries (*seanchadha*) of the Scotic nation (**cineadh Scuit**) that it is incumbent to follow up the ascertained genealogy of the nobles who sprang from (*do ghein ó*) Magog, and particularly of the posterity (*sliocht*) of Fenius Farsaidh, we shall here set down the genealogical account of the posterity (*sliocht*) of Magog, according to the Book of Invasion (*Leabhar Gabhála*)

The nouns *clann* 'family, children', *mac* 'son' (plural *mic*), *sliocht* 'descendants', as well as **cineadh** itself and the verb *geinid ó* 'is born from' (here in the past tense *do ghein*) evoke the KINSHIP frame, especially the idea of descent. There are two designations here representing the idea of an Irish nation. The first is *clann Mhíleadh* 'the children of Míl' (*clann* in the genitive case above). Míl of Spain (*Míl Easpáinne*) led the expedition to Ireland that captured it for the Gaelic Irish, who are henceforth known as the children or sons of Míl. This invasion is the final canonical one recognized by the Book of Invasions.[31] The second is **cineadh Scoit** 'the Scotic people/nation', a wider designation encompassing *all* the canonical invasions described in the Book of Invasions, including that of *Clann Mhíleadh*, the Gaelic Irish themselves. The nation is thus a temporally extended family.

The passage is otherwise concerned with origin in the form of the words **bunadhas** and **préamh**. The former is glossed by eDIL as "origin, source. Freq. of peoples, tribes"; the noun from which it is derived *bunad* also has a similar range of senses "origin, basis, source; Of families *etc.* origin, stock, race". [32] **Préamh** means most basically 'root', whence the

---

[31] For a concise discussion of the medieval view that the Irish originated in Spain, see John Carey, "Did the Irish Come from Spain? The Legend of the Milesians", *History Ireland*, 9.3 (2001): 8–11.

[32] eDIL *s.v. bunadas* and *bunad*; see also Peter McQuillan, *Native and Natural. Aspects of the Concepts of Right and Freedom in Irish* (Cork University Press, 2004), 58–60.

secondary meanings 'source, origin' and from there "root-stock (of a family or race), original or genuine stock: often loosely in the sense line or race."[33] The sense of 'a people' and the sense of that people's origins are conceptually coterminous and this is reflected in lexical structure. This process of the tracing of origins is implicated in the practices of the learned classes of medieval and early modern Ireland, through genealogy (*genealach; craobhsgaoileadh*) and historiography (as practiced by *seanchadha* 'historians') all in the context of the Gaelic origin legend *Leabhar Gabhála Éireann*, itself framed here by the origin of the world's nations in the Book of Genesis.[34] While much of this background is not immediately accessed through the lexical unit **cineadh**, it is still part of that word's deeper semantics, in that it frames (pun intended!) Céitinn's understanding of its deeper implications. This understanding is also conditioned by his engagement with the secular and religious learning of his day.

From the material presented thus far, it is clear that we are dealing here with a pervasive conceptual metaphor, A NATION IS A FAMILY. This involves mapping or projecting elements from a **source** frame (here A FAMILY) onto a **target** frame (here A NATION). "Cognition is embodied": the conceptual structure of our minds reflects our perceptual and sensory experience of the world. In this case, the intersubjective quotidian experience of belonging to a family is projected onto the more abstract idea of the extended family of nationhood.[35] We can note too that this mapping is characteristic not just of the frame as a whole but also of its constituent parts. So while 'family' is 'nation', the 'children' (*clann*) are the collective constituents of nation and the 'father' (*Míl*) is its leader or originator. So:

---

[33] eDIL *s.v. frém.*

[34] See note 23 above.

[35] See https://metaphor.icsi.berkeley.edu/pub/en/index.php/Metaphor:NATION_IS_ A_FAMILY (accessed online 30/5/2020); see Zoltán Kövecses, *Metaphor. A Practical Introduction* (Oxford University Press, 2002), 62–4; more extensively George Lakoff, *Moral Politics: what Conservatives Know and Liberals Don't* (University of Chicago Press, 1996).

Source (A FAMILY)   **Target** (A NATION)
Father of
Progenitor/Leader of (*Míl*)
Children of   Members of (*clann*)
Being born into   Becoming a member of

We will return to this metaphor below in the context of a broader discussion of kinship; first, however, I would like to comment further on the expression **cine Scuit**.

While Céitinn adopts the traditional Gaelic Irish belief that they originated in the eastern kingdom of Scythia, his use of this phrase to denote a "Scotic nation," an umbrella term to encompass all the canonical invaders, historic and pre-historic, of Ireland, is innovative.[36] This succession of invasions culminates in that of the Gaelic Irish themselves, who are therefore the historical representatives of that deeper nation. In a telling passage, Céitinn engages with two competing explanations of the designation **cine Scuit**. When the ancestors of the Gaelic Irish arrive in Scythia they are led by one Éibhear Scot:[37]

> a certain author says that Eibhear Scot was their leader in this expedition, and that it was from his cognomen, namely, Scot, that the Gaels are called the Scotic race (**cine Scuit**) .
> . . from this cognomen given him the name was given to his posterity (*sliocht*).

On this account, the Scotic nation is a matter of common biological descent, because their leader's 'surname' was *Scot*, his descendants (here *sliocht*) are 'the people of Scot' (**cine Scuit**). Céitinn, however, disagrees:[38]

> [B]ecause it is the common understanding of the historians that the reason that the descendants of Gaedheal (*sliocht Gaedhil*) are called the Scotic nation (**cine Scuit**) is because they came from Scythia according to their origin (*bunadhas*).

This is not so much a rejection of the principle of ethno-genetic descent, the Gaelic Irish are still *sliocht Gaedhil* after all, as an incorporation of it within

---

[36] See further McQuillan "Nation as word", 80–88; "Nation as 'pobal'", 14–15.

[37] Dinneen, *History*, vol. II, 26; 27 (editor's translation).

[38] Ibid. 26; this and all subsequent translations are my own.

the complementary principle of 'territorial descent,' vital for the validation of Céitinn's own Old English community as legitimate components of a Kingdom of Ireland. Nationhood stresses territorial descent, the identification with a shared territory and its culture, which facilitates the incorporation of multiple ethnic identities into the nation.[39] In addition, by including the non-Gaelic invaders from the Book of Invasions who preceded the Gaelic Irish, **cine Scuit** establishes the immemorial continuum of the nation and lays the basis for a more civic territorial sense of nationhood.[40] In addition to a common place of origin, all members of this Scotic nation share the same language (*Scoitbheurla* essentially the Irish language).[41]

While Céitinn cannot plausibly present his Old English community as members of a Scotic nation, it is the establishment of the *principle* of territoriality, of territorial descent, that is important here. I want to examine a further development of this principle in Céitinn's most famous political poem (Óm sceól ar ardmhagh Fáil "From my news on Fál's high plain"), composed in reaction to the turmoil caused by the New English conquest and colonization of Ireland in the seventeenth century. Here is the second stanza:[42]

> Brazen Fódla, it is a shame for you not to recognize that it
> is more proper to nurture (**tál ar**) the surpassing civil
> descendants (**sliocht**) of Míl; not a drop (**deór**) has been
> left in the expanse of your gentle fair breast (**brollach**) that
> the brood of every foreign sow has not sucked (**deól**)

The familiar word *sliocht* 'descendants' evokes the KINSHIP frame again here but the understanding of kinship is extended to include the idea of NURTURANCE (lexical units in brackets in the stanza prompt the idea of breast-feeding). Fódla, along with Banbha and Ériu, is one of the three

---

[39] Grosby, *Nationalism*, 14, 43 ff;

[40] It also helps to wards off Tudor claims that pre–Milesian Ireland had been part of an ancient British imperium. See Bradshaw, "Geoffrey Keating: Apologist", 166–90, 171–2; McQuillan, "Nation as word", 86–8.

[41] Comyn, *History* vol. I, 174.

[42] For the original text, see *Nua–Dhuanaire Cuid I*, ed. Breandán Ó Buachalla, Tomás Ó Concheanainn and Pádraig de Brún (Dublin; Dublin Institute of Advanced Studies, 1975), 18.

eponymous tutelary goddesses of Ireland in *Leabhar Gabhála*, members of the Tuatha Dé Danann, predecessors of the Gaels in Ireland. Having been defeated by the Gaelic Irish, the Tuatha Dé accept them as the legitimate inheritors of Ireland. Metaphorically, the goddesses are then conceived as the nurturing mothers of the descendants of Míl, who are consequently their adopted/fostered rather than genetic children. The complaint of the poet is that by the seventeenth century it is the New English ("the brood of every foreign sow") rather than the Gaelic Irish that are being nurtured as the nation's children. Based simply on this stanza, we can construct a KINSHIP NURTURE frame as follows:

- **Frame elements:** NURTURING MOTHER, CHILDREN, NURTURANCE
- **Lexical units:** *sliocht* 'family, descendants' (n) *Míl* "Milesius" (n) *Fódla* 'Goddess Ireland' (n) *deór* 'drop' (n), *brollach* 'breast' (n), *deól* 'suck' (v), *tál ar* 'suckle' (v)

Two things are immediately relevant here. First, Irish makes a lexical distinction between *máthair* 'birth mother' (also 'mother' generically) and *muime* (later form *buime*) 'foster mother, wet nurse', reflecting the importance of fosterage as an institution in medieval Ireland and the fact that birth and nurturance mother were frequently not the same woman.[43] Second, it is the latter that is almost invariably invoked in the present context of Ireland as mother. This leads to further associations. The nurture frame is most neatly illustrated as follows:

(like) a wet nurse (**buime**) nurturing (**ag altram**) her children (**clann**)

This example is taken from the Irish translation of St. Paul (I Thessalonians 7-8), where transmission of the gospel is likened to the loving devotion of a nurturing mother.[44] Paul further says that he and his disciples could have imposed God's word through their authority, but preferred, however, to be gentle and affectionate because the Thessalonians had become dear to them. Here all three core frame elements are represented lexically but comparison with Céitinn's example above underscores an important point: the priority

---

[43] See Fergus Kelly, *A Guide to Early Irish Law* (Dublin: Dublin Institute for Advanced Studies, 1988), 86–7.

[44] Uilliam Ó Domhnaill, *Tiomna Nuadh ár dTighearna* (Dublin: William Ussher, 1602).

of conceptual over lexical structure. Despite the absence of these three most central words, the frame is still present in Céitinn's poem.

That affection is central to NURTURANCE is borne out by the word *muime* itself. Languages often have a hypocoristic term for each of the parents of a family (English *mummy, mommy, daddy*). The term of affection in medieval Ireland (*muime*) is lexicalized to mean the nurturing rather than the birth mother, the latter retaining the inherited Indo-European etymon *máthair*. Céitinn's stanza has further significant implications for the 'nation-as-family' metaphor, especially in relation to the understanding of the nation's 'mother' as a nurturer. The nurturing of one's children is a moral responsibility within the family. Within A NATION IS A FAMILY, therefore, MORALITY IS NURTURANCE and MORAL AGENTS ARE NURTURING PARENTS; hence the poet's anger at Ireland the wet nurse nurturing "the brood of every foreign sow." It is a dereliction of her moral responsibility.[45] The nation is ideally a moral entity predicated on the 'nation-as-family' metaphor.

In a different poem, Céitinn refers to another of the eponymous goddesses, Banbha, as *seanbhuime mhaicne Mhílidh* "the old foster-mother of the sons of Míl".[46] In the preface to one of his historiographical works, the Franciscan Mícheál Ó Cléirigh expresses his desire to defend Ireland's reputation, referring to her as *mátharbhuime Éire* "mother nurse Ireland", a lexical compound of the two senses of birth and nurturance mother; the same passage also more elaborately describes Ireland as a *mathair accas muime gineamhna accas glanoilte* "mother and wet nurse of birth and of pure nurturance".[47] Early seventeenth-century texts invoke the names of each of the three goddesses as symbolic representations of the land itself, as nurturers of the Gaelic Irish, as transmitters of native culture from generation to generation. We can now update our metaphorical mapping A NATION IS A FAMILY to include the following metaphorical entailments:

---

[45] Kövesces, *Metaphor*, 63.

[46] Brain Ó Cuív (ed.), "Mo thruaighe mar tá Éire", *Éigse. A Journal of Irish Studies* 8/4 (1957): 302–8 at 305.

[47] Paul Walsh (ed.) *Genealogie Regum et Sanctorum Hiberniae* (Maynooth Catholic Record Society, 1916), 7.

THE CONCEPTUALIZATION OF NATIONHOOD

Source (A FAMILY)	**Target** (A NATION)
Father of	Leader/Origin(ator) of
Being born into	Becoming a member of
Children of	Members of
Mother of	Nurturance (culture) of
Being nurtured within	Becoming a member of

Since the three goddesses of the Tuatha Dé are personifications of Ireland, we can add the further ontological metaphor here of THE LAND IS A NURTURER. This further advances the principle of territorial descent. We may note that once again it is the *principle* that counts for Céitinn: the metaphor as such refers to the adoption of the Gaelic Irish as children of the Tuatha Dé Danann, the gods and goddesses who preceded them to Ireland, and does not as such include the Old English. Nonetheless, I think that we might see this principle at work in the final lines of *Foras Feasa*. As Céitinn expresses it, the Old English can justify their presence in Ireland because God, as reward for the sense of civic duty shown by the majority of the Anglo-Normans, has permitted their descendants to endure and prosper in Ireland (*do tug Dia do shochar dá chionn soin dóibh iomad do shleachtaibh do bheith ar a lorg aniú i nÉirinn*). No less than the Gaelic Irish, their presence is therefore divinely sanctioned, this time however by a Christian God. Each case is conceptually equivalent; a territorial descent by 'adoption'.[48]

To conclude this section and introduce the next, I want to look briefly at a text *not* by Céitinn, but by a Gaelic Irish nobleman, Domhnall Ó Súilleabháin Béirre; a letter written in December 1601 and addressed to the King of Spain, Philip III. A combined Irish-Spanish army had just been defeated in the decisive battle of the Nine Years War at Kinsale by the English, and Ó Súilleabháin Béirre is appealing for renewed Spanish aid. Here is the opening of his letter: [49]

---

[48] Dinneen, *The History*, III, 368.

[49] Brian Ó Cuív, "An appeal to Philip III of Spain by Ó Súilleabháin Béirre, December 1601", *Éigse* 27 (1993): 18–26; for further discussion, see McQuillan, *Native and Natural*, 57–60. This and all subsequent translations are my own.

PETER MCQUILLAN

It has always and eternally been affirmed among us the
Irish (*na hÉireannaigh*), from age to age as well as daily
custom, that there is no single thing that more powerfully
works in our hearts to merit and win our love and affection
than the natural love of the native land (**dúthchas**) and the
remembrance of the friendship (**caradradh**) that is
continuously in our minds, especially being renewed and
nourished and kept in memory . . . Since we, the preeminent Gaels of Ireland (*príomhGhaoighuil na hÉireann*),
have long drawn our root (**préamh**) and origin (**bunadhas**)
from the esteemed, truly noble race of the Spaniards, that
is, from Míl son of Bile son of Breóghon . . . according to
the evidence of our old books of traditional knowledge
(*seanchus*), the branches of our genealogy (*geinealach*),
our histories and chronicles . . .

The words **bunadhas** 'origin' and **préamh** 'root' have already been
encountered in the passage from *Foras Feasa* above outlining the descent
of the Gaelic Irish from Míl of Spain. These words evoke the same frame
of reference here, of knowledge of origins as derived from indigenous
learning and historiography, except that in the present context, the
invocation of the ancient Irish-Spanish genealogical connection is urgently
political. It is notable that here it is coupled with a reflection on the
animating power of natural affection for the native land (**dúthchas**), an
affection that has both daily efficacy and temporal depth, itself coupled with
an evaluation of the Spanish relationship as **caradradh**, a term that ranges
from 'friendship, alliance' to 'blood or marriage relationship.'[50]

Dúthchas 'inheritance; heritage; native land', is one of those words
that speakers of a language often deem 'untranslatable'. Including the
senses just listed, it extends in a number of directions to encompass traits
and characteristics inherited by bloodline, as well as emotive connections
based on relationships of long standing. Its core element is that which is
regarded as ineluctably natural and thus indefeasible and inalienable
because inherited personal attributes by blood or affective attachments,
whether that be material and cultural inheritance (the native land),
consolidated over time. While 'native land' is the most obvious translation

---

[50] eDIL s.v. caratrad.

245

here, the proximity of **caradradh** in relation to the Spanish connection may indicate that this affective connotation is 'subliminally' included in the remit of **dúthchas** as well.[51]

This concept will play an important role in the next section, and it occurs again later in the letter, where it clearly refers to the native land, as the author inveighs against the English enemy who is "diabolically extinguishing the Catholic faith, vengefully killing our nobles and unlawfully coveting our native land (**dúthchas**)".

There is an important distinction made in the letter between "the Irish" (*na hÉireannaigh*) and "the eminent Gaels of Ireland" (*príomhGhaoighuil na hÉireann*), the former a self-designation based primarily on territoriality, the latter on ethnicity within that territory. It is to the latter, and the latter only, that the Milesian Spanish connection is appropriate; however, Catholicism unites the Irish, including the Old English, within the ethos of a Protestant English state. It is to the relationship between the Catholic religion and Irish nationhood in the seventeenth century that we now turn.

Towards a frame analysis of pobal

The following is a summary of the relevant lexicographic information from eDIL for the noun **pobal** (Old Irish *popul*) in medieval and early modern Irish:[52]

(1) The people in general e.g. *an pobal coitcheann* "the common people"

(2) A people identified as belonging to a particular place or territory e.g. *pobal Israel* "the people of Israel"; *an pobal Rómhánach* "the Roman people"

(3) A large group of people united by a common interest or purpose e.g *pobal na gcreidmheach* "the community of believers"

These then are the three frames evoked by pobal. My argument here will be that senses (2) and (3) fuse in the seventeenth century under the pressures of English conquest and colonization. This involves the identification of

---

[51] eDIL s.v. dúthaig and dúthchas; for detailed discussion, see McQuillan, *Native and Natural*, passim.

[52] eDIL s.v. *popul*.

Irish Catholics as the pobal of a national church and hence the legitimate constituents of the Irish nation. This is clearly articulated in another of Céitinn's writings, his tract on how to prepare for a Christian death.[53] Having already characterized the Children of Israel as God's people (pobal Dé), Céitinn makes the analogy with the suffering of Irish Catholics explicitly:[54]

> Alas, I think that the misfortunes that God had visited upon the people of Israel (**pobal Israel**) are almost no more severe than the oppressive bondage that he allows to be inflicted on the distressed people of Ireland (**pobal imshníomhach Éireann**), so that they can legitimately establish their misfortune and complain of their oppression to God, as King David did long ago, when the Jewish people (**an pobal Iúdaidheach**) suffered tyranny . . . Every Irish Catholic (**gach Catoilice Éireannach**) can say just the same, being under the egregious persecution of the heretics, rejecting the false and fallacious religion of Calvin and Luther and their followers.

Pobal Éireann (the people of Ireland) is thus comprised of every Irish Catholic. As the Old English have overwhelmingly remained faithful to the Church of Rome, they are members of that **pobal**, along with the original (Gaelic) Irish. The broader context for this passage in Céitinn's text is the Babylonian captivity, to which we shall return shortly.

First, however, we go back briefly to FrameNet, which has a succession of frames (again uppercase) helpful, in a general way, in terms of the conceptual structure that could underlie the developing semantics of **pobal**. In frame (1), individuals form configurations of people whether intentionally or not (COME TOGETHER); in so doing, they create frame

---

[53] Osborn Bergin (ed.), *Trí Bior-ghaoithe an Bháis. The Three Shafts of Death* (Dublin Institute for Advanced Studies, 1992 [1931]), lines 6845–91; for discussion, see Tadhg Ó Dúshláine, *An Eoraip agus Litríocht na Gaeilge 1600–1650. Gnéithe den Bharóchachas Eorpach i Litríocht na Gaeilge* (Dublin: An Clóchomhar, 1987), 19–81; Brendan Kane, "Domesticating the Counter-Reformation: bridging the bardic and Catholic traditions in Geoffrey Keating's "Three Shafts of Death", *The Sixteenth-Century Journal* 40 (2009): 1029–44.

[54] Bergin (ed.), *Trí Bior-ghaoithe*, lines 6098–6110.

(2) an AGGREGATE of individuals (i.e. the act of congregating creates a "congregation"). In time this leads to frame (3) ORGANIZATION whereby social groups are formed intentionally; finally, as such organizations become more public and permanent, they lead to frame (4) **INSTITUTIONS**. The Anglo-Norman invasion of Ireland in the twelfth century is frame (1), subsequent conquest leads to frame (2); as the descendants of the invaders come to identify with Ireland as the land of their birth and unite with the Gaelic Irish through identification with a shared culture (through social institutions like marriage and fosterage), frames (3) and ultimately (4) result. By the seventeenth century, the important institution is the Catholic Church. While this schematic progression works tolerably well as a historical sketch, it is not fine-grained enough to account for the 'deep' semantic evolution of **pobal** and it is to aspects of this that we now turn.

We can start with the phrase **pobal an aifrinn** 'the people of the Catholic Mass' *(aifreann)*. Gillespie has discussed the importance of attendance at Mass in creating a sense of community in the early seventeenth century under pressure from the state for religious conformity to Anglican Protestantism. This produced "a wider sense of a sacramental community, based on the experience of the miraculous power of the eucharist, which helped define the nature of Catholicism in a rapidly changing world."[55] In like vein, Ó hAnnracháin and Armstrong speak of the language of community in early modern Ireland, as in Europe, as deriving from "Christian principles, as exemplified by the principles of sacramental communion".[56] In seventeenth-century Ireland, these sacramental communities, Catholic and Protestant, are in direct opposition to each another. That is the immediate context for the development of **pobal** to be explored further below.

The phrase **pobal an aifrinn** comes from a grammatical tract (of all places!), in which the author wishes to distinguish **pobal** from the

---

[55] Raymond Gillespie "Catholic religious cultures in the diocese of Dublin, 1614–97" in *History of the Catholic Diocese of Dublin*, ed. Dáire Keogh and James Kelly (Dublin: Four Courts Press, 2000), 127–43 at 143.

[56] Tadhg Ó hAnnracháin and Robert M. Armstrong, "Introduction: making and remaking community", in *Community in Early Modern Ireland*, ed. Tadhg Ó hAnnracháin and Robert M. Armstrong (Dublin: Four Courts Press, 2006) 13–33 at 20.

homophonous *puball* (borrowed from Latin *papilio* 'tent'). **Pobal** is distinguished from *puball* expressly by its identification with the Catholic Mass, "the people of the Mass".[57] As we have said, frames are schematizations of our experiences of the world, stored in the memory and evoked as needed. What our grammarian gives us here is a special kind of frame, identified by Lakoff as an **idealized cognitive model** (ICM).[58] Whereas a frame, by identification of component elements and linguistic units, aims at relative completeness in its description of a scenario, an ICM identifies the frame by extracting a prototypical example from it and using that example to identify the entire frame. This is what our grammarian has done here: the phrase **pobal an aifrinn** thus constitutes an 'idealization' in the speaker's mind of the entire concept on account of its perceived typicality: the quickest way to understand what a **pobal** is in early modern Ireland to visualize the congregation at Mass, even though there are other types of **pobal**. We can flesh out this understanding further from another of Céitinn's devotional texts, his tract on the Mass. Here he is describing the typical scene as the Mass is ending:[59]

> What *"Ite Missa est"* means is the granting of permission to the people (**an pobal**) to return home after hearing (**éisteacht**) the Mass (**aifreann**), articulating that the people (**an pobal**) are not allowed to leave the church (**eaglais**) from the divine office except with the priest's (**sagart**) agreement. And the priest's (**sagart**) face is cast downwards while saying those words, because it is to the people (**an pobal**) that the priest (**sagart**) is speaking. What *"Benedicamus Domino"* means is the priest's (**sagart**) injunction to the people to thank God (**altughadh**) after the sacrifice (**iodhbairt**) of the Mass (**aifreann**).

FrameNet has a frame RITE which "concerns rituals performed in line with religious beliefs or tradition". This is a very general frame in which *Mass*,

---

[57] Osborn Bergin (ed.) "Irish Grammatical Tracts", Supplement to *Ériu* 9 (1921/23): 61–124 at 71.

[58] See Lakoff, *Women, Fire*, 68–76; Croft and Cruse, "Frames", 28–32. See also Evans's characterization, *Glossary*, 105.

[59] Patrick O'Brien (ed.), *Eochair-sciath an Aifrinn: an Explanatory Defence of the Mass* (Dublin: P. O'Brien, 1898), 104.

sacrament and *sacrifice* appear as frame-evoking lexical units (RITE of course is not confined to particular liturgies or religions). For present purposes we might propose a frame MASS (as sub-frame of RITE) based simply on the above passage:

> **Frame elements:** CONGREGATION PRIEST SACRIFICE GOD
>
> **Lexical units:** *pobal* 'people' (n), *sagart* 'priest' (n), *aifreann* 'Mass' (n.), *iodhbairt* 'offering, sacrifice' (n), *eaglais* 'church' (n.); *éisteacht* 'listen' (v.), *altughadh* 'thank God' (v.) [60]

Consideration of Céitinn's tract as a whole would of course enable us to expand the frame further (to include 'eucharist' for instance).

I want to return now, however, to Céitinn's tract on death. Book III in general concerns the soul leaving the body after death; chapter nine addresses aspects of the appropriateness of weeping, or keening (*caoi*) over the dead body. Here is Céitinn's sixth reason justifying weeping: the mourner envies the soul departing for heaven:[61]

> The sixth reason why a person ought to weep is on account of the abundance of desire to go to heaven, which is everyone's inheritance/native land (**dúthaigh**). Because it is obvious that everyone desires to go to his own native land (**dá dhúthaigh féin**) . . . "I know not what sweetness is in the native land (**fonn dúthchasa**) that it draws all back to it and will not allow them to be forgetful of themselves."[62] From these words of Ovid is to be understood that that everyone loves his own native land (**a dhúthaigh féin**) and looks forward to returning to it from his exile (**a dheóraidheacht**).

---

[60] It may be noted that aifreann 'Mass' is a borrowing from Latin offerandum (cf. iodhbairt); the verbal noun éisteacht in the context of the Mass means 'attending'; altughadh is only used in the context of thanking God.

[61] Bergin, *Three Shafts*, lines 6845–91.

[62] Here Céitinn translates from Ovid *Epistulae Ex Ponto* (itself written in exile) 1.3.35–6: "*Nescio qua natale solum dulcedine cunctos ducit, et immemores non sinit esse sui*".

King David agrees with this, speaking of the Children of Israel (**Clann Israel**) when they were in foreign lands in the Babylonian captivity (**i gcoigcrích san bhroid Bháibhiolónda**) as Psalm 136[63] says . . . "We would sit over the rivers of Babylon and there we would weep, whenever we remembered you, Sion". Meaning that when the Children of Israel were in the captivity of Babylon, that they would go out *on the banks of the rivers and the lonely hills of the countryside to weep and lament when they would think of the music and sport and pastimes of the city of Jerusalem* ... And to crown every evil, *it grieved them terribly* to be without the brightly decorated sun-lit temple of Solomon in which they used to give offering (**iodhbairt**) to omnipotent God, while having nothing in its stead in that captivity of Babylon except watching in spite of themselves impure offerings (**iodhbarta amhghlana**) being made to idols and false gods after the practice of Gentiles.

And, alas, they had *no more cause to weep . . . than the cause to weep* that the poor families of Ireland now have on account of the persecution (**inghreim**) and compulsion (**coimhéigniughadh**) that is being inflicted on them, forcing them to abandon the precious offering of the Mass (**iodhbairt luachmhóir an aifrinn**) for the filthy communion of Luther and Calvin (**commaoin neamhghlan Lúitéir agus Chailbhín**), so that they would much rather be dead than seeing "Jerusalem", that is, the church (**an eaglais**) being devastated and the people (**an pobal**) being enslaved in the Babylonian captivity of heresy (**i mbroid Bháibhiolónda na heiriticeachta**).

A rich and evocative passage indeed, and a reminder that in his day Céitinn, a Jesuit-trained secular priest, was a famed preacher in the southern Irish province of Munster. We see clearly the antipathy of the one 'sacramental community' for the other, the liturgical purity of the one is the corruption of the other, in Céitinn's invocation of the MASS frame in the final section.

---

[63] Now Psalm 137.

The beginning of the passage is an intriguing evocation of the native land and its emotive power; this I am going to defer for a moment in order to consider the analogy that Céitinn makes, once again, between the Irish and the Israelites.

The heart of the passage is the comparison between the Israelites of the Old Testament and the Catholic Irish of the seventeenth century. We have another conceptual metaphor here but this one is based less on embodied experience than on a perceived similarity between two conceptual domains founded on common cultural knowledge: the centrality of the Bible as an exposition of God's will and plan for humankind.[64] 'Meaning is conceptualization': such knowledge serves the conceptualization and rationalization of a current predicament through the lens of myth and history as in the metaphor: THE CAPTIVITY OF THE ISRAELITES IN BABYLON IS THE CAPTIVITY OF THE CATHOLIC IRISH IN A HERETICAL STATE. This general projection also works in terms of detail: the Gentile worship of false gods then is the false liturgy of Protestants now; the destruction of Solomon's temple/Jerusalem then, is the destruction of the Irish Catholic Church now; the lamentation of the Jewish people then is the lamentation of the Catholic Irish now. As the biblical archetype of God's chosen people, the Israelites are the source frame which is mapped onto the target frame, the Catholic Irish, here the 'people' (**pobal**) of the 'church' (**eaglais**).

But if meaning is conceptualization, then cognition is also embodied, and we note here the recurring MASS frame at the end of the passage recalls the quote above on the centrality the sacramental communion in shaping Catholic identity at this time. Through the sociality of the sacrament, its "embodied intersubjectivity," this identity is grounded in the everyday experience of Mass attendance.[65]

When frame schematizations have a particularly dynamic sequential character, they are sometimes referred to as **scripts**.[66] Céitinn further explains that the Babylonian captivity was God's revenge (*díoghaltas*) on

---

[64] Kövecses, *Metaphor*, 243–5.

[65] See Jordan Zlatev "Embodied intersubjectivity," *Cambridge Handbook*, 172–87.

[66] Roger C. Shank and Peter C. Abelson, *Scripts, Plans, Goals and Understanding* (Hillsdale: Lawrence Erlbaum, 1977).

the Israelites for having permitted the worship of false gods.[67] Therefore, we might extrapolate the following script for 'God's chosen people':

GOD'S WRATH (through) FOREIGN POWER (results in) EXILE/CAPTIVITY/PERSECUTION (which results in) LAMENTATION

Divine providence represents the application of what Hastings terms "an Old Testament political economy" to an emerging early modern European nation, centered around the belief that, based on the Israelite prototype, a Christian nation can regard itself as being one of God's predilection, a chosen people, despite the vagaries of its own sinfulness.[68] This frame is replicated across a number of texts in early seventeenth-century Irish, especially in a series of secular poems reacting to the Plantation of Ulster and associated events.[69]

Similar to the cognitive linguistic approach of frame semantics, with its nodes of access to structured inventories of encyclopedic knowledge, is Busse's notion of the "discourse-semantic paradigm".[70] Discourses consist of the texts that comprise them; across this corpus of texts the elements that constitute individual texts tend to recur (also a guiding principle of FrameNet). These are the "emerging elements of a discourse", drawn from what Busse calls "the cognitive-epistemic make-up" of those producing the texts.[71] The cognitive-epistemic underpinnings of the providentialist paradigm lie in the early modern Europe of Reformation and Counter-Reformation, as well as in the Ireland of English conquest and colonization, both inextricably linked; their impact on Catholicism brings the Gaelic Irish and the Old English closer together. The *oeuvre* of the Old English Jesuit-

---

[67] Bergin, *Three Shafts*, lines 6082–89.

[68] Hastings, *Construction*, 195.

[69] As the script here is based solely on Céitinn's examples, it is necessarily incomplete. The complete script includes positive corollaries: repentance turns away God's anger, Ireland awaits a second Moses. See Marc Caball, "Providence and exile in seventeenth-century Ireland", *Irish Historical Studies* 29, no. 114 (1994): 174–88; "Dispossession and reaction: the Gaelic literati and the Plantation of Ulster", *History Ireland* 17, no. 6 (2009): 24–7; also Breandán Ó Buachalla, "'Anocht is uaigneach Éire'", *History Ireland* 15, no. 4 (2007): 32–7.

[70] Busse, *Conceptual History*, 120.

[71] Ibid. 122.

educated priest Céitinn, as a whole, both prose and poetry, his "cognitive-epistemic make-up" in fact, in itself illustrates this fusion. [72]

It remains now to treat the beginning of the passage, and here I want to apply Busse's idea of a "depth" semantics that seeks out those elements of meaning represented more obliquely. The most obvious elements of the passage are the Irish nouns highlighted that relate source frame (ISRAELITES) to target frame (IRISH). A further opposition at this level is that between 'native land' (*dúthaigh/fonn dúthchasa*[73]) and 'exile' (*deóraidheacht*) or 'foreignness' (*coigcríoch*): it is that which I wish to pursue briefly here. This is the general opposition at the conceptual level of which the Babylonian captivity is a more specific instance.

Nouns such as these are rich in specific semantic content and for that reason are known as 'content' words. There are other words in the above passage that perform more general grammatical and syntactic functions (articles, prepositions, pronouns) and are consequently referred to as 'function' words.[74] It is the contribution of such function words, specifically personal pronouns, to a deeper semantics of **pobal** in the passage that I wish to consider. As we have seen, the most 'obvious' surface sense of **pobal** here is its relation to the MASS frame.

The passage begins, however, with the identification of heaven as the soul's native land, because it is the yearning of the soul for this inheritance that justifies weeping over a corpse. Céitinn talks initially in individual terms in relation both to heaven (everyone's inheritance or *dúthaigh*) before referring the same desire to the native land on earth (everyone desires to go to his/her own *dúthaigh*). Grammatically, these pronominal forms are unambiguously singular, but their frame of reference is considered universal, applying to every single individual. When Céitinn cites Ovid on the ineffable attraction of the native land on earth, however, his Irish translation correctly reflects the plural forms of the Latin (*cunctos ducit . . . immemores sui* 'drawing all . . . never forgetting themselves'). Without narratorial comment, the meaningfulness of the native land has been silently collectivized. A collective yearning for and consciousness of the native land is subsequently grounded by the invocation of the Israelites in

---

[72] Kane, "Domesticating", passim.

[73] Literally "land (fonn) of dúthchas".

[74] Busse, *Conceptual History*, 121–22.

captivity. Nevertheless, the pronoun is third plural not first plural: the narrator as **sagart** (priest) retains a certain separation from the **pobal** (a 'separation' evident from our MASS frame). However, with the citation from Psalms the progression to a collective *self* is effectively, if obliquely realized, projected as it is on to the source frame of the Israelites ("*we* would sit and weep . . . whenever *we* remembered . . . "). The progression 'he/she' to 'they' and finally to 'we' represents subliminally the conceptual evolution of a **pobal**: individuals form a self-conscious collective united by a common cause before God; the priest (**sagart**), here the narrator, is the father of God's community on earth.[75]

The point in relation to a deep semantics, however, is that this progression in the passage relates not directly to **pobal**, but to **dúthaigh** and **dúthchas**, which returns us to the principle of 'territorial descent' already discussed. As we have seen, both words mean not only 'native land' but also indefeasible hereditary right: the native soil itself is inseparable on the lexical level from the claim to it based on descent, as is what is inherited by virtue of custom and tradition, including religion. Céitinn speaks of "the common age-old Catholic religion, which has been in the possession of our forebears and ancestors since planted in Ireland by St. Patrick" (*ó do plannduigheadh lé Pádraig naomhtha i nÉirinn é*). The metaphor of planting, of rooting Catholicism in the native soil emphasizes that 'it comes with the territory', as a more modern metaphor would have it.[76] Territorial descent forms the 'deep' semantics of **pobal** here.

Conclusion

We have talked about how in frame semantics words and their senses form lexical units, combinations of symbolic representation and meaning, and how these frames in turn constitute a recursively structured inventory of knowledge. Another way of saying much the same thing is Langacker's conception of **profile, base** and **domain**. A word is a profile against its immediate conceptual content, the base; the profile is thus the particular element of the base that is being foregrounded. The broader conceptual content triggered by the base is referred to as the **domain** which is not

---

[75] O'Brien, Eochair-sgiath, 41. Céitinn's tract on the Mass describes the priest as "father/head of household" (athair muinntire) to the **pobal**, which is characterized in turn as "God's household" (muinntir do Dhia).

[76] Bergin, *Three Shafts*, lines 6059–61.

directly activated by the profile but is the deeper conceptual structure that underpins it.[77]

The diagram below reads from left to right. In practice, bases are close to dictionary definitions, so the base in each case represents a combination of eDIL and FrameNet (or frames that I have modified from the latter) but with priority given to the former. The domain matrix is then the more 'encyclopedic' world knowledge that forms the epistemological background. So, I present the following representation of the semantic-conceptual structures of nationhood that underlie **cine** and **pobal**:

Profile	BASE		DOMAIN MATRIX
			CYCLE OF EXISTENCE SCENARIO
			CYCLE OF LIFE AND DEATH
	(1) BEING BORN		*COMING TO BE*
<u>cine</u>	(2) KINSHIP/FAMILY	*BIRTH SCENARIO*	*SEXUAL REPRODUCTION SCENARIO*
	(3) A PEOPLE BY DESCENT		
	(4) A PEOPLE BY TERRITORY		
<u>pobal</u>	(5) A PEOPLE BY RELIGION	*INSTITUTION*	
			ORGANIZATION
			AGGREGATE
			COME TOGETHER
	(6) POPULACE ('people')		

As the domain matrix for **pobal** has already been discussed, a word on that of **cine/cineadh**. As we have seen, what must have originally been its most basic sense, the frame BEING BORN (as verbal noun of *cinidh* 'is born') is by this period no longer directly evoked by **cineadh**. Nevertheless, that frame is still part of the deeper conceptual structure of nationhood (as witnessed by the 'nation-as-family' metaphor above). That is why, alone among the bases profiled above, BEING BORN is italicized. It leads, however, to broader frames such as COMING TO BE (a more general

---

[77] Langacker, "An introduction", 6–13; Croft and Cruse, "Frames, domains, spaces", 15–33.

abstract 'version' of being born, in turn part of the wider CYCLE OF LIFE AND DEATH), all applicable to the life-cycle of nations.

As we have seen, bases 1 and 2 are conceptually mapped on to the more abstract and extended domain of base 3 as the metaphor A NATION IS A FAMILY. This mapping is ultimately predicated on the idea of *territorial descent*, which then entails the fusion of bases 3 through 5 by a variety of means: kinship through ethno-genetic descent, through nurturance and adoption, through a sense of divine predilection and through identification of the land of birth as the land of birthright. These all represent potential frames more specific to the development of Irish national consciousness in the early modern period.

The important thing about frames, however, is not what we call them, but the coherent bodies of knowledge they represent. They are mental constructs as symbolized by language, not independent objective entities existing 'out there'. The advantage of the cognitive approach to semantics is that it provides an effective and principled account of the integration of linguistic and conceptual structure, of language and the world. In Fillmore's phrase, it is "the semantics of understanding"[78] in the broadest sense, indispensable to anyone who reads words (texts) with a view to recovering the worlds that produced them.

---

[78] Charles J. Fillmore, "Frames and the semantics of understanding", *Quaderni di Semantica* VI, no.2 (1985), 222–54; accessed through http://www.icsi.berkeley.edu/pubs/ai/framesand85.pdf (on 06/28/2020).

The Lost Memoir of a Blasket Islander

Tracey Ní Mhaonaigh

The Great Blasket island is in an archipelago collectively known as the Blaskets, situated off the south-west coast of Ireland. It is a small island, approximately five kilometres long and a kilometre at its widest point. The Great Blasket was officially inhabited until November 1953, although the final residents didn't leave until early 1954. The island has a recorded history dating back to the late thirteenth century when the Earl of Desmond leased the island to the Ferriter family, with whom it remained until the mid-seventeenth century. As to when the island was first inhabited, evidence would suggest as early as the end of the sixteenth century. But with a growth in population and a number of evictions on the mainland, an influx of inhabitants was recorded at the start of the nineteenth century.[1]

The Literature of the Blasket Islands

With a population of about 150 at its peak, in the early 1840s, just prior to the Great Famine, this tiny community would produce from among its number some of the greatest authors, and some of the greatest literary works, in the history of the Irish language. In the early twentieth century, visitors both from Ireland and further afield, began to go to the island and encouraged the inhabitants to tell their story–among them Carl Marstrander, Robin Flower, Brian Ó Ceallaigh, George Chambers and George Thomson.

In the catalogue of Blasket books penned by islanders, we find works by Eibhlís Ní Shúilleabháin (*Letters from the Great Blasket*, 1978), Eibhlín Ní Shúilleabháin (*Cín Lae Eibhlín Ní Shúilleabháin*, 2000), Seán Ó Criomhthain (*Lá dár Saol*, 1969), Máire Ní Ghuithín (*Bean an Oileáin*, 1986), Mícheál Ó Gaoithín (*Is Truagh ná Fanann an Óige*, 1953), Seán Pheats Tom Ó Cearnaigh (*Fiolar an Eireabaill Bháin*, 1992) and Seán Sheáin Í Chearnaigh (*An tOileán a Tréigeadh*, 1974; *Iarbhlascaodach ina*

---

[1] For a comprehensive history of the Blasket Islands see Mícheál de Mórdha, *Scéal agus Dán Oileáin* (Dublin: Coiscéim, 2012). For a photographic insight into Blasket life see Mícheál and Dáithí de Mórdha, *The Great Blasket/ An Blascaod Mór–A Photographic Portrait/ Portráid Pictiúr* (Cork: Collins Press, 2013).

Dheoraí, 1978).[2] In recent years Micheál Sheáin Tom Ó Ceárna added to the Blasket library with his book, co-authored with his son-in-law Gerald Hayes, entitled *From the Great Blasket to America: The Last Memoir by an Islander*.[3] Micheál Sheáin Tom Ó Ceárna, or Mike Carney, arrived in America in 1948 and settled in Hungry Hill, Springfield (MA). He played a pivotal role, following the death of his brother Seáinín in 1947, in the campaign for the relocation of the final residents in 1953. Throughout his life in the United States he advocated for the preservation of Blasket Heritage and worked tirelessly for the promotion of Irish language and culture, for which Maynooth University conferred on him an honorary doctorate in 2009.

Books relating to the Great Blasket Island and its residents continue to be produced, as is evident from the reference above to Mike Carney's memoir, which was published in 2013. Other recent works include, but are not limited to, Mícheál de Mórdha's comprehensive reference work in 2012 entitled *Scéal agus Dán Oileáin*, Gerald Hayes' *The Blasket Islandman: The Life and Legacy of Tomás Ó Criomhthain* (2018) and *The Last Blasket King–Pádraig Ó Catháin: An Rí* (2015), co-authored with Eliza Kane, Isobel Ní Riain's *Léiriú Socheolaíochtúil ar Litríocht an Bhlascaoid* (2019), and a new edition of *Beatha Pheig Sayers*, itself an expansion of *Peig: A Scéal Féin* (1936), edited by Liam P. Ó Murchú, which was launched at the 2019 "Ceiliúradh an Bhlascaoid" conference ("The Blasket Celebration/ Commemoration").[4] A series of lectures are given each year at Ceiliúradh an Bhlascaoid on a particular theme or topic relating to Blasket life and heritage. "Bláithín: Flower" was the theme of the inaugural conference which was held in 1996, and its proceedings were subsequently published in 1998.[5] The most recent conference was held in September 2019, on the subject of "Maidhc 'File' Ó Gaoithín–File, Fáidh agus Fear Feasa,"[6] Maidhc "File" is the aforementioned author of *Is Truagh ná*

---

[2] For full publication information, see the bibliography at the end of the article.

[3] Michael Carney (with Gerald Hayes), *From the Great Blasket to America: The Last Memoir by an Islander*. (Cork: The Collins Press, 2013).

[4] Liam P. Ó Murchú (eag.), *Beatha Pheig Sayers* (An Daingean: An Sagart, 2019). For full publication information for the other works cited here, see the bibliography.

[5] Mícheál de Mórdha (eag.), *Bláithín: Flower, Ceiliúradh an Bhlascaoid 1* (1998).

[6] "Poet, prophet and wise man."

Fanann an Óige and son of Peig Sayers. The publication of the proceedings of each conference alone ensures that both new work on Blasket life and reassessment of prior work is ongoing.

While many varying works have been produced by, and about, this island community over the years, the most renowned works are undoubtedly the memoirs of *"an triúr mór,"* "the big three," as Pádraig Ó Fiannachta described them in his article "Litríocht Chorca Duibhne"[7]–namely, *An tOileánach* by Tomás Ó Criomhthain (1855–1937),[8] *Peig: A Scéal Féin* by Peig Sayers (1873–1958)[9] and *Fiche Blian ag Fás* by Muiris Ó Súilleabháin (1904–1950).[10] It is the third of these writers, and the youngest, who is the subject of this article.

Muiris Ó Súilleabháin

Muiris Ó Súilleabháin was born in 1904 and after spending the first six years of his life in Dingle, following the death of his mother when he was a baby, he returned to the Great Blasket, where he remained until he left to join An Garda Síochána (the Irish police force). Encouraged by George Thomson, one of the aforementioned visitors to the island, and in the wake of the success of Ó Criomhthain's *An tOileánach*, Ó Súilleabháin penned his story and in 1933 *Fiche Blian ag Fás* was published. Thomson had first come to the island in 1923 to learn Irish, on the suggestion of Robin Flower,

---

[7] Pádraig Ó Fiannachta, "Litríocht Chorca Dhuibhne," *Irisleabhar Mhá Nuad* (1982): 21–35, at 25.

[8] This is not Tomás Ó Criomhthain's only work. He has also given us *Allagar na hInise, Dinnsheanchas na mBlascaodaí, Seanchas ón Oileán Tiar, Bloghanna ón mBlascaod, Allagar II, Scéilíní ón mBlascaod* and has been the subject of many scholarly articles and such works as *An tOileánach Léannta, Tomás Oileánach: Fear idir Dhá Thraidisiún,* and *The Blasket Islandman: The Life and Legacy of Tomás Ó Criomhthain.* [See bibliography for publication details.]

[9] From Peig we also have *Machtnamh Seana-mhná, Scéalta ón mBlascaod, Moirín* and "Labharfad le Cách: Scéalta agus Seanchas Taifeadta ag Radió Éireann agus an BBC"–I Will Speak to You All: Stories and Lore Recorded by Radió Éireann and the BBC. Her son Mícheál, Maidhc "File," played a central role in her telling of her life story and brought out a supplementary addition of *Peig: A Scéal Féin* in 1970 entitled *Beatha Pheig Sayers.* [See bibliography for publication details.]

[10] Muiris Ó Súilleabháin, *Fiche Blian ag Fás* (Dublin: Clólucht an Talbóidigh, 1933).

another English scholar who had arrived among the islanders in 1910.[11] Thomson was not only instrumental in encouraging his good friend to pen his story but he also co-translated it to English with Moya Llewelyn Davies, *Twenty Years a-Growing*, which was also published in 1933.[12] The work was subsequently translated into numerous languages, making it, arguably, the most successful Irish book ever.

Fiche Blian ag Fás, as the name suggests, tells the story of more-or-less the first twenty years of Ó Súilleabháin's life, beginning with his final days in Dingle before his father came to bring him back to the island. Chapter by chapter the book recounts his adventures and mishaps on the island and on the neighbouring mainland. Childhood innocence, hope and optimism are the backbone of this heart-warming, often funny, account of a young boy's youth on a tiny island in the Atlantic Ocean; his relationship with his grandfather at its core. In the closing chapters, we see a young man coming of age as he makes the decision to join the Gardaí rather than follow in the footsteps of the numerous islanders before him who had taken the *bád bán*, 'emigrant ship,' to America, to Springfield, Massachusetts in the case of many of them, in pursuit of a new life. Leaving the island behind, though not for the last time, we see Muiris take the train to Dublin where he begins his training as a recruit, before being assigned to Inverin in Connemara in the West of Ireland. It is at this stage that the work should have ended–but it doesn't. The closing chapter of the book, which George Thomson later admitted was added after it was finished and at his behest,[13] sees Muiris once again on the Great Blasket, where his final thoughts are of a sentimental nature as he contemplates the fate of the island and its people. This backward-looking chapter, focussing on an island way of life that was,

---

[11] Breandán Feiritéar, "Seoirse agus an tOileán," *Ceiliúradh an Bhlascaoid* 4 (2000): 31–46 at 32.

[12] Such was Muiris' admiration and respect for Moya Llewelyn Davies that, according to his wife Cáit, in an interview with Pádraig Tyers, he asked, on the birth of their daughter, if he could name her after her, a request to which Cáit consented, and she was thus named Máire Llewelyn Ní Shúilleabháin. (Pádraig Tyers, *Blasket Memories: The Life of an Irish Island Community* [Cork: Mercier Press, 1998], 186. First published in Irish, *Leoithne Aniar*, in 1982.)

[13] George Thomson, "Réamhrá an eagarthóra don dara heagrán," *Fiche Blian ag Fás* (An Daingean: An Sagart, 1975 [1998⁵]), 5–7 at 5. Also, George Thomson, "Fiche Blian ag Fás," *Comhar* 17, no. 11 (Samhain 1958): 4–6 at 4.

is out of place in a forward-looking work focussing on Muiris's life that will be. But this aside, *Fiche Blian ag Fás* is a well-written, heartening account of the carefree anticipation and expectancy of youth.

Ó Súilleabháin joined the Gardaí in 1927 but held ambitions of being a fulltime writer, and went that direction for a while. It is well known that he intended to write a trilogy, *Fiche Blian ag Fás, Fiche Bliadhan fé Bhláth* and, presumably, *Fiche Bliadhan ag Cromadh*; from the description his grandfather gave him of the phases of life, namely: twenty years a-growing, twenty years in bloom, twenty years a-stooping and twenty years declining.[14] Unfortunately Muiris had little more than begun the third phase of his life when he tragically drowned on the 25 June 1950, aged just 46, while swimming off the Galway coast. Had he lived beyond this point it is unlikely, however, that he would have written the third instalment of his trilogy, given his disappointment with the treatment of the second.

Having completed *Fiche Bliadhan fé Bhláth* (*Twenty Years in Bloom*) in 1938, he sent it to publishers in the hope that it would be as successful as his first work. His widow Cáit, in an interview with Pádraig Tyres, published in *Leoithne Aniar*, and translated to English in *Blasket Memories: The Life of an Irish Island Community*, told of how he started this second book "san áit ar fhág sé *Fiche Blian ag Fás*," "in the place where he left *Twenty Years a-Growing*."[15] But where exactly was that place? At the point mentioned already when he returned to the island at the very end of the first book, two years after he had gone to Connemara, or at the end of the second last chapter, the more natural endpoint, where we see the newly trained garda standing outside the barracks in Inverin "listening to the sound of the wind in the trees and watching the glitter of the moonlight on the sea"?[16] We shall return to this question presently.

In the same interview Cáit said that Muiris spent a lot of time on this second instalment and that he sent it to the publishers, but to what end? They were uninterested in it "toisc ná raibh sé cosúil le *Fiche Blian ag Fás*,"[17] because it wasn't like *Twenty Years A-Growing*. It could be argued,

---

[14] Muiris Ó Súilleabháin, *Fiche Bliadhan fé Bhláth* (Unpublished, 1938) 1.

[15] Pádraig Tyers, *Leoithne Aniar* (Baile an Fheirtéaraigh: Cló Dhuibhne, 1983), 170.

[16] Maurice O'Sullivan, *Twenty Years A-Growing*, trans. Moya Llewelyn Davis and George Thomson (Oxford: Oxford University Press, 1933), 296–7.

[17] Tyers, *Leoithne Aniar*, 170.

at this point, that this perhaps highlights the significance of the role played by George Thomson in the preparation of *Fiche Blian ag Fás* for publication. We have already mentioned how the closing chapter was added at Thomson's request, along with chapter eighteen entitled "An Tórramh Meiriceánach" ("The American Wake"),[18] and Thomson himself refers to the extent to which he edited the work in his preface to the second edition. In addition to the aforementioned chapters, he details how he reminded Muiris of events or occurrences which were then added in, and how he helped him to fill gaps created by the removal of certain sections of text. Thomson also tells us that he shortened the original work as it was too long to publish in its entirety, notwithstanding his addition of two additional chapters, and that he redrafted it before himself and Muiris went through it together "*á cheartú agus á athrú nó go raibh beirt againn sásta leis*"[19]– "correcting and changing it until we were both happy with it." He is cautious not to take away from the value of the original work, however, insisting that all he did was to give the guidance to Muiris that he needed to convert his story-telling ability into a more honed writing style.[20]

Had *Fiche Bliadhan fé Bhláth* been edited to the same extent, the publishers may have looked more favourably upon it, though I don't believe so. I feel that it was the differing content in the two works, and not the differing styles–*Fiche Blian ag Fás* having been polished significantly before publication–that the publishers had issue with. Having been rejected for publication, the manuscript of *Fiche Bliadhan fé Bhláth* was subsequently presumed lost, after countless searches over the years had proven fruitless. In his book *An tÚrscéal Gaeilge*, published in 1991, Alan Titley lamented its loss, not least, he wrote, as no consideration of its literary worth could be made if it no longer existed.[21] I'm not in a position to say exactly how many copies of the text exist, but the one that forms the basis of this paper was discovered in recent years, following the death of Monsignor Pádraig Ó Fiannachta, former head of both Early and Modern Irish in Maynooth University, and director of An Sagart publishers.

---

[18] Thomson, "Réamhrá an eagarthóra don dara heagrán," *Fiche Blian ag Fás* (1975 [1998⁵]), 5.

[19] Ibid.

[20] Ibid, 6.

[21] Alan Titley, *An tÚrscéal Gaeilge* (Dublin: An Clóchomhar Tta., 1991), 441.

LOST MEMOIR

Monsignor Ó Fiannachta died in July 2016, and when going through his papers, the interim director of An Sagart, Dr. Tadhg Ó Dúshláine, recently retired from the Modern Irish department in Maynooth, came across a typescript of *Fiche Bliadhan fé Bhláth.*

From the Great Blasket to Connemara: Fiche Bliadhan fé Bhláth

On the dedication page of the typescript, dated St. Patrick's Day 1938, is the message "*do mo bhean chéile síor ghrádhach agus do Eoghanín Íarlath, mo mhac ionmhain . . . as ocht mo cheanna agus mo g[h]rádh dhíobh*"–"to my ever loving wife and my beloved son Eoghanín Íarlath . . . with all my love." This page is followed by an introduction, before the work begins properly, wherein Muiris tells the reader of what he has come to know of life.

I would like to address, at this point, the publishers' assertion that *Fiche Bliadhan fé Bhláth* was not like *Fiche Blian ag Fás*, by acknowledging that they were correct. There is no doubt but the positive, hopeful voice of the young boy we hear in the first book is far-removed from the voice of the man we hear in the second–a man who has experienced more of life and who has come to accept the fate of mankind and the realisation that life is short and all too often challenging.

The following is taken from his introduction:

> Praise and thanks to God, but there is nothing surer than that he controls the life of the sinner from birth to death– just look at the change that comes over you unbeknown to yourself; look at the virtues and vices, the trouble and suffering, the difficult road you have to take; the knowledge and the understanding, the blunders and the mistakes, the satisfaction and the dissatisfaction–all of these you must endure . . . To that end I now understand, in my heart of hearts . . . that this life is but a sorrowful, unlucky moment which serves to test the sinner . . . This is exactly how I feel when I think back on the 20 years a-growing that I have left behind–I now see that those years are but a brisk and awkward moment, and yet I thank God for giving me those happy years. Dear reader, I am now in bloom, and oh, little did I think that I would ever get here that day when grandad described to me the stages of life,

i.e. twenty years a-growing, twenty years in bloom, twenty
years a-stooping and twenty years declining . . . but alas
grandad is no longer with us, Lord have mercy on his soul.
Little did he think that day that he would now be lifeless
and voiceless in a narrow grave in Ventry cemetery. I never
thought on that day that that time would come, but then,
what is life but a moment's reflection.

He then refers to the friends he had on the island in his youth, friends who,
like him, have come to know of the cruelty of life:

As all of you know I spent "Twenty years a-growing" on
the Great Blasket island, but alas, many of my companions
from those days are dead, more are thousands of miles
away. How often has it happened that while sitting on a
rock in west Connemara on a quiet moonlit night these
same companions have brought a tear to my eye as I have
recalled that time of our lives–a time that is, unfortunately,
well and truly gone.[22]

It is at this point that the story begins, with a conversation between the
author, a young garda in Inverin, and his sergeant:

"Muiris," said the Sergeant, "you should go for a walk. It's
a nice night and it will help to lighten your heart." Little
wonder that he noticed how lonely I was, it written all over
me as I stood starring out the window at the bright moon,
not a cloud in the sky, the moon having brought me down
memory lane. I could clearly see the Great Blasket before
me, the laughter of my companions ringing in my ears as
we all played together. "Perhaps you are right, Sergeant" I
said as I moved away from the window.

"But whatever else you do" he said, "do not stay out
later than eleven." "Why?" I asked . . . Know this," he said
. . . "there are six or seven people in authority over you and
if they were to come here tonight and to find you weren't
in, you would be severely punished–believe me that from

---

[22] Ó Súilleabháin, *Fiche Bliadhan fé Bhláth*, 1–2. (All translations from the text to
English are my own.)

this point on, for the rest of your life, you need to be mindful, always watching."[23]

This is most certainly not an explosive, captivating opening, but rather a pivotal moment in the narrator's life as he realises that life as it was is over and that things will never, can never, be the same again. The freedom he enjoyed on the Great Blasket has been replaced by the rigid rules and routine of adult working life.

Returning momentarily to a question I raised earlier about the starting point of the work, we find out, on page ten of the manuscript, that it is November 1927 and Muiris has just arrived in Connemara. Having gone out for the aforementioned walk, on the behest of his sergeant, he gets lost and is forced to ask for directions back:

> "Don't tell me you don't know where the Garda barracks is?" she said in surprise, "and you, surely here a good while". "Not at all" I replied, "I only arrived here yesterday."[24]

In terms of his writing style, Muiris Ó Súilleabháin has been accused in the past of being needlessly longwinded and wordy, of using, to quote Pádraig Ua Maoileoin,[25] "a dozen words where half a dozen would have sufficed."[26] I'm not sure that I agree with this assertion. Muiris Ó Súilleabháin is an artist of words–painting a picture, through his rich evocative language, in the mind of the reader. We find a lively style in *Fiche Blian ag Fás* and a livelier style again in *Fiche Bliadhan fé Bhláth*, as the author takes the reader with him on a journey through ten years (and not twenty as we might expect) of his life in Connemara. That is not to suggest that this wordy, descriptive style always works, and never slips into over-sentimentality, particularly in those passages that begin with the author taking a trip down memory lane–a trip he takes quite frequently throughout the text. But does that really come as a surprise to us? Muiris Ó Súilleabháin–at the start of the book, in particular–is a stranger, an exile. He

---

[23] Ibid, 3.

[24] Ibid, 10.

[25] For a biographical account of Ua Maoileoin see
https://www.ainm.ie/Bio.aspx?ID=1733.

[26] "[bhí sé] riamh leadránach ina stíl, easpa snoiteachta agus cruais air, dosaen focal aige nuair ab fhearr an laethdosaen . . . " Titley, *An tÚrscéal Gaeilge*, 440.

has left his own people behind and finds himself on the edge of his new community. Is it any wonder then that we see him looking back, coveting the community and the life he once had.

As a native Irish speaker in a native Irish speaking community, he thought that he would have little difficulty integrating, but he hadn't accounted for the dialectic differences in the language spoken by the two communities. He had a further challenge to his acceptance by the locals–as a member of An Garda Síochána people didn't trust him. They felt he was watching them, waiting for his opportunity to impose the law on them; something he didn't realise until he heard the following from a local man:

> "Hmm" he said, with a sarcastic smile that was anything but friendly, "I have always heard it said that you should never trust a policeman until he is seven years dead." . . . Oh how life has changed. Here I am, smartly turned out in my garda uniform, its buttons reflecting in the moonlight, but see how nobody trusts me, nor can they understand my Irish . . . Could I be any lonelier–nobody in west Connemara understands me and nobody trusts me.[27]

Eventually, however, he was accepted in Inverin and the community came to trust and understand him. But just as he was feeling settled and happy life threw him a curve, and he was moved to Carraroe, a different town in Connemara. In the following evocative piece we hear the extent to which the news of his transfer affected him:

> Dear reader, I got a lump in my throat and couldn't speak. My tongue stuck in my mouth, I saw stars before my eyes, I could see three suns on the horizon, I could see three streams racing across the rocks, I could hear thousands of sounds in my ears. I was flummoxed. I immediately thought of the friendships and acquaintances I had made with the locals–friendships and acquaintances which had taken a long year to form, and just like that I was to be taken away and sent to a place I had never been to before.

---

[27] Ó Súilleabháin, *Fiche Bliadhan fé Bhláth*, 75–76.

His anguish continued as he struggled to comprehend what he had just been told:

> ... [T]he joy left my heart. The sun darkened–the beautiful
> brightness of a moment hence extinguished. The voice of
> the stream was now tinged with sorrow and loneliness. I
> could no longer smell the sweet fragrance of the bracken so
> vibrant before now. The sea before me no longer held any
> joy for me. The world around me darkened. As far as I was
> concerned life as I knew it was coming to an end.[28]

In terms of the layout of this work, it is similar to *Fiche Blian ag Fás* in that the author puts before us a collection of individual stories–each one based on a particular event or occurrence–all knitted together in a finished work. Given that *Fiche Bliadhan fé Bhláth* is set during the period of his life spent in Connemara, it is hardly surprising that chronicles of his work as a garda account for quite a portion of it. We learn of his first court case, for example, which was against Seán Ó Flaithbheartaigh, from Baile Láir, who was found guilty of having an unshod donkey–the whole of the case written out by Ó Súilleabháin in the form of a script. We also learn of the time he had to brave the wild ocean to retrieve the bodies of two men who had died at sea, of the time he searched the mountains for a missing man, and of his countless attempts to apprehend the makers of *poitín*.

Along with accounts of his work, we are given a detailed romantic account of how he met his wife Cáit–an account, it must be said, that almost calls to mind the beguilement of the sirens of Greek mythology.

> Slash! slosh! slash! the sounds that I could hear from
> behind the big rock. At the same time I could hear the
> sound of a woman singing ... I stood up to get a good look
> at her ... and what did I see but a young maiden with her
> head down as she washed clothes ... all the time singing
> to herself. My, but she had the most beautiful voice–such a
> tall, comely girl the colour of roses, her hair black and
> curly. Her lips were as thin as an ivy leaf and as red as
> blood. She wore neither shoe nor stocking, and I can tell
> you that until that day I had never seen calves so shapely.

---

[28] Ibid, 126–127.

I was frozen to the spot. To this day I have yet to see any girl who won my heart as she did . . . As for her eyes–I had never seen ones so beguiling. The sky above me was the most beautiful alluring shade of blue, and yet it could not compete with the blue of those eyes; and though the lake before me was calm and crystal clear it could not compete with their clarity or with the blue sheen on her skin, and though the lark above my head sang so exquisitely it came nowhere near to the sweet voice of the maiden . . .[29]

Interestingly, when his wife spoke of their meeting in her interview with Pádraig Tyers, she gave a significantly different story.[30] She began with an account of the first time she met Garda Muiris Ó Súilleabháin:

[Cáit] When I was young my father kept me at home from school one time to give him a couple of days' help working in the field. Begor on the third day didn't the guard come and ask me why I wasn't at school. I quickly told him that my father kept me at home to help him pulling seaweed. "Well," he said in English, "you'll be at school tomorrow?" I didn't understand a word he said. "I have no English," I said to him. "Oh, my!" he said in Irish, "I hope you'll be in school tomorrow." "I will," I said, and the next thing was that I took to my heels and went ahide.

[Pádraig] Who was the guard?

[Cáit] Muiris Ó Súilleabháin.[31]

Life went on as normal after that, and she didn't encounter him again until after she had left school. She told Pádraig of how she started a cookery class one winter in Carraroe, but that local boys pestered her and her friends after class, for a taste of whatever it was they had made. If they didn't give them some, the boys would take it off them altogether.

---

[29] Ibid, 210–212.
[30] Tyers, *Blasket Memories*, 177–178.
[31] Ibid, 177.

[Cáit] Anyhow the teacher complained to the guards. One night I was going home after the class. I had a rhubarb pie and this lad–I don't know who he was because it was dark, about ten o'clock at night–made a drive at me to snatch a piece of the pie from me. Didn't the guard walk over, he caught him by the shoulder and said to him: "Go home, boy!" Then he said to me: "I'll go with you to the top of the road." We stood there talking for a while. "I'd go another bit of the road now with you," said he, "but I must go home." "That's all right, boy," I said. "But," he said, "I'll see you some night during the week." So I continued on with the cookery and Ó Súilleabháin used to meet me and walk me home.[32]

I think it is fair to say that Muiris' account is certainly more romantic! Cáit then explained how it was that she kept the fact that she was going out with a garda quiet, because she was concerned what people might think. There was a speak-easy close to her house and she was afraid that if anybody saw her talking to Muiris, or to any other garda, and that if the house was subsequently raided, she would be blamed for informing on them. By the time they got married, on 10 July 1934,[33] he had resigned from An Garda Síochána, though he would rejoin the force in March 1950.

The book of Job in the Bible contains the line "The Lord giveth and the Lord taketh away,"[34] and thus it was for Muiris–he was smitten with love, joyous in life, when death came and shattered his happiness. He tells us, in *Fiche Bliadhan fé Bhláth*, of the affect the deaths of both his father and his grandfather had on him. His description of the death of his father is one of openness and honesty–for the first time (as he had no recollection of the death of his mother) he had experienced the reality of true separation and the brevity of life–a reality that would hit him for a second time shortly afterwards, with the death of his beloved grandfather, one of the main characters in *Fiche Blian ag Fás*. The shock that he got when he heard that his father was dying was nothing to the shock he would get when he read of his grandfather's death in the newspaper *Scéala Éireann*:

---

[32] Ibid, 177–178.
[33] Ibid, 179.
[34] Job 1:21, Holy Bible: King James Version.

I sat down on the side of the bed and opened *Scéala Éireann*. My dearest reader, I was shaken to my very core, stars appeared before my eyes, the room darkened around me, I got pins and needles that started in the soles of my feet and travelled up to the crown of my head, because what did I see on the pages in front of me but grandad's smiling face. It was the following words in large print above it that caused my anguish, i.e. "The grandfather of Muiris Ó Súilleabháin, author of *Twenty Years a-Growing*, has died on the Great Blasket." I couldn't take my eyes away from it with the loneliness, grief and sorrow that enveloped me . . . with that the tears started to fall on grandad's picture. "Oh grandad, where is your strength and your agility now, where is your great mind and your storytelling; little did you think at one stage of your life that you would lie forever lifeless in a little, lime-white graveyard in Ventry."[35]

Encouraged by the strength and support of Cáit in his grief, Muiris, in due course, decided to visit his island home—his first visit since the death of the two men.

At midday the following day we arrived at the Great Blasket. . . . There wasn't a breath of air nor a cloud intruding on the beautiful blue sky, as the sun reflected upon the felt roofs of the houses, a little puff of smoke rising up from all the chimneys . . . but, alas, there was one house that had no sign of life in it or around it, my own home . . .

This was a particularly significant moment in his life, as he came to the sudden realisation that life had changed irrevocably and that the perceived constants in his world had proven to be fickle and vacillating:

It was then I realised that this was not the same island ... where I once felt comfort, solace and happiness coming into the Great Blasket I now felt lonely and intensely sorrowful.[36]

---

[35] Ó Súilleabháin, *Fiche Bliadhan fé Bhláth*, 230.
[36] Ibid, 238.

LOST MEMOIR

Fiche Bliadhan fé Bhláth ends with this journey home, as did *Fiche Blian ag Fás*, but it is a fitting ending on this occasion. At this stage of his life, Muiris Ó Súilleabháin has an understanding of the fragility and ephemerality of life. By the time he sits outside his grandfather's house, at the end of the second book, life has played the cruel trick of death on him twice–the two men who moulded and nurtured him no longer with him.

Conclusion

I mentioned earlier that the manuscript of *Fiche Bliadhan fé Bhláth* was rejected because it bore no similarity to the author's previous work. But how could it? His first book deals with the childish days of youth where life's great questions and mysteries have no place, where the concept of age and mortality mean nothing. As the years pass, we see the author coming of age. In *Fiche Bliadhan fé Bhláth* it is the voice of a man moulded by life– that is all too often difficult, challenging and lonely–that we hear. He is tormented by the uncertainty of human existence and is increasingly driven by a yearning for the days that once were.

This is a work in which the author speaks to the reader in a way he doesn't in *Fiche Blian ag Fás*. The narrator is a mature adult upon whom life has left its mark–there is an honesty, an openness and a sensitivity in this second work as Muiris Ó Súilleabháin grapples with the fate of man. His first book was an idealistic insight into a specific island people; but his second is a glance into humankind–a macroscopic rather than microscopic glance.

Fiche Bliadhan fé Bhláth is speckled with sentimentality and romanticism, and many will dislike the work as a result. But why are we so quick to find fault with these traits and to criticise an author for their presence in his/her work? Much of the sentimentality and romanticism in this work are borne from Muiris Ó Súilleabháin's evocative use of language, from his descriptions of the physical world around him in an attempt to reveal, explain and understand his emotions. But this physical world is part of his very essence–he was born and reared on a small island surrounded by the Atlantic Ocean; an ocean as turbulent as life itself. Connecting himself to the world around him is to connect himself to its people–to his own people; to focus, as he often does, on the moon overhead is to remind himself that this is the same moon that his family and friends on the Great Blasket can see, the same moon that his emigrated companions can see.

Romantic? Possibly so. Sentimental? Most likely. But above all it is innate, instinctive; and is at the very core of the Celtic mentality. The following quote from Matthew Arnold's *On the Study of Celtic Literature*, sums up nicely the virtue, as I see it, of the sentimentality of this work:

> *Sentiment* is, however, the word which marks where the Celtic races really touch and are one; sentimental, if the Celtic nature is to be characterised by a single term, is the best term to take. An organisation quick to feel impressions, and feeling them very strongly; a lively personality therefore, keenly sensitive to joy and to sorry; this is the main point. If the downs of life too much outnumber the ups, this temperament, just because it is so quickly and nearly conscious of all impressions, may no doubt be seen shy and wounded; it may be seen in wistful regret, it may be seen in passionate, penetrating melancholy; but its essence is to aspire ardently after life, light, and emotion, to be expansive, adventurous, and gay. . . . The Celt is often called sensual; but it is not so much the vulgar satisfactions of sense that attract him as emotion and excitement; he is truly, as I began by saying, sentimental.[37]

---

[37] Matthew Arnold, *On the Study of Celtic Literature* (London: Smith Elder & Co., 1867), 343.

LOST MEMOIR

Bibliography

Arnold, Matthew. *On the Study of Celtic Literature*. London: Smith Elder and Co., 1867.

Carney, Michael (with Gerald Hayes). *From the Great Blasket to America: The Last Memoir by an Islander*. Cork: The Collins Press, 2013.

Céitinn, Seosamh. *Tomás Oileánach: fear idir dhá thraidisiún*. Dublin: An Clóchomhar, 1992.

de Mórdha, Mícheál. Bláithín: Flower. Ceiliúradh an Bhlascaoid 1, 1998.

—. *Scéal agus Dán Oileáin*. Dublin: Coiscéim, 2012.

— and Dáithí de Mórdha. *The Great Blasket/ An Blascaod Mór–A Photographic Portrait/ Portráid Pictiúr*. Cork: Collins Press, 2013.

Feiritéar, Breandán. "Seoirse agus an tOileán." *Ceiliúradh an Bhlascaoid* 4 (2000): 31–46.

Hayes, Gerald and Kane, Eliza. *The Last Blasket King–Pádraig Ó Catháin, an rí*. Cork: The Collins Press, 2015.

—. *The Blasket Islandman: the life and legacy of Tomás Ó Criomhthain*. Cork: The Collins Press, 2018.

Í Chearnaigh, Seán Sheáin. *An tOileán a Tréigeadh*. Dublin: Sáirséal agus Dill, 1974.

—. *Iarbhlascaodach ina Dheoraí*. Dublin: Sáirséal agus Dill, 1978.

Nic Craith, Mairéad. *An tOileánach Léannta*. Dublin: An Clóchomhar, 1988.

Ní Ghuithín, Máire. *Bean an Oileáin*. Dublin: Coiscéim, 1986.

Ní Riain, Isobel. *Léiriú Socheolaíochtúil ar Litríocht an Bhlascaoid*. Dublin: Coiscéim, 2019.

Ní Shúilleabháin, Eibhlín. *Cín Lae Eibhlín Ní Shúilleabháin*. Dublin: Coiscéim, 2000.

Ní Shúilleabháin, Eibhlís. *Letters from the Great Blasket*. Cork: Mercier Press, 1978.

Ó Cearnaigh, Seán Pheats Tom. *Fiolar an Eireaball Bháin*. Dublin: Coiscéim, 1992.

Ó Criomhthain, Seán. *Lá dár Saol*. Dublin: Oifig an tSoláthair, 1969.

Ó Criomhthain, Tomás. *Allagar na hInise*. Dublin: Ó Fallamhain and Oifig an tSoláthair, 1928.

—. *An tOileánach*. Dublin: Clólucht an Talbóidigh, 1929.

—. *Dinnsheanchas na mBlascaodaí*. Dublin: Oifig Díolta Foillseacháin Rialtais, 1935.

—, Robin Flower and Séamus Ó Duilearga. *Seanchas ón Oileán Tiar*. Dublin: Comhlucht Oidhreachais na hÉireann, Tta., 1956.

— and Breandán Ó Conaire. *Bloghanna ón mBlascaod*. Dublin: Coiscéim, 1997.

— and Pádraig Ua Maoileoin. *Allagar II*. Dublin: Coiscéim, 1999.

TRACEY NI MHAONAIGH

— and Nollaig Mac Congáil. *Scéilíní ón mBlascaod.* Dublin: Coiscéim, 2004.

Ó Fiannachta, Pádraig. "Litríocht Chorca Dhuibhne." *Irisleabhar Mhá Nuad* (1982): 21–35.

Ó Gaoithín, Mícheál. *Is Truagh ná Fanann an Óige.* Dublin: Oifig an tSoláthair, 1953.

—. *Beatha Pheig Sayers.* Dublin: Foilseacháin Náisiúnta Tta, 1970.

Ó Murchú, Liam P. (eag.) *Beatha Pheig Sayers.* An Daingean: An Sagart, 2019.

Ó Súilleabháin, Muiris. *Fiche Blian ag Fás.* Dublin: Clólucht an Talbóidigh, 1933.

—. *Fiche Bliadhan fé Bhláth.* Unpublished typescript, 1938.

—. *Twenty Years A-Growing.* Translated by Moya Llewelyn Davis and George Thomson. Oxford: Oxford University Press, 1933.

Sayers, Peig and Máire Ní Chinnéide. *Peig: A Scéal Féin.* Dublin: Clólucht an Talbóidigh, 1936.

— and Máire Ní Chinnéide. *Machtnamh Seana-mhná.* Dublin: Oifig an tSoláthair, 1939.

— and Kenneth Jackson. *Scéalta ón mBlascaod.* Dublin: Cumann le Béaloideas Éireann, 1998.

—. *Móirín.* Dún Chaoin: Cló Dhún Chaoin, [n.d.].

—, Bo Almqvist and Pádraig Ó Héalaí. *Labharfad le Cách: scéalta agus seanchas taifeadta ag Radió Éireann agus an BBC–I will speak to you all: stories and lore recorded by Radió Éireann and the BBC.* Dublin: New Ireland Press, 2009.

Thomson, George. "Réamhrá an eagarthóra don dara heagrán." *Fiche Blian ag Fás* (1975 [1998⁵]): 5–7.

—. "Fiche Blian ag Fás." *Comhar* 17, no. 11 (November 1958): 4–6.

Titley, Alan. *An tÚrscéal Gaeilge.* Dublin: An Clóchomhar Tta., 1991.

Tyers, Pádraig. *Leoithne Aniar.* Ballyferriter: Cló Dhuibhne, 1982.

—. *Blasket Memories: The Life of an Irish Island Community.* Cork: Mercier Press, 1998.

Caílte's Weeping: Emotional Expressions of Cultural Change in Twefth-century Ireland

Graham David Sean O'Toole

The Middle Irish *dinnsenchas* text *Acallam na Senórach* (c. 1200) illuminates the cultural responses to changing economic and political dynamics in twelfth- to thirteenth-century Ireland. To do this, there must be a base understanding of texts in the tradition of *dinnsenchas* as defining place relative to their time of composition. In this nexus of space and time, the stories that transmit the lore of place names become reflections of both the place being defined and the times lived by the definers. Though composed roughly around the beginning of the thirteenth century, the prosimetric text considers the retinue of St. Patrick during the time of the conversion of Ireland around the middle of the fifth century.[1] The text introduces two simultaneous timelines: that of Caílte and Oisín and that of the native Irish during Patrick's conversion. The *Acallam* makes no mistake about the respective ages of Caílte and Oisín (approximately 200 years old), and their experience is described through living memory (i.e. *dinnsenchas* narratives from when the core members of the *fianaigecht* roamed Ireland). Further, this experience is contrasted with their interactions with the Irish of Patrick's present. The relationships between these temporalities describe the cultural difference between past and present in the terms of the compilers of the *Acallam*. As such, this essay is concerned with all of these periods and attempts to adequately describe them in their appropriate contexts. "Literary past" and "literary present" will be used broadly to highlight events which occur in the past and present as they exist in the text of the *Acallam*, whereas "past" and "present" refer to the past and present of the historical moment during which the *Acallam* was composed.

Using these terms, this essay will begin by outlining the translation of the donation of Cashel from its synodic context in 1101 to the time of

---

[1] Connon, Anne. "The Roscommon locus of Acallam na senórach and some thoughts as to tempus and persona" in Aidan Doyle and Kevin Murray (eds), *In Dialogue with the Agallamh: Essays in Honour of Seán Ó Coileáin* (Dublin: Four Courts Press, 2014) pp. 21–59.

Patrick's conversion of Ireland. While this is not the only instance of such translation of events through time in the text, it is key to the analysis that follows. The essay then discusses the terms of the second Synod of Cashel (c. 1172), as recounted by Gerald of Wales, with focus on the efforts to reform tithe practice and collection in Ireland. Those terms, from the Norman perspective, are then placed in contrast with the hunt scene at Seefin, during which Patrick institutes the tithe on the native Irish in the literary present of the *Acallam*'s narrative in central Munster.[2] This scene can elucidate the Irish attitude to changes in landscape and tax structure in the late-twelfth century through Caílte's extreme lamentation of the shifting results of hunts between the Fenians and those of Patrick's present.

Many scholars point to the mention of Mellifont Abbey for evidence that the *Acallam* was composed after 1142, but it also betrays its date of composition by referencing contemporaneous events regarding Cashel.[3] After being asked to "preach the gospel" by the king of Munster, Eogan Lethderg, Patrick ascends the Rock of Cashel and does so, at which point, "all the nobles of Munster did homage to Patrick, and entrusted their territory and patrimony to him, and put their land and wealth under his power."[4] Patrick is first to greet these men, and as the representative of the Irish Church, they immediately grant their lands to him, indicating a willingness to dedicate their faith in the form of property.

---

[2] For a fuller discussion on tithe reform in twelfth-century Europe, see Giles Constable, *Monastic Tithes: From their Origins to the Twelfth Century.* (Cambridge: Cambridge University Press, 1964).

[3] Ann Dooley and Harry Roe (Trans.). *Tales of the Elders of Ireland.* (Oxford: Oxford University Press, 1999). p. 225 (Henceforth "Dooley & Roe"). While Dooley and Roe claim that their translation of Acallam na Senórach is borne of the four extant manuscripts, they declare their indebtedness to the editions of Whitley Stokes and Standish Hayes O'Grady, pp. xxxi–xxxii. For the purposes of this essay, the Irish text of the Acallam remains faithful to Stoke's edition that is readily available to the public, but the author acknowledges minor differences between the Irish text and the English translation. Connon. p. 55.

[4] Dooley & Roe. pp. 150–1. For a thorough discussion on parochial organization, see Marie Therese Flanagan. *The Transformation of the Irish Church in the Twelfth Century.* (Suffolk: Boydell Press. 2010.) pp. 54–91. Flanagan's specific conversation about regulations regarding tithing can be found on pages 80–91.

EXPRESSIONS OF CULTURAL CHANGE

At this point, Benén, who according to Tirechán's *Collectanea de Sancto Patricio* is Patrick's handpicked successor to lead the new Irish church at Armagh, demands a *screpall soiscéla* (gospel-fee), which he defines as "a fee of territory and land to the cleric" from Éogan Lethderg.[5] The king's response reflects the decisions of the first synod of Cashel:

> *"In baile seo a tá & ina fuarusa h-é', ar rí Muman, 'do fognum dó co brath & da muintir ina diaid."* Is and **tuc rí Muman Caissil do Patraic** *mac Alpraind. "Cindus do- berar duind sin?"* ar Beineoin. *"Mar seo"*, ar in rí, *"tiacht don chleirech fein ar Lic na Cét,"* bar rí Muman, *"ʒ in neoch at-chífea do mín Muman ar cach leth do beith aici."*[6]

"This place in which he [St. Patrick] stands and in which I have found him", said the King of Munster, "shall be at his service until his death and thenceforth at the service of his people." At that time the **king of Munster gave Cashel to Patrick**, son of Calpurn. "How shall that be given to us?" asked Benén. "In this way", said the king. "The cleric himself shall go onto Cloch na Cét 'the Stone of the Hundreds', and whatever he sees of level Munster in any direction he shall have."[7]

Compare this language to that of the Annals of the Four Masters, where Muirchertach Ua Briain "granted Cashel of the Kings to the religious, without any claim of layman or cleric upon it, but to the religious of Ireland in general."[8] Here we see that the Annalistic tradition desires to remove

---

[5] "Tírechán's Text in English (Transl. L. Bieler): St. Patrick's Confessio." Transl. by Ludwig Bieler, *St. Patrick's Confessio*, 2011, www.confessio.ie/more/tirechan _english#; *eDIL*, s.v. "screpul(l), scripul(l)," accessed December 15, 2019, http://edil.qub.ac.uk/36628; *eDIL*, s.v. "soiscélae," accessed December 15, 2019, http://edil.qub.ac.uk/38384.

[6] *Acallam na Senórach.* ll. 5395–401. All Irish text quotations of the *Acallam* are copied from Whitley Stoke's edition of *Acallam na Senórach* (henceforth *AcS*) available online at celt.ucc.ie. My emphasis.

[7] Dooley and Roe. p. 151. my emphasis.

[8] *Annals of the Four Masters*. ed. J. O'Donovan (Dublin: Royal Irish Academy, 1848–51) vol. ii. p. 966–971. Other accounts suggest that the donation was explicitly to the Roman church, represented by St. Patrick. See *Chronicon Scotorum*, ed. W.M.

church ownership from the equation, where the *Acallam* specifies that Cashel is given to Patrick.

Patrick ascends the stone and expels eleven thousand demons from all the land he can see. Patrick blesses the place and nods toward the second synod of Cashel by giving it the gift of good counsel: "*bennaigis Pátraic in cloich iarsin, ₇ fácais buaid comairli do denam dí.*"[9] The donation of Cashel in the *Acallam* is shifted back by six centuries to the life of Patrick, removing it from the context of its donation to the Church in 1101 at the first synod of Cashel, and re-placing it in a setting where it can signify a rich heritage of ownership and cooperation between the historical church and the native Irish. Cashel's significance as an emerging episcopal see as well as its location for two notable ecclesiastical synods which concern tithing practice during twelfth-century reform marks it as an important episode in the *Acallam* for establishing the text's credibility in commenting on reform efforts.

Moreover, the blessing of good counsel serves as the foundation for all of the decisions made on the spot, as well as its position as the second archbishopric in what would be the Irish Church. It is this gesture which brings us to Gerald of Wales, who reports the findings of the second Synod of Cashel in 1172 and states that the Synod directed the collection of tithes: "*quod universi fideles Christi* **decimas animalium***, frugum, ceterarumque provencionum, ecclesie cuius fuerint parochiani persolvant*" (that all good Christians do pay the **tithe of beasts**, corn, and other produce, to the church of the parish in which they live).[10] Gerald's reports of the Synod and the language present in *Acallam na Senórach*, however, beg us to consider the perspectives of each.

Regarding the perspective of Gerald of Wales, his biases are plain to see. The product of the wealthy Norman noble de Barry family and an officer of the Church, Gerald positions himself in his texts so as to gain the

---

Hennessy, 1866.; *Annals of Tigernach,* ed. Whitley Stokes, in *Revue Celtique*, xvi–xviii, 1895–97.

[9] *AcS*. ll. 5405–06.; Dooley & Roe. p. 151.

[10] Giraldus Cambrensis. *Expugnatio Hibernica: The Conquest of Ireland.* Trans. by Thomas Forester. (Cambridge, ON: Medieval Latin Series, 2000). p. 36. I.34.5. My emphasis.

favor of both Crown and Church.[11] In his *Expugnatio Hibernica*, the second synod of Cashel is called by Henry II, which can in no way be seen as a Norman ratification of the independence of the Irish Church.[12] Rather, John of Salisbury's efforts to secure *Laudabiliter* for Henry II in 1154 indicates that the efforts to reform the Irish church under the jurisdiction of Canterbury and the forthcoming invasion of Ireland were similarly motivated and distinctly connected.[13] Clare Downham goes further to argue that the papal bull in question "authorised the invasion of Ireland in return for ecclesiastical taxes and Church reforms" though the invasion would not take place for another seventeen years. David Dumville similarly argues that under the close watch of Rome, Gaelic Christianity needed "to define itself organizationally as a single Church in relationship to papal authority . . . If the Irish church did not achieve such definition now, it would find itself being subsumed."[14] Therefore, following David Dumville's analysis of the relationship between the Irish Church and Canterbury, Gerald's depiction of the Second Synod of Cashel must be read as an effort to solidify the concept of economic ties between Irish Christians and the joint forces of the Norman invaders and reform efforts from Canterbury, after Pope Adrian IV, as Dumville puts it, "authorized a quasi-crusade into Ireland by King Henry II . . . on the grounds that [previous] reform in Ireland had been merely superficial."[15]

---

[11] Bartlett, Robert. *Gerald of Wales 1146–1223.* (Oxford: Clarendon Press, 1982.) p. 32–35. Additionally, Bartlett's discussion mentions Gerald's interest in issues relating to tithe reform among other matters during his time in Pembrokeshire, though the comment is made only in passing.

[12] *Expugnatio.* p. 36. I.33.1.

[13] Clare Downham. *Medieval Ireland* (Cambridge: Cambridge University Press, 2018). p. 281.

[14] Dumville, David N. Councils and Synods of the Gaelic Early and Central Middle Ages. *Quiggin Pamphlets on the Sources of Medieval Gaelic History*, 3. (Cambridge: Department of Anglo-Saxon, Norse, and Celtic, University of Cambridge). P. 50–51. Another excellent discussion of the relationship between the English and Irish churches is put forth by Marie Therese Flanagan in *Irish Society, Anglo-Norman Settlers, Angevin Kingship: Interactions in Ireland in the Late Twelfth Century.* (Oxford: Clarendon Press, 1989).

[15] Dumville. P. 51–52.

The *Acallam* indicates that its perspective is entirely the opposite. To discuss all the ways that this can be portrayed could constitute its own monograph, so this essay will focus on one particular scene. Early on in the narrative, during Patrick and Caílte's first foray around Ireland, the group comes to the place we now know as Ardpatrick in County Limerick. The scene brings together the converging themes of ecclesiastical reform of the tithe in Ireland, changes to the physical landscape during the period, and cultural differences between the Irish of literary past and those of literary present (as described earlier in this essay).

Caílte and Patrick arrive in Ardpatrick (just to the northeast of the mountain). They are approached by a local Irishman, Bran mac Derg, son of a king of Munster, who seeks wisdom from Patrick. Caílte is immediately curious about Bran's people's contemporary hunting methods. Bran gives a disheartening response suggesting that their hunts are not as successful as they might otherwise be: "*Iadhmait 'mon tulaig nó 'mon carn nó 'mon caill maigh-shlebhe, itir coin ₇ gilla ₇ óclach, ₇ bímit re h-edh in chaemh-lai a n-degaid an fhiadhraidh, ₇ marbhmait fiadh fecht ann, & feacht aile téit uainn.*"[16] ("We surround a hill or a mound or a high, level wood with our hounds, our servants and warriors, and spend the whole day chasing the game. At times we kill some game, but at other times it gets away").[17]

Caílte's response to this is to weep heavily "until both his shirt and his chest were wet" (*cur'bo fliuch blai ₇ bruinne dho*).[18] Kristen Mills's suggestion that these modes of sorrowful lamentation may represent an inability to "assimilate Patrick's message of salvation" as "survivors from the pre-Christian past" can perhaps be extended to an inability to assimilate to the social standards of the literary present.[19] His expression of weeping and tearful outrage permits Caílte to perform a social rite. They bring Bran up to the top of nearby Seefin mountain (also called Ballyhoura or *Osmetal*, which conveniently marks the border of Counties Cork and Limerick) to display the superior, hyper-masculine ancient Irish hunting methods:

---

[16] *AcS.* Ll. 884–887. My emphasis.

[17] Dooley & Roe. p. 29.

[18] Dooley & Roe. p. 29. *AcS.* l. 889.

[19] Kristen Mills, "Sorrow and Conversion in *Acallam na Senórach*" in *Éigse Vol. XXXVIII*, ed. Liam Mac Mathúna. (National University of Ireland, 2013) p. 14–15.

*tocbhais Cáilte a shuasán sealga ⁊ fiadhuigh ⁊ fian-
choscair ós aird, ⁊ ro léicestar a tri barann-ghlaedha
badhbha as, cu nach raibhi i comfhocraibh na a coimhnesa
dho fiadh fodil hain a maigh na a moin na a maigh-shléib
na a caill gan techt ina ruamannuibh roretha co n-
dechsat.*[20]

Caílte raised his cries of hunting and game and slaughter,
and three war-cries of anger came from him, so that there
was no game at large in the vicinity or near to him, in the
field or on the moor, or on the high ground or in the woods
that did not go dashing in a great frenzy.[21]

The frenzied animals described refresh themselves by drinking from a
nearby lake, at which place Caílte and company slaughter the lot: eight
hundred stags, does, and boar in total. The exaggerated bounty implies that
for some reason or another the temporal differences between Bran's more
'modern' hunting method and Caílte's traditional one make Bran's
markedly less successful.

Upon dividing the quarry, Bran is unwilling to give part of his share to
Benén. Upon refusal, Bran is immediately struck with a pain in his belly:

*"**Tabur dechmad in fhiadhuigh dun,**" ar Beneoin. Nír'
escaidh le Bran mac Deirg in cuid rainic do féin do roinn
re nech. Gabus galar ana broinn mac rígh Muman. "Do
lámh air-so, a naeim-chleirig," ar Bran. "Dar mu breiti,"
ar Cáilte,"no gu tarda a **luach** uait ní raga." "Gá **luagh**?"
ar Bran. "**Uair is at broinn atá in galar**," ar Cáilte "**tairr
gacha bó ⁊ gacha muice ⁊ gacha caerach uaid do Pátraic
⁊ don naeim-eclais co bráth.**" "Do-bér-sa sin," ar Bran,
"⁊ do-bhéra mo mhac am dhiaidh." Ocus do-chuaidh-sin a
n-gnáthugad ac feruibh Eirenn ó sin imach. Tuc iarsin
Pátraic a láimh ar broinn Brain meic Dheirg ⁊ ba slán
focétóir.*[22]

---

[20] *AcS.* ll. 907–11.
[21] Dooley & Roe. p. 29.
[22] *AcS.* ll. 919–929. My emphasis.

GRAHAM O'TOOLE

"A tenth of the hunt should be given to us," said Benén. But Bran, son of Derg, was unwilling to divide his share with anyone. The son of the King of Munster was then struck down by abdominal pain. "Put your hand on the pain," said Bran to Patrick. "By my word," said Caílte, "until you pay his fee he will not." "What fee?" asked Bran. **"Since the sickness is in your belly,"** said Caílte, **"you must give the belly of every cow and every pig and every sheep to Patrick and to the Holy Church henceforth."** "I shall do that," said Bran, "and my son after me." From that time on this custom prevailed among the men of Ireland. Patrick put his hand upon the stomach of Bran, son of Derg, and he was cured at once.[23]

Caílte only allows Patrick to relieve his pain if Bran agrees to pay a *lúach* (a fee) to Patrick and the Holy Church. This fee consisted of *"tairr gacha bhó ⁊ gacha mhuice ⁊ gacha chaerach uaid"*–the belly of all of Bran's livestock (cow, pig, and sheep respectively)–henceforth.[24]

While the kind of instruction present here has been noted before by a number of scholars including the most recent translators of the *Acallam*, this passage particularly diverges from the legal definition of consistent payments to the Irish Church. The respective obligations of church and layperson in pre-Norman Ireland are described in the eighth-century law text *Córus Bésgnai* which is extant in the Irish law compilation *Senchas Már*. The church is responsible for baptism, communion, praying for the dead, preaching the gospel, et cetera.[25] Meanwhile, according to the text, the Irish are responsible for "their donation, their tithe [*dechmad*], their first-fruits, their firstlings . . . every tenth plant of the plants of the earth and

---

[23] Dooley & Roe. p. 30. My emphasis.
[24] *eDIL*, s.v. "lóg," accessed April 26, 2020, http://edil.qub.ac.uk/30495.
[25] The translation is from Colmán Etchingham, *Church Organization in Ireland, AD 650–1000.* (Maynooth: Laigin Publications, 1999) p. 244., who curiously does not provide the citation for this entry from the *Corpus Iuris Hibernici* (CIH), 6 vols. ed. D.A. Binchy (Dublin: Royal Irish Academy, 1978). In Breatnach, Liam. "Córus Bésgnai: An Old Irish Law Tract on the Church and Society" (Dublin: DIAS, 2017), Breatnach translates the passages from this text largely in the same manner as Etchingham. In addition, it is worth nothing that the sections described in this essay are part of the main text in all manuscripts, not the glosses nor commentary.

283

offshoot of the animals every year . . ."[26] The work of the *Acallam* serves to redefine what constitutes the *dechmad*.[27] First, Benén draws our attention to the issue of tithes by using the legally charged word *dechmad* (cf. Latin *decimas*) when he demands his portion of the hunt. And second, Caílte re-negotiates the *luach* from every tenth whole animal to the belly of every animal as commensurate payment in exchange for Bran's health. This renegotiation transfers the idea of a "tenth" from an ordinal "every tenth animal" to a fraction "a tenth of every animal," that is, the belly. I argue that this suggests a need to reassess the abilities of twelfth-century Irish readers to pay their tithes to the church.

As Bran's sickness takes to his belly and the terms of his tithe are negotiated by Benén, Bran asks Patrick to put his hand on the pain. But Caílte steps in and designates the belly as both the origination point of the pain that has struck Bran, but also as the portion of his livestock to be given to the church. These terms are not unlike the eighth-century Irish law tract *Osbretha*. Fergus Kelly, in his monumental text *Early Irish Farming* (1997), recounts the mythological judgment that lies at the basis of the law:

> According to the preamble, the judgement was delivered by the legendary judge Amairgein to resolve a dispute between the invaders Éber and Éremón, who were brothers. Éber and his followers had gone hunting *(selg)* in the mountains, and had killed twelve deer. Éremón and his followers had in the meantime prepared a habitation. Éber's followers argued that they were not obliged to share any of the venison with the others. The matter was then submitted to Amargein. His judgement as preserved in the law text . . . does not seem to relate closely to the dispute described in the preamble. It deals rather with the division of the deer's carcass between the various persons involved in a hunt, as well as the owner of the land where the killing takes place. The first person who wounds the deer is entitled to the *clasach*, which presumably refers to some part of its body. The person who flays the deer gets its

---

[26] Breatnach. p. 37. Etchingham. p. 244–5.

[27] *Electronic Dictionary of the Irish Language (eDIL)*, s.v. "dechmad," accessed December 15, 2019. http://edil.qub.ac.uk/14893.

shoulder *(lethe)*, and the owner of the hounds gets the haunch *(cés)*. Another person–perhaps he who actually kills the deer–gets the neck *(muinél)*, and the hounds themselves get the legs *(cossa)*. The last man on the scene gets the intestines (*inathar*) and the rest of the hunting-party get the liver (*áe*). Finally, the landowner gets the belly (*tarr*).[28]

That the division of the carcass is adjudicated in this legendary context only solidifies its presence within the cultural milieu. It is worth noting, however, that *Osbretha* is the only law-text that relates to the division of bounty after a hunt and its contents are notoriously difficult to translate. Caílte's assertion of these terms, evoking past laws on a present period, gives necessary permission for the *Acallam* to reappropriate laws from a strictly Irish tradition on to the present circumstance of twelfth century ecclesiastical regulatory reform. *Osbretha* originally concerned the division of a carcass after a hunt, however, once put into the context of tithing, it takes on new meaning. "Every tenth animal, plant, et cetera" is reasonable when human population is low and animal populations are abundant. But, in Norman Ireland, that ratio was shifting in the opposite direction. Not only were Normans coming into and settling Ireland en masse, but the practice of hunting was slowly being privatized; land was being cordoned off for cultivation or even for deer parks, about which we know an increasing amount thanks to the work of scholars like Fiona Beglane.[29] Despite such work, the question of the effects of Norman colonization remains relatively under-studied. However, the Seefin hunt serves to connect the concept of hunting as a significant cultural and commercial piece of the early Irish economy to the regulation of tithes during twelfth-century reform.[30]

---

[28] *eDIL*, s.v. "tarr," accessed December 15, 2019, http://edil.qub.ac.uk/40128; Kelly, Fergus. *Early Irish Farming.* (Dublin: Four Courts Press. 1997). p. 275.

[29] See Beglane, Fiona. *Anglo-Norman Parks in Medieval Ireland.* (Dublin: Four Courts Press, 2015).

[30] The construction of hunting leading to tithing can also be seen in the hunt at *Maistiu* [Mullaghmast] whereupon The Hill of the Tithe is named. Dooley & Roe. pp. 134–5. While not strictly a hunt, Oisín's fishing expedition at Usnagh could also qualify as it deals with the division of both fish and crops (watercress and brooklime) between local leaders and the Church. Dooley & Roe. pp. 72.

Norman interference can be seen as a catalyst for the shifting dynamics that might cause changes in the locals' ability to hunt at scale as they did in the past, but such claims remain purely speculative. However, it may be fruitful to consider the effect of castellation and the expanded presence of monastic houses on the local populace. The hunt's regional setting provides ample room to consider this kind of effect. In the area surrounding Seefin, the colonizing Normans quickly set up a network of rectangular earthworks and motte-and-baileys:

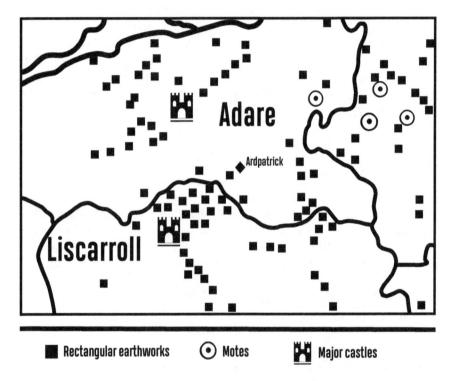

■ Rectangular earthworks   ⊙ Motes   ♜ Major castles

Figure 1: Area around Seefin[31]

Eventually, Gerald of Wales's own family would come to establish the largest castle in the region at Liscarroll, which is only twenty miles from

[31] Figure 1 adapted from F.H.A. Aalen. *Man and the Landscape in Ireland.* (London: Academic Press, 1978). p. 110.

Seefin and Ardpatrick. According to Gerald, subduing the Irish by castellation would *"legibus obtemperareet servire coegit"* (compel them to obey the laws).[32] That is, the presence of Norman castles would oblige the native Irish to comply with new regulations set up by the Norman colonizers or their proxies within the local ecclesiastical establishment. *Acallam na Senórach* notably does not directly mention either the issue of decreasing deer populations nor of Norman castellation. The subsequent passage does describe how Caílte notices a *dunad* (fort, stronghold) he's never seen before in the region, giving us direct reference to the changes to landscape.[33] The structure here is identified with the rulers of Fermoy, and could be related to the recently established Cistercian monastery there.[34] Those passages rather serve as gestures to trends in twelfth-century Ireland which are then interpreted through the lens of the monastic houses, local clergy, and laypersons struggling to conform to continental Church practices. Those who compiled the text were keenly aware of the need to reform the practice of tithing or risk being ostracized by Rome or worse: placed under the jurisdiction of Canterbury. So, they may have seen fit to imprint their changing circumstances onto the landscape of their text, however anachronistic these characteristics may be.

The tithe structures of pre-Norman Ireland were no longer appropriate to a land that was increasingly reliant on cultivation, and which exhibited a decrease in hunting lands and game. The *Acallam* is imbued with a sense of nostalgia for a more profitable past for the local Irish people and a just compromise for the institution of tithes paid to their local parish. Time and further research will tell what effect this change had on the prosperity of Irish persons under Norman rule, but, for now, the *Acallam* stands as a testament to the changing economic attitudes of the Irish Church and their congregations.

---

[32] Giraldus Cambrensis. *Expugnatio Hibernica: The Conquest of Ireland.* Trans. and ed. by A.B.
Scott and F.X. Martin. (Dublin: Royal Irish Academy, 1978). p. 190–1.

[33] *eDIL*, s.v. "dúnad", accessed December 15, 2019, http://edil.qub.ac.uk/19229. Dooley & Roe. p.31.

[34] Gwynn, Aubrey and R. Neville Hadcock. *Medieval Religious Houses: Ireland.* (Bristol: Longman Group, 1970). p. 132.

Abstracts of Other Papers Read at the Thirty-Ninth Harvard Celtic Colloquium

Reconsidering the Case of the Separating Sword in Irish Literature

Sarah Barnett

It is now considered all but a truism that the story of Tristan and Iseult is Celtic in origin. Since the earliest attestations of the tale survive in non-Celtic languages, however, the positive attribution of Celtic derivation for several elements of the legend is fraught with difficulty. Perhaps the most questionable literary feature is that of the separating sword motif, once thought to be Irish in origin, but now believed to be an entirely French invention. My paper seeks to question this foreign designation, arguing instead that the short, relatively obscure Irish tale, *Comrac Líadaine ocus Cuirithir*, provides a much clearer analogue for the sword's peculiar literary performance in its continental exemplars. The text's separating device, the *léignid becc*, is a figure whose symbolic intentions reflect the same anxieties of interpretation present throughout both *Comrac* and the Tristan and Iseult legend. Turning to Irish literature more broadly, I further demonstrate that such a thematic symbol also possesses an established history in Irish literature, appearing within a wide array of texts such as *Tochmarc Emire*, *Tochmarc Becfhola*, *Táin*, and even *Vǫlsungasaga*; a text, I argue, demonstrates Irish influence at the critical moment of the lover's separation by sword. From this survey, I seek to show not only that *Comrac* is an important missing witness to the transmutation of the Tristan legend abroad, but perhaps more significantly, that the motif of an ineffectual, falsely figurative separating device is one fundamentally rooted in the Irish imagination.

THIRTY-NINTH CELTIC COLLOQUIUM

The Breton Language in the Middle Ages,
Its perception and Explanation

Yves Coativy

At the end of the Middle Ages (twelfth–sixteenth centuries), the duchy of Brittany is one of the important western principalities of Europe. It is characterized by the continuous strengthening of its administrative structures, by the dynamic economy and by the social and cultural development equivalent to the rest of the West. From a linguistic point of view, Breton is used in the West of the peninsula while French dominates in the East. Between the two of them, it is difficult in the Middle Ages to define exactly which is the language used, from a lack of documentation. The origin and usage of the Breton language in the Middle Ages was not the subject of important research by medieval historians. However, from the twelfth to the middle of the sixteenth century, there are testimonies in the chronicles (like those by the Anonymous of the Saint-Brieuc, Pierre Le Baud, Alain Bouchard), the histories (that of Bertrand d'Argentré), the first travel stories (Ambroise Paré) and the contemporary Breton texts, especially those published recently (Between the rich and the poor, Saint Barba, Saint Nonne, Passion, etc.) and the Catholicon. The portulans and first maps even bring some geographical elements.

These sources provide some answers to three questions. The first is geographical: what is known about the difference between Breton and French-speaking Brittany? This question also makes it possible to pose the problem of the birth of the notions of Upper and Lower Brittany. The second relates to the mythical origin of Breton. In the intellectual and political construction of the late Middle Ages, Breton was the language of Troy. It was imported by Brutus, son of Ascagne and grandson of Aeneas, and his companions. Some nevertheless propose a beginning of rational explanation and we begin to see appear the first attempts to understand the origin of the Breton and even some etymologies of names of persons and places, more serious than the elucubrations born of the fertile spirit of Geoffroy de Monmouth. This presentation will consist, starting from the medieval and revival documentation, of trying to find out how the contemporaries perceive this original situation, from al-Idrisi (ca 1100–late-twelfth century) to Bertrand d'Argentré (1519–1590) This presentation will be an opportunity to take stock of the documentary corpus available to researchers, on whether or not these authors perceive the specific features of Brittany, on the bilingualism of the Duchy. It will shed light on the birth of the notions of Upper and Lower Brittany and on attempts to explain the usage of Breton.

From the Space of the Sea: Auralizing Coastal Communities in West Ireland

Eilish Cullen

The sound of the human voice as it interacts with the sea is the acoustic signature of the coastal periphery of the West of Ireland. Human beings perceive natural soundscapes within an acoustic environment. Indeed, every location has its own individual acoustic attributes. Aural architecture, as defined by Barry Blesser, consists of the "acoustic attributes of the environment that influence our social and emotional experience of sonic broadcasts."

For this paper, I will discuss how the human voice and natural soundscapes–the way sound transports us back into the past–have shaped and influenced the culture and the migratory experience within Irish coastal communities. I will be specifically focusing on examining the significance of the legacies and locations of communities in relationship to their surrounding acoustics. This study is anchored by Tim Robinson's work including the recent study, *Unfolding Irish Landscapes*, as well as the seminal writings of Michel de Certeau, Henri Lefebvre, David Harvey, Edward Soja, Paul Devereux's interests in archeology, and the cognitive aspects of the prehistoric mind, and Bissera Pentcheva's work exploring the relationship between the singing human voice and the resonant interiors of the Hagia Sophia–providing a lens through which to integrate the experience of sound, as people move through a given space within broader Irish historical and cultural narratives.

THIRTY-NINTH CELTIC COLLOQUIUM

On Medical Material in the *Acallam na Senórach*
Ranke de Vries

Much of what we know about medieval Irish medicine comes from two main sources: (1) legal tracts like *Bretha Déin Chécht* and *Bretha Crólige*, and (2) medical manuscripts that include material based on, translated, or extracted from, the works of famous physicians like Hippocrates, Galen, and Avicenna. However, other textual genres, including saga literature, also contain references to medical material. In this presentation, I would like to bring some of this material to light by discussing a number of references to medicine and medical conditions in the *Acallam na Senórach*. This is part of a larger research project on medicine and the body in medieval Irish non-medical sources.

The Murchuirthe 'Castaway' in Early Irish Law
Charlene Eska

The term 'muirchuirthe' can refer to both a castaway and anything which has washed up on shore. Considering the semantic overlap, i.e. a castaway is a subcategory of things which wash up on shore, it can be difficult to determine the exact meaning of the term in some legal contexts. In fact, no study has yet been done that examines all the attestations of the word within the larger legal context in which each appears. This paper will gather all of the instances of this word in the Irish legal corpus and seek to untangle, from a legal perspective, which precise meaning should be assigned to each legal example.

The Late Cornish Syntax of William Bodinar
Joe Eska and Benjamin Bruch

The bilingual English-Cornish letter written by William Bodinar to the Hon. Daines Barrington, dated 3 July 1776, is the last known example of traditional written Cornish prior to the death of the language. P. A. S. Pool & O. J. Padel, the most recent editors of the letter in 1976, state that Bodinar,

ABSTRACTS

"if not a native speaker of Cornish, . . . was probably its last natural writer" and, in examining his Cornish, describe it as "[o]n the whole, . . . authentic–better than that of John Boson some sixty years earlier."

In this paper, we will make some observations upon the Cornish of the letter not discussed by Pool & Padel, including the clausal configuration of the Cornish. We find that while there are some typically Brittonic features in the syntax, as well as what may be evidence of Late Cornish developments, there is considerably more English influence in the syntax of Bodinar's Cornish than has previously been discussed.

Brendan's Menagerie and the *Diversa Sua Secreta*

Seth Hunter Koproski

At the end of the *Navigatio sancti brendani* the mythologized St. Brendan of Clonfert reaches the Promised Land of the Saints after seven years of long, hard, and very circular voyaging. A heavenly steward there explains that God wanted Brendan to take this roundabout route in order that he may witness *diversa sua secreta*, that is, God's 'varied mysteries'. The function of these mysteries mirrors the function of the text itself, in that the reader has, along with Brendan, marveled at the strange happenings and wondrous inhabitants of the many Atlantic islands encountered in this voyage. But what, truly, is this function? What purpose does the author of the *Navigatio* desire these *diversa secreta* to accomplish?

This paper is a section of my dissertation, which focuses broadly on fantastic and imaginary animals in early medieval Britain and Ireland. Many of the creatures Brendan faces are related, both textually and thematically, to the animals of the Latin Physiologus, whence we get Jasconius the island-like whale, and other traditions active in this time period. This paper, and my dissertation as a whole, examines how religious texts like the *Navigatio* use the concepts of wonder and animality to reify and construct proper practices of Christian belief. Using connections to similar patterns of constructing animality in the lives of Sts. Cuthbert and Colum Cille, as well as theorizations on the nature of wonder and the fantastic by Caroline Walker Bynum, J.S. Mackley, and St. Augustine, I will argue that these *diversa secreta* are part of a particular discourse stretching back to the dawn of Christian exegesis and reveal the very foundations of how medieval Christians viewed the natural world.

Sound and Sense: Philosophy of Language in Early Irish Grammatical Tradition

Victoria Krivoshchekova

There is hardly a rival to Irish grammatical learning in the whole of early medieval Europe. *Auraicept na nÉces* and the vast corpus of Old Irish glosses on Priscian alone provide a wealth of material which, especially when it comes to the glosses, has not been fully studied in the context of medieval linguistic thought. While a significant part of vernacular grammatical theory developed in the image of its Latin prototype, the peculiarity of Irish grammar could not help but kindle profound reflections on the most fundamental aspects of how language functions. In this paper I will examine how the process of discourse creation was conceptualized by Irish scholars through the usage of nuanced terminology, particularly words for 'sound' and 'sense.' The two concepts often appear side by side as a pair, but their relationship is rather flexible. I will argue that the ostensible synonyms–*son* and *fogur* for 'sound' and *cíall, inne, séis* and *intliucht* for 'sense'–consistently reflect a multi-layered theoretical approach to the problems of semantics and phonetics as they interact to produce articulate speech. Additionally, and following in the footsteps of Martin Irvine, I will demonstrate how these grammatical ideas could inform and in turn be informed by the practices of biblical exegesis and hermeneutics as well as etymology. This study will show that Irish grammatical tradition was finely attuned to the subtleties of the relationship between speech and the work of the mind in the process of human cognition.

Saladin in Caer Ochren: J. Gwenogvryn Evans's "Preideu Annwfyn" and Otherworldly Orientalisms

Sam Lasman

The editor and translator J. Gwenogvryn Evans (1852–1930) remains well-known in Celtic Studies, particularly for his work in cataloging and publishing medieval Welsh manuscripts. Less attention has been paid to his highly unusual interpretations of the poems contained in *Llyfr Taliesin*. In his 1915 selected edition and translation of that manuscript, he advanced a theory which dated the corpus to the 1100's and identified it as a set of elaborate allegories for contemporary affairs of that century. Among the most striking of these is Evans's transformation of the poem "Preideu Annwfyn," generally interpreted as a description of a perilous otherworldly voyage undertaken by Arthur and his warriors, into an account of Richard I of England's 1191 sieges of Acre and Jaffa during the Third Crusade. Through a combination of speculative translation, creative filling of lacunae (including an insertion of the name "Saladin"), and a dense critical apparatus, he created a new work that blends erudition and fantasy, the Holy Land and Annwfyn, Welsh legend and British imperialism.

This paper uses Evans's text to explore the broader imbrication of Orientalism and Arthurian scholarship, particularly with regard to depictions and understandings of the 'Otherworld'. Drawing on the work of scholars including Geraldine Heng and Michelle R. Warren, it seeks to position Evans's re-fashioned poem not as an eccentric failure but rather as a fascinating site of interplay between text, history, and ideology, expressing themes that–given the ongoing prominence of Evans and his peers–continue to haunt Medieval Studies today.

Contested Succession at Iona (704–26)

Patrick McAlary

Prior to the death of Adomnán in 704 the abbacy of Iona had been held in perfect regularity, when an abbot died the appointment of a successor received no comment from the Annals. This state of affairs came crashing down following the death of Adomnán and the Annal entries for the 704–726 period record a series of overlapping successions indicating a period of contested succession. This period has garnered a lot of attention and explanations have ranged from a dispute in response to the Easter Controversy, dynastic strife in Scottish Dál Riata, organisational change, aging abbots, and the belief that we may simply never know. Given the plurality of explanations already circulating in scholarly discourse it may be viewed as ill-judged to forward another possibility. While previous commentators have focused on the eligibility criteria for the abbacy (most abbots had a Cenél Conaill genealogical affiliation), there has been a failure to consider the practical means of how the abbacy passed from one holder to his successor. I have found it to be extremely likely that in the 563–704 period the prevailing succession mechanism was one where an abbot designated his own successor. This paper proposes to view the period of contested succession through this lens. The first thing to be noted will be that the succession of Conamail (a non Cenél Conaill abbot) upon Adomnán's death was not as disruptive as has been assumed, and rather the disruption emerged from Dúnchad's interjection into the abbacy in 707. From this it will be argued that while contention was a product of a number of factors it had its basis in an internalised dynastic mindset.

Dindshenchas and Etymology: The Structure of Information

David McCay

This paper explores the role of etymology in dindshenchas; the *senchas*, 'history, traditional learning' of *dind*, the 'notable places' of Ireland. *Dindshenchas*, traditionally understood, is the name given to an aetiological narrative which purports to explain the origins of a place-name, and which links that narrative to the name by a type of etymology. This etymology, not to be confused with the modern linguistic kind, is usually explained as a vernacular Irish reflex of the Latinate, learned, 'Isidorean' etymology epitomised in the *Etymologiae* of Archbishop Isidore of Seville (d. 636).

Whilst the work of Isidore was foundational in the development of etymology as an analytical methodology, close examination of the use of etymology in dindshenchas texts suggests that, influenced though they likely were, the broader intellectual processes at work in their composers' wordplay were not identical to those of the archbishop.

In this paper, then, I will consider the *Dindshenchas*, not as an example of, but in relation to the Isidorean etymological practices characteristic of medieval writings, thereby developing a deeper understanding of the ways in which etymology might be used to diverse literary and analytical effects. Situated in the context of other–similarly etymological–Irish compilations such as *Cóir Anmann*, 'The Fitness of Names', and the *Banshenchas*,

'Lore/History of Women', I will demonstrate how etymology in dindshenchas deviates from its Isidorean roots, serving as a compelling mechanism by which information of many types might be brought together to many effects.

From "Strange Crosses" to "Great Miracles": Catholic Renewal, Manuscript Culture, and Women in Early Modern Wales and the Marches

Katharine Olson

This paper examines select aspects of Post-Tridentine efforts at Catholic renewal and reform in early modern Wales and the Welsh Marches, with a particular focus on the reign of Elizabeth (1558–1603). It considers the state of religion in later sixteenth-century Wales and the the Marches and the problems and challenges faced by both the Anglican Church and Welsh Catholics in implementing reforms during a period of substantial socio-economic change and religious turmoil in the British Isles and Europe. The role of Welsh-language recusant literature, gender, and manuscript culture in Catholic efforts to win converts and to reform is discussed, especially the use of sacred history and literature, and the role(s) of the native and universal saints in this. as well as gender and the role of women in religious renewal and recusancy. This paper also examines the sacred landscape as seen in a range of historical and other interdisciplinary evidence for popular religious practices like pilgrimages and devotions to the saints in Wales, and links this to other efforts at renewal. Lastly, it asses the complex nature and development of early modern religious identities and culture in sixteenth- and seventeenth-century Wales and the Marches and places these within a wider British, Irish, and European context.

THIRTY-NINTH CELTIC COLLOQUIUM

Yours at Power: Expressions of Social Hierarchy in the Early Modern Scottish Highlands

Roxanne Reddington-Wilde

"Be yours assurit at his command;"(#26) "Youris assuritly att his power;"(#27) "Your Ladyshipis to command at service;"(#40) . . . these closings and others acknowledging social hierarchy pervade the mid-sixteenth century Campbell of Glenorchy letter collection (edited Jane Dawson, Scottish Historical Society 1997). They are but one expression of social hierarchy and rank which pervaded social relations in the Early Modern Scottish Highlands. Men, women, chiefs and tenants knew their place and how to acknowledge that before others. Equality was not an ideal.

This paper, part of laying the groundwork for an historical ethnography of women in the Early Modern Highlands, shall explore how hierarchy was construed and expressed through Gaelic Poetry and Scots letters; Highland architecture and Scottish painting; legal contracts and English travel writings. What social function(s) did hierarchy serve? Was it ever set aside–within family, between friends or husband and wife? Without an understanding of and appreciation for the role of unequal power relations between people, one cannot begin to understand Highland society of the period.

The Past and the Present in Twelfth-Century Armagh

Patrick Wadden

This paper will discuss the short historical tract known as the "Short Annals of Armagh" (*Annála Gearra as Proibhinse Ard Macha*). The single surviving copy of this text survives in a fifteenth-century manuscript, whence it was edited by Gearóid Mac Niocaill, but the language and structure suggest that it was first written around the middle of the twelfth century. It begins with the story of St. Patrick's meeting with King Lóegaire mac Néill at Tara and ends in the second quarter of the twelfth century with St. Malachy's assumption of the bishopric of Armagh, though there are two significant gaps in coverage. Much of its content was apparently derived from texts similar to surviving annals, but it also contains unique references

ABSTRACTS

to events not reported elsewhere in Irish sources. This paper will briefly consider the sources used by the author/compiler of the tract before examining in greater detail its structure and content. Its goal will be to demonstrate the connection between the tract's approach to the past and contemporary political and cultural concerns of twelfth-century Armagh.

The Idea of Early Irish Verse
Thomas Walsh

Questions regarding genre in early Irish lyric regularly inquire about whether a poem exemplifies metrical phenomena that place it somewhere between an archaic and a later tradition: alliterative techniques, syllabic count, rhyme, etc. are appropriately brought into such discussions. At another level, terms like 'monastic' and 'secular' are often conscripted to serve as larger-scale generic demarcations, especially when needed for organizing anthologies or compilations of these poems. And, of course, the ubiquitous notion of 'nature poetry' remains a stand-by for characterizing early Irish verse, as do other references to kinds of thematics, for example, 'love,' 'exile', 'fame', 'the hermit', and the like.

As with many lyrical traditions in world literature, early Irish verse also presents, for want of a better term, 'ideas' set out by a poet for consideration by a reader. In this abstract, I point to examples of ideas in two familiar lyrics:

1.) "Pangur Ban" presents an occupational motif, whereby the monk composing the poem contrasts his daily work with that of a cat with whom he shares his space and time. The idea here is that, for both cat and person, the elements of labor are comparable in a way that highlights their activities, and, further, that the human occupation is particularly clarified as to its value by such a comparison.

2.) One can also identify, in this context, the famous quatrain beginning *Is acher in gáith innocht*. Note its epigrammatic turn in the third line where the poet declares that he does not fear (*ní agor*) the fierce (*acher*) weather because the implacable storm makes impossible any safe passage for the enemy. Like an epigram, moving to a 'point', an epigrammatic turn, the poem presents an idea that recasts the reader's expectations in an economically surprising manner. Just as does, I will argue, the *volta* in sonnets from completely different traditions—e.g., the moment between an octave and a sestet in a Petrarchan sonnet or the moment before the final couplet in a Shakespearean sonnet; and, in a fashion that resembles the methods of a Petrarch or a Shakespeare, this poet's skillful turn delicately manages the reader's perceptions in order to highlight the dramatic moment when nature (the storm) and culture (the invasions of a predatory enemy) meet each other. The idea is that nature, uncontrollable as it is by human beings, can, in a strikingly paradoxical way, work to keep us safe.

In this presentation I will identify some ideas of the kind identified above that are featured in early Irish lyric.